Current Biography

Cumulated Index 1940–2000

Current Biography

Cumulated Index 1940–2000

The H.W. Wilson Company
New York • Dublin
2001

PRINTED IN THE UNITED STATES OF AMERICA

International Standard Book No. 0-8242-0997-4

Library of Congress Catalog Card No. (40-27432)

PREFATORY NOTE

This index, covering the years from 1940 through 2000, cumulates and supersedes the *Current Biography Cumulated Index, 1940–1995*. The reader will need to consult only this index in order to locate a name.

The dates after the names indicate the monthly issue(s) and yearbooks containing the biographies and obituaries. If a subject was covered under a different name than the one listed here or in a joint article, the name that the biography appears under is listed in brackets after the date:

> Ali, Muhammad Sep 63 [Clay, Cassius] Nov 78
> Abbott, Bud Oct 41 [Abbott, Bud; and Costello, Lou] obit Jun 74
> Costello, Lou Oct 41 [Abbott, Bud; and Costello, Lou] obit May 59

When two subjects have exactly the same name, their occupations are listed in brackets after their names in order to distinguish between them:

> Segal, George [actor] Nov 75
> Segal, George [artist] Jan 72

We hope that readers will appreciate the convenience of this index to the first sixty volumes of Current Biography.

Current Biography

Cumulated Index 1940–2000

Adams, Eva Bertrand Sep 62 obit Oct 91

Adams, Franklin P. Jul 41 obit May 60

Adams, Gerry Sep 94

Adams, Grantley Herbert Sep 58 obit Jan 72

Adams, Herbert obit Jun 45

Adams, James Truslow Nov 41 obit Jul 49

Adams, John Cranford Sep 58 obit Jan 87

Adams, John May 88

Adams, Joseph H. obit Apr 41

Adams, Joseph Quincy obit Dec 46

Adams, Randolph G. Aug 43

Adams, Richard Oct 78

Adams, Roger Jun 47 obit Sep 71

Adams, Sherman Nov 52 obit Jan 87

Adams, Stanley Feb 54 obit Mar 94

Adams, Thomas obit Apr 40

Adamson, Joy Oct 72 obit Feb 80

Addams, Charles Jan 54 obit Nov 88

Addams, Clifford Isaac obit Jan 43

Adderley, Cannonball *see* Adderley, Julian E.

Adderley, Julian E. Jul 61 obit Oct 75

Addington, Sarah obit Yrbk 40

Additon, Henrietta Silvis Sep 40

Ade, George obit Jul 44

Adé, King Sunny Nov 94

Adelman, Kenneth L. Jul 85

Adenauer, Konrad Jul 49 Apr 58 obit Jun 67

Adjani, Isabelle Jan 90

Adkins, Bertha S. May 53 obit Mar 83

Adkins, Charles obit May 41

Adkinson, Burton W. Jun 59

Adler, Cyrus obit May 40

Adler, Guido obit May 41

Adler, Harry Clay obit Apr 40

Adler, Julius Ochs Jun 48 obit Dec 55 Yrbk 56

Adler, Kurt Herbert Mar 79 obit Apr 88

Adler, Larry Feb 44

Adler, Mortimer J. Apr 40 Sep 52

Adler, Renata Jun 84

Adler, Stella Aug 85 obit Feb 93

Adolfo Nov 72

Adoula, Cyrille Mar 62

Adrian, E. D. Feb 55 obit Oct 77

Adrian Feb 41 obit Nov 59

Adzhubei, Aleksei I. Sep 64 obit May 93

Affleck, Ben Mar 98 [Affleck, Ben; and Damon, Matt]

Afro Nov 58

Aga Khan, The May 46 obit Sep 57

Aga Khan IV, The Mar 60

Agam, Yaacov Apr 81

Agar, Herbert Mar 44 obit Jan 81

Agar, William May 49 obit Jul 72

Agassi, Andre Oct 89

Agnelli, Giovanni Jan 72

Agnew, Spiro T. Dec 68 obit Nov 96

Agnon, Shmuel Yosef Mar 67 obit Apr 70

Aguilera, Christina Aug 2000

Aguirre Cerda, Pedro Jan 41 obit Jan 41

Ahern, Bertie Jul 98

Aherne, Brian Feb 60 obit Apr 86

Ahlgren, Mildred Carlson Jul 52

Ahmad, Imam of Yemen Mar 56 obit Nov 62

Ahmadu, Alhaji, Sardauna of Sokoto Jul 57 [Ahmadu, Alhaji, Sardauna of Sokoto; Awolowo, Obafemi; and Azikiwe, Nnamdi]

Ahmed II, Sidi obit Aug 42

Aichi, Kiichi Jul 71 obit Jan 74

Aiello, Danny Jun 92

Aiken, Conrad May 70 obit Oct 73

Aiken, George D. Jun 47 obit Feb 85

Aiken, Howard Mar 47 obit May 73

Aiken, Loretta Mary *see* Mabley, Moms

Aikman, Troy May 95

Ailes, Roger E. Jan 89

Ailes, Stephen Jan 65

Ailey, Alvin Mar 68 obit Jan 90

Ainsworth, William Newman, Bishop obit Aug 42

Aitken, William Maxwell Jul 40 obit Sep 64

Akalaitis, Joanne Feb 93

Akebono Aug 99

Aked, Charles F., Rev. obit Oct 41

Akers, John F. May 88

Akihito, Emperor of Japan Apr 59 Aug 91

Aksyonov, Vassily Jan 90

Ala, Hussein May 51 obit Sep 64

Alagna, Roberto Jul 97

Alaïa, Azzedine Oct 92

Alain Sep 41

Alajalov, Constantin Jan 42 obit Jan 88

Alanis *see* Morissette, Alanis

Albanese, Licia Mar 46

Albee, Edward Feb 63 Apr 96

Albee, Fred H. May 43 obit Apr 45

Alberghetti, Anna Maria Jan 55

Albers, Josef Jun 62 obit May 76

Albert, Arthur William Patrick obit Mar 42

Albert, Carl Jun 57 obit Jun 2000

Albert, Eddie Jan 54

Alberti, Jules Jul 59

Alberto, Alvaro Mar 47

Albertson, Jack Mar 76 obit Jan 82

Albion, Robert Greenhalgh May 54 obit Oct 83

Albright, Ivan Feb 44 Dec 69 obit Jan 84

Albright, Madeleine Korbel May 95 Apr 2000

Albright, Tenley Sep 56

Albright, William F. Sep 55

Alcayaga, Lucila Godoy *see* Mistral, Gabriela

Alcindor, Lew *see* Abdul-Jabbar, Kareem

Alcock, Norman Z. Mar 63

Alcorn, Hugh Meade, Jr. May 57 obit Mar 92

Alda, Alan Jan 77

Aldredge, Theoni Feb 94

Aldrich, Chester Holmes obit Feb 41

Aldrich, Richard Jun 55 obit Jun 86

Aldrich, Richard S. obit Feb 42

Aldrich, Winthrop W. Oct 40 Mar 53 obit Apr 74

Aldridge, James Mar 43

Aldridge, John W. (WLB) Yrbk 58

Aldrin, Buzz Sep 93

Aldrin, Edwin E. Jr. *see* Aldrin, Buzz

Alechinsky, Pierre Sep 88

Alegría, Ciro Dec 41

Aleixandre, Vicente Mar 78 obit Mar 85

Alekhine, Alexander obit May 46

Alemán, Miguel Sep 46 obit Jul 83

Alepoudelis, Odysseus *see* Elytis, Odysseus

Alessandri, Jorge May 59 obit Oct 86

Alexander, Albert Victor Yrbk 40 obit Feb 65

Alexander, Archie A. Jun 55 obit Mar 58

Alexander, Clifford L., Jr. Sep 77

Alexander, Donald C. Dec 74

Alexander, Franz Aug 42 Sep 60 obit Apr 64

Alexander, Harold R. L. G. Oct 42 obit Sep 69 [Alexander of Tunis, Harold R. L. G. Alexander, 1st Earl]

Alexander, Harry Held obit Feb 41

Alexander, Holmes Sep 56

Alexander, Jane Feb 77

Alexander, Jason Jan 98

Alexander, Lamar Jul 91

Alexander, Madame Sep 57

Alexander, Margaret Walker *see* Walker, Margaret

Alexander, Ruth Mar 43

Alexander, Willis W. Jul 69 obit Jan 86

Alexander of Hillsborough, Albert Victor Alexander, 1st Earl *see* Alexander, Albert Victor

Alexander of Tunis, Harold R. L. G. Alexander, 1st E *see* Alexander, Harold R. L. G.

Alexanderson, Ernst F. W. Sep 55 obit Aug 75

Alexei, Patriarch of Russia Mar 53 obit Jun 70

Alexie, Sherman Oct 98

Alfonsín, Raúl Jul 84

Alfonso XIII obit Apr 41

Alfrink, Bernard May 66 obit Feb 88

Alger, Ellice M. obit Apr 45

Al-Hassan, Prince of The Yemen Feb 57

Al-Husseini, Faisal Jan 98

Ali, Asaf *see* Asaf Ali

Ali, Chaudhri Mohamad Feb 56

Ali, Mohammed Oct 52 obit Mar 63

Ali, Muhammad Sep 63 [Clay, Cassius] Nov 78

Alia, Ramiz Jan 91

Alice, Mary *see* Mary Alice

Alinsky, Saul Nov 68 obit Jul 72

Alioto, Joseph L. Sep 69 obit Apr 98

Aliyev, Heydar Sep 99

Al Kuwatly, Shukri *see* Kuwatly, Shukri Al

Allan, John J. Jan 50 obit Jan 61

Allee, Marjorie obit Jun 45

Allegro, John Dec 70 obit Apr 88

Allen, Arthur A. Jan 61 obit Mar 64

Allen, Betsy *see* Cavanna, Betty

Allen, Betty Nov 90

Allen, Debbie Feb 87

Allen, Dick May 73

Allen, Edgar obit Mar 43

Allen, Ethan Mar 54 obit Nov 93

Allen, Florence E. Feb 41 Jul 63 obit Nov 66

Allen, Frank A. Mar 45 obit Jan 80

Allen, Fred Feb 41 obit May 56

Allen, George E. Mar 46 obit Jun 73

Allen, George Jan 75 obit Mar 91

Allen, George V. Nov 48 obit Oct 70

Allen, Gracie Jul 40 [Burns, George; and Allen, Gracie] Mar 51 obit Oct 64

Allen, Helen Howe *see* Howe, Helen

Allen, James E., Jr. Jun 69 obit Dec 71

Allen, Jay Oct 41 obit Feb 73

Allen, Joel Nott obit Mar 40

Allen, Larry Jul 42

Allen, Leo E. Jun 48 obit Mar 73

Allen, Marcus Oct 86

Allen, Marion obit Feb 42

Allen, Martha F. Oct 59

Allen, Mel Oct 50 obit Aug 96

Allen, Paul Jul 98

Allen, Peter Mar 83 obit Aug 92

Allen, Ralph Jul 58 obit Feb 67

Allen, Raymond B. Mar 52 obit May 86

Allen, Robert May 41 [Pearson, Drew; and Allen, Robert]

Allen, Steve Jul 51 Mar 82

Allen, Terry Nov 43 obit Nov 69

Allen, Tim May 95

Allen, William L. Sep 53

Allen, William M. Mar 53 obit Jan 86

Allen, Woody Dec 66 Sep 79

Allende, Isabel Feb 88

Allende, Salvador Sep 71 obit Nov 73

Alley, Kirstie Jul 94

Alley, Rewi Oct 43 obit Feb 88

Alliluyeva, Svetlana Oct 68

Allison, John M. Mar 56 obit Feb 79

Allman, David B. Feb 58 obit May 71

Allon, Yigal Sep 75 obit Apr 80

Allott, Gordon May 55 obit Apr 89

Allport, Gordon Sep 60 obit Dec 67

Allsburg, Chris Van Sep 96

Allyn, Lewis B. obit Jan 40

Allyn, Stanley C. Mar 56 obit Dec 70

Allyson, June Jan 52

Almazan, Juan Andreu May 40 obit Dec 65

Almendros, Nestor Nov 89 obit May 92

Almirante, Giorgio Jan 74 obit Jul 88

Almodóvar, Pedro Sep 90

Almond, Edward M. Mar 51 obit Aug 79

Almond, J. Lindsay, Jr. Mar 58 obit Jun 86

Alonso, Alicia Jul 55 Jun 77

Alou, Felipe Jun 99

Alou, Moises Apr 99

Alpert, George Sep 61 obit Oct 88

Alpert, Herb Jan 67

Alphand, Hervé Nov 51 obit Mar 94

Al-Sabah, Jaber al-Ahmad al-Jaber see Sabah, Jaber Al-Ahmad Al-Jaber Al-, Sheik

Alsberg, Carl Lucas obit Yrbk 40

Al-Shabandar, Moussa see Shabandar, Moussa

Alsop, Joseph Oct 52 [Alsop, Joseph W., Jr.; and Alsop, Stewart] obit Oct 89

Alsop, Stewart Oct 52 [Alsop, Joseph W., Jr.; and Alsop, Stewart] obit Jul 74

Alsop Sture-Vasa, Mary O'Hara see O'Hara, Mary

Alstadt, W. R. Jul 58

Alston, Walter Jun 54 obit Nov 84

Altenburg, Alexander obit Mar 40

Alter, George Elias obit Oct 40

Altizer, Thomas J. J. Jun 67

Altman, Robert Feb 74

Altmeyer, Arthur J. Nov 46 obit Dec 72

Al-Turabi, Hassan see Turabi, Hassan al-

Alvarez, Luis W. May 47 obit Oct 88

Alvarez, Walter C. Sep 53 obit Aug 78

Alvarez Bravo, Manuel Jan 99

Alvarez Quintero, Joaquin obit Aug 44

Aly Khan, Prince May 60

Amado, Jorge Mar 86

Amalrik, Andrei Apr 74 obit Jan 81

Amanpour, Christiane Apr 96

Amato, Giuliano Sep 93

Amato, Pasquale obit Oct 42

Ambedkar, B. R. Nov 51 obit Feb 57

Ambler, Eric Jun 75 obit Jan 99

Amdahl, Gene Aug 82

Ameche, Don May 65 obit Feb 94

Amedeo, Duke of Aosta obit Apr 42

Ameling, Elly Oct 82

Amerasinghe, Hamilton Shirley Mar 77 obit Feb 81

Ameringer, Oscar obit Dec 43

Amery, L. S. Jul 42 obit Nov 55 Yrbk 56

Ames, Amyas Apr 72 obit Jun 2000

Ames, Bruce N. Oct 93

Ames, Joseph S. obit Aug 43

Ames, Louise Sep 56 [Ilg, Frances L; and Ames, Louise] obit Jan 97

Amherst, Alicia-Margaret obit Nov 41

Amichai, Yehuda Feb 98

Amies, Hardy Mar 62

Amin, Idi Feb 73

Amini, Ali Jan 62

Amis, Kingsley (WLB) Yrbk 58 Apr 87 obit Jan 96

Amis, Martin Jun 90

Ammann, O. H. Jan 63 obit Nov 65

Ammons, A. R. Feb 82

Amory, Derick Heathcoat Apr 58

Amos, Tori Sep 98

Amos, Wally Jul 95

Amos and Andy see Correll, Charles J.; Gosden, Freeman F.

Amram, David Nov 69

Amsden, Charles obit Apr 41

Amsterdam, Birdie Mar 40 obit Sep 96

Amulree, William Warrender Mackenzie, 1st Baron of Strathbraan obit Jun 42

Ananda Mahidol obit Jul 46

Anders, William A. Apr 69

Andersen, Hendrik Christian obit Feb 41

Andersen, Ib Aug 84

Anderson, Abraham Archibald obit Jan 40

Anderson, Alexander E. obit Feb 43

Anderson, Carl D. Jan 51 obit Mar 91

Anderson, Clinton P. Jun 45 obit Jan 76

Anderson, Constance May 48

Anderson, Dewey Jan 50

Anderson, Erica Feb 57 obit Nov 76

Anderson, Frances see Anderson, Judith

Anderson, Frederick L. May 44 obit Apr 69

Anderson, Gaylord W. Feb 53

Anderson, George Everett obit Apr 40

Anderson, George Lee see Anderson, Sparky

Anderson, George Whelan Nov 62 obit May 92

Anderson, Grete see Waitz, Grete

Anderson, Howard Jan 55

Anderson, Ian Feb 98

Anderson, Jack Jun 72

Anderson, John B. Sep 79

Anderson, John Crawford obit Jan 40

Anderson, John [drama critic] obit Sep 43 [Waverley, John Anderson, 1st Viscount]

Anderson, John [British cabinet member] Jul 41 obit Mar 58

Anderson, John W. Jul 53

Anderson, Judith Dec 41 Feb 61 obit Mar 92

Anderson, June May 91

Anderson, Kenneth A. N. Feb 43 obit Jul 59

Anderson, Laurie Jul 83

Anderson, Leroy Sep 52 obit Aug 75

Anderson, Lindsay Nov 75 obit Nov 94

Anderson, Marian May 40 Apr 50 obit Jun 93

Anderson, Mary see Navarro, Mary De Sep 40 obit Mar 64

Anderson, Maxwell Nov 42 Sep 53 obit May 59

Anderson, Mrs. Eugenie Jan 50

Anderson, Mrs. John Pierce see Anderson, Mrs. Eugenie

Anderson, Robert B. Jun 53 obit Oct 89

Anderson, Robert O. Sep 82

Anderson, Robert Sep 54

Anderson, Roy A. Aug 83

Anderson, Samuel W. Jun 54
obit Jan 63
Anderson, Sherwood obit
Apr 41
Anderson, Sigurd Sep 53 obit
Mar 91
Anderson, Sparky Apr 77
Anderson, Victor E. Sep 56
obit Oct 62
Anderson, W. French Oct 94
Anderson, William R. Apr 59
Andersson, Bibi Sep 78
Andino, Tiburcio Carías see
Carías Andino, Tiburcio
Ando, Tadao Jan 2000
Andrade, Victor Feb 53
Andre, Carl May 86
Andreadis, Christina see
Onassis, Christina
Andreas, Dwayne O. Mar 92
Andreessen, Marc Jun 97
[Andreessen, Marc; and
Clark, James H.]
Andreotti, Giulio Feb 77
Andresen, August H. Feb 56
obit Mar 58
Andretti, Mario Jul 68
Andrew, Duke of York Mar 87
Andrewes, William Sep 52
obit Jan 75
Andrews, Anthony Jun 91
Andrews, Bert Sep 48 obit
Oct 53
Andrews, C. M. obit Oct 43
Andrews, Charles O. obit
Nov 46
Andrews, Cicily Isabel see
West, Rebecca
Andrews, Dana Oct 59 obit
Feb 93
Andrews, Frank M. Feb 42
obit Jun 43
Andrews, John B. obit Feb 43
Andrews, Julie Jul 56 Apr 94
Andrews, Roy Chapman Jan
41 Jul 53 obit May 60
Andrews, Stanley Jun 52
Andrews, T. Coleman Apr 54
Andric, Ivo Feb 62 obit May
75
Andropov, Yuri May 83 obit
Apr 84
Andrus, Cecil D. Aug 77
Angarita, Isaías Medina see
Medina Angarita, Isaías
Angeles, Victoria de los Feb
55
Angell, James Rowland Yrbk
40 obit Mar 49

Angell, Norman May 48 obit
Dec 67
Angelou, Maya Jun 74 Feb 94
Angier, Natalie Aug 99
Angle, Paul McClelland Jul
55 obit Aug 75
Angoff, Charles (WLB) Yrbk
55 obit Jul 79
Anise see Strong, Anna Lou-
ise
Anka, Paul Feb 64
Annan, Kofi Mar 2000
Anne, Princess of Great Brit-
ain Oct 73
Annenberg, Walter H. Jan 70
Annis, Edward R. Apr 64
Ann-Margret Sep 75
Anouilh, Jean Apr 54 obit
Nov 87
Ansermet, Ernest Jul 49 obit
Apr 69
Anslinger, H. J. May 48 obit
Jan 76
Anspach, Charles L. Sep 56
Antall, József, Jr. Sep 90 obit
Feb 94
Antes, Horst Feb 86
Antheil, George Jul 54 obit
Apr 59
Anthony, John J. Jan 42 obit
Oct 70
Antoine, Josephine Aug 44
Antoine Jun 55 obit Sep 76
Antonescu, Ion Oct 40 obit
Jul 46
Antonioni, Michelangelo
Dec 64 May 93
Anuszkiewicz, Richard Oct
78
Aouita, Said May 90
Aoun, Michel Mar 90
Apgar, Virginia Feb 68 obit
Oct 74
Appel, James Z. Mar 66 obit
Oct 81
Appel, Karel Mar 61
Apple, R. W., Jr. Apr 93
Appleton, Edward Dale obit
Mar 42
Appleton, Edward Victor Sep
45 obit Jun 65
Appleton, Robert obit Mar 45
Appley, Lawrence A. Jul 50
obit Jun 97
Appleyard, Rollo obit Apr 43
Apted, Michael Feb 2000
Aquino, Corazon Aug 86
Arafat, Yasir Mar 71 Nov 94

Araki, Eikichi Oct 52 obit
Apr 59
Aramburu, Pedro Eugenio
Jan 57 obit Oct 70
Aranha, Oswaldo Mar 42 obit
Apr 60
Arantes do Nascimento,
Edson see Pelé
Aras, Tevfik Rüstü Jun 42
Araskog, Rand V. Nov 91
Arbenz Guzman, Jacobo Sep
53 obit Mar 71
Arcand, Denys Oct 90
Arcaro, Eddie Sep 58 obit Jan
98
Arcaro, George Edward see
Arcaro, Eddie
Arce, José Nov 47 obit Oct 68
Archambault, Louis Sep 59
Archer, Dennis W. Feb 97
Archer, Glenn Leroy May 49
Archer, Jeffrey Sep 88
Archer, Lane see Hauck, Lou-
ise Platt
Archipenko, Alexander Sep
53 obit Apr 64
Arciniegas, Germán May 54
obit Jun 2000
Arco, Georg Wilhelm Alex-
ander Hans Graf Von obit
Jan 40
Ardalan, Ali Gholi Apr 54
Arden, Elizabeth Jul 57 obit
Dec 66
Arden, Eve Sep 53 obit Jan 91
Arden, John Sep 88
Ardizzone, Edward May 64
obit Jan 80
Ardrey, Robert Jul 73 obit
Mar 80
Areilza, José Maria de, Count
of Motrico Apr 55 obit May
98
Arends, Leslie C. Feb 48 obit
Sep 85
Arendt, Hannah May 59 obit
Feb 76
Arens, Moshe Jul 89
Arfons, Art Feb 70
Argentinita Jun 42 obit Oct
45
Argento, Dominick May 77
Argerich, Martha Sep 99
Argeseanu, George obit Jan
41
Arias, Arnulfo May 41 obit
Sep 88
Arias Navarro, Carlos Oct 74
obit Jan 90

Arias Sánchez, Oscar Aug 87
Aristide, Jean-Bertrand May 91
Ariyoshi, George R. Jan 85
Arkin, Alan Oct 67
Arledge, Roone Feb 77
Arlen, Harold Jul 55 obit Jun 86
Arliss, George obit Mar 46
Armand, Louis Sep 57 [Armand, Louis; Etzel, Franz; and Giordani, Francesco] obit Oct 71
Armani, Giorgio Jan 83
Armetta, Henry obit Nov 45
Armey, Dick see Armey, Richard K.
Armey, Richard K. Jun 95
Armfield, Anne Constance see Smedley, Constance
Armitage, Kenneth Apr 57
Armour, Allison V. obit Apr 41
Armour, Norman Apr 45 obit Nov 82
Armour, Richard Nov 58 obit Apr 89
Armstrong, Anne Legendre May 76
Armstrong, C. Michael Jun 99
Armstrong, Charlotte (WLB) Yrbk 46 obit Sep 69
Armstrong, David W. Jul 49 obit Mar 63
Armstrong, Edwin Howard Apr 40 obit Mar 54
Armstrong, George E. Apr 52 obit Aug 79
Armstrong, Gillian Aug 95
Armstrong, Hamilton Fish Jan 48 obit Jun 73
Armstrong, Harry G. Jul 51
Armstrong, J. Sinclair Mar 58
Armstrong, Lance Sep 97
Armstrong, Louis Sep 44 Apr 66 obit Sep 71
Armstrong, Margaret obit Sep 44
Armstrong, Neil Oct 69
Armstrong-Jones, Antony Oct 60
Arnall, Ellis Aug 45 obit Feb 93
Arnault, Bernard Jun 98
Arnaz, Desi Sep 52 [Ball, Lucille; and Arnaz, Desi] obit Feb 87
Arne, Sigrid Oct 45
Arness, James Nov 73

Arnett, Peter Nov 91
Arno, Peter Aug 42 obit Apr 68
Arnold, Bion J. obit Mar 42
Arnold, Eddy Mar 70
Arnold, Edwin G. Sep 47 obit Jan 61
Arnold, George Stanleigh obit Mar 42
Arnold, Henry H. Feb 42 obit Feb 50
Arnold, Roseanne see Barr, Roseanne
Arnold, Thurman Wesley Jan-Feb 40 obit Dec 69
Arnold, William Richard, Mgr. May 42
Arnon, Daniel I. Jun 55 obit Mar 95
Arnow, Harriette Simpson (WLB) Yrbk 54 obit May 86
Arnstein, Daniel Mar 42
Aroldingen, Karin Von Jan 83
Aron, Raymond Jun 54 obit Jan 84
Aronin, Jeffrey Ellis Jan 55
Aronson, J. Hugo Feb 54
Aronson, Louis V. obit Yrbk 40
Aronson, Naoum obit Nov 43
Arp, Jean Hans May 54 obit Jul 66
Arpino, Gerald Oct 70
Arquette, Cliff Jun 61 obit Nov 74
Arquette, Patricia Oct 97
Arrabal, Fernando Sep 72
Arrau, Claudio Jan 42 Nov 86 obit Aug 91
Arroyo, Martina Feb 71
Arroyo Del Río, Carlos Alberto Jun 42
Arrupe, Pedro Feb 70 obit Apr 91
Arsonval, Jacques Arsène D' obit Feb 41
Arthur, Beatrice Dec 73
Arthur, George obit Mar 46
Arthur, J. C. obit Jun 42
Arthur, Jean Mar 45 obit Aug 91
Artschwager, Richard Jul 90
Artzybasheff, Boris Oct 45 obit Sep 65
Asaf Ali Jun 47 obit May 53
Asakai, Koichiro Sep 57
Ascher, Leo obit Apr 42
Ascoli, Max Feb 54 obit Mar 78

Asgeirsson, Asgeir Sep 52
Ash, Mary Kay May 95
Ash, Peter see Hauck, Louise Platt
Ash, Roy Jul 68
Ashbery, John Aug 76
Ashbrook, John M. Oct 73 obit Jun 82
Ashcroft, John Sep 99
Ashcroft, Peggy Sep 63 Jan 87 obit Aug 91
Ashdown, Jeremy John Durham see Ashdown, Paddy
Ashdown, Paddy Oct 92
Ashe, Arthur Nov 66 obit Mar 93
Ashford, Nickolas Apr 97 [Ashford, Nickolas; and Simpson, Valerie]
Ashford and Simpson see Ashford, Nickolas; Simpson, Valerie
Ashida, Hitoshi Jun 48 obit Sep 59
Ashkenazy, Vladimir Jul 67
Ashley, Elizabeth Mar 78
Ashley, Maurice Sep 99
Ashley, Merrill Nov 81
Ashley, Thomas Ludlow May 79
Ashmore, Harry S. Sep 58 obit Apr 98
Ashmun, Margaret Eliza obit Apr 40
Ashrawi, Hanan Mar 92
Ashton, Frederick May 51 obit Sep 88
Asimov, Isaac (WLB) Yrbk 53 Oct 68 obit May 92
Askew, Reubin Apr 73
Askey, E. Vincent Feb 61 obit Feb 75
Askwith, George Ranken Askwith, 1st Baron obit Jul 42
Asner, Edward Aug 78
Aspin, Les Feb 86 obit Jul 95
Aspinall, Wayne N. Apr 68 obit Nov 83
Asquith, Margot obit Sep 45
Assad, Hafez Al- Jul 75 Apr 92 obit Aug 2000
Assis Chateaubriand Jun 57
Astaire, Fred Sep 45 Apr 64 obit Aug 87
Astin, Allen V. May 56 obit Apr 84

Astin, Patty Duke *see* Duke, Patty

Aston, Francis William obit Jan 46

Astor, Brooke Jan 87

Astor, John Jacob, 1st Baron of Hever May 54 obit Sep 71

Astor, Mary Nov 61 obit Nov 87

Astor, Nancy Witcher, Viscountess Nov 40 obit Jul 64

Asturias, Miguel Angel Oct 68 obit Jul 74

Aswell, James (WLB) Yrbk 51 obit Apr 55

Atalena *see* Jabotinsky, Vladimir Evgenevich

Atcheson, George, Jr. Sep 46 obit Oct 47

Athenagoras I, Patriarch Mar 49 obit Sep 72

Atherton, Gertrude Franklin Horn Nov 40 obit Sep 48

Atherton, Warren H. Dec 43 obit May 76

Atkins, Chet Jan 75

Atkinson, Brooks Apr 42 Feb 61 obit Mar 84

Atkinson, Eleanor obit Jan 43

Atkinson, Joseph Hampton May 56

Atkinson, Oriana (WLB) Yrbk 53 obit Oct 89

Atoll, John George Stewart-Murray, 8th Duke of obit May 42

Attaway, William Dec 41

Attenborough, David Apr 83

Attenborough, Richard May 84

Attlee, Clement Richard Attlee, 1st Earl May 40 Feb 47 obit Dec 67

Attwood, William Jan 68 obit Jul 89

Atwater, Lee Jun 89 obit May 91

Atwell, Wayne J. obit May 41

Atwill, Lionel obit Jun 46

Atwood, Donna May 54

Atwood, Margaret May 84

Aubrey, James T., Jr. Mar 72 obit Nov 94

Auchincloss, Louis (WLB) Yrbk 54 Aug 78

Auchinleck, Claude John Eyre Feb 42 obit May 81

Auden, W. H. Sep 71 obit Nov 73

Auel, Jean M. Feb 91

Auerbach, Arnold *see* Auerbach, Red'

Auerbach, Red' Feb 69

Auerbach-Levy, William Feb 48 obit Sep 64

Augér, Arleen Feb 89 obit Aug 93

Aughinbaugh, William obit Feb 41

Augstein, Rudolf Jun 66

August, John *see* De Voto, Bernard

Augustine, Norman R. Jun 98

Aulaire, Edgar Parin d' Aug 40 [Aulaire, Ingri d'; and Aulaire, Edgar Parin d']

Aulaire, Ingri d' Aug 40 [Aulaire, Ingri d'; and Aulaire, Edgar Parin d']

Aulenti, Gae Sep 99

Aung San Suu Kyi Feb 92

Auriol, Jacqueline Sep 53 obit Jun 2000

Auriol, Vincent Mar 47 obit Feb 66

Auster, Paul Mar 96

Austerlitz, Fred *see* Astaire, Fred

Austin, F. Britten obit May 41

Austin, Herbert Austin, 1st Baron obit Jul 41

Austin, Margretta Feb 54

Austin, Tracy May 81

Austin, Warren R. Jan 44 obit Feb 63

Austin, William Lane Apr 40

Autry, Gene Dec 47 obit Jan 99

Avedon, Richard Feb 75

Avenol, Joseph Jan-Feb 40 obit Oct 52

Averoff-Tossiza, Evangelos May 57 obit Mar 90

Avery, Milton Jun 58 obit Feb 65

Avery, Sewell Jun 44 obit Jan 61

Avila Camacho, Manuel Sep 40 obit Yrbk 56

Avon, Anthony Eden, 1st Earl of *see* Eden, Anthony

Awolowo, Obafemi Jul 57 [Ahmadu, Alhaji, Sardauna of Sokoto; Awolowo, Obafemi; and

Azikiwe, Nnamdi] obit Jul 87

Ax, Emanuel Mar 84

Ayala, Eusebio obit Jul 42

Ayala, Julio César Turbay *see* Turbay Ayala, Julio César

Ayckbourn, Alan Jan 80

Aydelotte, Frank Oct 41 Apr 52 obit Feb 57

Ayer, A. J. May 64 obit Aug 89

Aykroyd, Dan Jan 92

Aylwin, Patricio Aug 90

Ayres, Agnes obit Feb 41

Ayres, Leonard Porter May 40 obit Dec 46

Ayub Khan, Mohammad Apr 59 obit Jun 74

Azad, Abul Kalam, Maulana *see* Abul Kalam Azad, Maulana

Azana, Manuel obit Yrbk 40

Azcona Hoyo, José Feb 88

Azikiwe, Nnamdi Jul 57 [Ahmadu, Alhaji, Sardauna of Sokoto; Awolowo, Obafemi; and Azikiwe, Nnamdi] obit Aug 96

Aziz, Tariq May 91

Aznavour, Charles Feb 68

Azuma IV, Tokuho Apr 54

Azzam, Abdul Rahman Apr 47

Babangida, Ibrahim Sep 90

Babb, James T. Jul 55 obit Oct 68

Babbitt, Bruce E. Apr 87

Babbitt, Milton Sep 62

Babcock, Edward Chester *see* Van Heusen, Jimmy

Babson, Naomi Lane (WLB) Yrbk 52

Babson, Roger W. Feb 45 obit May 67

Babyface Jul 98

Baca-Flor, Carlos obit Jul 41

Bacall, Lauren Mar 70

Baccaloni, Salvatore Oct 44 obit Feb 70

Bach, P. D. Q. *see* Schickele, Peter

Bach, Reginald obit Feb 41

Bach, Richard Oct 73

Bacharach, Burt Dec 57 Oct 70

Bachauer, Gina Jun 54 obit Sep 77

Bache, Harold L. May 59
Bache, Jules S. obit May 44
Bacher, Robert F. Feb 47
Bachman, Richard *see* King, Stephen
Bachrach, Elise Wald obit Mar 40
Backe, John D. Apr 78
Backman, Jules Apr 52 obit Jun 82
Backstrand, C. J. Feb 54 obit Dec 68
Backstreet Boys May 2000
Bacon, Charles L. May 62
Bacon, Charles R. obit Jun 43
Bacon, Francis Feb 57 Aug 85 obit Jun 92
Bacon, George P. obit Nov 41
Bacon, Leonard Jun 41 obit Mar 54
Bacon, Peggy Jan-Feb 40 obit Mar 87
Bacon, Selden D. May 52 obit Feb 93
Bada, Angelo obit May 41
Baden-Powell, Lady May 46
Badger, Oscar C. May 49 obit Feb 59
Badillo, Herman May 71
Badoglio, Pietro Oct 40 obit Jan 57
Badu, Erykah Apr 98
Baehr, George May 42
Baekeland, Leo H. obit Apr 44
Baer, William J. obit Nov 41
Baez, Joan Nov 63
Bagley, William Chandler obit Jul 46
Bagnold, Enid Jun 64 obit May 81
Bagramyan, Ivan C. Dec 44 obit Jan 83
Bagwell, Jeff Aug 2000
Bahcall, John N. Apr 2000
Bailar, Benjamin F. Jul 76
Bailar, John C., Jr. Jul 59
Bailey, Abe obit Sep 40
Bailey, Carolyn Sherwin (WLB) Yrbk 48
Bailey, Consuelo Northrop Jun 54
Bailey, Donald Coleman Oct 45 obit Jul 85
Bailey, F. Lee Dec 67
Bailey, Guy Winfred obit Yrbk 40
Bailey, John M. Jun 62 obit Jun 75

Bailey, Josiah W. Apr 45 obit Jan 47
Bailey, L. H. Jun 48 obit Mar 55
Bailey, Pearl Jun 55 Oct 69 obit Oct 90
Bailey, Thomas L. obit Dec 46
Bailey, Vernon obit Jun 42
Baillie, Hugh Feb 46 obit Mar 66
Bainton, Roland H. Jun 62 obit Jun 84
Baird, Bil Mar 54 [Baird, Bil; and Baird, Cora] obit May 87
Baird, Cora Mar 54 [Baird, Bil; and Baird, Cora] obit Feb 68
Baird, John Lawrence obit Oct 41
Baker, Anita Apr 89
Baker, Asa George obit Oct 40
Baker, Charles Whiting obit Aug 41
Baker, Dorothy Dec 43 obit Sep 68
Baker, Frank (WLB) Yrbk 48
Baker, George Nov 44 obit Aug 75
Baker, George T. Jun 53 obit Jan 64
Baker, Howard H. Mar 74 Aug 87
Baker, James A., 3d Feb 82
Baker, Janet Jun 71
Baker, John H. May 49
Baker, Josephine Jul 64 obit Jun 75
Baker, Louise (WLB) Yrbk 54
Baker, Melvin H. Feb 60
Baker, Mrs. Sydney J. *see* Baker, Nina Brown
Baker, Nicholson Aug 94
Baker, Nina Brown (WLB) Yrbk 47 obit Nov 57
Baker, Norma Jean *see* Monroe, Marilyn
Baker, Phil Nov 46 obit Jan 64
Baker, Ray Stannard Jan-Feb 40 obit Sep 46
Baker, Richard A. *see* Baker, Rick
Baker, Rick Mar 97
Baker, Roy G. Nov 48
Baker, Russell Mar 80
Baker, S. Josephine obit Apr 45
Bakke, E. Wight Sep 53 obit Jan 72

Bakker, Robert T. Aug 95
Bakshi, Ghulam Mohammad Jun 56 obit Sep 72
Bakshi, Ralph Mar 79
Balaban, Barney Oct 46 obit Apr 71
Balaguer, Joaquín Nov 66
Balanchine, George Nov 42 Jun 54 obit Jun 83
Balbo, Italo obit Aug 40
Balch, Emily Greene Jan 47 obit Mar 61
Balchen, Bernt Jan 49 obit Dec 73
Balderston, William Sep 49 obit Oct 83
Baldessari, John Jun 91
Baldomir, Alfredo Jun 42 obit Mar 48
Baldrige, Letitia Feb 88
Baldrige, Malcolm Aug 82 obit Sep 87
Baldwin, Alec Jul 92
Baldwin, C. B. Nov 43
Baldwin, Hanson W. Aug 42 obit Jan 92
Baldwin, James (WLB) Yrbk 59 Jul 64 obit Jan 88
Baldwin, Raymond E. Jul 46 obit Nov 86
Baldwin, Roger Nash Jan-Feb 40 obit Oct 81
Baldwin, William H. Nov 45
Balenciaga May 54 obit May 72
Balewa, Abubakar Tafawa Sep 61 obit Feb 66
Baline, Israel *see* Berlin, Irving
Ball, George W. Feb 62 obit Jul 94
Ball, Joseph H. Oct 43 obit Feb 94
Ball, Lucille Sep 52 [Ball, Lucille; and Arnaz, Desi] Jan 78 obit Jun 89
Ball, Robert M. Jan 68
Ball, Stuart S. Jul 52
Ball, William May 74 obit Oct 91
Ball, Zachary (WLB) Yrbk 53
Balladur, Edouard Feb 94
Ballantine, Ian May 54 obit May 95
Ballantine, Stuart obit Jun 44
Ballard, J. G. May 88
Ballard, Kaye Sep 69
Ballard, Robert D. Jun 86

Ballesterios, Seve *see* Ballesteros, Severiano

Ballesteros, Severiano Sep 80

Balmain, Pierre Jul 54 obit Aug 82

Balthus Nov 79

Baltimore, David Jul 83

Bampton, Rose Mar 40

Bancroft, Anne Jun 60

Bancroft, Ann Jul 2000

Banda, Hastings Jan 63 obit Feb 98

Bandaranaike, S. W. R. D. Sep 56 obit Nov 59

Bandaranaike, Sirimavo May 61

Banderas, Antonio Mar 97

Banfield, Edward C. May 72 obit Feb 2000

Banfield, Jillian Feb 2000

Bani-Sadr, Abolhassan Feb 81

Bankhead, John H. May 43 obit Jul 46

Bankhead, Tallulah Jul 41 Jan 53 obit Feb 69

Bankhead, William Brockman Oct 40 obit Oct 40

Banks, Dennis Jun 92

Banks, Ernie May 59

Banks, Russell Jan 92

Banning, Kendall obit Feb 45

Banning, Margaret Culkin May 40 obit Feb 82

Bannister, Constance Jul 55

Bannister, Roger Apr 56

Bannow, Rudolph F. Dec 60 obit Sep 62

Banting, Frederick Grant obit Apr 41

Bantock, Granville obit Dec 46

Banville, John May 92

Banzer Suárez, Hugo Sep 73

Banzhaf, John F., 3d Dec 73

Bao Dai Nov 49 obit Oct 97

Barad, Jill E. Sep 95

Baragwanath, Mrs. John Gordon *see* McMein, Neysa

Barak, Ehud Aug 97

Baraka, Amiri *see* Jones, Leroi

Barber, Anthony Jan 71

Barber, Carl Jerome *see* Barber, Jerry

Barber, Jerry Apr 62 obit Nov 94

Barber, Mary I. Jul 41 obit Apr 63

Barber, Red Jul 43 obit Jan 93

Barber, Samuel Sep 44 Sep 63 obit Mar 81

Barber, Walter Lanier *see* Barber, Red

Barbey, Daniel E. Jan 45 obit Jun 69

Barbier, George W. obit Aug 45

Barbieri, Fedora Feb 57

Barbirolli, John Yrbk 40 obit Oct 70

Barbour, Haley Nov 96

Barbour, Henry Gray obit Nov 43

Barbour, Ralph Henry obit Apr 44

Barbour, W. Warren obit Jan 44

Barclay, McClelland Sep 40 obit Yrbk 46

Barco Vargas, Virgilio Feb 90 obit Aug 97

Bard, Mary (WLB) Yrbk 56

Bardeen, John Sep 57 obit Apr 91

Barden, Graham A. Sep 49 obit Mar 67

Bardot, Brigitte Jan 60

Barenboim, Daniel Apr 69

Bari, Joe *see* Bennett, Tony

Baring, George Rowland Stanley May 71 obit May 91

Barker, Bob Nov 99

Barker, Lewellys Franklin obit Sep 43

Barkley, Alben W. May 41 Jan 49 obit Jul 56

Barkley, Charles Oct 91

Barlow, Howard Jan-Feb 40 Jul 54 obit Mar 72

Barlow, Reginald obit Aug 43

Barnard, Chester I. Mar 45 obit Sep 61

Barnard, Christiaan N. May 68

Barnard, Elinor M. obit Apr 42

Barnard, James Lynn obit Oct 41

Barnes, Albert Coombs Mar 45 obit Sep 51

Barnes, Clifford W. obit Nov 44

Barnes, Clive Mar 72

Barnes, Henry A. Jun 55 obit Nov 68

Barnes, Julian Mar 88

Barnes, Margaret Campbell (WLB) Yrbk 53

Barnes, Roy Jan 2000

Barnes, Stanley N. Sep 53

Barnes, Wendell B. Jun 57 obit Aug 85

Barnes, William R. obit Mar 45

Barnet, Will Jun 85

Barnett, Eugene E. May 41

Barnett, M. Robert Jan 50

Barnett, Ross Sep 61 obit Jan 88

Barney, Samuel E. obit Mar 40

Barnhart, Clarence L. Sep 54 obit Jan 94

Barnouw, Erik Nov 40

Barnsley, Alan Gabriel *see* Fielding, Gabriel

Baron Franks of Headington *see* Franks, Oliver Shewell

Barr, Alfred H., Jr. Jan 61 obit Oct 81

Barr, John A. Jan 61 obit Mar 79

Barr, Joseph W. Jan 68 obit May 96

Barr, Norman B., Rev. obit May 43

Barr, Roseanne May 89

Barr, Stringfellow Aug 40 obit Apr 82

Barr, William P. Jun 92

Barratt, Arthur Sheridan Jan 41

Barrault, Jean-Louis Mar 53 [Barrault, Jean-Louis; and Renaud, Madeleine] obit Mar 94

Barre, Raymond Jul 77

Barrere, Camille Eugene Pierre obit Yrbk 40

Barrère, Georges obit Aug 44

Barrett, C. Waller Mar 65

Barrett, Craig Mar 99

Barrett, Edward W. Feb 47 obit Feb 90

Barrett, Frank A. Jul 56 obit Jul 62

Barrett, William Aug 82 obit Nov 92

Barrett, Wilton Agnew obit Mar 40

Barrette, Antonio Jul 60 obit Feb 69

Barringer, Emily Dunning Mar 40 obit Jun 61

Barringer, Paul Brandon obit Mar 41

Barros Hurtado, César Jan 59

Barrow, Errol W. Sep 68 obit Jul 87

Barrow, Joseph Louis *see* Louis, Joe

Barry, Dave May 98

Barry, John Mar 2000

Barry, Lynda Nov 94

Barry, Marion May 87

Barry, Patrick Frank, Bishop obit Sep 40

Barry, Rick Mar 71

Barry, William Bernard obit Dec 46

Barrymore, Drew Oct 98

Barrymore, Ethel Mar 41 obit Sep 59

Barrymore, John obit Jul 42

Barrymore, Lionel Jul 43 obit Jan 55

Barshefsky, Charlene Feb 2000

Barth, John May 69

Barth, Karl Nov 62 obit Feb 69

Barthé, Richmond Jul 40 obit May 89

Barthelme, Donald Mar 76 obit Sep 89

Barthes, Roland Feb 79 obit May 80

Bartlett, E. L. Jun 51 obit Mar 69

Bartlett, Jennifer Nov 85

Bartlett, Robert A. obit Jun 46

Bartók, Béla Sep 40 obit Oct 45

Bartol, William Cyrus obit Yrbk 40

Bartoli, Cecilia Jun 92

Barton, Bruce Feb 61 obit Oct 67

Barton, George A. May 53

Barton, George obit Apr 40

Barton, Robert B. M. Apr 59 obit Apr 95

Barton, William H., Jr. obit Aug 44

Bartz, Carol Jul 99

Baruch, Bernard M. Aug 41 Jul 50 obit Sep 65

Baryshnikov, Mikhail Feb 75

Barzel, Rainer May 67

Barzin, Leon May 51 obit Aug 99

Barzini, Luigi Jul 72 obit May 84

Barzun, Jacques Sep 64

Basaldella, Afro *see* Afro

Basdevant, Jules Feb 50 obit Mar 68

Basie, Count Jun 42 obit Jun 84

Basie, William *see* Basie, Count

Basinger, Kim Feb 90

Baskin, Leonard May 64 obit Aug 2000

Basoalto, Ricardo Elizier Neftali Reyes *see* Neruda, Pablo

Bass, George Mar 2000

Bass, Lance *see* 'N Sync

Bass, Robert M. Jul 89

Bassett, Angela May 96

Bassett, Sara Ware (WLB) YRBK 56

Batcheller, Hiland G. Apr 49 obit Jul 61

Bates, Alan Mar 69

Bates, Blanche obit Feb 42

Bates, Ernest Sutherland obit Jan 40

Bates, Granville obit Sep 40

Bates, H. E. Sep 44 obit Mar 74

Bates, Kathy Sep 91

Bates, Marston Apr 56 obit May 74

Bates, Sanford Jan 61 obit Nov 72

Bateson, Mrs. Gregory *see* Mead, Margaret

Bathgate, Andy Feb 64

Batista, Fulgencio Sep 40 Apr 52 obit Oct 73

Batt, William L., Jr. Sep 62

Batt, William L. Feb 42 obit Mar 65

Battle, John S. Nov 50 obit Jun 72

Battle, Kathleen Nov 84

Baudouin Sep 50 obit Oct 93

Baudrillard, Jean Jun 93

Baudrillart, Henri Marie Alfred, Cardinal obit Jul 42

Bauer, Erwin A. Feb 93 [Bauer, Erwin A.; and Bauer, Peggy]

Bauer, Gary L. Jan 99

Bauer, Hank Feb 67

Bauer, Louis Hopewell Oct 48 obit Mar 64

Bauer, Peggy Feb 93 [Bauer, Erwin A.; and Bauer, Peggy]

Baulieu, Etienne-Emile Nov 95

Baum, Kurt Sep 56 obit Feb 90

Baum, William Cardinal Oct 76

Baumer, Marie (WLB) Yrbk 58

Baumgartner, Leona Jan 50 obit Mar 91

Baur, Bertha obit Nov 40

Baur, Harry obit May 43

Baur, John I. H. Dec 69 obit Jul 87

Bausch, Edward obit Sep 44

Bausch, Pina Sep 86

Bausch, William obit Dec 44

Bausher, Mrs J. Lee *see* Jordan, Mildred

Bax, Arnold Sep 43 obit Jan 54

Baxter, Anne May 72 obit Feb 86

Baxter, Frank C. Mar 55

Baxter, James P., 3d Jul 47 obit Aug 75

Bay, Mrs. Charles Ulrick Jun 57

Bayar, Celal Jul 50 obit Oct 86

Bayard, Thomas F. obit Sep 42

Bayh, Birch E., Jr. Jun 65

Bayh, Evan Nov 98

Bayne, Stephen F., Jr. Jan 64 obit Mar 74

Bazelon, David L. Jan 71 obit Apr 93

Bazin, Germain Jan 59 obit Jul 90

Bea, Augustin, Cardinal Sep 64 obit Jan 69

Beach, Amy Marcy *see* Beach, Mrs. H. H. A.

Beach, Edward Oct 60

Beach, Mrs. H. H. A. obit Feb 45

Beadle, George W. Apr 56 obit Aug 89

Beale, Howard Mar 59

Beall, J. Glenn Apr 55 obit Mar 71

Beall, Lester Nov 49 obit Sep 69

Beals, Carleton Jun 41 Yrbk 42 obit Aug 79

Beals, Ralph A. Feb 47 obit Dec 54

Beam, Jacob D. Jul 59 obit Oct 93

Bell Burnell, Jocelyn May 95
Belli, Melvin M. Jul 79 obit Sep 96
Bellmon, Henry Jul 63
Bellow, Saul Feb 65 Nov 88
Belluschi, Pietro Feb 59 obit Apr 94
Belmondo, Jean-Paul Dec 65
Belmont, Eleanor Robson Jul 44 obit Jan 80
Belmore, Alice obit Sep 43
Belt, Guillermo Nov 47 obit Sep 89
Beltrán, Pedro G. Apr 67 obit Apr 79
Belushi, James Jan 95
Belushi, John Jan 80 obit Apr 82
Belyayev, Pavel Jul 65 obit Mar 70
Bemelmans, Ludwig Apr 41 obit Dec 62
Bemis, Samuel Flagg Jun 50 obit Nov 73
Ben and Jerry see Cohen, Ben; Greenfield, Jerry
Benavente, Jacinto Jun 53 obit Sep 54
Benavides, Oscar obit Aug 45
Ben Bella, Ahmed Feb 63
Bench, Johnny Oct 71
Benchley, Belle Jennings Oct 40
Benchley, Nathaniel Sep 53 obit Feb 82
Benchley, Peter Jul 76
Benchley, Robert Sep 41 obit Jan 46
Bender, George H. Jan 52 obit Sep 61
Bender, James F. May 49 obit Mar 98
Bendetsen, Karl R. May 52 obit Sep 89
Bendix, Vincent obit May 45
Bendix, William Sep 48 obit Feb 65
Benedict, Ruth May 41 obit Nov 48
Benelli, Cardinal see Benelli, Giovanni
Benelli, Giovanni Sep 77 obit Jan 83
Benes, Eduard Jan 42 obit Oct 48
Benesh, Joan Jul 57 [Benesh, Rudolf; and Benesh, Joan]

Benesh, Rudolf Jul 57 [Benesh, Rudolf; and Benesh, Joan]
Benét, Stephen Vincent obit Apr 43
Bengough, Percy R. Apr 51
Ben-Gurion, David Oct 47 Jan 57 obit Jan 74
Benigni, Roberto Jun 99
Benjamin, William Evarts obit Mar 40
Benn, Tony Jun 65 Nov 82
Bennett, H. Stanley Apr 66 obit Oct 92
Bennett, Henry G. Feb 51 obit Feb 52
Bennett, Henry Gordon Mar 42 obit Oct 62
Bennett, Hugh Hammond Dec 46 obit Oct 60
Bennett, Ivan L. Nov 52 obit Aug 80
Bennett, James O'Donnell obit Mar 40
Bennett, James V. Apr 49 obit Feb 79
Bennett, John C. Jan 61 obit Jul 95
Bennett, John W. F. obit Oct 43
Bennett, Michael Mar 81 obit Aug 87
Bennett, Rawson, 2d Sep 58 obit Feb 68
Bennett, Richard obit Dec 44
Bennett, Richard Rodney Mar 92
Bennett, Robert L. Sep 67
Bennett, Robert Russell Apr 42 May 62 obit Oct 81
Bennett, Tony Mar 65 Jun 95
Bennett, W. A. C. May 53 obit May 79
Bennett, W. J. Jun 54
Bennett, Wallace F. Feb 49 obit Feb 94
Bennett, William J. Sep 85
Benny, Jack Aug 41 Nov 63 obit Feb 75
Benoit-Lévy, Jean Oct 47 obit Nov 59
Benrimo, J. Harry obit May 42
Bensin, Basil M. Jul 48
Benson, Allan Louis obit Oct 40
Benson, Edward Frederic obit Mar 40

Benson, Ezra Taft Feb 53 obit Aug 94
Benson, Francis Colgate, Jr. obit Apr 41
Benson, John Apr 40 obit Nov 62
Benson, Sally Aug 41 obit Sep 72
Bentley, Helen Delich Dec 71
Bentley, Irene obit Jul 40
Benton, Thomas Hart Oct 40 obit Mar 75
Benton, William Dec 45 obit May 73
Bentsen, Lloyd Sep 73 Apr 93
Ben-Zvi, Isaac Apr 53 obit Jun 63
Beranek, Leo L. Mar 63
Berding, Andrew H. Apr 60
Bérégovoy, Pierre Feb 93 obit Feb 93
Berelson, Bernard Jul 61 obit Nov 79
Berendsen, Carl August Oct 48 obit Dec 73
Berendt, John Apr 98
Beresford, Bruce Mar 93
Berg, Elizabeth Nov 99
Berg, Ernst J. obit Nov 41
Berg, Gertrude Jul 41 Sep 60 obit Nov 66
Berg, Hart O. obit Feb 42
Berg, Irving H. obit Nov 41
Berg, Patricia Jane Sep 40
Berganza, Teresa Jan 79
Bergé, Pierre Jan 90
Berge, Wendell Feb 46 obit Dec 55 Yrbk 56
Bergen, Candice Aug 76
Bergen, Edgar May 45 obit Nov 78
Bergen, John J. Jun 61 obit Feb 81
Bergen, Polly Sep 58
Berger, Meyer Jan 43 obit Apr 59
Berger, Peter L. Mar 83
Berger, Sandy Feb 98
Berger, Thomas Jun 88
Berggrav, Eivind Oct 50 obit Mar 59
Bergland, Bob Sep 77
Bergman, Ingmar Apr 60 Oct 81
Bergman, Ingrid Jan-Feb 40 Sep 65 obit Oct 82
Bergonzi, Carlo Nov 92
Bergquist, Kenneth P. Mar 61

Bergson, Henri obit Feb 41
Bergson, Herbert A. Sep 50
Beria, Lavrenti P. Dec 42 obit Sep 54
Berigan, Bunny obit Jul 42
Berio, Luciano Mar 71
Beriosova, Svetlana Sep 60 obit Feb 99
Berkeley, Busby Apr 71 obit May 76
Berkner, Lloyd V. Sep 49 obit Oct 67
Berkson, Seymour Oct 49 obit Mar 59
Berle, Adolf A., Jr. Jul 40 Jun 61 obit Apr 71
Berle, Milton Jun 49
Berlin, Ellin Aug 44 obit Sep 88
Berlin, Irving May 42 May 63 obit Nov 89
Berlin, Isaiah Jul 64 obit Jan 98
Berlinguer, Enrico Jul 76 obit Aug 84
Berlitz, Charles F. Feb 57
Berlosconi, Silvio Aug 94
Berman, Chris Aug 98
Berman, Emile Zola Jun 72 obit Aug 81
Berman, Eugene Jun 65 obit Feb 73
Berman, Lazar Sep 77
Bernadotte, Folke, Count May 45 obit Nov 48
Bernard, Émile obit Jun 41
Bernardin, Joseph L. Oct 82 obit Jan 97
Bernardino, Minerva Mar 50 obit Nov 98
Bernays, Edward L. Feb 42 Sep 60 obit May 95
Bernbach, William Mar 67 obit Nov 82
Bernhard, Prince of The Netherlands Jun 50
Bernhard, Sandra Sep 90
Bernheim, Bertram M. Sep 43
Bernie, Ben Dec 41 obit Dec 43
Bernier, Rosamond Feb 88
Bernstein, Carl Oct 76
Bernstein, Leonard Feb 44 Feb 60 obit Nov 90
Bernstein, Philip S. Nov 51 obit Feb 86
Bernstein, Robert L. Jul 87
Berra, Lawrence May 52

Berra, Yogi see Berra, Lawrence
Berri, Claude Mar 89
Berri, Nabih Nov 85
Berrigan, Daniel Sep 70
Berrigan, Philip Feb 76
Berry, Charles A. Apr 69
Berry, Chuck Apr 77
Berry, Edward Wilber obit Oct 45
Berry, George L. Jan 48 obit Jan 49
Berry, Halle May 99
Berry, James Gomer Jan 51 obit Mar 68
Berry, Martha McChesney Apr 40 obit Apr 42
Berry, Mary Frances Jun 99
Berry, Wendell May 86
Berry, William Ewert Oct 41 obit Sep 54
Berryman, James Thomas Jul 50 obit Oct 71
Berryman, John May 69 obit Feb 72
Bertolucci, Bernardo Jul 74
Berton, Pierre Oct 91
Bertram, Adolf, Cardinal obit Aug 45
Bertrand, Louis obit Feb 42
Bess, Demaree Jan 43 obit Sep 62
Bessmertnova, Natalya Jan 88
Bessmertnykh, Aleksandr A. Jun 91
Best, Charles H. Jun 57 obit May 78
Best, Edna Jul 54 obit Nov 74
Besteiro Y Fernandez, Julian obit Nov 40
Bestor, Arthur E. obit Mar 44
Bestor, Arthur Sep 58 obit Feb 95
Betancourt, Romulo May 60 obit Nov 81
Betancur, Belisario Apr 85
Bethe, Hans A. Jan-Feb 40 Apr 50
Bethune, Mary McLeod Jan 42 obit Jul 55
Betjeman, John Mar 73 obit Jul 84
Bettelheim, Bruno Jul 61 obit May 90
Betteridge, Don see Newman, Bernard
Bettis, Valerie May 53 obit Nov 82
Bettman, Gary B. Mar 99

Bettmann, Otto L. Nov 61 obit Jul 98
Betts, Rome A. Mar 49
Beuys, Joseph Jul 80 obit Mar 86
Bevan, Aneurin May 43 obit Oct 60
Bevan, Arthur D. obit Aug 43
Bevan, Mrs. Aneurin see Lee, Jennie
Beveridge, William Henry Jan 43 obit May 63
Bevier, Isabel obit May 42
Bevin, Ernest Sep 40 Jun 49 obit May 51
Bevis, Howard L. Jan-Feb 40 Nov 50 obit Jun 68
Bevis, Palmer Apr 53
Beyen, J. W. Feb 53 obit Jun 76
Bezos, Jeff Jun 98
Bhabha, Homi J. Sep 56 obit Feb 66
Bhave, Vinoba Sep 53 obit Jan 83
Bhumibol Adulyadej see Rama IX, King of Thailand
Bhutto, Benazir Jul 86
Bhutto, Zulfikar Ali Apr 72 obit May 79
Biaggi, Mario Jan 86
Bialk, Elisa (WLB) Yrbk 54 obit May 90
Bible, Alan Feb 57 obit Oct 88
Bickel, George L. obit Aug 41
Bidault, Georges May 45 obit Mar 83
Biddle, Anthony J. Drexel Mar 41 obit Jan 62
Biddle, Francis Sep 41 obit Dec 68
Biddle, George Feb 42 obit Jan 74
Biddle, Katherine Garrison Chapin Oct 43 obit Jan 84
Biden, Joseph R., Jr. Jan 87
Bieber, Owen F. Apr 86
Bierut, Boleslaw Sep 49 obit May 56
Biffle, Leslie L. Sep 46 obit May 66
Bigart, Homer Jun 51 obit Jul 91
Bigelow, Karl W. Feb 49 obit Jun 80
Bigelow, William obit May 41
Biggers, John D. Sep 41 obit Feb 74

Biggs, E. Power Nov 50 obit May 77

Bikel, Theodore Mar 60

Bilandic, Michael A. Feb 79

Bilbo, Theodore G. Apr 43 obit Oct 47

Bildt, Carl Jan 93

Biller, Moe Jun 87

Billingsley, Sherman Feb 46 obit Dec 66

Billington, James H. May 89

Billwiller, Henrietta Hudson *see* Hudson, Henrietta

Bimson, Carl A. Mar 61

Binchy, Maeve Nov 95

Binder, Carroll May 51 obit Jul 56

Binder, Theodor Sep 64

Binet-Valmer, Jean obit Sep 40

Bing, Rudolf Feb 50 obit Nov 97

Bingham, Barry Sep 49 obit Sep 88

Bingham, Hiram Mar 51 obit Sep 56

Bingham, Jonathan B. Jul 54 obit Aug 86

Bingham, Millicent Todd Jun 61 obit Jan 69

Binh, Nguyen Thi *see* Nguyen Thi Binh

Binkley, Robert Cedric obit May 40

Binns, Joseph Patterson Jun 54 obit Mar 81

Binyon, Laurence obit Apr 43

Birch, Reginald B. obit Aug 43

Bird, Caroline Jul 76

Bird, Larry Jun 82

Bird, Rose E. May 84 obit May 2000

Bird, Will R. Sep 54

Birdseye, Clarence Mar 46 obit Dec 56 Yrbk 57

Birdseye, Claude Hale obit Jul 41

Birdwell, Russell Jul 46 obit Mar 78

Birendra Bir Bikram Shah Dev, King of Nepal Aug 75

Birge, Raymond Thayer Mar 40

Birmingham, Stephen May 74

Birnbaum, Nathan *see* Burns, George

Birnie, William A. H. Sep 52 obit Oct 79

Birren, Faber May 56 obit Feb 89

Bishop, André Jul 99

Bishop, Elizabeth Sep 77 obit Nov 79

Bishop, Hazel Sep 57 obit Feb 99

Bishop, Isabel Oct 77 obit Apr 88

Bishop, Jim Jun 69 obit Sep 87

Bishop, Joey Apr 62

Bishop, William Avery Sep 41

Bissell, Claude T. May 59

Bissell, Clayton L. Feb 43

Bisset, Jacqueline May 77

Bisset, James G. P. Dec 46

Bitar, Salah Eddin Feb 58 obit Sep 80

Bittner, Van A. Mar 47 obit Sep 49

Bjoerling, Jussi Sep 47 obit Nov 60

Björnsson, Sveinn Aug 44 obit Mar 52

Black, Alexander obit Jan 40

Black, Cathleen P. Jan 98

Black, Clint Aug 94

Black, Conrad M. Aug 92

Black, Eugene R. Jan 50 obit Apr 92

Black, Hugo LaFayette Sep 41 May 64 obit Nov 71

Black, Karen Mar 76

Black, Shirley Temple Oct 45 Apr 70

Black, William Jul 64 obit May 83

Blackall, Frederick S., Jr. Jan 53

Blackett, Patrick M. S. Feb 49 obit Sep 74

Blackfan, K. D. obit Jan 42

Blackie, Ernest Morell, Bishop obit Apr 43

Blackmun, Harry A. Oct 70 obit May 99

Blackton, J. Stuart obit Oct 41

Blackwell, Betsy Talbot Jun 54 obit Apr 85

Blackwell, Earl, Jr. Nov 60 obit May 95

Blades, Rubén May 86

Blaese, R. Michael Mar 2000

Blagonravov, A. A. Feb 58 obit Apr 75

Blaik, Earl H. Jan 45 obit Jul 89

Blain, Daniel Sep 47

Blair, Bonnie Jul 92

Blair, David H. obit Nov 44

Blair, David Jan 61 obit May 76

Blair, James T., Jr. Apr 58 obit Sep 62

Blair, Tony Aug 96

Blaisdell, Thomas C. Jul 49 obit Feb 89

Blake, Doris Nov 41

Blake, Edgar, Bishop obit Jul 43

Blake, Eubie Apr 74 obit Apr 83

Blake, Eugene Carson Sep 55 obit Oct 85

Blake, Francis G. Jan 43 obit Mar 52

Blake, Nicholas *see* Day-Lewis, C.

Blake, Robert Oct 75

Blake, Tiffany obit Nov 43

Blaker, Richard obit Mar 40

Blakeslee, A. F. Oct 41 obit Jan 55

Blakeslee, Francis D. obit Nov 42

Blakey, Art Sep 88 obit Jan 91

Blakey, Michael L. Sep 2000

Blalock, Alfred Sep 46 [Blalock, Alfred; and Taussig, Helen B.] obit Nov 64

Blalock, Mrs. Richard W. May 50

Blamauer, Karoline *see* Lenya, Lotte

Blamey, Thomas Albert Jun 42 obit Jul 51

Blanc, Mel Jun 76 obit Sep 89

Blanch, Arnold May 40 Jan 54 obit Dec 68

Blanch, Mrs. Arnold (Alder) *see* Lee, Doris

Blanchard, Doc *see* Blanchard, Felix A.

Blanchard, Felix A. Mar 46

Blanchard, Hazel A. Jun 63

Blanche, Jacques obit Nov 42

Blanchett, Cate Aug 99

Blanchfield, Florence A. Sep 43 obit Jun 71

Blancke, Harold Jun 57

Blanco Galindo, Carlos obit Nov 43

Blanda, George Sep 72

Blandford, John B., Jr. May 42 obit Mar 72

Blanding, Don Jan 57

Blanding, Sarah Gibson Jun 46 obit Apr 85

Blandy, W. H. P. Nov 42 obit Mar 54

Blank, Theodor Sep 52 obit Jul 72

Blankenhorn, Herbert Apr 56

Blanton, Smiley Jun 56 obit Jan 67

Blass, Bill Sep 66

Blatch, Harriot Stanton obit Jan 41

Blatchford, Joseph H. Mar 71

Blatchley, Willis Stanley obit Jul 40

Blatnik, John A. Feb 58 obit Feb 92

Blattenberger, Raymond Mar 58 obit Jun 71

Blatty, William Peter Jun 74

Blau, Bela obit Yrbk 40

Blaustein, Jacob Apr 49 obit Jan 71

Blease, Cole L. obit Mar 42

Bledsoe, Jules obit Sep 43

Blegen, Judith Jun 77

Blier, Bertrand Oct 88

Bliss, A. Richard, Jr. obit Oct 41

Bliss, Anthony A. Apr 79 obit Nov 91

Bliss, Henry Evelyn Sep 53 obit Oct 55

Bliss, Ray C. Jan 66 obit Oct 81

Bliss, Raymond W. Jan 51 obit Jan 66

Blitch, Iris F. Apr 56 obit Oct 93

Blitzstein, Marc Jul 40 obit Mar 64

Bliven, Bruce Dec 41 obit Jul 77

Bloch, Charles Edward obit Oct 40

Bloch, Claude C. Feb 42 obit Dec 67

Bloch, Ernest Sep 53 obit Oct 59

Bloch, Felix Sep 54 obit Nov 83

Block, Herbert L. Jul 54

Block, John R. Apr 82

Block, Joseph L. Jun 61 obit Feb 93

Block, Paul obit Aug 41

Block, Rudolph *see* Lessing, Bruno

Blodgett, Katharine Burr Jan-Feb 40 May 52 obit Jan 80

Blomfield, Reginald obit Feb 43

Bloodworth-Thomason, Linda Feb 93

Bloom, Allan David Mar 88 obit Nov 92

Bloom, Claire May 56

Bloom, Harold Apr 87

Bloom, Sol May 43 obit Mar 49

Bloomberg, Michael Jun 96

Bloomgarden, Kermit Dec 58 obit Nov 76

Blough, Roger M. Jul 55 obit Jan 86

Blough, Roy Jul 50 obit Sep 2000

Blount, Winton M. Apr 69

Bloustein, Edward J. Nov 65 obit Feb 90

Blücher, Franz Jan 56 obit Jun 59

Blue, Robert D. Dec 48 obit Feb 90

Blue, Vida Mar 72

Bluford, Guion S., Jr. Sep 84

Blum, Léon Nov 40 obit May 50

Blumberg, Baruch S. Nov 77

Blume, Judy Apr 80

Blume, Peter Mar 56 obit Jan 93

Blumenthal, George [financier] obit Yrbk 41

Blumenthal, George [theatrical producer] obit Sep 43

Blumenthal, Hugo obit Sep 43

Blumenthal, W. Michael Jul 77

Blumer, George Alder obit Jan 40

Blundell, Michael Mar 54

Blunt, Katharine Dec 46 obit Oct 54

Bly, Robert Mar 84 Mar 93

Boardman, Mabel Aug 44 obit Apr 46

Boas, Franz May 40 obit Feb 43

Boatner, Haydon L. Jul 52

Bobst, Elmer H. Dec 73 obit Sep 78

Bochco, Steven May 91

Bocher, Main Rousseau *see* Mainbocher

Bock, Fedor Von Oct 42 obit Jun 45

Bocuse, Paul Jan 88

Bodansky, Meyer obit Aug 41

Bodanzky, Artur obit Jan 40

Bodet, Jaime Torres Feb 48 obit Jul 74

Boe, Lars Wilhelm, Rev. obit Feb 43

Boerma, Addeke H. Dec 74

Boesak, Allan Nov 86

Boeschenstein, Harold Feb 61 obit Dec 72

Boff, Leonardo Jan 88

Bogarde, Dirk Jul 67 obit Jul 99

Bogart, Anne Feb 99

Bogart, Humphrey May 42 obit Mar 57

Bogdanovich, Peter Jun 72

Bogert, George H. obit Feb 45

Boggiani, Tommaso Pio, Cardinal obit Apr 42

Boggs, Charles Reid obit Apr 40

Boggs, Hale Apr 58 obit Mar 73

Boggs, J. Caleb Jul 56

Boggs, Wade Aug 90

Bogosian, Eric Sep 87

Boguslawski, Moissaye obit Oct 44

Bohan, Marc Apr 65

Boheman, Erik Mar 51

Bohlen, Charles E. Jun 48 May 60 obit Feb 74

Böhm, Karl Jun 68 obit Oct 81

Bohr, Niels Sep 45 obit Jan 63

Bohrod, Aaron Feb 55 obit Jun 92

Boileau, Ethel obit Mar 42

Boisson, Pierre Feb 43 obit Sep 48

Boitano, Brian Nov 89

Bojan, Willy *see* Stekel, Wilhelm

Bojaxhiu, Agnes Gonxha *see* Teresa, Mother

Bok, Derek C. Jul 71

Bok, Sissela Jan 96

Bok, William Curtis May 54 obit Jul 62

Bokassa, Jean-Bedel Apr 78 obit Jan 97

Bokassa I, Emperor *see* Bokassa, Jean-Bedel

Boland, Edward P. Oct 87

Boland, Frederick H. Feb 61 obit Feb 86

Boland, Patrick J. obit Jul 42

Bolcom, William Apr 90

Boles, Ewing T. Apr 53

Boles, Paul Darcy (WLB) Yrbk 56 obit Jun 84

Bolger, Ray Aug 42 obit Mar 87

Bolger, William F. Oct 79 obit Oct 89

Bolkiah, Muda Hassanal Oct 89

Böll, Heinrich Jul 72 obit Sep 85

Bolles, Stephen obit Sep 41

Bolling, Richard Walker Mar 60 obit Jul 91

Bolotowsky, Ilya Apr 75 obit Jan 82

Bolt, Richard H. Jun 54

Bolt, Robert Jul 63 obit Apr 95

Bolté, Charles G. Oct 45 obit May 94

Bolte, Charles L. Jan 54 obit May 89

Bolton, Frances P. Mar 40 Apr 54 obit May 77

Bolton, Michael Aug 93

Bolz, Lothar Sep 59 obit Apr 87

Bombeck, Erma Feb 79 obit Jun 96

Bonci, Alessandro obit Sep 40

Bond, Edward Jun 78

Bond, Horace Mann Mar 54

Bond, Jessie obit Aug 42

Bond, Julian Dec 69

Bonds, Barry Jun 94

Bonesteel, Charles H. Jun 42 obit Sep 64

Bonham, Milledge Louis, Jr. obit Mar 41

Bonham Carter, Helena Jan 98

Bonine, Frederick N. obit Oct 41

Bon Jovi, Jon Jan 90

Bonnell, John Sutherland Jun 45 obit Apr 92

Bonner, Elena see Bonner, Yelena

Bonner, Herbert C. Jul 56 obit Jan 66

Bonner, Mary Graham (WLB) Yrbk 50

Bonner, Paul Hyde (WLB) Yrbk 55 obit Mar 69

Bonner, Yelena Apr 87

Bonnet, Henri Feb 45 obit Feb 79

Bonney, Therese Feb 44

Bono, Cher see Cher

Bono, Emilio De see De Bono, Emilio (Giuseppe Gaspare Giovanni)

Bono, Sonny Feb 74 obit Mar 98

Bonomi, Ivanoe Aug 44 obit May 51

Bonomi, Maria Jul 60

Bonsal, Philip Wilson Jun 59 obit Sep 95

Bonsal, Stephen Aug 45 obit Jul 51

Bontemps, Arna (WLB) Yrbk 46 obit Jul 73

Bonynge, Richard Feb 81

Booker, Edna Lee Apr 40

Boone, J. T. Mar 51 obit Jun 74

Boone, Pat Jul 59

Boone, Richard Feb 64 obit Mar 81

Boorman, John Jun 88

Boorstin, Daniel J. Sep 68 Jan 84

Boosler, Elayne May 93

Booth, Arch N. Dec 61

Booth, Ballington obit Nov 40

Booth, Evangeline Feb 41 obit Sep 50

Booth, Shirley Nov 42 Apr 53 obit Jan 93

Borah, William Edgar obit Jan 40

Borberg, William Nov 52 obit Sep 58

Borch, Fred J. Oct 71

Borcherds, Richard Feb 99

Bordaberry, Juan M. Apr 75

Borde, Jean de la see De La Borde, Jean

Borden, Neil H. May 54

Bordes, Pierre-Louis obit Sep 43

Boren, David L. Nov 89

Borg, Björn Dec 74

Borge, Victor Mar 46 May 93

Borges, Jorge Luis Jan 70 obit Aug 86

Borgese, G. A. Dec 47 obit Jan 53

Borglum, Gutzon obit Apr 41

Borgnine, Ernest Apr 56

Boring, Edwin G. Mar 62 obit Sep 68

Boris III, King of Bulgaria Feb 41 obit Yrbk 91 (died Aug 43)

Boris Vladimirovitch, Grand Duke of Russia obit Dec 43

Borlaug, Norman E. Jul 71

Borman, Frank Mar 69 Apr 80

Born, Max May 55 obit Feb 70

Borne, Mortimer Apr 54

Bornó, Louis obit Sep 42

Borofsky, Jonathan Jul 85

Boros, Julius Nov 68 obit Aug 94

Borst, Lyle B. Jul 54

Bortz, Edward Leroy Sep 47 obit Apr 70

Borysenko, Joan Oct 96

Borzage, Frank Dec 46 obit Sep 62

Bosch, Carl obit Jan 40

Bosch, Juan Jun 63

Bosch, Robert obit Apr 42

Bose, Subhas Chandra Jun 44 obit Dec 45

Boskin, Michael J. Sep 89

Bosone, Reva Beck Jan 49

Bossy, Mike Jun 81

Bostwick, Arthur E. obit Apr 42

Bosustow, Stephen Jun 58

Bosworth, Hobart obit Feb 44

Botero, Fernando Mar 80

Botha, P. W. Sep 79

Botha, Roelof F. May 84

Botha Pik see Botha, Roelof F.

Bothe, Walther May 55 obit Apr 57

Bothwell, Jean (WLB) Yrbk 46

Botstein, Leon Aug 96

Botvinnik, Mikhail Jun 65 obit Jul 95

Bouchard, Lucien Apr 99

Boucher, Anthony Jun 62 obit Jun 68

Bouchles, Olympia Jean see Snowe, Olympia J.

Boudreau, Lou Aug 42

Boulanger, Nadia May 62 obit Jan 80

Boulding, Kenneth E. Mar 65 obit May 93

Boulez, Pierre Mar 69

Boult, Adrian Cedric Mar 46 obit Apr 83

Boumedienne, Houari Jan 71 obit Feb 79

Bourassa, Robert Sep 76 obit Jan 97

Bourgeois, Louise Oct 83

Bourgès-Maunoury, Maurice Jul 57

Bourguiba, Habib ben Ali Sep 55 obit Aug 2000

Bourke-White, Margaret Jan 40 [White, Margaret Bourke] obit Oct 71

Bourne, Jonathan Jr. obit Oct 40

Bourne, St. Clair Jun 2000

Bourtzev, Vladimir L. obit Dec 42

Bouteflika, Abdelaziz Feb 76

Boutell, Clarence B. Jul 46

Boutell, Clip see Boutell, Clarence B.

Boutelle, Richard S. Sep 51

Bouton, Jim Oct 71

Boutros-Ghali, Boutros Apr 92

Bovet, Daniele Jan 58 obit Jun 92

Bowater, Eric Sep 56 obit Nov 62

Bowden, Bobby Nov 96

Bowditch, Richard L. Jul 53 obit Nov 59

Bowe, Riddick Jun 96

Bowen, Catherine Drinker Jul 44 obit Dec 73

Bowen, Ira Sprague Jun 51 obit Apr 73

Bowen, Otis R. Nov 86

Bowen, William G. May 73

Bower, Bertha Muzzy obit Sep 40

Bowers, Claude Gernade Sep 41 obit Mar 58

Bowers, Faubion Sep 59 obit May 2000

Bowes, Edward Mar 41 obit Jul 46

Bowes-Lyon, Claud George obit Dec 44

Bowie, David Oct 76 Nov 94

Bowie, Edward Hall obit Sep 43

Bowker, Albert H. Jan 66

Bowles, Chester Sep 43 Jan 57 obit Jul 86

Bowles, Erskine Aug 98

Bowles, Paul Oct 90 obit Feb 2000

Bowman, George E. obit Nov 41

Bowman, Isaiah Jan 45 obit Feb 50

Bowman, Scotty Jan 99

Bowron, Fletcher Feb 50 obit Nov 68

Boxer, Barbara Apr 94

Boyce, Westray Battle Sep 45 obit Mar 72

Boyd, Alan S. Mar 65

Boyd, Bill Mar 50 obit Nov 72

Boyd, James [geophysicist] Mar 49

Boyd, James [historical novelist] obit Apr 44

Boyd, Julian P. Jun 76 obit Aug 80

Boyd, Louise A. Sep 60 obit Nov 72

Boyd, Malcolm Mar 68

Boyd, Stephen Dec 61 obit Aug 77

Boyd, William see Boyd, Bill

Boyd of Merton, Viscount see Lennox-Boyd, Alan Tindal

Boyd-Orr, John Boyd Orr Jun 46 obit Sep 71

Boyer, Charles Feb 43 obit Oct 78

Boyer, Ernest L. Jan 88 obit Feb 96

Boyer, Harold Raymond Feb 52

Boyer, Ken Mar 66 obit Oct 82

Boyer, Lucien obit Aug 42

Boyer, Marion W. Jan 51 obit Jan 83

Boy George Oct 85

Boylan, Robert P. Apr 50

Boyle, Hal Jun 45 obit May 74

Boyle, Kay Jun 42 obit Feb 93

Boyle, T. Coraghessan Jan 91

Boyle, Tony see Boyle, W. A.

Boyle, W. A. Jul 70 obit Jul 85

Boyle, William M., Jr. Jun 49 obit Nov 61

Boylston, Helen Dore Jul 42 obit Nov 84

Bracco, Roberto obit Jun 43

Brace, Gerald Warner (WLB) Yrbk 47 obit Sep 78

Bracken, Brendan Dec 41

Bracken, Eddie Oct 44

Brackett, Charles Feb 51 obit Apr 69

Brackman, Robert Jul 53 obit Sep 80

Bradbury, James H. obit Yrbk 40

Bradbury, Norris E. Apr 49 obit Nov 97

Bradbury, Ray Jun 53 Jul 82

Braddock, Bessie see Braddock, E. M.

Braddock, E. M. Jul 57 obit Jan 71

Brademas, John May 77

Braden, Spruille Sep 45 obit Mar 78

Bradford, Barbara Taylor Oct 91

Bradford, Robert F. Dec 48 obit May 83

Bradlee, Benjamin C. Sep 75

Bradley, Bill Jul 65 Sep 82

Bradley, David Apr 49

Bradley, Ed May 88

Bradley, Omar Nelson Jul 43 obit May 81

Bradley, Pat Feb 94

Bradley, Preston Mar 56

Bradley, Tom Nov 73 Oct 92 obit Jan 99

Bradshaw, John E. Apr 93

Bradshaw, Lillian Moore Jun 70

Bradshaw, Terry Apr 79

Bradshaw, Thornton F. Jun 82 obit Feb 89

Brady, James S. Oct 91

Brady, Nicholas F. Nov 88

Brady, Sarah Oct 96

Brady, William T. Jan 61 obit Jul 84

Bragdon, Claude obit Oct 46

Bragdon, Helen D. Feb 51

Bragg, William Henry obit Apr 42

Brahdy, Mrs. Leopold see Rees, Mina S.

Brailowsky, Alexander Jun 56 obit Jun 76

Brainered, Norman see Fuller, S. R., Jr.

Bramah, Ernest obit Sep 42

Brameld, Theodore Jun 67 obit Jan 88

Bramuglia, Juan A. May 49 obit Nov 62

Branagh, Kenneth Apr 97

Brancusi, Constantin Sep 55 obit Jun 57

Brand, Max see Faust, Frederick

Brand, Oscar Jun 62
Brandauer, Klaus Maria Jul 90
Brandeis, Louis D. obit Nov 41
Brandenburg, William A. obit Yrbk 40
Brando, Marlon Apr 52 Mar 74
Brandt, Bill Aug 81 obit Feb 84
Brandt, Willy Jun 58 Dec 73 obit Nov 92
Braniff, T. E. Apr 52 obit Mar 54
Branly, Edouard obit Apr 40
Brannaman, Ray H. Nov 47
Brannan, Charles F. Sep 48
Bransome, Edwin D. Apr 52
Branson, Richard Feb 95
Branzell, Karin Feb 46 obit Feb 75
Braque, Georges Nov 49 obit Oct 63
Brattain, Walter Sep 57 obit Nov 87
Brauchitsch, Heinrich Alfred Hermann Walther Von Mar 40 obit Dec 48
Braudel, Fernand Apr 85 obit Jan 86
Braun, Werner Jun 57 obit Jan 73
Bravo, Ellen Aug 97
Braxton, Toni Sep 2000
Bray, Robert S. Feb 66 obit Feb 75
Brazelton, T. Berry Oct 93
Brazzi, Rossano May 61 obit Mar 95
Bream, Julian Mar 68
Breathitt, Edward T. Jul 64
Breckenridge, Lester Paige obit Oct 40
Breckinridge, Aida De Acosta Jun 54 obit Jul 62
Breech, Ernest R. Sep 55 obit Aug 78
Breedlove, Craig Sep 66
Breen, Joseph I. Jul 50 obit Jan 66
Breitmeyer, Philip obit Jan 42
Brel, Jacques Mar 71 obit Nov 78
Brenan, Gerald Jul 86 obit Mar 87
Brendel, Alfred Jul 77
Brennan, Edward A. Nov 90

Brennan, Francis, Cardinal Oct 67 obit Sep 68
Brennan, Peter J. Apr 73 obit Jan 97
Brennan, Walter May 41 obit Nov 74
Brennan, William J. Jun 57 obit Oct 97
Brenner, Charles H. Oct 2000
Brenner, David Mar 87
Brentano, Arthur obit Mar 44
Brentano, Heinrich Von Feb 55 obit Jan 65
Brenton, W. Harold Jan 53
Brereton, Lewis H. Dec 43 obit Oct 67
Breslin, Howard (WLB) Yrbk 58 obit Jul 64
Breslin, Jimmy Dec 73
Bresson, Robert Jan 71 obit Jun 2000
Brett, George H. Jun 42
Brett, George Jul 81
Brett, George P., Jr. Dec 48 obit May 84
Breuer, Lee Oct 99
Breuer, Marcel Sep 41 Jun 60 obit Aug 81
Brewer, Roy M. Sep 53
Brewster, Benjamin, Bishop obit Mar 41
Brewster, Chauncey Bunce, Bishop obit Jun 41
Brewster, Kingman, Jr. May 64 Sep 79 obit Jan 89
Brewster, Owen May 47 obit Feb 62
Breyer, Stephen G. Jun 96
Breytenbach, Breyten Jun 86
Brezhnev, Leonid I. Jan 63 Nov 78 obit Jan 83
Brice, Fanny Jun 46 obit Jul 51
Brick, John (WLB) Yrbk 53 obit Dec 73
Brickell, Herschel Nov 45 obit Jul 52
Bricker, John W. Apr 43 Jul 56 obit May 86
Brickner, Richard M. Sep 43
Brico, Antonia Sep 48 obit Oct 89
Bridge, Frank obit Mar 41
Bridges, Alfred Bryant Renton see Bridges, Harry
Bridges, Harry Nov 40 May 50 obit May 90
Bridges, Jeff Mar 91

Bridges, Lloyd Jul 90 obit May 98
Bridges, Robert obit Nov 41
Bridges, Styles Mar 48 obit Jan 62
Bridgman, P. W. Apr 55 obit Nov 61
Brier, Howard M. (WLB) Yrbk 51
Briggs, Ellis O. Apr 65 obit Apr 76
Briggs, Eugene S. Oct 48
Briggs, James E. Jun 57 obit Aug 79
Brigham, Carl Campbell obit Mar 43
Brigham, Clarence S. Jul 59 obit Oct 63
Brill, Steven Nov 97
Brimmer, Andrew Jul 68
Brind, Patrick Nov 52 obit Jan 64
Briney, Nancy Jan 54
Brink, Carol (WLB) Yrbk 46
Brinkley, Christie Feb 94
Brinkley, David Mar 60 Sep 87
Brinkley, John R. obit Jul 42
Brinkley, Nell obit Dec 44
Brinton, Crane Jun 59 obit Nov 68
Brinton, Howard H. Jul 49 obit Yrbk 84 (died Apr 73)
Briscoe, Connie Jan 2000
Briscoe, Robert May 57 obit Jul 69
Bristol, Arthur Leroy obit Jun 42
Bristol, Lee H. Sep 62
Bristow, Gwen Yrbk 40 obit Yrbk 84 (died Aug 80)
Bristow, Joseph Little obit Sep 44
Brittan, Leon Aug 94
Britten, Benjamin Oct 42 Apr 61 obit Feb 77
Britton, Edgar C. Apr 52 obit Oct 62
Bro, Margueritte Harmon (WLB) Yrbk 52
Broad, William Michael Albert see Idol, Billy
Broadbent, John Edward May 88
Broadhurst, Harry May 43
Brock, Lou Jun 75
Brock, William Emerson, 3d May 71
Brode, Mildred H. Sep 63

Brode, Wallace Jun 58 obit Oct 74

Broder, Samuel Aug 92

Broderick, Matthew May 87

Brodie, Bernard B. Sep 69 obit May 89

Brodkey, Harold Apr 89 obit Apr 96

Brodsky, Joseph Jul 82 obit Apr 96

Brody, Jane E. Feb 86

Brogan, Denis William (WLB) Yrbk 47 obit Feb 74

Broglie, Louis De Sep 55 obit May 87

Brokaw, Tom May 81

Brokenshire, Norman May 50 obit Jun 65

Bromfield, Louis Jul 44 obit May 56

Bromley, Dorothy Dunbar Apr 46 obit Feb 86

Bronfman, Edgar M., Jr. Oct 95

Bronfman, Edgar M. Jul 74

Bronk, Detlev W. Oct 49 obit Jan 76

Bronowski, J. Sep 58 obit Oct 74

Bronson, Charles Mar 75

Bronstein, Lev Davidovich see Trotsky, Leon

Brook, Alexander Apr 41 obit Apr 80

Brook, Peter May 61

Brooke, Alan Jan 41 obit Sep 63

Brooke, Basil Stanlake Jun 48 obit Oct 73

Brooke, Edward William, III Apr 67

Brookeborough, Basil Stanlake Brooke, 1st Viscount see Brooke, Basil Stanlake

Brooke-Popham, Robert Oct 41 obit Jan 54

Brookes, George S., Rev. Aug 40

Brookhart, Smith W. obit Jan 45

Brookner, Anita Feb 89

Brooks, Albert Apr 97

Brooks, Angie Mar 70

Brooks, C. Wayland Sep 47 obit Mar 57

Brooks, D. W. Jun 51

Brooks, Diana D. Jun 98

Brooks, Donald Mar 72

Brooks, Garth Mar 92

Brooks, Gwendolyn Jun 50 Jul 77

Brooks, Jack Jun 92

Brooks, James Feb 59 obit May 92

Brooks, James L. Apr 98

Brooks, Louise Apr 84 obit Oct 85

Brooks, Matilda M. Nov 41

Brooks, Mel Sep 74

Brooks, Overton Jun 57 obit Dec 61

Brooks, Robert C. obit Apr 41

Brooks, Van Wyck Jun 41 Sep 60 obit Jun 63

Brophy, Thomas D'arcy Sep 52 obit Oct 67

Brosio, Manlio Sep 55 obit May 80

Brosnan, Jim Nov 64

Brosnan, Pierce Jan 97

Brossard, Edgar B. Jul 54

Brothers, Joyce Apr 71

Brough, Louise Jun 48

Broun, Heywood obit Jan 40

Brouwer, Dirk Mar 51 obit Mar 66

Browder, Earl Oct 44 obit Sep 73

Browdy, Benjamin G. Jul 51

Brower, Charles Feb 65 obit Nov 84

Brower, David Jun 73

Brown, A. Ten Eyck obit Jul 40

Brown, Alberta L. May 58

Brown, Albert Eger Jan 48

Brown, Angeline see Dickinson, Angie

Brown, Bobby Apr 91

Brown, Carleton obit Aug 41

Brown, Cecil Mar 42 obit Jan 88

Brown, Charles H. Aug 41 obit Mar 60

Brown, Charles L. Sep 81

Brown, Charles R. Jul 58

Brown, Clarence J. Feb 47 obit Nov 65

Brown, Claude Nov 67

Brown, David M. Jun 50

Brown, Dee Aug 79

Brown, Edmund G., Jr. Apr 75

Brown, Edmund G. Mar 60 obit Apr 96

Brown, Francis Shunk obit Jan 40

Brown, George Dec 63 obit Jul 85

Brown, George H. Jan 71

Brown, George S. Oct 75 obit Feb 79

Brown, Gilmor Jul 44

Brown, Harold Sep 61 Oct 77

Brown, Harrison Jul 55 obit Feb 87

Brown, Helen Dawes obit Nov 41

Brown, Helen Gurley Nov 69

Brown, Helen Hayes see Hayes, Helen

Brown, Irving Jul 51 obit May 89

Brown, J. Carter Apr 76

Brown, James Mar 92

Brown, Jerry see Brown, Edmund G., Jr.

Brown, Jesse Nov 93

Brown, Jim Sep 64

Brown, Joe E. Feb 45 obit Sep 73

Brown, John Franklin obit Mar 40

Brown, John Mason Apr 42 obit May 69

Brown, Larry [football player] Mar 73

Brown, Larry [basketball coach] Apr 96

Brown, Lester R. Jan 93

Brown, Lewis H. Oct 47 obit Mar 51

Brown, Newell Sep 59 obit Sep 2000

Brown, Pat see Brown, Edmund G.

Brown, Perry see Brown, Sanford Perry

Brown, Prentiss M. Jan 43 obit Feb 74

Brown, Rita Mae Sep 86

Brown, Robert McAfee May 65

Brown, Ron Jul 89 obit Jun 96

Brown, Sanford Perry Apr 49

Brown, Sterling Aug 82 obit Apr 89

Brown, Tina Feb 90

Brown, Tony Feb 97

Brown, Trisha Apr 97

Brown, Virginia Mae Jul 70 obit May 91

Brown, Willie Apr 97

Browne, Coral Dec 59 obit Jul 91

Browne, Edward E. obit Jan 46

Browne, George Elmer obit Sep 46

Browne, Jackson Oct 89

Browne, Mary Mumpere Shaver *see* Shaver, Mary

Browne, Sidney Jane obit Oct 41

Brownell, Herbert, Jr. Aug 44 Feb 54 obit Aug 96

Brownell, Samuel Miller Feb 54 obit Jan 91

Browner, Carol M. May 94

Browning, Frederick A. M. Jun 43 obit Apr 65

Browning, Jean *see* Madeira, Jean

Browning, John May 69

Browning, Webster E. obit Jun 42

Brownlow, Kevin Mar 92

Brownmiller, Susan Jan 78

Brownson, Charles B. Jul 55

Brownson, Josephine Mar 40

Broyhill, Joel T. May 74

Broz, Joseph *see* Broz, Tito Josip

Broz, Tito Josip Nov 43 Mar 55 obit Jun 80

Brozovich, Josip *see* Broz, Tito Josip

Brubeck, Dave Mar 56 Apr 93

Bruce, David K. E. Jun 49 Sep 61 obit Feb 78

Bruce, Howard Sep 48 obit Sep 61

Bruce, James Jan 49 obit Sep 80

Bruce, Louis R., Jr. May 72 obit Jul 89

Bruce, Robert Randolph obit Apr 42

Bruce, William Cabell obit Jun 46

Brucker, Wilbur M. Sep 55 obit Dec 68

Bruckheimer, Jerry Mar 99

Bruckner, Henry obit Jun 42

Bruhn, Erik Apr 59 obit May 86

Brumel, Valeri Apr 63

Brunauer, Esther C. Nov 47 obit Sep 59

Brundage, Avery Jan 48 obit Aug 75

Brundage, Percival F. Apr 57

Brundtland, Gro Harlem Nov 81

Bruner, Jerome Seymour Oct 84

Brunner, Edmund De S. Sep 58 obit Feb 74

Brunner, Jean Adam Sep 45 obit Jun 51

Bruns, Franklin R., Jr. May 54

Brunsdale, Norman Sep 54

Brush, George De Forest obit Jun 41

Brustein, Robert Aug 75

Bruton, John Nov 96

Bryan, Charles W. obit Apr 45

Bryan, Ernest R. Jul 50 obit Feb 55

Bryan, George Sands obit Feb 44

Bryan, James E. Jun 62

Bryan, Julien Jul 40 obit Jan 75

Bryant, Anita Nov 75

Bryant, Bear *see* Bryant, Paul W.

Bryant, Benjamin Nov 43

Bryant, C. Farris Sep 61

Bryant, Paul W. Jun 80 obit Mar 83

Bryce, Elizabeth Marion, Viscountess obit Jan 40

Brynner, Yul Sep 56 obit Nov 85

Bryson, Lyman Sep 40 Sep 51 obit Feb 60

Brzezinski, Zbigniew Apr 70

Buatta, Mario May 91

Buber, Martin Jun 53 obit Jul 65

Bubka, Sergei Jul 96

Buchan, John Jan 40

Buchanan, Edna Sep 97

Buchanan, Frank Feb 51

Buchanan, Patrick J. Aug 85

Buchanan, Scott Sep 62 obit May 68

Buchanan, Thomas Drysdale obit Apr 40

Buchanan, Wiley T., Jr. Nov 57 obit Mar 86

Bucher, Walter H. Feb 57 obit Apr 65

Buchholz, Horst Mar 60

Buchinsky, Charles *see* Bronson, Charles

Buchman, Frank N. D. Oct 40 obit Nov 61

Buchwald, Art Jan 60

Buck, Dorothea Dutcher *see* Buck, Mrs. J. L. Blair

Buck, Frank Jun 43 obit Apr 50

Buck, Gene Feb 41 obit May 57

Buck, Mrs. J. L. Blair Sep 47

Buck, Paul Herman Jul 55 obit Apr 89

Buck, Pearl Jul 56 obit Apr 73

Buck, Solon J. May 47 obit Jul 62

Buckley, Christopher Apr 97

Buckley, James L. Oct 71

Buckley, William F., Jr. Jun 62 Oct 82

Buckmaster, Henrietta (WLB) Yrbk 46 obit Jun 83

Buckner, Emory R. obit May 41

Buckner, Simon Bolivar, Jr. Oct 42 obit Jul 45

Budd, Edward G., Jr. Jul 49 obit Jul 71

Budd, Ralph Jul 40 obit Mar 62

Budenny, Semyon M. Sep 41 obit Dec 73

Budenz, Louis F. Jun 51 obit Jun 72

Budge, Donald Jun 41 obit Jun 2000

Budge, Hamer H. Dec 70

Budington, William S. Jun 64

Buechner, Frederick (WLB) Yrbk 59

Buechner, Thomas S. Feb 61

Buell, Raymond Leslie obit Apr 46

Bueno, Maria Apr 65

Buetow, Herbert P. Mar 60 obit Mar 72

Buffet, Bernard Apr 59 obit Feb 2000

Buffett, Jimmy Mar 99

Buffett, Warren E. Nov 87

Buffum, Charles A. obit Sep 41

Buford, John Lester Apr 56

Bugas, John S. Dec 47 obit Feb 83

Bugher, John C. Apr 53

Buitoni, Giovanni Jun 62 obit Mar 79

Bujones, Fernando Jan 76

Bukovsky, Vladimir Mar 78

Bukovsky, Volodya *see* Bukovsky, Vladimir

Bukowski, Charles Apr 94 obit Apr 94

Buley, R. Carlyle Jul 51 obit Jun 68

Bulgakov, Mikhail Afa-nasievich obit Mar 40

Bulganin, Nikolai A. Feb 55 obit Apr 75

Bull, Johan obit Oct 45

Bull, Odd Nov 68

Bullard, Edward Crisp Sep 54 obit May 80

Bullins, Ed May 77

Bullis, Harry A. Oct 46 obit Jan 64

Bullitt, William Christian Jul 40 obit Apr 67

Bullock, Sandra Aug 97

Bulosan, Carlos (WLB) Yrbk 46 obit Nov 56

Bultmann, Rudolf Jan 72 obit Sep 76

Bumbry, Grace Mar 64

Bumgarner, James see Garner, James

Bumpers, Dale Aug 79

Bunau-Varilla, Philippe obit Jul 40

Bunche, Ralph J. Feb 48 obit Jan 72

Bundesen, Herman Niels Oct 48 obit Nov 60

Bundy, McGeorge Mar 62 obit Jan 97

Bundy, William P. Jun 64

Bunge, Alejandro E. obit Jul 43

Bunker, Ellsworth Apr 54 Mar 78 obit Nov 84

Bunker, George M. Apr 57

Bunshaft, Gordon Mar 89 obit Oct 90

Bunting, Earl Feb 47

Bunting, Mary I. Jun 67 obit Apr 98

Bunting-Smith, Mary Ingra-ham see Bunting, Mary I.

Buñuel, Luis Mar 65 obit Sep 83

Burbidge, E. Margaret Nov 2000

Burchard, John E. Apr 58 obit Mar 76

Burchfield, Charles May 42 May 61 obit Mar 67

Burdell, Edwin S. Feb 52

Burdett, Winston Oct 43 obit Jul 93

Burdick, Charles Kellogg obit Aug 40

Burdick, Quentin N. May 63 obit Nov 92

Burdick, Usher L. Apr 52 obit Nov 60

Burford, Anne McGill see Gorsuch, Anne

Burger, Warren E. Nov 69 obit Aug 95

Burgess, Anthony May 72 obit Jan 94

Burgess, Carter L. Apr 57

Burgess, Robert W. Jul 60 obit Jul 69

Burgess, W. Randolph Jun 49 obit Nov 78

Burghley, David George Brownlow Cecil, Lord Jan 56

Burgin, William O. obit May 46

Burke, Arleigh A. Sep 55 obit Aug 96

Burke, Charles H. obit May 44

Burke, Edmund J., Father obit Feb 41

Burke, Edward Raymond Sep 40 obit Dec 68

Burke, Michael Apr 72 obit Mar 87

Burke, Thomas A. Jul 54 obit Jan 72

Burke, Thomas obit Oct 45

Burke, William R. Jul 61

Burke, Yvonne Brathwaite Oct 75

Burleigh, George William obit Apr 40

Burleigh, Harry T. Aug 41 obit Oct 49

Burliuk, David Apr 40 obit Mar 67

Burnet, Macfarlane May 54 obit Oct 85

Burnett, Carol Jan 62 Nov 90

Burnett, Charles Sep 95

Burnett, Hallie Southgate (WLB) Yrbk 54 obit Nov 91

Burnett, Whit Apr 41 [Foley, Martha; and Burnett, Whit] obit Jun 73

Burney, Leroy E. Jul 57 obit Oct 98

Burnham, Donald C. Nov 68

Burnham, Forbes Nov 66 obit Oct 85

Burnham, James Nov 41 obit Jan 88

Burns, Alan Sep 53

Burns, Arthur F. Sep 53 Aug 76 obit Aug 87

Burns, Cecil Delisle obit Mar 42

Burns, E. L. M. Feb 55

Burns, Edward McN Feb 54

Burns, Eveline Mabel Nov 60 obit Jan 86

Burns, George Mar 51 [Burns, George; and Allen, Gracie] Jul 76 obit Nov 96

Burns, H. S. M. May 54 obit Dec 71

Burns, James Aloysius, Father obit Oct 40

Burns, James Mac Gregor Dec 62

Burns, John A. Feb 72 obit Jun 75

Burns, John L. Apr 60 obit Aug 96

Burns, Ken May 92

Burnseig, Arthur Frank see Burns, Arthur F.

Burpee, David Mar 55 obit Aug 80

Burr, Donald C. Sep 86

Burr, Henry obit May 41

Burr, Raymond Sep 61 obit Nov 93

Burrell, Stanley Kirk see Hammer

Burroughs, William S. Nov 71 obit Nov 97

Burrows, Abe Nov 51 obit Jul 85

Burrows, Millar Jul 56 obit Jul 80

Burstyn, Ellen Jun 75

Burton, Alan C. Sep 56

Burton, Charles Emerson, Rev. obit Oct 40

Burton, Dan Sep 98

Burton, Harold H. Apr 45 obit Jan 65

Burton, Jean (WLB) Yrbk 48

Burton, LeVar Mar 2000

Burton, Lewis William, Bishop obit Yrbk 40

Burton, Richard [writer] obit May 40

Burton, Richard [actor] Dec 60 obit Sep 84

Burton, Tim Jul 91

Burton, Virginia Lee Sep 43 obit Dec 68

Burwash, Lachlin Taylor obit Feb 41

Buscaglia, Leo Oct 83 obit Aug 98

Buscemi, Steve Apr 99

Busch, August A. Jul 73 obit Nov 89

Busch, Carl obit Feb 44

Busch, Charles Jun 95

Busch, Fritz Jan 46 obit Oct 51

Bush, Barbara Oct 89

Bush, George Jan 72 Sep 83

Bush, George W. Apr 97

Bush, Jeb Feb 99

Bush, John Ellis *see* Bush, Jeb

Bush, Kate Mar 95

Bush, Prescott S. May 42 Jan 54 obit Dec 72

Bush, Vannevar Sep 40 May 47 obit Sep 74

Bush, Wendell T. obit Mar 41

Bushnell, Asa S. Jul 52 obit May 75

Bustamante, Alexander May 65 obit Sep 77

Butcher, Susan Jun 91

Butcher, Willard C. Jul 80

Buthelezi, Gatsha *see* Buthelezi, Mangosuthu G.

Buthelezi, Mangosuthu G. Oct 86

Butler, Hugh Feb 50 obit Sep 54

Butler, John Jun 55 obit Nov 93

Butler, John M. May 54 obit May 78

Butler, Nevile Apr 41

Butler, Nicholas Murray Nov 40 obit Dec 47

Butler, Paul M. May 55 obit Feb 62

Butler, Reg Sep 56

Butler, Richard Austen May 44 Sep 64 obit May 82

Butler, Robert N. Jan 97

Butler, Sally Dec 46

Butler, Smedley Darlington obit Aug 40

Butler of Saffron Walden, Richard Austen Butler, Baron *see* Butler, Richard Austen

Buttenwieser, Benjamin J. Nov 50 obit Mar 92

Butterfield, Roger Place Mar 48 obit Yrbk 91 (died Jan 81)

Butterfly, Julia *see* Hill, Julia "Butterfly"

Butterworth, Charles obit Jul 46

Button, Richard Mar 49

Buttons, Red Sep 58

Butts, Alfred M. Jul 54 obit Jun 93

Butts, Calvin O. Feb 99

Butz, Earl L. Jul 72

Buzzi-Peccia, Arturo obit Oct 43

Byas, Hugh Mar 43 obit Apr 45

Byatt, A. S. Sep 91

Byers, Margaretta Sep 41

Byington, Spring Sep 56 obit Oct 71

Bykovsky, Valery Jan 65

Byrd, Charlie Oct 67 obit Mar 2000

Byrd, Harry F. Apr 42 Sep 55 obit Dec 66

Byrd, Richard E. Oct 42 May 56 obit May 57

Byrd, Robert C. Mar 60 Feb 78

Byrd, Sam Nov 42 obit Jan 56

Byrne, Brendan T. May 74

Byrne, Gabriel May 99

Byrne, Jane Jan 80

Byrne, John Keyes *see* Leonard, Hugh

Byrne, John Oct 2000

Byrnes, James F. Jun 41 Oct 51 obit Jun 72

Byrnes, John W. Oct 60 obit Mar 85

Byroade, Henry A. Feb 52 obit Mar 94

Byron, Arthur W. obit Sep 43

Byron, Don Sep 2000

Byron, William D. obit Apr 41

C. R. *see* Rajagopalachari, Chakravarti

Caan, James May 76

Caballé, Montserrat Jun 67

Cabot, John M. Sep 53 obit Apr 81

Cabot, Thomas D. Jun 51 obit Aug 95

Caccia, Harold Anthony Feb 57 obit Jan 91

Cacoyannis, Michael May 66

Caddell, Patrick H. Nov 79

Cadell, Elizabeth (WLB) Yrbk 51

Cadle, E. Howard obit Feb 43

Cadmus, Paul Jul 42 obit Mar 2000

Cadogan, Alexander Oct 44 obit Sep 68

Caesar, Sid Apr 51

Caetano, Marcello Mar 70 obit Jan 81

Café Filho, Joao Jan 55 obit Apr 70

Caffery, Jefferson Nov 43 obit Jun 74

Caffrey, James J. Jun 47 obit May 61

Cage, John Sep 61 obit Sep 92

Cage, Nicolas Apr 94

Cagney, James Dec 42 obit May 86

Cahill, Michael Harrison obit Apr 40

Cahill, William T. Jun 70 obit Sep 96

Cahn, Sammy Nov 74 obit Mar 93

Caillaux, Joseph obit Jan 45

Cain, Harry P. Apr 49 obit May 79

Cain, James M. Dec 47 obit Jan 78

Caine, Michael May 68 Jan 88

Cairns, Huntington Nov 40

Cai Yuanpei obit Mar 40

Calatrava, Santiago Aug 97

Calder, A. Stirling obit Feb 45

Calder, Alexander Apr 46 Jul 66 obit Jan 77

Calder, Nigel Jun 86

Calder, Ritchie Apr 63 obit May 86

Calder, William M. obit Apr 45

Caldera, Rafael Jul 69

Calderone, Frank A. Jul 52 obit Apr 87

Calderone, Mary S. Nov 67 obit Jan 99

Calderón Guardia, Rafael Ángel Jun 42 obit Sep 70

Caldicott, Helen Oct 83

Caldwell, Erskine Oct 40 obit May 87

Caldwell, Millard F. Nov 48 obit Feb 85

Caldwell, Mrs. Leslie Godfrey *see* Caldwell, Sarah C.

Caldwell, Sarah C. Jan 53

Caldwell, Sarah Oct 73

Caldwell, Taylor Jan-Feb 40 obit Oct 85

Caldwell, William E. obit May 43

Caldwell, Zoe Dec 70

Calero, Adolfo Oct 87

Calfee, John Edward obit Jan 41

Calhern, Louis Jul 51 obit Jul 56

Califano, Joseph A., Jr. Jun 77

Calisher, Hortense Nov 73

Calkins, Robert D. Oct 52 obit Sep 92

Callaghan, Daniel J. obit Jan 43

Callaghan, James Feb 68

Callahan, Harry M. Nov 84 obit Jul 99

Callahan, John Sep 98

Callander, W. F. Oct 48

Callas, Maria Sep 56 obit Nov 77

Callender, John Hancock Sep 55 obit Jun 95

Callery, Mary Jul 55

Calles, Plutarco Ellias obit Nov 45

Callow, John Michael obit Sep 40

Calloway, Cab Nov 45 obit Jan 95

Calvé, Emma obit Mar 42

Calverton, V. F. obit Jan 41

Calvin, Melvin Apr 62 obit Mar 97

Calvino, Italo Feb 84 obit Nov 85

Calvo Sotelo, Leopoldo Aug 81

Calwell, Arthur A. Oct 47

Cam, Helen M. Sep 48 obit Apr 68

Camac, Charles Nicoll Bancker obit Nov 40

Camacho, Manuel Avila see Avila Camacho, Manuel

Câmara, Helder Pessora Jul 71 obit Jan 2000

Camargo, Alberto Lleras see Lleras Camargo, Alberto

Cambridge, Godfrey Mar 69 obit Feb 77

Camby, Marcus Jan 2000

Camden, Harry P., Jr. obit Sep 43

Cameron, Basil Apr 43

Cameron, Charles S. Sep 54

Cameron, Hugh obit Jan 42

Cameron, James Jan 98

Camm, Sydney Apr 42 obit Apr 66

Cammerer, Arno B. obit Jun 41

Campa, Miguel Angel Sep 57 obit Nov 65

Campanella, Roy Jun 53 obit Aug 93

Campbell, Bebe Moore Apr 2000

Campbell, Ben Nighthorse Oct 94

Campbell, Bill Jul 96

Campbell, Boyd May 56

Campbell, Donald Feb 64 obit Feb 67

Campbell, Douglas Jun 58

Campbell, E. Simms Jan 41 obit Mar 71

Campbell, Earl Apr 83

Campbell, Gerald Mar 41 obit Sep 64

Campbell, Glen Jul 69

Campbell, Grace (WLB) Yrbk 48 obit Jul 63

Campbell, Harold G. obit Aug 42

Campbell, Joseph Jun 84 obit Jan 88

Campbell, Malcolm Sep 47 obit Feb 49

Campbell, Mrs. Harvey see Campbell, Grace

Campbell, Mrs. Patrick obit May 40

Campbell, Mrs. W. E. Burton see Campbell, Patricia

Campbell, Naomi Feb 97

Campbell, Neve Jan 2000

Campbell, Patricia (WLB) Yrbk 57

Campbell, Philip P. obit Jul 41

Campbell, Willis C. obit Jun 41

Campeau, Robert Mar 89

Campinchi, César obit Apr 41

Campion, Jane Apr 94

Campney, Ralph Osborne Sep 55 obit Dec 67

Campora, Giuseppe Jul 57

Cámpora, Héctor José Oct 73 obit Feb 81

Camrose, William Ewert Berry, 1st Viscount see Berry, William Ewert

Canaday, John May 62 obit Sep 85

Canaday, Ward M. Mar 51 obit Apr 76

Canady, Alexa Aug 2000

Canavan, Joseph J. obit Yrbk 40

Canby, Al H. obit Yrbk 40

Canby, Henry Seidel Sep 42 obit Jun 61

Candau, Marcolino G. Sep 54

Candee, Robert C. May 44

Candela, Félix Jul 60

Candia, Alfredo Ovanda see Ovanda Candia, Alfredo

Candler, Warren A. obit Nov 41

Candy, John Feb 90 obit May 94

Canegata, Leonard Lionel Cornelius see Lee, Canada

Canetti, Elias Jan 83 obit Oct 94

Canfield, Cass Apr 54 obit May 86

Canham, Erwin D. Jul 45 Jan 60 obit Feb 82

Caniff, Milton A. Jan 44 obit May 88

Cannon, Annie J. obit Jun 41

Cannon, Cavendish W. Jul 57 obit Dec 62

Cannon, Clarence Nov 49 obit Jul 64

Cannon, Howard W. Feb 60

Cannon, James, Jr., Bishop obit Nov 44

Cannon, Legrand, Jr. Mar 43

Cannon, Sarah Ophelia Colley see Pearl, Minnie

Cannon, Walter Bradford obit Nov 45

Canseco, José Nov 91

Canterbury, Hewlett Johnson, Dean of see Johnson, Hewlett

Cantinflas Jun 53 obit Jun 93

Canton, Allen A. obit Apr 40

Cantor, Eddie Nov 41 May 54 obit Jan 65

Cantu, Giuseppe obit Yrbk 40

Capehart, Homer E. Apr 47 obit Oct 79

Caperton, William B. obit Feb 42

Caplin, Mortimer M. Sep 61

Capogrossi, Giuseppe Dec 57

Capote, Truman Sep 51 Mar 68 obit Oct 84

Capp, Al May 47 obit Jan 80

Capper, Arthur Sep 46 obit Feb 52

Capra, Frank Apr 48 obit Oct 91

Caputo, Philip Apr 96

Caradon, Hugh Foot *see* Foot, Hugh

Caramanlis, Constantine May 56 Apr 76 obit Jul 98

Caras, Roger A. Apr 88

Caraway, Hattie W. Mar 45 obit Jan 51

Cardin, Pierre Mar 65

Cardon, P. V. May 54 obit Dec 65

Cardoso, Fernando Henrique Oct 96

Carew, Rod Jan 78

Carewe, Edwin obit Jan 40

Carey, Charles Henry obit Oct 41

Carey, Drew Mar 98

Carey, Ernestine Gilbreth May 49 [Gilbreth, Frank B.; and Carey, Ernestine Gilbreth]

Carey, George Aug 91

Carey, Hugh L. Sep 65

Carey, James B. Nov 41 Jul 51 obit Nov 73

Carey, Mariah Jul 92

Carey, Ron May 92

Carey, Walter F. Feb 65

Carías Andino, Tiburcio Jun 42 obit Feb 70

Carl XVI Gustaf, King of Sweden Feb 74

Carle, Richard obit Aug 41

Carlin, George Oct 76

Carlino, Lewis John May 83

Carlisle, Kitty *see* Hart, Kitty Carlisle

Carlos, Juan Oct 51 obit Jun 93

Carlos, Prince Juan Oct 64

Carlson, A. J. Jan 48 obit Nov 56

Carlson, Evans F. Oct 43 obit Jun 47

Carlson, Frank Apr 49 obit Jul 87

Carlson, John F. obit May 45

Carlson, John Roy Oct 43

Carlson, William S. Jul 52 obit Jul 94

Carlsson, Ingvar Feb 88

Carlton, William Newnham Chattin obit Mar 43

Carlucci, Frank Oct 81

Carlyle, Alexander James, Rev. obit Jul 43

Carmack, John Mar 2000

Carmichael, Hoagy May 41 obit Feb 82

Carmichael, Oliver C. Jan 46 obit Dec 66

Carmichael, Stokely Apr 70 obit Feb 99

Carmines, Al Sep 72

Carmody, John Michael May 40 obit Jan 64

Carmona, Antonio Oscar De Fragoso Nov 50 obit May 51

Carnarvon, Countess of *see* Losch, Tilly

Carnegie, Dale Dec 41 Sep 55

Carnegie, Dorothy Sep 55 obit Jan 99

Carnegie, Hattie Oct 42 obit May 56

Carney, Art Apr 58

Carney, Robert B. Oct 51 obit Aug 90

Carnovsky, Morris Jan 91

Caro, Anthony Nov 81

Caro, Robert A. Jan 84

Carol II, King of Romania Aug 40 obit May 53

Caroline, Princess of Monaco Nov 89

Caron, Leslie Sep 54

Carpenter, George L. Jan 43 obit May 48

Carpenter, Henry Cort Harold obit Nov 40

Carpenter, J. Henry Feb 43 obit Sep 54

Carpenter, John Alden May 47 obit May 51

Carpenter, Lewis Van obit Jul 40

Carpenter, Malcolm Scott Sep 62

Carpenter, Mary Chapin Feb 94

Carpentier, Marcel-Maurice Apr 51

Carr, Alexander obit Dec 46

Carr, Emma Perry Apr 59

Carr, Robert Jan 73

Carr, Robert K. Apr 61

Carr, Wilbur J. obit Aug 42

Carr, William G. Sep 52 obit May 96

Carradine, Keith Aug 91

Carraway, Gertrude S. Jan 54

Carrel, Alexis Mar 40 obit Dec 44

Carreras, José Jun 79

Carrero Blanco, Luis Oct 73 obit Feb 74

Carrey, Jim Feb 96

Carrillo, Santiago Jun 77

Carrington, 6th Baron Jun 71

Carrington, Elaine Feb 44 obit Jul 58

Carroll, Diahann Sep 62

Carroll, James May 97

Carroll, Jim Oct 95

Carroll, John A. May 58 obit Oct 83

Carroll, John Jul 55 obit Jan 60

Carroll, Joseph F. Apr 62 obit Mar 91

Carroll, Madeleine Apr 49 obit Nov 87

Carroll, Pat Aug 80

Carroll, Thomas H. Jul 62 obit Oct 64

Carroll, Vinnette Sep 83

Carroll-Abbing, J. Patrick Jul 67

Carruth, Hayden Apr 92

Carsey, Marcy Jan 97

Carson, Benjamin S., Sr. May 97

Carson, Johnny Jan 64 Apr 82

Carson, John Renshaw obit Yrbk 40

Carson, Rachel Nov 51 obit Jun 64

Carstens, Karl Apr 80 obit Aug 92

Cartas, María Estela Martínez *see* Perón, Isabel

Carter, Betty Mar 82 obit Jan 99

Carter, Boake Jan 42 obit Yrbk 47

Carter, Don Mar 63

Carter, Elliott Nov 60

Carter, Hodding, 3rd Aug 81

Carter, Huntly obit May 42

Carter, James Earl, Jr. *see* Carter, Jimmy

Carter, James Feb 97

Carter, Jimmy Sep 71 Nov 77

Carter, John Franklin *see* Franklin, Jay

Carter, John May 59 obit May 75

Carter, John Ridgely obit Jul 44

Cerezo, Marco Vinicio Mar 87

Cerezo Arévalo, Vinicio *see* Cerezo, Marco Vinicio

Cerf, Bennett Nov 41 Sep 58 obit Oct 71

Cerf, Vinton G. Sep 98

Cernan, Eugene A. May 73

Chaban-Delmas, Jacques Jul 58

Chabrol, Claude Jan 75

Chaddock, Robert Emmet obit Yrbk 40

Chadli, Bendjedid Apr 91

Chadourne, Marc obit Feb 41

Chadwick, Florence Oct 50 obit May 95

Chadwick, Helene obit Oct 40

Chadwick, James Nov 45 obit Oct 74

Chafee, John H. Nov 69 obit Jan 2000

Chafee, Zechariah, Jr. Aug 42 obit Apr 57

Chagall, Marc Nov 43 Nov 60 obit May 85

Chagla, Mahomed Ali Currim Jun 59 obit Jan 84

Chaikin, Joseph Jul 81

Chaikin, Sol C. Apr 79 obit Jun 91

Chailly, Riccardo Jun 91

Chain, Ernst Boris Nov 65 obit Oct 79

Chalk, O. Roy Nov 71 obit Feb 96

Challans, Mary *see* Renault, Mary

Chalmers, Philip O. obit Mar 46

Chamberlain, Francis L. Jul 59

Chamberlain, John Rensselaer Apr 40 obit Jun 95

Chamberlain, Neville obit Yrbk 40

Chamberlain, Owen Mar 60

Chamberlain, Paul Mellen obit Jul 40

Chamberlain, Richard Jul 63 Nov 87

Chamberlain, Samuel Sep 54 obit Mar 75

Chamberlain, Wilt Jun 60 obit Jan 2000

Chamberlin, Georgia Louise obit Oct 43

Chambers, Raymond Wilson obit Jun 42

Chaminade, Cecile obit Jun 44

Chamorro, Violeta Barrios De Jun 90

Chamoun, Camille N. Jul 56 obit Sep 87

Champion, George Apr 61 obit Jan 98

Champion, Gower Sep 53 [Champion, Marge; and Champion, Gower] obit Oct 80

Champion, Marge Sep 53 [Champion, Marge; and Champion, Gower]

Champion, Pierre Honoré Jean Baptiste obit Aug 42

Chan, Jackie Nov 97

Chan, Kong Sun *see* Chan, Jackie

Chance, Dean Jul 69

Chancellor, John Jan 62 Nov 88 obit Sep 96

Chandler, Albert Benjamin *see* Chandler, Happy

Chandler, Dorothy Buffum Jul 57 [Chandler, Dorothy Buffum; and Chandler, Norman] obit Sep 97

Chandler, Happy Aug 43 Sep 56 obit Aug 91

Chandler, Norman Jul 57 [Chandler, Dorothy Buffum; and Chandler, Norman] obit Dec 73

Chandler, Otis Nov 68

Chandler, Raymond (WLB) Yrbk 46 obit Jun 59

Chandos, Oliver Lyttelton, 1st Viscount *see* Lyttelton, Oliver

Chandrasekhar, Sripati Oct 69

Chandrasekhar, Subrahmanyan Mar 86 obit Oct 95

Chandy, Anna Apr 60

Chanel, Coco Sep 54 obit Feb 71

Chaney, John Mar 99

Chang, John M. Jun 49 obit Jul 66

Chang, Michael Jul 97

Chang Shan-Tze obit Yrbk 40

Channing, Carol Sep 64

Channing, Stockard Apr 91

Chapin, Charles Value obit Mar 41

Chapin, James Mar 40 obit Sep 75

Chapin, Katherine Garrison *see* Biddle, Katherine Garrison Chapin

Chapin, Schuyler G. Feb 74

Chaplin, Charlie Yrbk 40 Mar 61 obit Feb 78

Chaplin, Geraldine Jul 79

Chapman, Albert K. Sep 52 obit Yrbk 84

Chapman, Blanche obit Aug 41

Chapman, Charles F. May 58 obit Yrbk 84 (died Mar 76)

Chapman, Daniel A. Apr 59

Chapman, Frank Michler obit Jan 46

Chapman, Gilbert W. Jun 57 obit Feb 80

Chapman, Helen Louise Busch *see* Chapman, Mrs. Theodore S.

Chapman, Leonard F. Jr. Jul 68 obit Sep 2000

Chapman, Mrs. Theodore S. Apr 55

Chapman, Oscar L. Feb 49 obit Apr 78

Chapman, Sydney Jul 57 obit Sep 70

Chapman, Tracy Aug 89

Chappedelaine, Louis De obit Jan 40

Chappell, Tom May 94

Charisse, Cyd Jan 54

Charles, Eugenia Oct 86

Charles, Ezzard Jun 49 obit Aug 75

Charles, Prince of Belgium May 46 obit Jul 83

Charles, Prince of Wales Nov 69

Charles, Ray Apr 65 Jun 92

Charles-Roux, François

Charlesworth, James C. Sep 54 obit Mar 74

Charlot, Jean Sep 45 obit Yrbk 84 (died Mar 79)

Charlotte, Grand Duchess of Luxembourg Apr 49 obit Aug 85

Charnwood, Godfrey Rathbone Benson, Ist Baron obit Mar 45

Charques, Dorothy (WLB) Yrbk 58

Charques, Mrs. Robert Denis *see* Charques, Dorothy

Charters, Spencer obit Mar 43

Charyk, Joseph V. Dec 70

Chase, Charley obit Aug 40

Chase, Chevy Mar 79

Chase, Edna Woolman Nov 40 obit Jun 57

Chase, Harry Woodburn Jun 48 obit Jun 55

Chase, Ilka May 42 obit Apr 78

Chase, Joseph Cummings May 55

Chase, Lucia Jul 47 Aug 75 obit Mar 86

Chase, Mary Ellen May 40 obit Oct 73

Chase, Mary Oct 45 obit Jan 82

Chase, Mrs. Hamilton see Seton, Anya

Chase, Stuart Oct 40 obit Jan 86

Chase, William C. Nov 52

Chase, William Sheafe, Rev. obit Sep 40

Chasez, JC see 'N Sync

Chasins, Abram Feb 60 obit Aug 87

Chast, Roz Jul 97

Chastain, Madye Lee (WLB) Yrbk 58

Chateaubriand, Assis see Assis Chateaubriand

Chatel, Yves obit Dec 44

Chatwin, Bruce Jan 88 obit Mar 89

Chauncey, Henry Jul 51

Chauvel, Jean Oct 50 obit Jul 79

Chavan, Y. B. Apr 63

Chavarri, Emperatriz see Sumac, Yma

Chavchavadze, George Mar 43 obit Apr 62

Chávez, Carlos May 49 obit Sep 78

Chavez, Cesar Feb 69 obit Jun 93

Chavez, Dennis Mar 46 obit Jan 63

Chávez, Hugo May 2000

Chávez, Julio César Apr 99

Chavez, Linda Nov 99

Chavez-Thompson, Linda Mar 2000

Chavis, Benjamin F. Jan 94

Chayefsky, Paddy Sep 57 obit Sep 81

Chayefsky, Sidney see Chayefsky, Paddy

Cheadle, Don Sep 99

Cheatham, Kitty obit Feb 46

Cheever, John Sep 75 obit Aug 82

Chelf, Frank L. Jun 52

Chen, Eugene obit Jul 44

Chen, Joan Sep 99

Chenault, Kenneth I. Jun 98

Chen Cheng Sep 41 obit Apr 65

Cheney, Brainard (WLB) Yrbk 59 obit Mar 90

Cheney, Lynne V. Oct 92

Cheney, Richard B. Aug 89

Cheney, Russell obit Aug 45

Chennault, Claire Lee Oct 42 obit Oct 58

Chen Ning Yang see Yang, Chen Ning

Chen Shui-bian Sep 2000

Chen Yi Oct 59 obit Feb 72

Chéreau, Patrice Jan 90

Cher Jan 74 Jun 91

Cherkassky, Shura Oct 90 obit Mar 96

Cherne, Leo M. Yrbk 40 obit Mar 99

Chernenko, Konstantin U. Aug 84 obit May 85

Chernomyrdin, Viktor Aug 98

Chernyakhovsky, Ivan D. Oct 44 obit Apr 45

Cherry, Addie obit Dec 42

Cherry, Francis A. Jul 54 obit Sep 65

Cherwell, Frederick Alexander Lindemann, 1st Baron see Lindemann, Frederick Alexander

Cheshire, Leonard Jan 62 obit Sep 92

Chesser, Elizabeth Sloan obit Mar 40

Chester, Edmund Mar 41

Chevalier, Elizabeth Pickett Jan 43

Chevalier, Maurice Jan 48 Mar 69 obit Feb 72

Chevrier, Lionel Jun 52

Chevrolet, Louis obit Aug 41

Chia, Sandro Jun 90

Chiang Ching-Kuo Sep 54 obit Mar 88

Chiang Kai-shek, Mme see Chiang Mei-Ling

Chiang Kai-Shek Jan-Jun 40 May 53 obit May 75

Chiang Mei-Ling May 40

Chiang T'ing-fu see Tsiang, T. F.

Chiang Tso-Pin obit Feb 43

Chiappe, Jean obit Jan 41

Chiari, Roberto F. Feb 61

Chicago, Judy Feb 81

Chichester, Francis Dec 67 obit Oct 72

Chidlaw, Benjamin W. Mar 55

Chifley, Joseph B. Aug 45 obit Jul 51

Chihuly, Dale Aug 95

Chih-Yuan Yang see Yang, Jerry

Child, Julia Feb 67

Childs, Lucinda Apr 84

Childs, Marquis William Jan 43 obit Sep 90

Childs, Richard Spencer Sep 55 obit Jan 79

Chiles, Lawton Sep 71 obit Mar 99

Chillida, Eduardo Sep 85

Chiluba, Frederick May 92

Chin, Frank Mar 99

Ch'ing, Chiang see Jiang Qing

Ching, Cyrus S. Jan 48 obit Feb 68

Ching-Kuo, Chiang see Chiang Ching-Kuo

Chinmoy, Sri Apr 76

Chiperfield, Robert B. Sep 56 obit May 71

Chipp, Mrs. Rodney Duane see Hicks, Beatrice A.

Chirac, Jacques Jun 75 Apr 93

Chirico, Giorgio de see De Chirico, Giorgio

Chisholm, Brock Jul 48 obit Mar 71

Chisholm, Shirley Oct 69

Chissano, Joaquim Alberto Nov 90

Chi-tien, Mao see Yoshida, Shigeru

Cho, Margaret Oct 2000

Chodorov, Edward Apr 44 obit Nov 88

Chomsky, Noam Oct 70 Aug 95

Chopra, Deepak Oct 95

Chotzinoff, Samuel Apr 40 obit Apr 64

Chou En-Lai Sep 46 Jul 57 obit Feb 76

Chouinard, Yvon Jun 98
Chow Yun-Fat May 98
Chrebet, Wayne Feb 99
Chrétien, Jean Apr 90
Christenberry, Robert K. Mar 52 obit Jun 73
Christian X, King of Denmark Nov 43 obit May 47
Christians, Mady May 45 obit Dec 51
Christie, Agatha Sep 40 Jul 64 obit Mar 76
Christie, John Walter obit Feb 44
Christie, Julie Sep 66
Christie, William Jan 92
Christison, Philip Nov 45 obit Feb 94
Christman, Elisabeth Jan 47
Christofilos, Nicholas C. Nov 65 obit Nov 72
Christo Mar 77
Christopher, George Feb 58 obit Yrbk 2000
Christopher, George T. Nov 47 obit Jul 54
Christopher, Warren M. Jun 81 Nov 95
Chrysler, Walter Percy obit Oct 40
Chryssa Nov 78
Chuan Leekpai Nov 98
Chubb, L. Warrington Feb 47 obit May 52
Chuikov, Vasili May 43 obit May 82
Chun Doo Hwan Mar 81
Chung, Connie Jul 89
Chung, Myung-Whun Aug 90
Church, Frank Mar 58 Mar 78 obit May 84
Church, Marguerite Stitt Feb 51 obit Jul 90
Church, Sam, Jr. Oct 81
Church, Samuel Harden obit Nov 43
Churchill, Berton obit Yrbk 40
Churchill, Caryl Jun 85
Churchill, Edward D. Feb 63
Churchill, Gordon Sep 58
Churchill, Lady see Spencer-Churchill, Clementine Ogilvy Hozier
Churchill, Randolph Oct 47 obit Sep 68
Churchill, Sarah May 55 obit Jan 83

Churchill, Winston Jul 40 Mar 42 Jul 53 obit Mar 65
Chu Shen obit Aug 43
Chute, B. J. (WLB) Yrbk 50 obit Oct 87
Chute, Charles Lionel Sep 49 obit Jan 54
Chute, Joy see Chute, B. J.
Chute, Marchette Gaylord (WLB) Yrbk 50 obit Jul 94
Chu Teh Nov 42 obit Aug 76
Chwast, Seymour Sep 95
Chwatt, Aaron see Buttons, Red
Ciano, Galeazzo, Conte Jul 40 obit Feb 44
Ciardi, John Oct 67 obit May 86
Cicognani, Amleto Giovanni Cardinal Jul 51 obit Feb 74
Çiller, Tansu Sep 94
Cimino, Michael Jan 81
Cisler, Walker Sep 55 obit Jan 95
Cisneros, Henry Aug 87
Citrine, Walter McLennan Citrine Feb 41 obit Apr 83
Civiletti, Benjamin R. Feb 80
Clague, Ewan Jul 47 obit Jun 87
Claiborne, Craig Sep 69 obit Apr 2000
Claiborne, Liz Jun 89
Claiborne, Loretta Jul 96
Clair, René Nov 41 obit May 81
Claire, Ina May 54 obit Apr 85
Clampitt, Amy Feb 92 obit Nov 94
Clancy, Mrs. Carl Stearns see Lownsbery, Eloise
Clancy, Tom Apr 88
Clapp, Gordon R. Feb 47 obit Jun 63
Clapp, Margaret Jun 48 obit Jun 74
Clapp, Verner W. Mar 59 obit Sep 72
Clapper, Mrs. Raymond see Clapper, Olive Ewing
Clapper, Olive Ewing Sep 46 obit Jan 69
Clapper, Raymond Mar 40 obit Mar 44
Clapton, Eric Jun 87
Clark, Bennett Champ Nov 41 obit Sep 54

Clark, Bobby May 49 obit Apr 60
Clark, Charles E. Jul 59 obit Mar 64
Clark, Dick May 59 Jan 87
Clark, Dorothy Park (WLB) Yrbk 57 [McMeekin, Isabel McLennan; and Clark, Dorothy Park]
Clark, Eleanor May 78 obit Apr 96
Clark, Eugenie Sep 53
Clark, Evans Sep 47 obit Nov 70
Clark, Fred G. Oct 49
Clark, Georgia Neese Sep 49 obit Feb 96
Clark, Helen Nov 2000
Clark, J. J. Jan 54 obit Sep 71
Clark, James H. Jun 97 [Andreessen, Marc; and Clark, James H.]
Clark, James Nov 65 obit Jun 68
Clark, Joe Oct 76
Clark, John Apr 52
Clark, John D. Jan 47
Clark, Joseph S. Jun 52 obit Mar 90
Clark, Kenneth B. Sep 64
Clark, Kenneth Sep 63 obit Jul 83
Clark, Leonard Jan 56 obit Sep 57
Clark, Marguerite obit Nov 40
Clark, Mark W. Nov 42 obit Jun 84
Clark, Mary Higgins Jan 94
Clark, Paul F. Apr 55 obit Mar 73
Clark, Petula Feb 70
Clark, Ramsey Oct 67
Clark, Richard Wagstaff see Clark, Dick
Clark, Robert L. Nov 52
Clark, Roy Jun 78
Clark, Sydney Sep 56
Clark, Tom C. Jul 45 obit Aug 77
Clark, Wesley K. Jul 99
Clark, William P. Jul 82
Clarke, Arthur C. Oct 66
Clarke, John Hessin obit May 45
Clarke, Martha Jan 89
Clarke, Robert see Indiana, Robert
Clarke, Ron May 71

Clarke, Walter May 47 obit Jan 65

Clash, Kevin Jun 2000

Clausen, A. W. Nov 81

Claussen, Julia obit Jun 41

Clavell, James Oct 81 obit Nov 94

Claxton, Brooke Dec 47 obit Sep 60

Clay, Cassius *see* Ali, Muhammad

Clay, Laura obit Aug 41

Clay, Lucius D. May 45 Jun 63 obit Jun 78

Clayburgh, Jill Sep 79

Clayton, Eva McPherson Jun 2000

Clayton, Mrs. Joseph E. *see* Sampson, Edith S.

Clayton, P. B. May 55 obit Mar 73

Clayton, William L. Apr 44 obit Mar 66

Claytor, W. Graham, Jr. May 79 obit Jul 94

Cleaver, Eldridge Mar 70 obit Jul 98

Cleese, John Jan 84

Cleland, Max Feb 78

Clemens, Roger Nov 88

Clemensen, Erik Christian obit Jul 41

Clement, Frank G. Jul 55 obit Dec 69

Clement, M. W. Nov 46 obit Nov 66

Clement, Rufus E. Jun 46 obit Jan 68

Clemente, Roberto Feb 72 obit Feb 73

Clements, Earle C. Sep 55 obit May 85

Clendening, Logan obit Mar 45

Cleveland, Harlan Sep 61

Cleveland, James Aug 85 obit Apr 91

Cliburn, Van Sep 58

Clifford, Clark Mar 47 Sep 68 obit Jan 99

Clifford, John Nov 72

Clift, David H. Jun 52 obit Dec 73

Clift, Montgomery Jul 54 obit Sep 66

Clinchy, Everett R. Apr 41 obit Mar 86

Cline, John Wesley Jun 51 obit Sep 74

Clinton, Bill Apr 88 Nov 94

Clinton, George Jul 93

Clinton, Hillary Rodham Nov 93

Clinton, William Jefferson *see* Clinton, Bill

Clive, Edward E. obit Jul 40

Clooney, Rosemary Feb 57

Close, Chuck Jul 83

Close, Glenn Nov 84

Close, Upton Dec 44 obit Jan 61

Clurman, Harold Feb 59 obit Nov 80

Clyde, George D. Jul 58 obit May 72

Coaldigger, Adam *see* Ameringer, Oscar

Coanda, Henri Jul 56 obit Feb 73

Coates, John obit Oct 41

Coates, Joseph Gordon obit Jul 43

Cobb, Geraldyn M. *see* Cobb, Jerrie

Cobb, Irvin S. obit Apr 44

Cobb, Jerrie Feb 61

Cobb, Lee J. Feb 60 obit Apr 76

Cobb, Ty Sep 51 obit Oct 61

Cobham, Charles John Lyttelton, 10th Viscount Apr 62

Coblentz, Stanton A. Jun 54

Coblentz, W. W. Mar 54 obit Nov 62

Cobo, Albert E. Nov 51 obit Dec 57 Yrbk 58

Coburn, Charles Jun 44 obit Nov 61

Coburn, James Jun 99

Coca, Imogene Apr 51

Cochran, Charles Blake Oct 40 obit Mar 51

Cochran, H. Merle Feb 50 obit Nov 73

Cochran, Jacqueline Sep 40 Jun 63 obit Oct 80

Cochran, Johnnie L., Jr. Jun 99

Cochrane, Edward L. Mar 51 obit Jan 60

Cockcroft, John Nov 48 obit Nov 67

Cocke, C. Francis Mar 52

Cocke, Erle, Jr. Jan 51 obit Sep 2000

Cocker, Jarvis Nov 98

Cockrell, Ewing May 51 obit Apr 62

Coco, James May 74 obit Apr 87

Cody, John Patrick Cardinal Nov 65 obit Jun 82

Coe, Fred Jan 59 obit Jun 79

Coe, Sebastian Nov 80

Coe, Sue Aug 97

Coen, Ethan Sep 94 [Coen, Ethan; and Coen, Joel]

Coen, Joel Sep 94 [Coen, Ethan; and Coen, Joel]

Coetzee, J. M. Jan 87

Coffee, John M. Oct 46

Coffin, Frank M. Apr 59

Coffin, Haskell obit Jul 41

Coffin, Henry Sloane, Rev. Dr Apr 44 obit Jan 55

Coffin, William Sloane, Jr. Jul 68 Apr 80

Coggan, F. Donald Jul 74 obit Sep 2000

Coggeshall, Lowell T. Sep 63 obit Jan 88

Cogswell, Charles N. obit Feb 42

Cohan, George M. obit Jan 43

Cohen, Abby Joseph Jun 98

Cohen, Alexander H. Jun 65 obit Aug 2000

Cohen, Arthur A. Sep 60 obit Jan 87

Cohen, Barbara May 57 [Cohen, Barbara; and Roney, Marianne]

Cohen, Ben Apr 94 [Cohen, Ben; and Greenfield, Jerry]

Cohen, Benjamin A. May 48 obit May 60

Cohen, Benjamin V. Apr 41 obit Oct 83

Cohen, Howard William *see* Cosell, Howard

Cohen, Judy *see* Chicago, Judy

Cohen, Leonard Jun 69

Cohen, Manuel F. Apr 67 obit Aug 77

Cohen, Wilbur J. Sep 68 obit Jul 87

Cohen, William S. Apr 82 Jan 98

Cohu, La Motte T. Apr 51 obit Nov 68

Coit, Margaret Louise Jun 51

Coker, Elizabeth Boatwright (WLB) Yrbk 59 obit Nov 93

Colbert, Claudette Jan 45 May 64 obit Oct 96

Colbert, Edwin H. Sep 65

Colbert, Lester L. Apr 51 obit Nov 95

Colby, Charles Dewitt obit Nov 41

Colby, Nathalie S. obit Jul 42

Colby, William E. Jan 75 obit Jul 96

Coldwell, M. J. Sep 43 obit Oct 74

Cole, Albert M. Jan 54

Cole, David L. Jan 49 obit Mar 78

Cole, Edward N. Jul 72 obit Jul 77

Cole, Janet see Hunter, Kim

Cole, Jessie Duncan Savage obit Yrbk 40

Cole, Johnnetta B. Aug 94

Cole, Natalie Nov 91

Cole, Nat King Feb 56 obit Mar 65

Cole, W. Sterling Mar 54 obit May 87

Cole-Hamilton, J. B. obit Sep 45

Coleman, Cy Aug 90

Coleman, Georgia obit Nov 40

Coleman, J. P. Sep 56 obit Nov 91

Coleman, James S. Oct 70 obit Jun 95

Coleman, John R. Oct 74

Coleman, John S. Apr 53 obit Jul 58

Coleman, Lonnie (WLB) Yrbk 58 obit Oct 82

Coleman, Ornette Jun 61

Coleman, William T., Jr. Mar 76

Coles, Nathaniel Adams see Cole, Nat King

Coles, Robert Nov 69

Colijn, Hendricus obit Jan 45

Colina, Rafael De La Jan 51

Coller, Taube see Davis, Tobé Coller

Colles, Henry Cope obit Apr 43

Collet, John C. Feb 46 obit Feb 56

Collier, Constance Jul 54 obit Jun 55

Collier, John Mar 41 obit Jul 68

Collier, William, Sr. obit Mar 44

Collingwood, Charles Jun 43 obit Nov 85

Collingwood, R. G. obit Mar 43

Collins, Cardiss Feb 97

Collins, Eddie obit Oct 40

Collins, Edward Day obit Jan 40

Collins, Francis S. Jun 94

Collins, Gail Mar 99

Collins, George Lewis obit Aug 40

Collins, Hunt see Hunter, Evan

Collins, J. Lawton Nov 49 obit Oct 87

Collins, Jackie Jul 2000

Collins, James Dec 63

Collins, James J. obit Apr 43

Collins, Joan Jan 84

Collins, John F. Jan 65 obit Feb 96

Collins, Judy Apr 69

Collins, LeRoy Jun 56 Apr 65 obit May 91

Collins, Lorin Cone obit Yrbk 40

Collins, Martha Layne Jan 86

Collins, Marva Nov 86

Collins, Michael May 75

Collins, Phil Nov 86

Collins, Seaborn P. Apr 55

Collins, Susan May 2000

Collison, Wilson obit Jul 41

Collor De Mello, Fernando Mar 90

Collyer, John L. Mar 47

Colman, Ronald Jul 43 obit Sep 58

Colombo, Emilio Apr 71

Colonna, Simonetta see Simonetta

Colquitt, Oscar Branch obit Mar 40

Colville, Alex Mar 85

Colvin, Mamie White Dec 44 obit Jan 56

Colvin, Mrs. D. Leigh see Colvin, Mamie White

Colvin, Shawn Mar 99

Colwell, Eileen Jul 63

Colwell, Rita R. May 99

Comaneci, Nadia Feb 77

Comber, Elizabeth see Han Suyin

Combs, Bert Thomas Jun 60 obit Feb 92

Combs, Sean see Puff Daddy

Comden, Betty Mar 45 [Comden, Betty; and Green, Adolph]

Comer, James P. Aug 91

Comfort, Alex Sep 74 obit Aug 2000

Commager, Henry Steele Jan 46 obit May 98

Commoner, Barry Sep 70

Como, Perry Apr 47

Companys, Luis obit Yrbk 40

Compton, Arthur H. Aug 40 Sep 58 obit May 62

Compton, Karl T. Mar 41 obit Sep 54

Compton, Wilson Apr 52 obit May 67

Conable, Barber B., Jr. Jul 84

Conant, James Bryant Mar 41 Feb 51 obit Apr 78

Concheso, Aurelio Fernández May 42 obit Jan 56

Condon, E. U. Apr 46 obit May 74

Condon, Eddie Oct 44 obit Oct 73

Condon, Frank obit Feb 41

Condon, Richard Feb 89 obit Jun 96

Cone, David Feb 98

Cone, Fairfax M. Jul 66 obit Aug 77

Conerly, Charles Apr 60 obit Apr 96

Congdon, William May 67 obit Jul 98

Conigliaro, Tony Feb 71 obit Apr 90

Coningham, Arthur Nov 44 obit Feb 48

Conley, Eugene Jul 54 obit Feb 82

Conley, William Gustavus obit Yrbk 40

Conn, Billy Aug 41 obit Aug 93

Connah, Douglas John obit Oct 41

Connally, John B. Jul 61 obit Aug 93

Connally, Tom Dec 41 Apr 49 obit Jan 64

Connaught, Arthur William Patrick Albert, Duke of see Albert, Arthur William Patrick

Connell, Arthur J. Feb 54

Connell, Karl obit Dec 41

Connelly, Marc Nov 69 obit Feb 81

Conner, Dennis Nov 87

Conner, Nadine Jan 55

Connerly, Ward Nov 2000

Connery, Lawrence J. obit Dec 41

Connery, Sean Jan 66 Jun 93

Conness, Robert obit Mar 41

Connick, Harry, Jr. Nov 90

Connolly, Cyril (WLB) Yrbk 47

Connolly, Maureen Nov 51 obit Sep 69

Connolly, Paul see Wicker, Tom

Connolly, Walter obit Jul 40

Connor, John T. Apr 61

Connors, Jimmy Sep 75

Conover, Harry Feb 49 obit Oct 65

Conrad, Barnaby, Jr. Sep 59

Conrad, Charles, Jr. Dec 65

Conroy, Pat [Canadian government official] Jul 54

Conroy, Pat [novelist] Jan 96

Considine, Robert Dec 47 obit Nov 75

Considine, Thomas Terry see Considine, Robert

Constantine II, King of The Hellenes Apr 67

Constanza, Midge see Costanza, Midge

Contadin, Fernand Joseph Desire see Fernandel

Conti, Tom Jun 85

Converse, Frederick Shepherd obit Aug 40

Conway, Jill Ker Jun 91

Conway, Thomas see Conway, Tim

Conway, Tim Apr 81

Conyers, John, Jr. Sep 70

Cook, Barbara Feb 63

Cook, Donald C. May 52 obit Feb 82

Cook, Donald Jul 54 obit Dec 61

Cook, Fannie (WLB) Yrbk 46 obit Oct 49

Cook, Frederick Albert obit Sep 40

Cook, Marlow W. Jan 72

Cook, Mrs. Jerome E. see Cook, Fannie

Cook, W. W. obit Dec 43

Cooke, Alistair Jun 52 May 74

Cooke, Cardinal see Cooke, Terence J.

Cooke, Hope see Hope Namgyal, Maharani of Sikkim

Cooke, Leslie E. Jun 62 obit Apr 67

Cooke, Morris Llewellyn May 50 obit May 60

Cooke, Terence J. Sep 68 obit Nov 83

Cooley, Denton A. Jan 76

Cooley, Harold D. Mar 51 obit Mar 74

Coolidge, Dane obit Sep 40

Coolidge, Elizabeth Sprague Aug 41 obit Jan 54

Coolidge, William David Jun 47 obit Mar 75

Coolio Aug 98

Coon, Carleton S. Sep 55 obit Jul 81

Cooney, Joan Ganz Jul 70

Coons, Albert H. Jun 60

Cooper, Alfred Duff Aug 40 obit Mar 54 [Norwich, Alfred Duff Cooper, 1st Viscount]

Cooper, Courtney Ryley obit Nov 40

Cooper, Cynthia Aug 98

Cooper, Edwin obit Aug 42

Cooper, Gary Dec 41 obit Jul 61

Cooper, Gladys Feb 56 obit Jan 72

Cooper, Irving S. Apr 74 obit Jan 86

Cooper, Jere Mar 55 obit Feb 58

Cooper, John Sherman Jun 50 obit Apr 91

Cooper, Joseph D. Feb 52

Cooper, Kent Oct 44 obit Mar 65

Cooper, Leroy Gordon, Jr. Sep 63

Cooper, Louise Field (WLB) Yrbk 50 obit Jan 93

Cooper, R. Conrad Jan 60

Coover, Robert Feb 91

Copeland, Benjamin, Rev. obit Jan 41

Copeland, Lammot Du Pont May 63

Copland, Aaron Sep 40 Mar 51 obit Jan 91

Copperfield, David Jul 92

Coppers, George H. May 52

Coppola, Francis Ford May 74 Jul 91

Coppola, Nicholas see Cage, Nicolas

Corbett, Jim May 46 obit Jun 55

Corbusier see Le Corbusier

Corcoran, Thomas Gardiner Mar 40 obit Feb 82

Cordero, Angel Oct 75

Cordier, Andrew W. Apr 50 obit Sep 75

Cordier, Constant obit Mar 40

Cordier, Gilbert see Rohmer, Eric

Cordiner, Ralph J. Jan 51 obit Jan 74

Cordon, Guy Apr 52 obit Jul 69

Corea, Chick Oct 88

Corea, Claude Mar 61 obit Nov 62

Corella, Angel Mar 99

Corelli, Franco Feb 64

Corey, Paul Yrbk 40

Cori, Carl F. Dec 47 [Cori, Carl F; and Cori, Gerty T] obit Feb 85

Cori, Gerty T. Dec 47 [Cori, Carl F; and Cori, Gerty T] obit Jan 58

Corigliano, John Jun 89

Corita see Kent, Corita

Corman, Roger Feb 83

Cornelius, John C. Jun 60

Cornell, Katharine May 41 Mar 52 obit Jul 74

Cornwell, David John Moore see Le Carré, John

Cornwell, Patricia May 97

Correll, Charles J. Dec 47 [Gosden, Freeman F.; and Correll, Charles J.] obit Nov 72

Corrigan, Joseph M., Bishop obit Aug 42

Corrigan, Mairead Apr 78

Corsaro, Frank Aug 75

Corson, Fred Pierce May 61 obit Apr 85

Cortázar, Julio Feb 74 obit Apr 84

Cortelyou, George Bruce obit Yrbk 40

Cortines, Adolfo Ruiz see Ruiz Cortines, Adolfo

Cortney, Philip Jan 58 obit Jul 71

Corwin, Norman Yrbk 40

Cory, John Mackenzie Sep 49 obit May 88

Cosby, Bill Apr 67 Oct 86
Cosell, Howard Nov 72 obit Jul 95
Cosgrave, Liam Jun 77
Cossiga, Francesco Jan 81
Cost, March Jan 58 obit Apr 73
Costa E Silva, Arthur Da Sep 67 obit Feb 70
Costa-Gavras Sep 72
Costa Gomes, Francisco Da May 76
Costain, Thomas B. May 53 obit Dec 65
Costanza, Midge Jun 78
Costas, Bob Jan 93
Costello, Elvis Sep 83
Costello, John A. Apr 48 obit Feb 76
Costello, Lou Oct 41 [Abbott, Bud; and Costello, Lou] obit May 59
Costle, Douglas M. Jun 80
Costner, Kevin Jun 90
Cot, Pierre Jun 44 obit Oct 77
Cothran, James W. Sep 53
Cotnareanu, Philippe see Cortney, Philip
Cotrubas, Ileana Oct 81
Cotten, Joseph Jul 43 obit Apr 94
Cottenham, Mark Everard Pepys, 6th Earl of see Pepys, Mark Everard
Cotter, Audrey see Meadows, Audrey
Cotter, Jayne see Meadows, Jayne
Cotterell, Geoffrey (WLB) Yrbk 54
Cotton, Joseph Bell obit Sep 40
Cotton, Norris Feb 56 obit May 89
Cottrell, Dorothy (WLB) Yrbk 55 obit Sep 57
Coty, René Apr 54 obit Jan 63
Coudenhove-Kalergi, Richard N., Count Feb 48 obit Oct 72
Coudert, Frederic René, Jr. Jun 41 obit Jul 72
Cougar, John see Mellencamp, John
Coughlin, Charles Edward Sep 40 obit Jan 80
Coulter, Calvin Brewster obit Jan 40
Coulter, John B. Jun 54

Counts, George S. Dec 41 obit Jan 75
Couples, Fred Jul 93
Courant, Richard Sep 66 obit Mar 72
Couric, Katie Mar 93
Cournand, André F. Mar 57 obit Apr 88
Courrèges, André Jan 70
Court, Margaret Sep 73
Courtenay, Tom May 64
Cousins, Frank Feb 60 obit Jul 86
Cousins, Margaret Jun 54 obit Oct 96
Cousins, Norman Aug 43 Aug 77 obit Jan 91
Cousteau, Jacques-Yves Jun 53 Jan 76 obit Sep 97
Cousy, Bob Sep 58
Coutts, Frederick Mar 64
Couve de Murville, Maurice Apr 55 obit Jun 2000
Covarrubias, Miguel Jul 40 obit Apr 57
Covey, Stephen R. Jan 98
Cowan, Minna G. Feb 48
Coward, Noel Jan 41 Mar 62 obit May 73
Cowden, Howard A. Mar 52
Cowdry, E. V. Jan 48
Cowen, Joshua Lionel Sep 54 obit Nov 65
Cowles, Fleur Apr 52
Cowles, Gardner, Jr. Jun 43 obit Aug 85
Cowles, John Jun 54 obit Apr 83
Cowles, Mike see Cowles, Gardner, Jr.
Cowles, Virginia May 42 obit Nov 83
Cowley, Malcolm Jun 79 obit May 89
Cox, Allyn Jul 54 obit Jan 83
Cox, Archibald Jul 61
Cox, Bobby Feb 98
Cox, Christopher Jul 99
Cox, E. Eugene Apr 43 obit Feb 53
Cox, Harvey Nov 68
Cox, Herald R. Apr 61
Cox, Wally Feb 54 obit Apr 73
Cox, William Trevor see Trevor, William
Coxe, Howard obit Jan 41
Coy, Wayne Mar 48 obit Dec 57 Yrbk 58

Coyne, James E. Jul 55
Cozzens, James Gould Jun 49 obit Oct 78
Crabtree, James W. obit Jul 45
Craft, Robert Mar 84
Craig, Cleo F. Sep 51 obit Jun 78
Craig, Elizabeth May Jun 49 obit Sep 75
Craig, George N. Feb 50 obit Feb 93
Craig, Lyman C. Apr 64 obit Sep 74
Craig, Malin Mar 44 obit Aug 45
Craig, Walter E. Jun 64 obit Sep 86
Craigavon, James Craig, 1st Viscount obit Jan 41
Craigie, Robert Jul 42 obit Jul 59
Crain, Jeanne Nov 51
Cram, Ralph Adams Oct 42 obit Oct 42
Cramer, Stuart Warren obit Aug 40
Crandall, Robert L. Nov 92
Crane, Eva Aug 93
Crane, Philip M. May 80
Cranko, John Jul 70 obit Sep 73
Cranston, Alan Feb 50 Oct 69
Cravath, Paul Drennan obit Aug 40
Craveiro Lopes, Francisco Higino Mar 56 obit Nov 64
Craven, Frank obit Oct 45
Craven, Thomas Apr 44 obit Apr 69
Crawford, Broderick Apr 50 obit Jun 86
Crawford, Cheryl Dec 45 obit Nov 86
Crawford, Cindy Aug 93
Crawford, Frederick C. Feb 43 obit Feb 95
Crawford, Joan Jan 46 Sep 66 obit Jul 77
Crawford, Michael Jan 92
Crawford, Morris Barker obit Yrbk 40
Crawford, Phyllis Nov 40
Crawshaw, William Henry obit Aug 40
Craxi, Bettino Feb 84 obit Jun 2000
Crayencour, Marguerite de see Yourcenar, Marguerite

Cream, Arnola Raymond *see* Walcott, Joe

Creasey, John Sep 63 obit Jul 73

Creeft, José De *see* de Creeft, José

Creel, George Jun 44 obit Jan 54

Creeley, Robert Oct 88

Cregar, Laird obit Jan 45

Crenshaw, Ben Sep 85

Crerar, H. D. G. Nov 44 obit May 65

Cresap, Mark W., Jr. Oct 59 obit Sep 63

Crespin, Régine Sep 79

Cresson, Edith Sep 91

Cresswell, Robert obit Nov 43

Cret, Paul Philippe Nov 42 obit Nov 45

Crewe, Albert V. Feb 64

Crewe, Robert Offley Ashburton Crewe-Milnes, 1st Marquis of obit Jul 45

Crews, Laura Hope obit Jan 43

Crichton, Michael Apr 76 Nov 93

Crick, Francis Mar 83

Crider, John H. Jun 49 obit Sep 66

Crile, George obit Feb 43

Cripps, Stafford Jul 40 Apr 48 obit Jun 52

Crisler, Fritz *see* Crisler, Herbert Orin

Crisler, Herbert Orin Feb 48 obit Oct 82

Crispin, Edmund (WLB) Yrbk 49

Criss, Peter *see* Kiss

Crist, William E. Nov 45

Cristiani, Alfredo Jan 90

Croce, Benedetto Jan 44 obit Jan 53

Crocetti, Dino *see* Martin, Dean

Crocker, Chester A. Jul 90

Crockett, Lucy Herndon (WLB) Yrbk 53

Croft, Arthur C. Jun 52

Cromer, 3d Earl of *see* Baring, George Rowland Stanley

Crompton, Rookes Evelyn Bell obit Mar 40

Cromwell, James H. R. Mar 40 obit May 90

Cronenberg, David May 92

Cronin, A. J. Jul 42 obit Mar 81

Cronin, Joe Mar 65 obit Nov 84

Cronkite, Walter Jan 56 Nov 75

Cronyn, Hume Mar 56 Jun 88

Crosbie, John Carnell Jan 90

Crosby, Bing Sep 41 Jun 53 obit Jan 78

Crosby, John C. Jun 53

Crosby, John Nov 81

Crosby, Robert Jun 54

Crosland, Anthony Sep 63 obit Apr 77

Crosley, Powel, Jr. Jun 47 obit Jun 61

Cross, Amanda *see* Heilbrun, Carolyn G.

Cross, Ben Aug 84

Cross, Burton M. Apr 54 obit Jan 99

Cross, Milton John Jan-Feb 40 obit Feb 75

Cross, Ronald H. Jun 41

Crosser, Robert Mar 53 obit Sep 57

Crossfield, A. Scott Oct 69

Crossley, Archibald M. Dec 41 obit Jul 85

Crossman, R. H. S. May 47 obit Jun 74

Crouch, Stanley Mar 94

Crouse, Russel Jun 41 obit May 66

Crow, Carl Oct 41 obit Jul 45

Crow, John O. Mar 69

Crow, Sheryl May 98

Crowe, Cameron Mar 96

Crowe, Russell May 2000

Crowe, William J., Jr. Jul 88

Crowell, T. Irving obit Mar 42

Crowley, John J., Father obit Apr 40

Crowley, Leo T. Jun 43 obit Jun 72

Crown, Henry Jan 72 obit Oct 90

Crownfield, Gertrude obit Jul 45

Crowther, Bosley Jul 57 obit Apr 81

Cruise, Tom Apr 87

Crum, Bartley C. May 47 obit Feb 60

Crumb, George Dec 74

Crumb, R. Apr 95

Crumit, Frank obit Oct 43

Crump, N. R. Sep 57

Cruyff, Johan Nov 81

Cruz, Celia Jul 83

Cruz, Hernan Santa *see* Santa Cruz, Hernan

Cruze, James obit Sep 42

Cruzen, Richard H. Mar 47 obit Jun 70

Crystal, Billy Feb 87

Csáky, Stephen obit Mar 41

Csermanck, János *see* Kádár, János

Csonka, Larry Feb 77

Cubberley, Ellwood P. obit Nov 41

Cudahy, John C. obit Oct 43

Cuevas, José Luis Jan 68

Cugat, Xavier May 42 obit Jan 91

Cukor, George Apr 43 obit Mar 83

Culbertson, Ely May 40 obit Mar 56

Culkin, Francis D. obit Sep 43

Cullberg, Birgit Nov 82 obit Nov 99

Cullen, Bill Jan 60 obit Sep 90

Cullen, Countee obit Mar 46

Cullen, Glenn Ernest obit May 40

Cullen, Hugh Roy Jul 55 obit Sep 57

Cullen, Thomas H. obit Apr 44

Cullis, Winifred C. Nov 43 obit Jan 57

Cullman, Howard S. Jun 51 obit Sep 72

Culshaw, John Jun 68 obit Jun 80

Culver, Essae Martha Sep 40

Culver, John C. Nov 79

Cummings, Robert Jan 56 obit Feb 91

Cuneo, John F. Jun 50

Cunhal, Alvaro Sep 75

Cunningham, Alan Jun 46 obit Apr 83

Cunningham, Andrew Browne, 1st Viscount Cunningham May 41 obit Sep 63

Cunningham, Graham Sep 49

Cunningham, Mary Nov 84

Cunningham, Merce May 66

Cunningham, Michael Jul 99

Cunningham, Mrs. James L. *see* Jenkins, Sara

Cunningham, Randall Mar 91

Cunningham, William Francis obit Jan 41

Cuomo, Andrew M. Oct 98

Cuomo, Mario Aug 83

Curie, Eve Mar 40

Curie, Irène *see* Joliot-Curie, Irène

Curran, Charles C. obit Jan 43

Curran, Charles E. Jan 87

Curran, Joseph E. Apr 45 obit Oct 81

Curran, Pearl Gildersleeve obit Jun 41

Currie, Lauchlin Bernard May 41 obit Mar 94

Curry, John Jul 79 obit Jun 94

Curry, John Steuart Apr 41 obit Oct 46

Curry, Mrs. William Seeright *see* Curry, Peggy Simon

Curry, Peggy Simon (WLB) Yrbk 58

Curtice, Harlow H. Mar 53 obit Jan 63

Curtin, Jane Jan 97

Curtin, John Jul 41 obit Aug 45

Curtin, Phyllis Sep 64

Curtis, Ann Jun 45

Curtis, Carl T. Sep 54 obit Jun 2000

Curtis, George Vaughan obit Oct 43

Curtis, Heber D. obit Mar 42

Curtis, Jamie Lee Nov 98

Curtis, Thomas B. Mar 65 obit Mar 93

Curtis, Tony May 59

Curzon, Clifford May 50 obit Oct 82

Cusack, Joan Jul 98

Cusack, John Jun 96

Cushing, Charles C. S. obit Apr 41

Cushing, Richard Cardinal Jun 52 obit Dec 70

Cushing, Tom *see* Cushing, Charles C. S.

Cushman, Robert E., Jr. Nov 72 obit Apr 85

Cussler, Clive Nov 2000

Custin, Mildred Nov 67 obit Jun 97

Cuthbert, Margaret May 47 obit Oct 68

Cyrankiewicz, Józef Feb 57

Czettel, Ladislas Mar 41 obit Apr 49

Dabney, Virginius Sep 48 obit Mar 96

Daché, Lilly Jul 41 obit Mar 90

Dacre of Glanton, Baron *see* Trevor-Roper, H. R.

Dae Jung, Kim *see* Kim Dae Jung

Dafoe, Allan obit Jul 43

Dafoe, John Wesley obit Feb 44

Dafoe, Willem Apr 90

Dahanayake, W. Apr 60

Dahlberg, Edwin T. May 58 obit Oct 86

Dai, Bao *see* Bao Dai

Daladier, Edouard Apr 40 obit Dec 70

Dalai Lama Jul 51 Jun 82

Dale, Benjamin J. obit Sep 43

Dale, Chester Sep 58 obit Jan 63

Dale, Clamma Apr 79

Dale, Jim Jul 81

Daley, Arthur Sep 56 obit Feb 74

Daley, Richard J. Sep 55 Jun 76 (died Dec 76)

Daley, Richard M. Aug 92

Daley, William M. Mar 98

Dali, Salvador Sep 40 Apr 51 obit Mar 89

Dallapiccola, Luigi Feb 66

Dallas, C. Donald Apr 49 obit Jun 59

Dallin, Cyrus Edwin obit Jan 45

Dalmia, Ramkrishna Dec 48

Dalrymple, Jean Sep 53 obit Feb 99

Dalton, Charles obit Aug 42

Dalton, Hugh Dalton, Baron Aug 45 obit Apr 62

Dalton, Timothy May 88

Daluege, Kurt obit Dec 46

Daly, Chuck Apr 91

Daly, James Oct 59 obit Sep 78

Daly, John May 48 obit May 91

Daly, Maureen Jan 46

Daly, Thomas A., Father obit Mar 41

Daly, Tyne Mar 92

Dam, Henrik Sep 49 obit Jun 76

Damadian, Raymond V. Jan 2000

Damaskinos, Archbishop Nov 45 obit Jul 49

D'amato, Alfonse Sep 83

D'amboise, Jacques Sep 64

Damerel, Donna obit Apr 41

Damon, Lindsay Todd obit Jan 40

Damon, Matt Mar 98 [Affleck, Ben; and Damon, Matt]

Damon, Ralph S. Jul 49 obit Mar 56

Damrosch, Walter Mar 44 obit Jan 51

Dancer, Stanley Jun 73

Dandurand, Raoul obit Apr 42

Dandy, Walter E. obit May 46

Danforth, John C. Jan 92

Danforth, William obit Jun 41

Dangerfield, George Sep 53 obit Mar 87

Daniel, Clifton Mar 66 obit Jul 2000

Daniel, Price Jan 56 obit Oct 88

Daniel, Robert Prentiss May 52 obit Mar 68

Daniel, W. C. Dan Jun 57

Daniell, Raymond Mar 44 obit Jun 69

Danielovitch, Issur *see* Douglas, Kirk

Daniel-Rops, Henry Mar 57 obit Oct 65

Daniels, Arthur Hill obit Apr 40

Daniels, Charles N. obit Mar 43

Daniels, Farrington Jul 65 obit Sep 72

Daniels, Grace B. Sep 59

Daniels, Jonathan Apr 42 obit Jan 82

Daniels, Josephus Oct 44 obit Feb 48

Däniken, Erich Von *see* Von Däniken, Erich

Danilova, Alexandra Jul 87 obit Sep 97

Dannay, Frederic Jul 40 [Dannay, Frederic; and Lee, Manfred B.] obit Oct 82

Danner, Blythe Jan 81

Danner, Louise Rutledge obit Nov 43

Danson, Ted Oct 90

Dantchenko, Vladimir Nemirovich- *see* Nemirov-

Davis, Sammy, Jr. Sep 56 Jul 78 obit Jul 90

Davis, Stuart Aug 40 Jul 64

Davis, Tobé Coller Dec 59 obit Feb 63

Davis, Watson Dec 45 obit Oct 67

Davis, Westmoreland obit Oct 42

Davis, William Ellsworth Apr 40

Davis, William H. Jun 41 obit Oct 64

Davis, William May 73

Davis, William Rhodes Mar 41 obit Mar 41

Davison, F. Trubee Dec 45

Davison, Frederic E. Feb 74

Dawes, Rufus Cutler obit Jan 40

Dawkins, Richard Aug 97

Dawson, Bertrand, 1st Viscount Dawson of Penn see Dawson of Penn, Bertrand Dawson, 1st Viscount

Dawson, John A. Sep 52

Dawson, William Apr 41 obit Sep 72

Dawson, William Levi Apr 45 obit Dec 70

Dawson of Penn, Bertrand Dawson, 1st Viscount obit Apr 45

Day, Albert M. Dec 48

Day, Doris Apr 54

Day, Dorothy May 62 obit Jan 81

Day, Edmund Ezra Sep 46 obit Apr 51

Day, J. Edward May 62 obit Jan 97

Day, Laraine Sep 53

Day, Pat Oct 97

Dayal, Rajeshwar Feb 61

Dayan, Moshe Mar 57 obit Jan 82

Dayan, Yaël Apr 97

Day-Lewis, C. Jan-Feb 40 Jul 69 obit Jul 72

Day-Lewis, Daniel Jul 90

Deakin, Arthur Jan 48 obit Jun 55

De Alvear, Marcelo T. obit May 42

Dean, Arthur Hobson Mar 54 obit Jan 88

Dean, Dizzy Sep 51 obit Sep 74

Dean, Erica see Burstyn, Ellen

Dean, Gordon Sep 50 obit Nov 58

Dean, H. Trendley Jun 57 obit Jul 62

Dean, Jay Hanna see Dean, Dizzy

Dean, Jerome Herman see Dean, Dizzy

Dean, Jimmy Dec 65

Dean, Laura Oct 88

Dean, Patrick May 61 obit Jan 95

Dean, Vera Micheles May 43 obit Dec 72

Dean, William F. Sep 54 obit Oct 81

Deane, Martha [radio personality, 1889-1976] see McBride, Mary Margaret

Deane, Martha [radio personality, 1909-73] see Young, Marian

Deane, Sidney N. obit Jun 43

de Angeli, Marguerite (WLB) Yrbk 47

De Angeli, Mrs. John see de Angeli, Marguerite

Dearborn, Ned H. Jan 47 obit Oct 62

Dearden, John Jul 69 obit Sep 88

Dearie, Blossom Feb 89

Deasy, Luere B. obit Apr 40

Deasy, Mary (WLB) Yrbk 58

Déat, Marcel Jan 42 obit May 55

De Bakey, Michael E. Mar 64

De Beck, William Morgan obit Jan 43

De Benedetti, Carlo May 90

De Bono, Emilio (Giuseppe Gaspare Giovanni) obit Feb 44

Debray, Régis Jun 82

Debre, Michel May 59 obit Oct 96

De Broglie, Louis, Prince see Broglie, Louis De

Debus, Kurt H. Nov 73 obit Nov 83

Debusschere, Dave Oct 73

Debutts, Harry A. Apr 53

Debye, Peter J. W. Jul 63 obit Jan 67

De Cartier (de Marchienne, Emile), Baron see Cartier, Baron

De Casseres, Benjamin obit Feb 46

De Castelnau, Edouard de Curieres see Castelnau, Edouard De Curieres De

De Castro, Morris F. May 50

De Chappedelaine, Louis see Chappedelaine, Louis De

De Chirico, Giorgio Jan 56 Jun 72 obit Jan 79

Decker, George H. Jan 61

Decker, Karl obit Feb 42

Decker, Mary Oct 83

Deconcini, Dennis Feb 92

Decoursey, Elbert Sep 54

de Crayencour, Marguerite see Yourcenar, Marguerite

de Creeft, José Dec 42 obit Yrbk 91 (died Sep 82)

Decter, Midge Apr 82

Dee, Ruby Nov 70

Deer, Ada E. Sep 94

Dees, Morris S., Jr. Jan 95

De Falla, Manuel see Falla, Manuel de

Defauw, Désiré Jan-Feb 40 obit Oct 60

Defferre, Gaston Sep 67 obit Jun 86

Deford, Frank Aug 96

De Forest, Lee May 41 obit Oct 61

DeGaetani, Jan Oct 77

De Galard Terraube, Geneviève see Galard Terraube, Geneviève De

De Gasperi, Alcide see Gasperi, Alcide De

De Gaulle, Charles see Gaulle, Charles De

De Geer, Gerard obit Sep 43

Degeneres, Ellen Apr 96

De Graff, Robert F. May 43

De Groot, Adriaan M. see Groot, Adriaan M. De

De Guise, Jean Pierre Clément Marie, Duc see Guise, Jean Pierre Clement Marie, Duc De

De Hartog, Jan Feb 70

De Hauteclocque, Jacques-Philippe Leclerc see Leclerc, Jacques-Philippe

De Havilland, Olivia May 44 [Fontaine, Joan; and de Havilland, Olivia] Nov 66

De Hevesy, George see Hevesy, George De

Dehler, Thomas Jul 55 obit Oct 67

Dehn, Adolf Apr 41 obit Jul 68

Deighton, Len Sep 84

Dejong, David C. Jul 44 obit Nov 67

De Jong, Dola (WLB) Yrbk 47

Dejong, Meindert (WLB) Yrbk 52 obit Sep 91

De Kauffmann, Henrik see Kauffmann, Henrik

De Kiewiet, Cornelis W. Jul 53 obit Apr 86

De Kleine, William Apr 41 obit Dec 57 Yrbk 58

De Klerk, F. W. Feb 90

De Kooning, Elaine Jul 82 obit Mar 89

De Kooning, Willem Jun 55 Sep 84 obit May 97

De Kruif, Paul May 42 Jul 63 obit Apr 71

De La Borde, Jean Feb 43

De La Colina, Rafael see Colina, Rafael De La

Delacorte, George T. Nov 65 obit Jul 91

Delafield, E. M. obit Jan 44

De la Guardia, Ernesto, Jr. see Guardia, Ernesto De La, Jr.

De La Guardia, Ricardo Adolfo May 42 obit Feb 70

De La Hoya, Oscar Jan 97

De La Madrid, Miguel Apr 83

Deland, Margaret Wade obit Mar 45

Delaney, Shelagh Apr 62

Delany, Annie Elizabeth see Delany, Bessie

Delany, Bessie Nov 95 [Delany, Sadie; and Delany, Bessie] obit Jan 96

Delany, Sadie Nov 95 [Delany, Sadie; and Delany, Bessie] obit Apr 99

Delany, Sarah see Delany, Sadie

Delany, Walter S. Dec 52

De La Renta, Oscar Mar 70

De Larrocha, Alicia see Larrocha, Alicia de

De la Torre, Lillian (WLB) Yrbk 49 obit Nov 93

Delaunay, Sonia Aug 77 obit Feb 80

De Laurentiis, Dino May 65

DeLauro, Rosa Mar 2000

De Lavallade, Carmen Dec 67

Delay, Tom May 99

Del Castillo, Antonio see Castillo, Antonio

De Leath, Vaughn obit Jul 43

Delgado, José Feb 76

Delillo, Don Jan 89

de Lima, Sigrid (WLB) Yrbk 58 obit Feb 2000

Dell, Michael Jun 98

Dell, Robert Edward obit Sep 40

Della Casa, Lisa Jul 56

Della Chiesa, Vivian Nov 43

Della Femina, Jerry Nov 79

Dellinger, David Aug 76

Dello Joio, Norman Sep 57

Dellums, Ronald V. Sep 72 Sep 93

Del Monaco, Mario Feb 57 obit Jan 83

Delon, Alain Apr 64

Deloncle, Eugene obit Feb 44

De Long, Emma J. Wotton obit Jan 41

Delorean, John Z. Mar 76

Deloria, Vine, Jr. Sep 74

Delors, Jacques Jun 89

De los Angeles, Victoria see Angeles, Victoria de los

Del Tredici, David Mar 83

De Luca, Giuseppe Mar 47 obit Oct 50

De Luce, Daniel Jun 44

De Maizière, Lothar Aug 90

De Menthon, François see Menthon, Francois De

Demikhov, Vladimir P. Jun 60 obit Feb 99

De Mille, Agnes Oct 43 Jan 85 obit Jan 94

De Mille, Cecil B. May 42 obit Mar 59

Deming, Dorothy May 43

Deming, Edwin W. obit Dec 42

Deming, W. Edwards Sep 93 obit Mar 94

Demirel, Süleyman Feb 80

Demme, Jonathan Apr 85

De Montebello, Philippe Apr 81

Demott, Richard H. Feb 51 obit Nov 68

De Moya, Manuel A. see Moya, Manuel A. De

Dempsey, Jack Feb 45 obit Jul 83

Dempsey, John Jun 61 obit Sep 89

Dempsey, Miles Christopher Oct 44 obit Jul 69

Dempsey, William Harrison see Dempsey, Jack

De Navarro, Mary see Navarro, Mary De

Dench, Judi Jan 99

Dendramis, Vassili Jun 47 obit Jul 56

Denebrink, Francis C. Feb 56 obit Jun 87

Denenberg, Herbert S. Dec 72

Deneuve, Catherine Feb 78

Denfeld, Louis E. Dec 47 obit May 72

Deng Xiaoping May 76 Jun 94 obit Apr 97

Denham, R. N. Oct 47 obit Sep 54

Deniel, Enrique, Pla y see Pla Y Deniel, Enrique

De Niro, Robert Aug 76 May 93

Dennehy, Brian Jul 91

Denning, Alfred Thompson Jul 65 obit Jun 99

Dennis, Charles Henry obit Nov 43

Dennis, Eugene May 49 obit Mar 61

Dennis, Felix Apr 2000

Dennis, Lawrence Mar 41 obit Oct 77

Dennis, Olive Wetzel Jun 41

Dennis, Patrick see Tanner, Edward Everett, 3d

Dennis, Sandy Jan 69 obit May 92

Dennison, Robert Lee Apr 60 obit May 80

Denniston, Reynolds obit Mar 43

Denny, Charles R., Jr. May 47

Denny, Collins, Bishop obit Jul 43

Denny, George V., Jr. Sep 50 obit Jan 60

Denny, George Vernon Jr. Sep 40

De Noue, Jehan, Comte see Noue, Jehan De, Comte

Densen-Gerber, Judianne Nov 83

Densford, Katharine J. Feb 47

Dent, Allie Beth see Martin, Allie Beth

Dent, Frederick B. Apr 74

Denton, Jeremiah A., Jr. May 82

Denver, John Jan 75 obit Jan 98

De Onís, Harriet Apr 57 obit May 69

De Palencia, Isabel *see* Palencia, Isabel De

De Palma, Brian Sep 82

DePaola, Tomie Feb 99

Depardieu, Gérard Oct 87

De Pauw, Gommar A. May 74

Depinet, Ned E. Jun 50

De Poncins, Gontran Jean-Pierre de Montaigne, Vicomte *see* Poncins, Gontran, Vicomte De

De Pourtalès, Guy, Count *see* Pourtalès, Guy, Count De

Depp, Johnny May 91

Depreist, James Oct 90

De Quay, Jan Eduard *see* Quay, Jan Eduard de

Der Harootian, Koren Jan 55

Dermot, Jessie *see* Elliott, Maxine

Dern, Bruce Oct 78

Dern, Laura Oct 92

De Rochemont, Louis Nov 49 obit Feb 79

De Rochemont, Richard Oct 45 obit Sep 82

De Roussy De Sales, Raoul obit Jan 43

Derrida, Jacques Jul 93

Dershowitz, Alan M. Sep 86

Derthick, Lawrence Gridley Apr 57 obit Mar 93

Derwent, Clarence Nov 47 obit Nov 59

Derwinski, Edward J. Aug 91

Desai, Morarji Sep 58 Jan 78 obit Jun 95

De Sapio, Carmine G. Sep 55

De Selincourt, Ernest obit Jul 43

De Seversky, Alexander Feb 41 obit Oct 74

Des Graz, Charles Louis obit Yrbk 40

De Sherbinin, Betty (WLB) Yrbk 48

De Sica, Vittorio Jul 52 obit Jan 75

D'esperey, Franchet obit Sep 42

Des Portes, Fay Allen obit Nov 44

Dessès, Jean Jan 56 obit Oct 70

De Sylva, Buddy Sep 43 obit Sep 50

De Sylva, George Gard *see* De Sylva, Buddy

De Tirtoff, Romaine *see* Erté

De Toledano, Ralph *see* Toledano, Ralph De

Dett, R. Nathaniel obit Nov 43

Deuel, Wallace R. Aug 42

Deukmejian, George Jun 83

Deupree, Richard R. Apr 46 obit May 74

Deutsch, Julius Nov 44 obit Mar 68

Deutschendorf, Henry John, Jr. *see* Denver, John

De Valera, Eamon Nov 40 Sep 51 obit Oct 75

De Valois, Ninette Dec 49

Devaney, John Patrick obit Nov 41

Dever, Paul A. May 49 obit Jul 58

Devereaux, William Charles obit Sep 41

Devers, Gail Jul 96

Devers, Jacob Loucks Sep 42 obit Jan 80

Devi, Gayatri *see* Jaipur, Maharani of

Devine, John M. Jan 48

Deviny, John J. Sep 48 obit Apr 55

Devito, Danny Feb 88

Devlin, Bernadette Jan 70

Devoe, Ralph G. Oct 44 obit Nov 66

De Voto, Bernard Sep 43 obit Jan 56

De Vries, Peter (WLB) Yrbk 59 obit Jan 94

Devries, William C. Jan 85

De Vry, Herman A. obit May 41

de Waart, Edo Mar 90

Dewart, William T. obit Mar 44

Dewey, Charles S. Jan 49 obit Feb 81

Dewey, John Aug 44 obit Jul 52

Dewey, Thomas E. Jul 40 Sep 44 obit Apr 71

Dewhurst, Colleen Jul 74 obit Oct 91

Dewhurst, J. Frederic Jan 48 obit Jul 67

De Wiart, Adrian Carton *see* Carton De Wiart, Adrian

De Witt, John L. Jul 42

De Wohl, Louis (WLB) Yrbk 55 obit Oct 61

De Wolfe, James P. Aug 42 obit Mar 66

Dexheimer, W. A. Feb 55

Dexter, John Jul 76 obit May 90

Dhaliwal, Daljit Nov 2000

D'harnoncourt, René Sep 52 obit Oct 68

Dhebar, U. N. Jun 55

Dial, Morse G. Mar 56 obit Jan 83

Diamant, Gertrude Nov 42

Diamond, David Nov 66

Diamond, Neil May 81

Diana, Princess of Wales Jan 83 obit Nov 97

Díaz Ordaz, Gustavo May 65 obit Sep 79

Dibelius, Otto May 53 obit Mar 67

DiCaprio, Leonardo Mar 97

Dichter, Ernest Jan 61 obit Jan 92

Dick, Charles obit May 45

Dickerson, Ernest Jul 2000

Dickerson, Nancy Hanschman Sep 62 obit Jan 98

Dickerson, Roy E. obit Apr 44

Dickey, James Apr 68 obit Mar 97

Dickey, John Sloan Apr 55 obit Apr 91

Dickinson, Angie Feb 81

Dickinson, Edwin Sep 63 obit Feb 79

Dickinson, Lucy Jennings Nov 45

Dickinson, Luren D. obit Jun 43

Dickinson, Mrs. LaFell *see* Dickinson, Lucy Jennings

Dickinson, Robert L. Mar 50 obit Jan 51

Dickinson, Willoughby Hyett Dickinson, 1st Baron obit Jul 43

Dickson, Lovat Sep 62

Dickson, Marguerite (WLB) Yrbk 52 obit Jan 54

Diddley, Bo Jun 89

Didion, Joan Sep 78

Didrikson, Babe *see* Zaharias, Babe Didrikson

Diebenkorn, Richard Dec 71 obit May 93
Diebold, John Mar 67
Diefenbaker, John George May 57 obit Oct 79
Diefendorf, Allen Ross obit Sep 43
Diehl, Frances White Oct 47
Diehl, Mrs. Ambrose N. *see* Diehl, Frances White
Diem, Ngo Dinh *see* Ngo Dinh Diem
Dies, Martin Apr 40 obit Jan 73
Dieterich, William H. obit Yrbk 40
Dieterle, William Sep 43 obit Feb 73
Dietrich, Marlene Jun 53 Feb 68 obit Jun 92
Dietz, David Oct 40 obit Apr 85
Dietz, Howard Oct 65 obit Sep 83
DiFiglia, Michael Bennett *see* Bennett, Michael
Difranco, Ani Aug 97
Diggs, Charles C., Jr. Jul 57 obit Nov 98
Dike, Phil Dec 42
Dill, John Greer Feb 41 obit Dec 44
Dillard, Annie Jan 83
Dillard, James Hardy obit Sep 40
Diller, Barry Apr 86
Diller, Phyllis Jul 67
Dillman, Bradford Jan 60
Dillon, C. Douglas Apr 53
Dillon, Matt May 85
DiMaggio, Joe Jun 41 Jul 51 obit May 99
DiMaggio, Joseph Paul *see* DiMaggio, Joe
Dimechkie, Nadim Feb 60
Dimitrov, Georgi May 49
Dine, Jim Jun 69
Dinehart, Alan obit Sep 44
Ding, J. N. *see* Darling, Jay Norwood
Dingell, John D., Jr. Aug 83
Dingell, John D. Mar 49 obit Nov 55 Yrbk 56
Dinkins, David Mar 90
Dinsmore, Charles Allen obit Oct 41
Dior, Christian Oct 48 obit Jan 58

Dirksen, Everett McKinley Apr 41 Sep 57 obit Nov 69
Disalle, Michael V. Jan 51 obit Nov 81
Disney, Anthea Jun 98
Disney, Doris Miles (WLB) Yrbk 54
Disney, Walt Aug 40 Apr 52 obit Feb 67
Di Suvero, Mark Nov 79
Ditchy, Clair W. Mar 54 obit Oct 67
Dith Pran Oct 96
Ditka, Mike Oct 87
Ditmars, Raymond Lee Sep 40 obit Jul 42
Ditter, J. William obit Jan 44
Divine, Frank H. obit May 41
Dix, Dorothy Jan-Jun 40 obit Feb 52
Dix, William S. Jun 69 obit Apr 78
Dixey, Henry E. obit Apr 43
Dixie Chicks July 2000
Dixon, Dean Apr 43 obit Jan 77
Dixon, Jeane Feb 73 obit Mar 97
Dixon, Owen Aug 42
Dixon, Paul Rand Jan 68
Dixon, Pierson Sep 54 obit Jun 65
Dixon, Thomas obit May 46
Dixon, Willie May 89 obit Apr 92
Djanira Jan 61
Djilas, Milovan Sep 58 obit Jul 95
Djuanda Apr 58 obit Jan 64
Dmitri, Ivan *see* West, Levon
Doan, Leland I. Oct 52 obit May 74
Dobbie, William Jul 45
Dobbs, Mattiwilda Sep 55
Dobie, J. Frank Dec 45 obit Nov 64
Dobnievski, David *see* Dubinsky, David
Dobrynin, Anatoly F. Sep 62
Dobson, James C. Aug 98
Dobson, William Alexander obit Jul 43
Dobzhansky, Theodosius Sep 62 obit Feb 76
Docking, George Jun 58 obit Mar 64
Doctorow, E. L. Jul 76
Dodd, Alvin E. Nov 47 obit Jul 51

Dodd, Christopher J. Oct 89
Dodd, Martha (WLB) Yrbk 46 obit Jan 91
Dodd, Norris E. Feb 49 obit Sep 68
Dodd, Thomas J. Sep 59 obit Jul 71
Dodd, William Edward obit Mar 40
Dodds, Gil Jun 47 obit Apr 77
Dodds, Harold W. Dec 45 obit Jan 81
Dodge, Bayard Feb 48 obit Jul 72
Dodge, Cleveland E. Mar 54 obit Feb 83
Dodge, David (WLB) Yrbk 56
Dodge, John V. Jul 60
Dodge, Joseph Morrell Nov 47 obit Jan 65
Dodge, Raymond obit May 42
Doe, Samuel Kanyon May 81 obit Nov 90
Doenitz, Karl Nov 42 obit Feb 81
Doherty, Henry Latham obit Jan 40
Doherty, Robert E. Sep 49 obit Dec 50
Dohnányi, Christoph von Oct 85
Doi, Peter Tatsuo Nov 60
Doi, Takako Jul 92
Doihara, Kenji Mar 42 obit Feb 49
Doisy, Edward A. Mar 49 obit Jan 87
Dolan, D. Leo Sep 56
Dolbier, Maurice (WLB) Yrbk 56 obit Jan 94
Dolci, Danilo Sep 61 obit Mar 98
Dole, Elizabeth Hanford Jun 83 Jan 97
Dole, Robert J. Apr 72 Oct 87
Dolin, Anton Jan 46 obit Jan 84
Dollard, Charles Dec 48 obit Apr 77
Dolly, Jenny obit Jul 41
Domagk, Gerhard Mar 58 obit Jun 64
Domenici, Pete V. Jun 82
Domingo, Placido Mar 72
Dominguín, Luis Miguel Mar 72 obit Jul 96
Doms, Keith Jun 71
Donahey, Vic obit May 46
Donahue, Phil May 80

Donald, David Sep 61
Donald, W. H. Jul 46
Donaldson, Jesse M. Jan 48 obit May 70
Donaldson, Sam Sep 87
Donegan, Horace W. B. Jul 54 obit Jan 92
Dongen, Cornélius Théodorus Marie van *see* Dongen, Kees Van
Dongen, Kees Van Sep 60 obit Jul 68
Donleavy, J. P. Jul 79
Donlon, Mary Jul 49 obit May 77
Donnadieu, Marguerite *see* Duras, Marguerite
Donnell, Forrest C. Sep 49
Donnelly, Antoinette *see* Blake, Doris
Donnelly, Phil M. Jun 56 obit Nov 61
Donnelly, Walter J. Sep 52 obit Jan 71
Donner, Frederic G. Jan 59 obit Apr 87
Donoso, José Feb 78 obit Feb 97
Donovan, Carrie Sep 99
Donovan, Hedley May 65 obit Oct 90
Donovan, James B. Jun 61 obit Mar 70
Donovan, Raymond J. Jan 82
Donovan, William J. Mar 41 Sep 54 obit Apr 59
Dooley, Thomas A. Jul 57 obit Mar 61
Doolittle, James H. Aug 42 Mar 57 obit Jan 94
Dooyeweerd, H. Sep 58
Dorati, Antal Jul 48 obit Jan 89
Doriot, Jacques Nov 40
Dorman, Gerald D. Jun 70
Dornay, Louis obit Sep 40
Dornberger, Walter R. Feb 65 obit Sep 80
Dorough, Howie D. *see* Backstreet Boys
Dorpfeld, Wilhelm obit Jan 40
Dorris, Michael Mar 95 obit Jun 97
Dorsett, Tony Apr 80
Dorsey, Jimmy Apr 42 [Dorsey, Jimmy; and Dorsey, Tommy] obit Sep 57

Dorsey, Tommy Apr 42 [Dorsey, Jimmy; and Dorsey, Tommy] obit Feb 57
Dorticós, Osvaldo Feb 63 obit Aug 83
Dos Passos, John Aug 40 obit Nov 70
dos Santos, José Eduardo *see* Santos, José Edwardo Dos
Doster, James J. obit Dec 42
Doten, Carroll Warren obit Aug 42
Doubleday, Nelson May 87
Dougherty, Dora Mar 63
Doughton, Robert L. Jul 42 obit Dec 54 Yrbk 55
Douglas, Arthur F. Nov 50 obit May 56
Douglas, Donald W. Nov 41 Dec 50 obit Mar 81
Douglas, Emily Taft Apr 45 obit Mar 94
Douglas, Helen Gahagan Sep 44 obit Aug 80
Douglas, James H. Sep 57 obit Apr 88
Douglas, Kirk Mar 52
Douglas, Lewis W. Mar 47 obit May 74
Douglas, Marjory Stoneman Jul 53 obit Jul 98
Douglas, Melvyn May 42 obit Sep 81
Douglas, Michael *see* Crichton, Michael Apr 87
Douglas, Mike May 68
Douglas, Paul H. Apr 49 obit Nov 76
Douglas, Sholto Jun 43 obit Dec 69
Douglas, T. C. *see* Thompson, William
Douglas, Walter J. obit Sep 41
Douglas, William O. Oct 41 Nov 50 obit Mar 80
Douglas-Home, Alexander Frederick Feb 58 obit Jan 96 [Home, Alexander Frederick Douglas-Home, 14th Earl of]
Douglas of Kirtleside, William Sholto Douglas, 1st Baron *see* Douglas, Sholto
Dove, Rita May 94
Dover, Elmer obit Nov 40
Dow, Willard H. Feb 44 obit May 49
Dowd, Maureen Sep 96

Dowding, Hugh Caswell Tremenheere, 1st Baron Nov 40 obit Apr 70
Dowell, Anthony May 71
Dowling, Eddie Feb 46 obit Apr 76
Dowling, Robert W. Oct 52 obit Nov 73
Dowling, Walter C. Mar 63 obit Sep 77
Downes, Olin Mar 43 obit Oct 55
Downey, Fairfax (WLB) Yrbk 49 obit Aug 90
Downey, Morton Jul 49 obit Jan 86
Downey, Robert Jr. Aug 98
Downey, Sheridan Oct 49 obit Jan 62
Downs, Hugh Mar 65
Downs, Robert B. Jan 41 Jun 52 obit Apr 91
Doxiadis, Constantinos A. Sep 64 obit Sep 75
Doyle, Adrian Conan Sep 54
Doyle, Roddy Oct 97
D'oyly Carte, Rupert Feb 48
Dr. Seuss *see* Geisel, Theodor Seuss
Drabble, Margaret May 81
Drabinsky, Garth Oct 97
Drake, Alfred Apr 44 obit Sep 92
Drake, Frank Donald Jan 63
Drake, St. Clair Jan 46 [Cayton, Horace R; and Drake, St. Clair] obit Aug 90
Drapeau, Jean Dec 67 obit Oct 99
Draper, Charles Stark Dec 65 obit Sep 87
Draper, Dorothy May 41 obit Apr 69
Draper, Paul Feb 44 obit Jan 97
Draper, William H., Jr. Mar 52 obit Feb 75
Drees, Willem Jan 49 obit Jul 88
Dreiser, Theodore obit Feb 46
Drescher, Fran Apr 98
Dressen, Chuck Jul 51 obit Nov 66
Drew, Charles R. May 44 obit May 50
Drew, Elizabeth Oct 79
Drew, George A. Dec 48 obit May 84
Drexler, Clyde Jan 96

Drexler, Millard S. Jan 93

Dreyfus, Camille May 55 obit Dec 56 Yrbk 57

Dreyfus, Pierre Jul 58 obit Mar 95

Dreyfuss, Henry May 48 Oct 59 obit Dec 72

Dreyfuss, Richard Jan 76

Dridzo, Solomon Abramovichch see Lozovsky, S. A.

Driesch, Hans obit Jun 41

Drinan, Robert F. Jun 71

Driscoll, Alfred E. Jan 49 obit May 75

Driskell, David C. Aug 2000

Droch see Bridges, Robert

Drossaerts, Arthur Jerome obit Oct 40

Drouet, Bessie Clarke obit Oct 40

Drozniak, Edward Jul 62 obit Jan 67

Drucker, Peter F. May 64

Druckman, Jacob May 81 obit Aug 96

Drum, Hugh A. Jul 41 obit Nov 51

Drummond, Roscoe Nov 49 obit Nov 83

Dryden, Hugh L. Apr 59 obit Jan 66

Dryden, Lennox see Steen, Marguerite

Dryfoos, Orvil E. Jan 62 obit Jul 63

Drysdale, Don Feb 65 obit Sep 93

Duarte, José Napoleón Sep 81 obit Apr 90

Dubcek, Alexander Nov 68

Dubilier, William Sep 57 obit Oct 69

Dubinsky, David Dec 42 Jun 57 obit Jan 83

Dublin, Louis Israel Oct 42 obit Yrbk 91 (died Mar 69)

Dubois, Eugéne obit May 41

Du Bois, Guy Péne Oct 46 obit Oct 58

Du Bois, Shirley Graham Oct 46 [Graham, Shirley] obit Jun 77

Du Bois, W. E. B. Jan-Jun 40 obit Oct 63

Dubos, René J. Oct 52 Jan 73 obit Apr 82

Du Bose, Horace Mellard obit Mar 41

Dubridge, L. A. Jun 48 obit Mar 94

Dubuffet, Jean Jul 62 obit Jul 85

Duchamp, Gaston Emile see Villon, Jacques

Duchamp, Marcel Jun 60 obit Dec 68

Duchin, Eddy Jan 47 obit Mar 51

Duchin, Peter Jan 77

Duclos, Jacques Feb 46 obit Jun 75

Duc Tho, Le see Le Duc Tho

Dudley, Bide obit Feb 44

Dudley, Walter Bronson see Dudley, Bide

Duerk, Alene Sep 73

Dufek, George J. Mar 57

Duff, James H. Apr 48 obit Feb 70

Duffey, Joseph D. Mar 71

Duffy, Bernard C. Jul 52 obit Nov 72

Duffy, Edmund Jan-Jun 40 obit Nov 62

Duffy, James J. obit Feb 42

Du Fournet, Louis Rene Marie Charles Dartige obit Mar 40

Dufy, Raoul Mar 51 obit May 53

Dugan, Alan Nov 90

Dugan, Raymond Smith obit Oct 40

Duggan, Ervin S. Oct 98

Duggan, Laurence May 47 obit Jan 49

Duggar, Benjamin Minge Nov 52 obit Nov 56

Du Jardin, Rosamond (WLB) Yrbk 53

Dukakis, Michael S. Feb 78

Dukakis, Olympia Jul 91

Duke, Angier Biddle Feb 62 obit Jul 95

Duke, Patty Sep 63

Duke, Vernon Jun 41 obit Mar 69

Dukelsky, Vladimir see Duke, Vernon

Dullea, Keir Jun 70

Dulles, Allen W. Mar 49 obit Mar 69

Dulles, Eleanor Lansing Sep 62 obit Jan 97

Dulles, John Foster Aug 44 Sep 53 obit Jul 59

Dumas, Roland Oct 90

Du Maurier, Daphne May 40 obit Jun 89

Du Mont, Allen B. Jun 46 obit Jan 66

Dunaway, Faye Feb 72

Dunbar, Paul B. Jul 49 obit Nov 68

Dunbar, Rudolph Oct 46

Duncan, Andrew Rae Jul 41 obit May 52

Duncan, Charles W. Apr 80

Duncan, David Douglas Nov 68

Duncan, Malcolm obit Jun 42

Duncan, Michael Clarke Aug 2000

Duncan, Patrick obit Sep 43

Duncan, Sandy Jan 80

Duncan, Thomas W. Dec 47

Duncan, Tim Nov 99

Duncan, Todd Jul 42 obit May 98

Dunham, Charles L. Mar 66

Dunham, Franklin Jan 42 obit Jan 62

Dunham, Katherine Mar 41

Dunkerley, William Arthur see Oxenham, John

Dunlap, John B. Dec 51 obit Feb 65

Dunlop, John T. Apr 51

Dunn, Gordon E. May 66

Dunn, J. Allan obit May 41

Dunn, James Clement May 43 obit Jun 79

Dunn, Jennifer Mar 99

Dunn, Loula F. Mar 51

Dunne, Dominick May 99

Dunne, Irene Aug 45 obit Nov 90

Dunne, John Gregory Jun 83

Dunning, John R. May 48 obit Oct 75

Dunninger, Joseph Sep 44 obit May 75

Dunnock, Mildred Sep 55 obit Sep 91

Dunrossil, William Shepherd Morrison, 1st Viscount see Morrison, William Shepherd

Dunton, A. Davidson Jan 59 obit Apr 87

Duplessis, Maurice Oct 48 obit Nov 59

Du Pont, Francis Irénée obit May 42

Du Pont, Pierre Samuel Sep 40 obit May 54

Du Pré, Jacqueline May 70 obit Nov 87

Du Puy, William Atherton obit Oct 41

Durán, Roberto Sep 80

Durang, Christopher Jun 87

Durant, Will Sep 64 obit Jan 82

Durante, Jimmy Sep 46 obit Mar 80

Duranty, Walter Jan 43 obit Dec 57 Yrbk 58

Duras, Marguerite Nov 85 obit May 96

Durbin, Deanna Jun 41

Durenberger, David F. Oct 88

Durgin, C. T. Sep 54 obit May 65

Durham, Carl Jul 57 obit Jun 74

Durkin, Martin P. Feb 53 obit Jan 56

Durning, Charles Sep 97

Durocher, Leo Sep 40 Jul 50 obit Nov 91

Durocher, Mrs. Leo see Day, Laraine

Durrell, Gerald May 85 obit Apr 95

Durrell, Lawrence Jul 63 obit Jan 91

Dürrenmatt, Friedrich Feb 59 obit Apr 91

D'usseau, Arnaud Mar 44 [Gow, James; and d'Usseau, Arnaud] obit Apr 90

Dusser De Barenne, Joannes Gregorius obit Aug 40

Dutoit, Charles Feb 87

Dutra, Eurico Gaspar Mar 46 obit Sep 74

Dutton, Charles S. Oct 2000

Duva, Lou Nov 99

Duval, David Oct 99

Duvalier, François

Duvalier, Jean-Claude Jun 72

Duvall, Evelyn Millis Oct 47

Duvall, Mrs. Sylvanus Milne see Duvall, Evelyn Millis

Duvall, Robert Jul 77

Duvieusart, Jean Sep 50

Du Vigneaud, Vincent Jan 56 obit Feb 79

Duvivier, Julien Jul 43 obit Jan 68

Dwight, Reginald Kenneth see John, Elton

Dwinell, Lane Jun 56 obit Jun 97

Dworkin, Andrea Oct 94

Dworshak, Henry C. Jan 50 obit Oct 62

Dye, Marie Dec 48

Dyer-Bennet, Richard Jun 44 obit Feb 92

Dyhrenfurth, Norman G. Apr 65

Dyke, Cornelius G. obit Jun 43

Dykstra, Clarence A. Jan 41 obit Jun 50

Dykstra, John Apr 63 obit May 72

Dylan, Bob May 65 Oct 91

Dyson, Esther Aug 97

Dyson, Freeman J. Jan 80

Dyson, Michael Eric Oct 97

Dzhugashvili, Iosif Vissarionovich see Stalin, Joseph

Eady, Wilfrid Oct 47 obit Feb 62

Eagleburger, Lawrence S. Nov 92

Eagleton, Thomas Nov 73

Eaker, Ira Clarence Oct 42 obit Sep 87

Eames, Charles Jan 65 obit Oct 78

Eanes, António Ramalho Apr 79

Earle, Steve Oct 98

Earle, Sylvia A. May 92

Early, Gerald May 95

Early, Stephen T. Jul 41 Dec 49 obit Sep 51

Early, William Ashby Mar 54

Easley, Claudius M. obit Jul 45

Eastland, James O. Jan 49 obit Apr 86

Eastman, Joseph B. Jul 42 obit May 44

Eastman, Max Apr 69 obit Apr 69

Eastwood, Clint Oct 71 Mar 89

Eaton, Charles A. May 45 obit Mar 53

Eaton, Cyrus S. Jul 48 obit Jul 79

Eban, Abba Oct 48 May 57

Ebbers, Bernard J. Feb 98

Ebbott, Percy J. Oct 54

Eberhart, Richard Jan 61

Eberle, Irmengarde (WLB) Yrbk 46

Ebersol, Dick Jul 96

Eberstadt, Ferdinand Dec 42 obit Jan 70

Ebert, Roger Mar 97

Eboue, Felix Adolphe obit Jul 44

Ebsen, Buddy Jan 77

Ebsen, Christian Rudolph, Jr. see Ebsen, Buddy

Eccles, David Jan 52 obit May 99

Eccles, John C. Oct 72 obit Jul 97

Eccles, Marriner S. Apr 41 obit Feb 78

Ecevit, Bülent Jan 75

Echeverría Álvarez, Luis Nov 72

Echols, Oliver P. Dec 47 obit Jul 54

Eckardt, Felix Von Jan 56

Ecker, Frederick H. Jun 48 obit May 64

Eckstein, Gustav May 42 obit Nov 81

Eckstein, Otto Feb 67 obit May 84

Eckstine, Billy Jul 52 obit Apr 93

Eco, Umberto Apr 85

Edberg, Stefan Jan 94

Eddington, Arthur Stanley Apr 41 obit Yrbk 91 (died Nov 44)

Eddy, Manton S. Feb 51 obit Jun 62

Eddy, Nelson Feb 43 obit May 67

Ede, James Chuter May 46 obit Jan 66

Edel, Leon Jul 63 obit Nov 97

Edelman, Gerald M. Apr 95

Edelman, Marian Wright Sep 92

Edelman, Maurice Jan 54 obit Feb 76

Eden, Anthony Yrbk 40 Apr 51 obit Mar 77

Edey, Birdsall Otis obit Aug 40

Edge, Walter Evans Jun 45 obit Jan 57

Edgerton, Harold E. Nov 66 obit Mar 90

Edinburgh, Philip, 3d Duke of see Mountbatten, Philip

Edison, Charles Jul 40 obit Oct 69

Edman, Irwin Jul 53 obit Oct 54

Edmonds, Walter Dumaux Sep 42

Edwards, Blake Jan 83

Edwards, Charles C. Oct 73

Edwards, Don Mar 83

Edwards, Douglas Aug 88 obit Jan 91

Edwards, Gus obit Dec 45

Edwards, India Sep 49 obit Mar 90

Edwards, James B. Nov 82

Edwards, Joan Oct 53 obit Oct 81

Edwards, John H. obit Yrbk 45

Edwards, Ralph L. Jul 43

Edwards, Teresa Mar 98

Edwards, Vincent Oct 62 obit May 96

Edwards, Waldo B. Jun 43 [Hingson, Robert A.; Edwards, Waldo B.; and Southworth, James L.]

Egan, William Allen Sep 59 obit Jul 84

Egbert, Sherwood H. Jun 63 obit Oct 69

Egeberg, Roger O. Jan 70 obit Nov 97

Eger, Ernst Oct 42

Eggers, Dave Jul 2000

Eggerth, Marta Nov 43

Eggleston, Edward Mason obit Mar 41

Eghbal, Manouchehr May 59 obit Feb 78

Eglevsky, Andre Feb 53 obit Feb 78

Egloff, Gustav Sep 40

Egorov, Boris (Borisovitch) see Yegorov, Boris

Egoyan, Atom May 94

Ehrenburg, Ilya Jun 66 obit Nov 67

Ehrenreich, Barbara Mar 95

Ehricke, Krafft A. Jun 58 obit Feb 85

Ehrlich, Paul R. Sep 70

Ehrlichman, John D. Oct 79 obit Apr 99

Eichelberger, Clark M. Jan 47 obit Mar 80

Eichelberger, Robert L. Jan 43 obit Dec 61

Eicher, Edward C. May 41 obit Jan 45

Eichheim, Henry obit Oct 42

Eidmann, Frank Lewis obit Nov 41

Eilshemius, Louis Michel Apr 40 obit Feb 42

Einaudi, Luigi Jul 48 obit Jan 62

Einem, Gottfried Von Jul 53 obit Sep 96

Einstein, Albert Nov 41 May 53 obit Jun 55

Eiseley, Loren Jun 60 obit Sep 77

Eisen, Gustav obit Yrbk 40

Eisendrath, Maurice N. May 50 obit Jan 74

Eisenhower, Dwight D. Aug 42 Feb 48 Sep 57 obit May 69

Eisenhower, John S. D. Jul 69

Eisenhower, Mamie May 53 obit Jan 80

Eisenhower, Milton S. Dec 46 obit Jul 85

Eisenhower, Mrs. Dwight D. see Eisenhower, Mamie

Eisenman, Peter Oct 97

Eisenschiml, Otto Oct 63 obit Jan 64

Eisenstaedt, Alfred Jan 75 obit Oct 95

Eisenstein, Sergei May 46 obit Mar 48

Eisler, Hanns May 42 obit Nov 62

Eisner, Michael D. Nov 87

Eisner, Thomas Mar 93

Eisner, Will Oct 94

Eklund, John M. Dec 49 obit Mar 97

Eklund, Sigvard Jul 62

Ekman, Carl Gustaf obit Jul 45

Elath, Eliahu see Epstein, Eliahu

El-Bitar, Salah see Bitar, Salah Eddin

El Cordobés Jan 66

Elder, Albert L. Sep 60

Elder, Lee Aug 76

Elders, Joycelyn Mar 94

Eldridge, Edward H. obit Jun 41

Eldridge, Florence Mar 43 [March, Fredric; and Eldridge, Florence] obit Sep 88

Eldridge, Roy Mar 87 obit Apr 89

El-Glaoui, Thami El-Mezouari, Pasha of Marrakech Sep 54 obit Mar 56

Eliade, Mircea Nov 85 obit Jun 86

Elias, Leona Baumgartner see Baumgartner, Leona

Elias, Rosalind Jan 67

Elion, Gertrude B. Mar 95 obit May 99

Eliot, George Fielding Jan-Feb 40 obit Jun 71

Eliot, Martha May Oct 48 obit Apr 78

Eliot, T. S. Oct 62 obit Feb 65

Eliot, Thomas H. May 42 obit Jan 92

Elisofon, Eliot Jan 72 obit May 73

Elizabeth, Princess of Great Britain see Elizabeth II, Queen of Great Britain

Elizabeth, Queen Mother of Great Britain Aug 81

Elizabeth II, Queen of Great Britain Jun 44 Jun 55

Elizalde, Joaquin M. Feb 48 obit Mar 65

Elizondo, Hector Jan 92

El-Khoury, Bechara see Khoury, Bechara El-

Elkin, Stanley Jul 87 obit Aug 95

Ellender, Allen J. Jul 46 obit Oct 72

Ellerbee, Linda Oct 86

Ellerman, Ferdinand obit Apr 40

Ellingson, Mark Sep 57 obit Apr 93

Ellington, Buford Sep 60 obit May 72

Ellington, Duke Mar 41 Jan 70 obit Jul 74

Elliot, Kathleen Morrow Mar 40

Elliott, Bob Oct 57 [Elliott, Bob; and Goulding, Ray]

Elliott, Harriet Wiseman Jul 40 obit Sep 47

Elliott, Herbert Jul 60

Elliott, John Lovejoy obit Jun 42

Elliott, Maxine Mar 40

Elliott, Osborn Jan 78

Elliott, William Thompson obit Aug 40

Ellis, Albert Jul 94
Ellis, Bret Easton Nov 94
Ellis, Carleton obit Mar 41
Ellis, Elmer Jul 62
Ellis, John Tracy Mar 90 obit Jan 93
Ellis, Perry Jan 86 obit Jan 86
Ellis, Ruth Sep 2000
Ellison, Lawrence J. Jan 98
Ellison, Ralph Oct 68 Jun 93 obit Jun 94
Elliston, Herbert Jun 49 obit Mar 57
Ellroy, James Apr 98
Ellroy, Lee Earle see Ellroy, James
Ellsberg, Daniel Dec 73
Ellsberg, Edward Nov 42 obit Yrbk 91 (died Jan 83)
El Mallakh, Kamal Oct 54 obit Jan 88
Elman, Mischa Oct 45 obit Jun 67
El-Solh, Sami see Solh, Sami
Elson, Arthur Mar 40
Elson, Edward L. R. Nov 67 obit Nov 93
Eltinge, Julian obit Apr 41
Elvehjem, C. A. May 48 obit Oct 62
Elway, John Nov 90
Ely, Paul Oct 54 obit Mar 75
Ely, Richard Theodore obit Nov 43
El-Yafi, Abdullah see Yafi, Abdullah El-
Elytis, Odysseus Sep 80 obit Jun 96
Elzy, Ruby obit Aug 43
Emanuel, Rahm Apr 98
Emanuel, Victor May 51 obit Jan 61
Embree, Edwin R. Dec 48 obit Mar 50
Emeny, Brooks Nov 47
Emerson, Faye Sep 51 obit May 83
Emerson, Lee E. Oct 53
Emerson, Roy Jun 65
Emerson, Victor Lee obit Jul 41
Emery, Ann (WLB) Yrbk 52
Emery, Dewitt Oct 46 obit Oct 55
Emmerich, Roland Nov 2000
Emmerson, Louis Lincoln obit Mar 41
Emmet, Evelyn Mar 53

Emmet, Mrs. Thomas Addis see Emmet, Evelyn
Emmet, William L. obit Nov 41
Emmons, Delos C. Mar 42 obit Dec 65
Emmons, Glenn L. Oct 54
Empie, Paul C. Oct 58
Emrich, Duncan Mar 55
Enckell, Carl J. A. Apr 50 obit Jun 59
Endara, Guillermo Feb 91
Endeley, E. M. L. Jul 59
Enders, John F. Jun 55 [Enders, John F.; Robbins, Frederick C.; and Weller, Thomas H.] obit Jan 86
Engel, Carl obit Jun 44
Engel, Kurt obit Mar 42
Engelbreit, Mary Oct 99
Engle, Clair Mar 57 obit Oct 64
Engle, Paul Jun 42 obit May 91
Englebright, Harry L. obit Jul 43
Engleman, James Ozro obit Nov 43
English, Diane Jun 93
English, Mrs. William D. see Kelly, Judith
Englund, Robert Mar 90
Engstrom, E. W. Dec 51 obit Feb 85
En-lai, Chou see Chou En-Lai
Enright, Elizabeth (WLB) Yrbk 47 obit Sep 68
Enrique Tarancón, Vicente Oct 72 obit Feb 95
Ensor, James, Baron obit Feb 43
Enters, Angna Jan-Feb 40 Jun 52 obit Apr 89
Entezam, Nasrollah Dec 50
Entremont, Philippe Mar 77
Ephron, Nora Jan 90
Epstein, Abraham obit Jun 42
Epstein, Eliahu Dec 48 obit Aug 90
Epstein, Jacob Jul 45 obit Nov 59
Epstein, Jason Aug 90
Epstein, Joseph Mar 90
Ercoli, Ercole see Togliatti, Palmiro
Erdman, Jean Sep 71
Erdrich, Louise Apr 89
Erhard, Ludwig Jan 50 Jun 64 obit Jul 77

Erhard, Werner Apr 77
Erickson, John Edward obit Jun 46
Erikson, Erik H. see Erikson, Erik H. May 71 obit Jul 94
Erikson, Leonard F. Oct 53
Erkin, Feridun C. Jan 52
Erlander, Tage Oct 47 obit Aug 85
Erlanger, Mitchell Louis obit Oct 40
Ernst, Jimmy Mar 66 obit Apr 84
Ernst, Max Dec 42 Oct 61 obit May 76
Ernst, Morris L. Aug 40 Feb 61 obit Jul 76
Ershad, Hussain Mohammad Nov 84
Erskine, G. B. Jul 46 obit Jul 73
Erskine, George Jan 52 obit Nov 65
Ertegun, Mehmet Munir obit Jan 45
Erté Nov 80 obit Jun 90
Ervin, Sam J., Jr. Jan 55 Oct 73 obit Jun 85
Erving, Julius May 75
Esch, John J. obit Jun 41
Eschenbach, Christoph Aug 89
Escobar, Marisol see Marisol
Eshelman, W. W. May 60
Eshkol, Levi Oct 63 obit Apr 69
Esiason, Boomer Nov 95
Esiason, Norman Julius see Esiason, Boomer
Esposito, Phil May 73
Espy, A. Michael "Mike" Oct 93
Estefan, Gloria Oct 95
Estenssoro, Victor Paz see Paz Estenssoro, Victor
Estes, Eleanor (WLB) Yrbk 46 obit Sep 88
Estes, Elliott M. Jan 79 obit May 88
Estes, Harlow Mar 41
Estes, Mrs. Rice see Estes, Eleanor
Estes, Richard Nov 95
Estes, Simon Aug 86
Esteven, John see Shellabarger, Samuel
Estevez, Ramon see Sheen, Martin

Estigarribia, Jose Felix Mar 40 obit Mar 40

Estrada, Joseph Feb 2000

Eszterhas, Joe Apr 98

Etheridge, Melissa May 95

Etherington, Edwin D. Apr 66

Ethridge, Mark Jan 46 obit Jun 81

Ettinger, Richard P. Dec 51 obit Apr 71

Ettinghausen, Walter *see* Eytan, Walter

Ettl, John obit Feb 41

Etzel, Franz Sep 57 [Armand, Louis; Etzel, Franz; and Giordani, Francesco]

Etzioni, Amitai Mar 80

Eurich, Alvin C. Jun 49 obit Aug 87

Eustis, Helen (WLB) Yrbk 55

Evans, Alice Catherine Oct 43 obit Oct 75

Evans, Anne obit Feb 41

Evans, Arthur obit Sep 41

Evans, Bergen (WLB) Yrbk 55 obit Apr 78

Evans, Dale *see* Rogers, Dale Evans

Evans, Daniel Aug 75

Evans, Edith Jun 56 obit Jan 77

Evans, Edward R. G. R. May 41 obit Nov 57 [Mountevans, Edward R. G. R. Evans, 1st Baron]

Evans, Faith Feb 99

Evans, Harold Apr 85

Evans, Herbert M. Jul 59 obit Apr 71

Evans, Hugh Ivan Nov 50 obit Jul 58

Evans, Janet Jul 96

Evans, Linda Mar 86

Evans, Luther H. Aug 45 obit Feb 82

Evans, Maurice May 40 Jun 61 obit May 89

Evans, Nancy Mar 2000

Evans, Poncé Cruse *see* Heloise

Evans, Walker Sep 71 obit Jun 75

Evarts, Esther *see* Benson, Sally

Evatt, Harriet (WLB) Yrbk 59

Evatt, Herbert V. May 42 obit Jan 66

Evatt, Mrs. William S. *see* Evatt, Harriet

Evergood, Philip Oct 44 Oct 60 obit Apr 73

Evers, James Charles Apr 69

Evers-Williams, Myrlie Aug 95

Evert, Chris Apr 73

Eves, Reginald Grenville Sep 40 obit Aug 41

Evren, Kenan Apr 84

Ewbank, Weeb Jun 69 obit Feb 99

Ewell, Tom May 61 obit Nov 94

Ewing, James obit Jul 43

Ewing, Maria Apr 90

Ewing, Maurice Jan 53 obit Jun 74

Ewing, Oscar R. Jul 48 obit Mar 80

Ewing, Patrick May 91

Exeter, David George Brownlow Cecil, 6th Marquis of *see* Burghley, David George Brownlow Cecil, Lord

Exley, Frederick Oct 89 obit Aug 92

Exner, Max J. obit Nov 43

Exon, James Nov 96

Eyde, Samuel obit Aug 40

Eyler, John Aug 2000

Eyre, Katherine Wigmore (WLB) Yrbk 49 (WLB) Yrbk 57

Eyre, Mrs. Dean Atherton *see* Eyre, Katherine Wigmore

Eyring, Henry Oct 61

Eysenck, Hans J. Nov 72 obit Nov 97

Eyskens, Gaston Nov 49 obit Feb 88

Eytan, Walter Oct 58

Eyüboglu, Bedri Rahmi Sep 54

F. P. A. *see* Adams, Franklin P.

Fabares, Nanette *see* Fabray, Nanette

Fabian, Robert Apr 54 obit Aug 78

Fabius, Laurent Feb 85

Fabray, Nanette Jan 56

Fackenthal, Frank D. Feb 49 obit Nov 68

Fadiman, Clifton May 41 Oct 55 obit Sep 99

Fagan, Garth Aug 98

Fagerholm, Karl August Oct 48 obit Jul 84

Fagg, Fred D., Jr. Feb 56 obit Jan 82

Fagnani, Charles P. obit Mar 41

Fahd, Crown Prince of Saudi Arabia May 79

Fahd, King of Saudi Arabia *see* Fahd, Crown Prince of Saudi Arabia

Fahy, Charles Jan 42 obit Nov 79

Fair, A. A. *see* Gardner, Erle Stanley

Fairbank, John King Oct 66 obit Nov 91

Fairbanks, Douglas Jan 40

Fairbanks, Douglas Jr. Nov 41 Feb 56 obit Aug 2000 obit Aug 20000

Fairchild, Benjamin Lewis obit Dec 46

Fairchild, David Jul 53 obit Oct 54

Fairchild, Henry Pratt Dec 42 obit Dec 56 Yrbk 57

Fairchild, John B. Jun 71

Fairclough, Ellen Oct 57

Fairclough, Mrs. Gordon *see* Fairclough, Ellen

Fairfax, Beatrice Aug 44 obit Jan 46

Fairfield, Cecily Isabel *see* West, Rebecca

Fairless, Benjamin F. Jun 42 May 57 obit Feb 62

Faisal, King of Saudi Arabia May 66 obit May 75

Faisal II, King of Iraq *see* Feisal II, King of Iraq

Faisal Ibn Abdul-Aziz Al Saud, Prince Jan 48

Faldo, Nick Sep 92

Falk, Maurice obit Apr 46

Falk, Peter Jul 72

Falkner, Roland Post obit Jan 41

Fall, Albert B. obit Jan 45

Falla, Manuel de obit Dec 46

Fallaci, Oriana Feb 77

Fälldin, Thorbjörn May 78

Fallows, James Nov 96

Faludi, Susan Feb 93

Falwell, Jerry Jan 81

Fanfani, Amintore Oct 58 obit Mar 2000

Fang Lizhi Nov 89

Fanning, Shawn Sep 2000
Farah Diba Pahlevi Mar 76
Farber, Sidney Sep 67 obit
  May 73
Faricy, William T. Jun 48
Farish, William S. obit Jan 43
Farley, James A. Sep 44 obit
  Aug 76
Farley, Walter (WLB) Yrbk 49
  obit Feb 90
Farmer, Guy Feb 55
Farmer, James Feb 64 obit
  Sep 99
Farnsworth, Arthur obit Oct
  43
Farnsworth, Jerry Oct 54
Farnsworth, Mrs. Jerry see
  Sawyer, Helen
Farny, George W. obit Oct 41
Farouk Oct 42 obit May 65
Farrakhan, Louis Apr 92
Farrar, John Jun 54 obit Jan
  75
Farrar, Margaret Jul 55 obit
  Aug 84
Farrell, Eileen Feb 61
Farrell, James T. Sep 42 obit
  Oct 79
Farrell, Suzanne Sep 67
Farrington, Joseph R. May 48
  obit Sep 54
Farrington, Mary Elizabeth
  Pruett Jun 55 obit Sep 84
Farrington, Mrs. Joseph R see
  Farrington, Mary Elizabeth
  Pruett
Farrow, Mia Apr 70
Fasanella, Ralph Jun 75 obit
  Mar 98
Fascell, Dante B. Apr 60 obit
  Feb 99
Fassbaender, Brigitte Jun 94
Fassbinder, Rainer Werner
  May 77 obit Aug 82
Fassett, Kaffe Jun 95
Fast, Howard Apr 43 Apr 91
Fatemi, Hossein May 53 obit
  Jan 55
Fath, Jacques Apr 51 obit Jan
  55
Fatone, Joey see 'N Sync
Faubus, Orval E. Oct 56 obit
  Feb 95
Fauci, Anthony S. Aug 88
Fauley, Wilbur F. obit Feb 43
Faulkner, Brian Feb 72 obit
  May 77
Faulkner, Nancy (WLB) Yrbk
  56

Faulkner, William Jan 51 obit
  Sep 62
Fauntroy, Walter E. Feb 79
Faure, Edgar Feb 52 obit May
  88
Faurot, Joseph A. obit Jan 43
Faust, Clarence H. Mar 52
  obit Aug 75
Faust, Frederick obit Jul 44
Faversham, William obit
  May 40
Favre, Brett Nov 96
Fawcett, Edward obit Nov 42
Fawcett, Farrah see Fawcett-
  Majors, Farrah
Fawcett, Sherwood L. Dec 72
Fawcett-Majors, Farrah Feb
  78
Fawley, Wilbur see Fauley,
  Wilbur F.
Fawzi, Mahmoud Dec 51
Fay, Frank Aug 45 obit Dec
  61
Feather, Vic Mar 73 obit Sep
  76
Fechteler, William M. Sep 51
  obit Oct 67
Fedorenko, Nikolai T. Dec 67
Fedorova, Nina Nov 40
Feifel, Herman Aug 94
Feiffer, Jules Oct 61
Feikema, Feike (WLB) Yrbk
  50
Feingold, Russell D. Jul 98
Feininger, Andreas Oct 57
  obit May 99
Feininger, Lyonel Jul 55 obit
  Mar 56
Feinsinger, Nathan P. May 52
  obit Jan 84
Feinstein, Dianne Jun 79 Aug
  95
Feinstein, Isidor see Stone, I.
  F.
Feinstein, John Jul 98
Feinstein, Michael Apr 88
Feis, Herbert Oct 61 obit May
  72
Feisal II, King of Iraq Jul 55
  obit Oct 58
Feld, Eliot Oct 71
Feld, Irvin Feb 79 obit Nov
  84
Feldmann, Markus Jun 56
  obit Jan 59
Feldstein, Martin May 83
Feldt, Gloria Jul 2000
Feliciano, José Jul 69

Felix, Robert H. Apr 57 obit
  May 90
Felker, Clay S. Feb 75
Feller, Abraham H. Nov 46
  obit Jan 53
Feller, Bob Aug 41
Fellini, Federico Jun 57 Oct
  80 obit Jan 94
Fellows, George Emory obit
  Mar 42
Fellows, Harold E. Feb 52
  obit May 60
Fels, William C. Apr 59 obit
  Jan 65
Felt, Harry D. Mar 59
Feltin, Maurice Cardinal May
  54 obit Nov 75
Felton, Ralph A. Sep 57
Feltsman, Vladimir Apr 88
Fenimore-Cooper, Susan De
  Lancey obit Mar 40
Fenwick, Millicent Apr 77
  obit Nov 92
Feoktistov, Konstantin Nov
  67
Ferber, Herbert Nov 60 obit
  Oct 91
Ferguson, Elsie Feb 44 obit
  Jan 62
Ferguson, Garland S. Jul 49
  obit Jun 63
Ferguson, Harriet Jan 47 obit
  Feb 66
Ferguson, Harry Mar 56 obit
  Jan 61
Ferguson, Homer May 43 obit
  Mar 83
Ferguson, Howard obit Apr
  46
Ferguson, James Edward obit
  Nov 44
Ferguson, Malcolm P. May 57
Ferguson, Maynard Feb 80
Fergusson, Erna (WLB) Yrbk
  55
Ferlinghetti, Lawrence Jun
  91
Fermi, Enrico Oct 45 obit Jan
  55
Fermi, Laura May 58
Fermi, Mrs. Enrico see Fermi,
  Laura
Fermor, Patrick Leigh (WLB)
  Yrbk 55
Fernandel Oct 55 obit Apr 71
Fernandes, L. Esteves Oct 50
Fernandez Concheso, Aure-
  lio see Concheso, Aurelio
  Fernández

Fisketjon, Gary cb

Fister, George M. Jun 63 obit Jul 76

Fitch, Aubrey Oct 45 obit Jul 78

Fitch, Robert Elliot Apr 62

Fittipaldi, Emerson Apr 92

Fitzgerald, Albert J. Oct 48 obit Jul 82

Fitzgerald, Barry Feb 45 obit Feb 61

Fitzgerald, Cissy obit Jul 41

Fitzgerald, Ed Apr 47 [Fitzgerald, Ed; and Fitzgerald, Pegeen] obit Jun 82

Fitzgerald, Ella Oct 56 Jul 90 obit Aug 96

Fitzgerald, F. Scott obit Feb 41

Fitzgerald, Frances Jun 87

Fitzgerald, Garret Aug 84

Fitzgerald, Geraldine Oct 76

Fitz Gerald, Leslie M. Sep 54

Fitzgerald, Pegeen Apr 47 [Fitzgerald, Ed; and Fitzgerald, Pegeen] obit Apr 89

Fitzgerald, Robert Sep 76 obit Mar 85

Fitzgibbons, John obit Oct 41

Fitzmaurice, George obit Aug 40

Fitzpatrick, D. R. Jul 41 obit Jul 69

Fitzpatrick, George L. obit Jun 41

Fitzroy, Edward Algernon obit Apr 43

Fitzsimmons, Frank E. May 71 obit Jul 81

Fitzwater, Marlin May 88

Fivoosiovitch, Edith Gregor see Halpert, Edith Gregor

Flack, Roberta Nov 73

Flagg, James Montgomery Nov 40 obit Sep 60

Flagstad, Kirsten May 47 obit Jan 63

Flaherty, Robert Mar 49 obit Sep 51

Flair, Ric Mar 2000

Flanagan, Edward Joseph Sep 41 obit Jun 48

Flanagan, Tommy Apr 95

Flanders, Michael Jan 70 obit Jun 75

Flanders, Ralph E. Jan 48 obit Apr 70

Flandin, Pierre-étienne Jan 41 obit Oct 58

Flannagan, John B. obit Mar 42

Flanner, Janet May 43 obit Jan 79

Flannery, Harry W. Oct 43

Flansburgh, John see They Might Be Giants

Flavin, Martin Dec 43 obit Feb 68

Fleck, Alexander Fleck, 1st Baron Apr 56 obit Oct 68

Fleck, Béla Nov 96

Fleck, Jack Sep 55

Fleeson, Doris May 59 obit Oct 70

Fleischman, Ruth Geri see Hagy, Ruth Geri

Fleischmann, Manly Jul 51

Fleisher, Leon Jan 71

Fleming, Alexander Apr 44 [Fleming, Alexander; and Florey, Howard W.] obit May 55

Fleming, Amalia Nov 72 obit Apr 86

Fleming, Ambrose obit May 45

Fleming, Arthur Henry obit Sep 40

Fleming, Berry (WLB) Yrbk 53 obit Nov 89

Fleming, Donald M. Feb 59 obit Mar 87

Fleming, Ian Jan 64

Fleming, John A. May 40 obit Oct 56

Fleming, Peggy Jul 68

Fleming, Philip Bracken Apr 40 obit Dec 55 Yrbk 56

Fleming, Renée May 97

Fleming, Robben W. Dec 70

Fleming, Sam M. Jun 62

Flemming, Arthur S. Jun 51 Apr 60 obit Nov 96

Flesch, Carl obit Jan 45

Flesch, Rudolf Apr 48 obit Nov 86

Fletcher, Angus Sep 46 obit Nov 60

Fletcher, Arthur A. Nov 71

Fletcher, C. Scott Feb 53

Fletcher, Inglis (WLB) Yrbk 47 obit Jul 69

Fletcher, James May 72 obit Feb 92

Fletcher, Mrs. John George see Fletcher, Inglis

Flexner, Abraham Jun 41 obit Nov 59

Flexner, Bernard obit Jun 45

Flexner, Jennie M. obit Jan 45

Flexner, Simon obit Jun 46

Flickinger, Roy C. obit Aug 42

Flikke, Julia O. Jul 42

Flinders Petrie, William Matthew see Petrie, William Matthew Flinders

Flood, Daniel J. Aug 78 obit Aug 94

Flore, Edward F. obit Oct 45

Florence, Fred F. Jun 56 obit Feb 61

Florey, Howard Apr 44 [Fleming, Alexander; and Florey, Howard W.] obit Apr 68

Florinsky, Michael T. Oct 41 obit Jan 82

Florio, James J. May 90

Flory, Paul J. Mar 75 obit Nov 85

Floyd, Carlisle Jul 60

Floyd, William obit Jan 44

Flutie, Doug Oct 85

Fly, James Lawrence Sep 40 obit Feb 66

Flying Officer X see Bates, H. E.

Flynn, Edward J. Sep 40 obit Oct 53

Flynn, Elizabeth Gurley Oct 61 obit Nov 64

Flynn, Keri see Burstyn, Ellen

Flynn, Raymond Oct 93

Flynt, Larry Sep 99

Fo, Dario Nov 86

Fodor, Eugene Apr 76

Foerster, Friedrich Wilhelm Jul 62 obit Feb 66

Fogarty, Anne Oct 58 obit Mar 80

Fogarty, John E. Apr 64 obit Mar 67

Fokine, Michel obit Oct 42

Foley, Martha Apr 41 [Foley, Martha; and Burnett, Whit] obit Oct 77

Foley, Raymond M. Oct 49 obit Apr 75

Foley, Thomas S. Sep 89

Folger, A. D. obit Jun 41

Folkers, Karl Oct 62

Folkman, Judah May 98

Folks, Homer Yrbk 40

Follett, Ken Jan 90

Folliard, Edward T. Nov 47 obit Feb 77

Folon, Jean-Michel Feb 81

Folsom, Frank M. Feb 49 obit Mar 70

Folsom, James Elisha Sep 49 obit Jan 88

Folsom, Marion B. Jan 50 obit Nov 76

Fonda, Bridget Jan 94

Fonda, Henry Dec 48 Nov 74 obit Sep 82

Fonda, Jane Jul 64 Jun 86

Fonda, Peter Mar 98

Fong, Hiram L. Feb 60

Fontaine, Joan May 44 [Fontaine, Joan; and de Havilland, Olivia]

Fontana, Tom Aug 2000

Fontanne, Lynn Jun 41 [Lunt, Alfred; and Fontanne, Lynn] obit Sep 83

Fonteyn, Margot Dec 49 Mar 72 obit Apr 91

Foot, Hugh Oct 53 obit Nov 90

Foot, Michael Dec 50 May 81

Foote, H. W. obit Mar 42

Foote, Horton Aug 86

Foote, Shelby Apr 91

Forand, Aime J. Jun 60 obit Mar 72

Forbes, B. C. Mar 50 obit Jul 54

Forbes, Guillaume, Archbishop obit Jul 40

Forbes, John J. Apr 52

Forbes, Kathryn Dec 44 obit Jun 66

Forbes, Malcolm S. Feb 75 obit Apr 90

Forbes, Steve May 96

Force, Juliana Mar 41 obit Oct 48

Ford, Benson Feb 52 obit Sep 78

Ford, Betty see Ford, Elizabeth

Ford, Blanche Chapman see Chapman, Blanche

Ford, Edsel obit Jul 43

Ford, Edward Charles see Ford, Whitey

Ford, Eileen Oct 71

Ford, Elizabeth Sep 75

Ford, Frederick W. Nov 60 obit Sep 86

Ford, Gerald R. Mar 61 Nov 75

Ford, Glenn Jun 59

Ford, Harold E. Jr. Nov 99

Ford, Harrison Sep 84

Ford, Henry Dec 44 obit May 47

Ford, Henry, II Apr 46 Jun 78 obit Nov 87

Ford, John Feb 41 obit Nov 73

Ford, Richard Sep 95

Ford, Tennessee Ernie Mar 58 obit Jan 92

Ford, Tom May 98

Ford, W. W. obit Aug 41

Ford, Whitey Apr 62

Ford, Worthington C. obit Apr 41

Foreman, Clark Oct 48 obit Aug 77

Foreman, George May 74 Aug 95

Foreman, Richard Jul 88

Forest, Lee de see De Forest, Lee

Forman, Milos Dec 71

Fornos, Werner H. Jul 93

Forrest, Allan obit Sep 41

Forrest, Wilbur S. May 48 obit May 77

Forrestal, James V. Feb 42 Jan 48 obit Jul 49

Forrester, Maureen Jul 62

Forssmann, Werner Mar 57 obit Aug 79

Forster, E. M. Apr 64 obit Sep 70

Forster, Rudolph obit Aug 43

Forsyth, Bill Jan 89

Forsyth, Cecil obit Feb 42

Forsyth, Frederick May 86

Forsyth, W. D. Apr 52

Forsythe, John May 73

Forsythe, Robert S. obit Aug 41

Fortas, Abe Feb 66 obit May 82

Fosdick, Harry Emerson Oct 40 obit Nov 69

Fosdick, Raymond B. Feb 45 obit Sep 72

Foss, Joe see Foss, Joseph Jacob

Foss, Joseph Jacob Oct 55

Foss, Lukas Jun 66

Fosse, Bob Jun 72 obit Nov 87

Fossey, Dian May 85 obit Feb 86

Foster, Harry Hylton- see Hylton-Foster, Harry

Foster, Jodie Jun 81 Aug 92

Foster, John see Furcolo, Foster

Foster, John S., Jr. Dec 71

Foster, Maximilian obit Nov 43

Foster, Norman Sep 2000

Foster, Richard C. obit Jan 42

Foster, William C. Nov 50

Foster, William Zebulon Jul 45 obit Nov 61

Fougner, G. Selmer obit May 41

Fouilhoux, J. Andre obit Jul 45

Fournet, Louis Rene Marie Charles Dartige du see Du Fournet, Louis Rene Marie Charles Dartige

Fowler, Alfred obit Aug 40

Fowler, Gene Mar 44 obit Sep 60

Fowler, Henry H. Sep 52 obit May 2000

Fowler, Mark S. Mar 86

Fowler, R. M. Oct 54

Fowler, William A. Sep 74 obit May 95

Fowler-Billings, Katharine Jan 40

Fowles, John Mar 77

Fox, Carol Jul 78 obit Sep 81

Fox, Genevieve (WLB) Yrbk 49 obit Dec 59

Fox, Jacob Nelson see Fox, Nellie

Fox, Jay see Carewe, Edwin

Fox, John McDill obit May 40

Fox, Michael Feb 77

Fox, Michael J. Nov 87

Fox, Nellie Mar 60 obit Feb 76

Fox, Robert J. May 70 obit Jun 84

Fox, Sidney obit Jan 43

Fox, Virgil Jan 64 obit Jan 81

Foxx, Redd Dec 72 obit Jan 92

Foyle, Gilbert Jun 54 [Foyle, Gilbert; and Foyle William Alfred] obit Jan 72

Foyle, William Alfred Jun 54 [Foyle, Gilbert; and Foyle William Alfred] obit Jul 63

Foyt, A. J. Nov 67

Fracci, Carla Feb 75

Fraga Iribarne, Manuel May 65

Frager, Malcolm Apr 67 obit Aug 91

Frahm, Herbert *see* Brandt, Willy

Frakes, Jonathan Jul 99

Frampton, Peter May 78

Franca, Celia May 56

France, Pierre Mendès- *see* Mendès-France, Pierre

Francescatti, Zino Oct 47 obit Nov 91

Franciosa, Anthony Jul 61

Francis, Arlene May 56

Francis, Clarence Feb 48 obit Mar 86

Francis, Connie Jul 62

Francis, Dick Aug 81

Francis, Emile Apr 68

Francis, Frank Jul 59 obit Apr 89

Francis, Sam Oct 73 obit Jan 95

Francis-Williams Mar 46 obit Sep 70

Franck, James May 57 obit Jul 64

Franco, Afranio de Mello *see* Mello Franco, Afranio De

Franco, Francisco Mar 42 Mar 54 obit Jan 76

Francois-Poncet, Andre Oct 49 obit Mar 78

Frank, Anthony M. Aug 91

Frank, Barney Apr 95

Frank, Glenn obit Nov 40

Frank, Hans Mar 41 obit Nov 46

Frank, Jerome N. Apr 41 obit Mar 57

Frank, Lawrence K. Jan 58 [Frank, Lawrence K; and Frank, Mary] obit Nov 68

Frank, Louis obit May 41

Frank, Mary Jan 58 [Frank, Lawrence K.; and Frank, Mary]

Frank, Reuven Jun 73

Frank, Robert Aug 97

Frank, Waldo David Nov 40 obit Mar 67

Franke, William B. Sep 59 obit Aug 79

Frankel, Bernice *see* Arthur, Beatrice

Frankel, Charles Apr 66 obit Jul 79

Frankel, Felice Apr 98

Frankel, Max Apr 87

Franken, Al Jun 99

Franken, Rose Yrbk 41 (WLB) Yrbk 47 obit Aug 88

Frankenberg, Mrs. Lloyd *see* Maciver, Loren

Frankenheimer, John Oct 64

Frankensteen, Richard T. Dec 45

Frankenthaler, Helen Apr 66

Frankfurter, Felix Jun 41 Jul 57 obit Apr 65

Frankl, Viktor E. Jul 97 obit Nov 97

Franklin, Aretha Dec 68 May 92

Franklin, Frederic Sep 43

Franklin, Irene obit Aug 41

Franklin, Jay Oct 41 obit Jan 68

Franklin, John Hope Oct 63

Franklin, John M. Sep 49 obit Aug 75

Franklin, Kirk Mar 2000

Franklin, Walter S. Feb 50 obit Oct 72

Franks, Oliver Shewell Mar 48 obit Jan 93

Franz, Dennis Jul 95

Fraser, Antonia Oct 74

Fraser, Brad Jul 95

Fraser, Bruce Jul 43 obit Apr 81

Fraser, Douglas Andrew Oct 77

Fraser, Hugh Russell Jun 43

Fraser, Ian Dec 47

Fraser, Ian Forbes Jun 54

Fraser, James Earle Jul 51 obit Jan 54

Fraser, Leon obit May 45

Fraser, Malcolm Mar 76

Fraser, Peter May 42 obit Jan 51

Fraser, Robert Oct 56

Fraser of North Cape, Bruce Austin Fraser, 1st Baron *see* Fraser, Bruce

Fratellini, Paul obit Yrbk 40

Frayn, Michael Jan 85

Frazer, James obit Jul 41

Frazer, Joseph W. Mar 46 obit Sep 71

Frazer, Spaulding obit Apr 40

Frazier, Edward Franklin Jul 40

Frazier, Ian Aug 96

Frazier, Joe Apr 71

Frazier, Walt Feb 73

Frear, J. Allen, Jr. Oct 54

Frears, Stephen Apr 90

Fred, E. B. Dec 50

Fredenthal, David Sep 42 obit Jan 59

Frederick, John T. Jun 41

Frederick, Pauline Oct 54 obit Jul 90

Frederik IX, King of Denmark Nov 47 obit Mar 72

Frederika, Consort of Paul I, King of The Hellenes Jan 55 obit Apr 81

Fredman, Samuel, Rabbi obit Jun 41

Freed, James Ingo. Nov 94

Freedlander, Arthur R. obit Aug 40

Freedley, George Sep 47 obit Nov 67

Freedman, Benedict Sep 47 [Freedman, Benedict; and Freedman, Nancy]

Freedman, Nancy Sep 47 [Freedman, Benedict; and Freedman, Nancy]

Freeh, Louis J. May 96

Freehafer, Edward G. Jun 55 obit Feb 86

Freeman, James Edward, Bishop obit Jul 43

Freeman, John Jun 69

Freeman, Lucy Oct 53

Freeman, Morgan Feb 91

Freeman, Orville L. Jun 56

Freeman, R. Austin obit Nov 43

Freeman-Thomas, Freeman, 1st Marquess of Willingdon *see* Willingdon, Freeman Freeman-Thomas, 1st Marquess of

Frehley, Ace *see* Kiss

Frehley, Paul *see* Frehley, Ace

Frei, Eduardo Apr 65 obit Mar 82

Freilicher, Jane Nov 89

Freitag, Walter Jan 54 obit Oct 58

Fremantle, Francis Edward obit Oct 43

French, Hollis obit Jan 41

French, Marilyn Sep 92

French, Paul *see* Asimov, Isaac

French, Paul Comly May 51 obit Sep 60

French, Robert W. Oct 59

Freni, Mirella Apr 77
Fresnay, Pierre Feb 59 obit Feb 75
Freud, Anna Apr 79 obit Mar 83
Freud, Lucian Jul 88
Freund, Philip (WLB) Yrbk 48
Freundlich, Herbert obit May 41
Freyberg, Bernard Cyril, 1st Baron Freyberg Oct 40 obit Sep 63
Frick, Ford May 45 obit Jun 78
Frick, Wilhelm Aug 42 obit Nov 46
Friday, William Apr 58
Friedan, Betty Nov 70 Mar 89
Friedkin, William Jun 87
Friedman, Bruce Jay Jun 72
Friedman, Herbert Sep 63 obit Nov 2000
Friedman, Milton Oct 69
Friedman, Thomas L. Oct 95
Friel, Brian Jun 74
Friendly, Edwin S. Jul 49 obit Sep 70
Friendly, Fred W. Sep 57 Aug 87 obit May 98
Frings, Ketti Jan 60 obit Apr 81
Frisch, Karl Von Feb 74 obit Yrbk 83 (died Jun 82)
Frisch, Max Jan 65 obit Jun 91
Frische, Carl A. Oct 62
Frissell, Toni Jun 47 obit Jun 88
Froehlich, Jack E. Jul 59
Frohman, Daniel obit Feb 41
Frohnmayer, John E. Apr 90
Fromm, Erich Apr 67 obit May 80
Frondizi, Arturo Oct 58 obit Jun 95
Frost, David Jul 69
Frost, Frances Mary (WLB) Yrbk 50 obit Apr 59
Frost, Jack see Erhard, Werner
Frost, Leslie M. Oct 53 obit Jul 73
Frost, Robert Sep 42 obit Mar 63
Frothingham, Channing Mar 48 obit Nov 59
Frowick, Roy Halston see Halston

Fruehauf, Roy Feb 53 obit Jan 66
Fry, Christopher Feb 51
Fry, Franklin Clark Jun 46 obit Sep 68
Fry, Kenneth D. Apr 47
Fry, Stephen Sep 98
Frye, David Mar 75
Frye, Jack Apr 45 obit Apr 59
Frye, Northrop Aug 83 obit Mar 91
Fuchs, Joseph Oct 62 obit May 97
Fuchs, Michael J. Feb 96
Fuchs, Vivian E. Oct 58 obit Jan 2000
Fudge, Ann M. Jun 98
Fuentes, Carlos Oct 72
Fuentes, Miguel Ydígoras see Ydígoras Fuentes, Miguel
Fugard, Athol Jun 75
Fujimori, Alberto Nov 90
Fujiyama, Aiichiro Apr 58 obit May 85
Fukuda, Takeo Jun 74 obit Sep 95
Fulani, Lenora Mar 2000
Fulbright, J. William Nov 43 Oct 55 obit Apr 95
Fulghum, Robert Jul 94
Fuller, Alfred C. Oct 50 obit Jan 74
Fuller, Bonnie May 2000
Fuller, Charles E. Dec 51 obit May 68
Fuller, Charles Jun 89
Fuller, Clara Cornelia obit Yrbk 40
Fuller, George Washington obit Yrbk 40
Fuller, John L. Mar 59
Fuller, Kathryn S. Jan 94
Fuller, Margaret H. Jun 59
Fuller, Millard Apr 95
Fuller, Mrs. Raymond G. see Fox, Genevieve
Fuller, R. Buckminster Jan 60 Feb 76 obit Aug 83
Fuller, S. R., Jr. May 41 obit Mar 66
Fuller, Samuel Aug 92 obit Jan 98
Fuller, Walter Deane Mar 41 obit Jan 65
Fulmer, Hampton Pitts obit Dec 44
Fulton, E. D. Jan 59
Funk, Casimir May 45 obit Jan 68

Funk, Charles Earle Jun 47 obit Jul 57
Funk, Walther Oct 40 obit Sep 60
Funk, Wilfred Jan 55 obit Jul 65
Funston, Keith Jul 51 obit Jul 92
Funt, Allen Dec 66 obit Nov 99
Fuoss, Robert M. Feb 59 obit Mar 80
Fuqua, Stephen Ogden Feb 43
Furcolo, Foster Jan 58 obit Sep 95
Furey, Warren W. May 50 obit Jan 59
Furman, N. Howell Dec 51 obit Oct 65
Furnas, Clifford Cook Oct 56 obit Jun 69
Furness, Betty Feb 68 obit Jun 94
Furstenberg, Diane von see Von Fürstenberg, Diane
Furtseva, Ekaterina A. Jun 56 obit Dec 74
Futter, Ellen V. Oct 85
Fyan, Loleta D. Dec 51
Fyfe, H. Hamilton Yrbk 40 obit Jul 51

G, Kenny see Kenny G
Gabin, Jean Jun 41 obit Jan 77
Gable, Clark May 45 obit Jan 61
Gable, Dan Aug 97
Gabo, Naum Apr 72 obit Oct 77
Gabor, Dennis Oct 72 obit Apr 79
Gabor, Eva Jul 68 obit Sep 95
Gabor, Zsa Zsa Mar 88
Gabriel, Peter Jan 90
Gabriel, Roman Nov 75
Gabrielson, Guy Oct 49 obit Jun 76
Gaddafi, Moamar al- see Qaddafi, Muammar Al-
Gaddis, William Nov 87 obit Mar 99
Gades, Antonio Feb 73
Gaer, Joseph (WLB) Yrbk 51
Gaffney, T. St. John obit Mar 45
Gág, Wanda obit Jul 46
Gagarin, Yuri Oct 61 obit May 68

Gage, Nicholas Mar 90

Gahagan, Helen *see* Douglas, Helen Gahagan

Gaillard, Félix Feb 58 obit Oct 70

Gaines, Ernest J. Mar 94

Gainza Paz, Alberto Apr 51 obit Feb 78

Gaither, Frances (WLB) Yrbk 50 obit Jan 56

Gaither, H. Rowan, Jr. May 53 obit Jun 61

Gaitskell, Hugh Jun 50 obit Feb 63

Gajdusek, D. Carleton Jun 81

Galanos, James Sep 70

Galard Terraube, Geneviève De Oct 54

Galassi, Jonathan Sep 99

Galbraith, John Kenneth Mar 59 May 75

Galdikas, Biruté M. F. Mar 95

Gale, Henry Gordon obit Jan 43

Gale, Robert Jan 87

Galen, Clemens August Von obit Apr 46

Galindo, Carlos Blanco *see* Blanco Galindo, Carlos

Gallagher, Buell Gordon May 53 obit Jan 79

Gallagher, William J. obit Oct 46

Gallagher, William M. Oct 53 obit Nov 75

Gallant, Mavis May 90

Gallegos Freire, Rómulo May 48 obit May 69

Gallery, Daniel V. Apr 66 obit Mar 77

Galli, Rosina obit Jan 40

Galliano, John Oct 96

Gallico, Paul Apr 46 obit Sep 76

Gallo, Fortune Oct 49 obit May 70

Gallo, Robert C. Oct 86

Galloway, Irene O. May 53 obit Feb 63

Gallup, George Mar 40 Dec 52 obit Sep 84

Galtieri, Leopoldo Aug 82

Galvin, Robert W. Mar 60

Galway, James Jun 80

Gamble, Ralph A. Jan 53 obit May 59

Gambling, John B. Mar 50 obit Jan 75

Gambrell, E. Smythe Jun 56

Gamelin, Marie Gustave *see* Gamelin, Maurice Gustave

Gamelin, Maurice Gustave Jan-Jun 40 obit Jul 58

Gamow, George Oct 51 obit Oct 68

Gandhi, Indira Oct 59 Jun 66 obit Jan 85

Gandhi, Mohandas Dec 42 obit Feb 48

Gandhi, Rajiv Apr 85 obit Jul 91

Gandhi, Sonia May 98

Gandolfini, James Feb 2000

Ganfield, William Arthur obit Yrbk 40

Gannett, Frank Ernest Mar 45 obit Feb 58

Gannett, Lewis Aug 41 obit Mar 66

Gannon, Robert I., Rev. Mar 45 obit May 78

Ganso, Emil obit Jun 41

Gaposchkin, Cecilia Payne-*see* Payne-Gaposchkin, Cecilia

Garagiola, Joe Jan 76

Garand, John C. Aug 45 obit Apr 74

Garbett, Cyril Forster, Archbishop of York Feb 51 obit Mar 56

Garbo, Greta Apr 55 obit Jun 90

Garbus, Martin Nov 2000

Garcia, Carlos P. Jun 57 obit Jul 71

Garcia, Cristina Aug 99

Garcia, Jerry May 90 obit Oct 95

García Márquez, Gabriel Jul 73

Garciaparra, Nomar Jun 2000

García Pérez, Alan Nov 85

Gardiner, James Garfield Jun 56 obit Mar 62

Gardiner, Robert K. Jul 75

Gardner, Arthur Jan 56 obit Jun 67

Gardner, Ava Mar 65 obit Mar 90

Gardner, Ed Sep 43 obit Oct 63

Gardner, Erle Stanley Jun 44 obit Apr 70

Gardner, Howard Oct 98

Gardner, John Oct 78 obit Nov 82

Gardner, John W. Mar 56 Mar 76

Gardner, Lester D. Sep 47 obit Feb 57

Gardner, Martin Sep 99

Gardner, Matthias B. Jun 52

Gardner, O. Max Jan 47

Garfield, Harry A. obit Feb 43

Garfield, John Apr 48 obit Jul 52

Garfunkel, Art Jun 74

Gargan, William Jan 69 obit Apr 79

Garland, Hamlin Mar 40

Garland, Judy Nov 41 Dec 52 obit Sep 69

Garn, Edwin *see* Garn, Jake

Garn, Jake Aug 85

Garner, Erroll Sep 59 obit Mar 77

Garner, James Nov 66

Garnett, Kevin Sep 98

Garnsey, Elmer Ellsworth obit Dec 46

Garratt, Geoffrey Theodore obit Jun 42

Garreau, Roger Apr 50

Garrels, Arthur obit Aug 43

Garrison, Lloyd K. Jun 47 obit Nov 91

Garroway, Dave May 52 obit Sep 82

Garson, Greer Sep 42 obit Jun 96

Garst, Jonathan Oct 64

Garst, Roswell Apr 64 obit Jan 78

Garst, Shannon (WLB) Yrbk 47

Garth, David [political consultant] Jan 81

Garth, David [writer] (WLB) Yrbk 57

Gartner, Michael May 90

Garvey, Jane P. Sep 2000

Garvey, Marcus obit Aug 40

Garvin, Clifton Canter, Jr. Nov 80

Garwin, Richard L. Mar 89

Gary, John Jul 67 obit Mar 98

Gary, Raymond Oct 55 obit Feb 94

Garzarelli, Elaine Sep 95

Gasch, Marie Manning *see* Fairfax, Beatrice

Gaselee, Stephen obit Aug 43

Gasparotti, Mrs. John J. *see* Seifert, Elizabeth

Gasperi, Alcide De Dec 46 obit Oct 54

Gass, William H. Apr 86

Gasser, Herbert S. Oct 45 obit Jul 63

Gassman, Vittorio Oct 64 obit Oct 2000

Gassner, John Jan 47 obit Jun 67

Gaston, Cito Apr 93

Gaston, Clarence Edwin *see* Gaston, Cito

Gatch, Lee Mar 66 obit Jan 69

Gates, Bill May 91

Gates, Henry Louis Oct 92

Gates, Ralph F. Sep 47

Gates, Robert M. Apr 92

Gates, Thomas S., Jr. Sep 57 obit May 83

Gates, William H. *see* Gates, Bill

Gates, William obit Jan 40

Gatti-Casazza, Giulio obit Oct 40

Gaud, William S. Jan 69 obit Feb 78

Gaulle, Charles De Sep 40 Jun 49 Apr 60 obit Dec 70

Gaultier, Jean-Paul Jan 99

Gaumont, Leon Ernest obit Sep 46

Gauss, Christian Apr 45 obit Dec 51

Gauss, Clarence E. Jan 41 obit Jun 60

Gauthier, Joseph Alexandre George, Archbishop obit Oct 40

Gautier, Felisa Rincón De Oct 56 obit Nov 94

Gaver, Mary Virginia Jun 66 obit Mar 92

Gavin, James M. Feb 45 Sep 61 obit Apr 90

Gavin, John Sep 62

Gavras, Costa *see* Costa-Gavras

Gavrilov, Andrei Oct 2000

Gavrilovic, Stoyan May 46 obit Mar 65

Gay, Peter Feb 86

Gayda, Virginio Sep 40 obit Sep 43

Gayle, Crystal Mar 86

Gaylord, Robert Mar 44

Gazzaniga, Michael S. Apr 99

Gazzara, Ben Nov 67

Gebel-Williams, Gunther Dec 71

Gebrselassie, Haile Jul 99

Gedda, Nicolai Nov 65

Geddes, Barbara Bel Jul 48

Geddes, Norman Bel May 40 obit Jul 58

Geer, Alpheus obit Oct 41

Geffen, David Jan 92

Gehrig, Lou Jan-Jun 40 obit Jul 41

Gehrmann, Don Oct 52 (see also correction p. 664 YRBK 52)

Gehry, Frank Jun 87

Geiger, Roy S. Jul 45 obit Mar 47

Geijer, Arne Jul 64

Geis, Bernard Sep 60

Geisel, Ernesto Aug 75 obit Nov 96

Geisel, Theodor Seuss Feb 68 obit Nov 91

Geldof, Bob Mar 86

Geldzahler, Henry Sep 78 obit Oct 94

Geller, Margaret J. Jun 97

Geller, Uri Sep 78

Gellhorn, Walter May 67 obit Feb 96

Gell-Mann, Murray Feb 66 Oct 98

Gemayel, Amin Mar 83

Geneen, Harold S. Feb 74 obit Jan 98

Genet *see* Flanner, Janet

Genet, Jean Apr 74 obit Jun 86

Gennaro, Peter Jun 64

Genscher, Hans-Dietrich Jun 75

Gentele, Goeran Sep 72

Genthe, Arnold obit Oct 42

George II, King of Greece Dec 43 obit Apr 47

George VI, King of Great Britain Mar 42 obit Mar 52

George, Albert Bailey obit Apr 40

George, Boy *see* Boy George

George, David Lloyd Nov 44 obit May 45

George, Elizabeth Mar 2000

George, Harold L. Dec 42

George, Manfred Oct 65 obit Feb 66

George, Walter F. Jun 43 Jun 55 obit Oct 57

George, Zelma W. Oct 61 obit Sep 94

George-Brown, Baron *see* Brown, George

George Tupou, King of Tonga *see* Taufa'ahau Tupou IV

Gephardt, Richard A. Oct 87

Gerard, Ralph W. May 65 obit Apr 74

Geraud, André Sep 40 obit Jan 75

Gerbner, George Aug 83

Gere, Richard Aug 80

Gergen, David Feb 94

Gergiev, Valery Jan 98

Gerhardsen, Einar Mar 49 obit Nov 87

Gernreich, Rudi Dec 68 obit Jun 85

Gerow, Leonard Townsend Apr 45 obit Dec 72

Gerowitz, Judy *see* Chicago, Judy

Gershwin, Ira Jan 56 obit Oct 83

Gerstacker, Carl A. Oct 61 obit Jul 95

Gerstenmaier, Eugen Feb 58 obit May 86

Gerstner, Louis V. Jun 91

Gerulaitis, Vitas Jun 79 obit Nov 94

Gervasi, Frank Jun 42 obit Mar 90

Gesell, Arnold L. Nov 40 obit Sep 61

Gest, Morris obit Jul 42

Getman, F. H. obit Jan 42

Getty, Estelle Mar 90

Getty, Gordon P. Feb 85

Getz, Stan Apr 71 obit Aug 91

Geyer, Georgie Anne Aug 86

Gheerbrant, Alain Feb 59

Gheorghiu-Dej, Gheorghe Oct 58 obit May 65

Ghezali, Salima May 98

Ghormley, Robert Lee Oct 42 obit Oct 58

Ghose, Sri Chinmoy Kumar *see* Chinmoy, Sri

Ghulam Mohammed *see* Mohammed, Ghulam

Giacometti, Alberto Feb 56 obit Feb 66

Giacomin, Edward Mar 68

Giamatti, A. Bartlett Apr 78 obit Oct 89

Giannini, A. P. Mar 47 obit Jul 49

Giannini, Giancarlo Jun 79

Giannini, L. M. Nov 50 obit Oct 52

Giap, Vo Nguyen *see* Vo Nguyen Giap

Giauque, William F. Jan 50 obit May 82

Gibb, Barry Sep 81

Gibbings, Robert (WLB) Yrbk 48 obit Mar 58

Gibbings, Terence Harold Robsjohn *see* Robsjohn-Gibbings, T. H.

Gibbs, Constance *see* Bannister, Constance

Gibbs, George obit Jul 40

Gibbs, Joe Apr 92

Gibbs, Lois Sep 99

Gibbs, William Francis Apr 44 obit Nov 67

Gibson, Althea Oct 57

Gibson, Bob Dec 68

Gibson, Charles Dana obit Feb 45

Gibson, Ernest W. Jul 49 obit Dec 69

Gibson, Ernest Willard obit Aug 40

Gibson, Hugh Jan 53 obit Feb 55

Gibson, John W. Oct 47

Gibson, Kenneth A. May 71

Gibson, Mel Apr 84

Gibson, Robert W., Jr. May 69

Gibson, Virginia *see* Johnson, Virginia E.

Gibson, William Jul 83

Gibstein, Yaacov *see* Agam, Yaacov

Giddens, Anthony Apr 98

Gideonse, Harry D. May 40 obit May 85

Gidney, Ray M. Oct 53

Giegengack, A. E. Nov 44 obit Sep 74

Gielgud, John Apr 47 Feb 84 obit Aug 2000

Gierek, Edward May 71

Gieseking, Walter Oct 56 obit Jan 57

Gifford, Chloe Mar 59

Gifford, Francis Newton *see* Gifford, Frank

Gifford, Frank May 64 Jan 95

Gifford, Kathie Lee Nov 94

Gifford, Sanford R. obit Apr 44

Gifford, Walter S. Jan 45 obit Jun 66

Gigli, Romeo Aug 98

Gilbert, George obit May 43

Gilbert, Martin Feb 91

Gilbert, Rod Jul 69

Gilbert, Walter Nov 92

Gilbreth, Frank B. Jr. May 49 [Gilbreth, Frank B.; and Carey, Ernestine Gilbreth]

Gilbreth, Lillian M. May 40 Sep 51 obit Feb 72

Gilbreth, Mrs. Frank Bunker *see* Gilbreth, Lillian M.

Gilchrist, Brad Jan 99

Gilchrist, Guy Jan 99

Gilchrist, Huntington Apr 49 obit Mar 75

Gilder, George Oct 81

Gilder, Robert Fletcher obit Mar 40

Gilder, Rosamond Nov 45 obit Oct 86

Gildersleeve, Virginia C. Aug 41 obit Sep 65

Gilels, Emil Oct 56 obit Jan 86

Giles, Barney McKinney Jul 44 obit Aug 84

Giles, Janice Holt (WLB) Yrbk 58

Giles, Mrs. Henry Earl *see* Giles, Janice Holt

Gil Fortoul, José obit Aug 43

Gill, Eric obit Jan 41

Gillespie, Dizzy Apr 57 Jan 93 obit Jan 93

Gillespie, John Birks *see* Gillespie, Dizzy

Gillespie, Louis John obit Mar 41

Gillet, Louis obit Aug 43

Gillette, Guy M. Sep 46 obit Apr 73

Gillham, Mrs. Robert Marty *see* Enright, Elizabeth

Gilligan, Carol May 97

Gilligan, John J. May 72

Gillis, James M., Rev. Jun 56 obit Jun 57

Gillmore, Frank obit May 43

Gillooly, Edna Rae *see* Burstyn, Ellen

Gilmer, Elizabeth Meriwether *see* Dix, Dorothy

Gilmore, Eddy Jun 47 obit Dec 67

Gilmore, John Washington obit Aug 42

Gilmore, Melvin Randolph obit Sep 40

Gilmore, Voit Feb 62

Gilmour, John obit Apr 40

Gilpatric, Roswell L. Mar 64 obit May 96

Gilroy, Frank D. Oct 65

Gilruth, Robert R. Oct 63 obit Yrbk 2000

Gimbel, Bernard F. Mar 50 obit Dec 66

Gimbel, Peter Jan 82 obit Aug 87

Ginastera, Alberto Jan 71

Ginger, Lyman V. May 58

Gingold, Hermione Oct 58 obit Jul 87

Gingrich, Arnold Feb 61 obit Sep 76

Gingrich, Newt Jul 89

Ginsberg, Allen Apr 70 Apr 87 obit Jun 97

Ginsberg, Mitchell I. Jun 71 obit May 96

Ginsberg, Samuel *see* Krivitsky, Walter G.

Ginsburg, Ruth Bader Feb 94

Ginzberg, Eli Mar 66

Ginzburg, Natalia Jul 90 obit Nov 91

Giordani, Francesco Sep 57 [Armand, Louis; Etzel, Franz; and Giordani, Francesco] obit Mar 61

Giovanna, Ella Rosa *see* Grasso, Ella

Giovanni, Nikki Apr 73

Gipson, Fred (WLB) Yrbk 57

Gipson, Lawrence Henry Oct 54 obit Nov 71

Giral, Jose May 46

Giraud, Henri Honore Dec 42 obit Apr 49

Giraudoux, Jean obit Mar 44

Girdler, Tom M. Apr 44 obit Mar 65

Giri, V. V. Jan 70 obit Aug 80

Giroud, Françoise

Giroux, Robert Nov 82

Giscard D'estaing, Valéry Jul 67 Oct 74

Gish, Dorothy Aug 44 [Gish, Dorothy; and Gish, Lillian] obit Sep 68

Gish, Lillian Aug 44 [Gish, Dorothy; and Gish, Lillian] Aug 78 obit Apr 93

Giuliani, Rudolph W. Apr 88

Giulini, Carlo Maria Mar 78

Givenchy, Hubert De May 55

Givens, Willard E. Sep 48 obit Jul 71

Gjesdal, Cornelia *see* Knutson, Coya

Glaoui, Thami el-Mezouari el- *see* El-Glaoui, Thami El-Mezouari, Pasha of Marrakech

Glaser, Donald A. Mar 61

Glaser, Milton May 80

Glasgow, Ellen obit Jan 46

Glass, Carter Oct 41 obit Jun 46

Glass, H. Bentley Apr 66

Glass, Philip Mar 81

Glasser, Ira Jan 86

Glazer, Nathan Dec 70

Gleason, C. W. obit Dec 42

Gleason, Herbert John *see* Gleason, Jackie

Gleason, Jackie Oct 55 obit Aug 87

Gleason, John S., Jr. Jun 58

Gleason, Thomas W. Oct 65 obit Mar 93

Glemp, Jozef Sep 82

Glenn, John H., Jr. Jun 62 Mar 76 Jan 99

Glenn, Mary Wilcox obit Yrbk 40

Glennan, T. Keith Oct 50 obit Jun 95

Glennie, Evelyn Jul 97

Glennon, John obit Apr 46

Glicenstein, Enrico obit Feb 43

Glicenstein, Henryk *see* Glicenstein, Enrico

Glick, Mrs. Frank *see* Kirkus, Virginia

Glintenkamp, H. obit May 46

Glover, Danny Apr 92

Glover, Savion Mar 96

Glubb, John Bagot Sep 51 obit May 86

Glueck, Eleanor Touroff Oct 57 [Glueck, Sheldon; and Glueck, Eleanor T.] obit Nov 72

Glueck, Nelson Oct 48 Jul 69 obit Mar 71

Glueck, Sheldon Oct 57 [Glueck, Sheldon; and Glueck, Eleanor T.] obit May 80

Glyn, Elinor obit Nov 43

Gmeiner, Hermann May 63 obit Jun 86

Gobbi, Tito Jan 57 obit May 84

Gobel, George Mar 55 obit Apr 91

Godard, Jean-Luc May 69 Oct 93

Goddard, James L. Oct 68

Goddard, Paulette obit Jun 90

Goddard, Robert H. obit Sep 45

Godden, Rumer Aug 76

Godfrey, Arthur Jul 48 obit May 83

Godoy, Alcayaga Lucila *see* Mistral, Gabriela

Godunov, Alexander Feb 83 obit Jul 95

Godwin, Gail Oct 95

Goebbels, Joseph Sep 41 obit Yrbk 91 (died May 45)

Goedhart, G. J. van Heuven *see* Heuven Goedhart, G. J. Van

Goertz, Arthémise (WLB) Yrbk 53

Goetz, Delia (WLB) Yrbk 49 obit Sep 96

Goetz, George *see* Calverton, V. F.

Gogarty, Oliver St. John Jul 41 obit Dec 57

Goheen, Robert F. Jan 58

Goizueta, Roberto C. Aug 96 obit Jan 98

Gold, Herbert (WLB) Yrbk 55

Gold, Thomas Jun 66

Goldberg, Arthur J. Jul 49 Jul 61 obit Mar 90

Goldberg, Emmanuel *see* Robinson, Edward G.

Goldberg, Reuben Lucius *see* Goldberg, Rube

Goldberg, Rube Sep 48 obit Jan 71

Goldberg, Whoopi Mar 85

Goldblum, Jeff Jul 97

Goldbogen, Avrom Hirsch *see* Todd, Mike

Golden, Clinton S. Apr 48 obit Sep 61

Golden, Harry Jan 59 obit Nov 81

Golden, John Mar 44 obit Sep 55

Goldenson, Leonard H. Sep 57 obit May 2000

Goldenweiser, Alexander A. obit Sep 40

Goldin, Daniel S. Jun 93

Golding, William Mar 64 obit Aug 93

Goldman, Edwin Franko Sep 42 obit May 56

Goldman, Emma obit Jan 40

Goldman, Eric F. Jul 64 obit Apr 89

Goldman, Frank Jan 53 obit Apr 65

Goldman, Mrs. Marcus Selden *see* Goldman, Mrs. Olive Remington

Goldman, Olive Remington Sep 50 [Goldman, Mrs. Marcus Selden]

Goldman, William Jan 95

Goldmann, Nahum May 57 obit Oct 82

Goldmark, Henry obit Mar 41

Goldmark, Peter C. Nov 40 Dec 50 obit Feb 78

Goldovsky, Boris Dec 66

Goldsborough, John Byron obit May 43

Goldsborough, Phillips Lee obit Dec 46

Goldsborough, T. Alan Jun 48 obit Jul 51

Goldschmidt, Neil Aug 80

Goldsmith, James Feb 88 obit Oct 97

Goldsmith, Jimmy *see* Goldsmith, James

Goldsmith, Lester Morris Apr 40

Goldsmith, Peter *see* Priestley, J. B.

Goldstein, Betty Naomi *see* Friedan, Betty

Goldstein, Elliott *see* Gould, Elliott

Goldstein, Israel Jul 46 obit Jun 86

Goldstein, Joseph L. Jul 87

Goldstine, Herman Heine Nov 52

Goldsworthy, Andy Oct 2000

Goldthwaite, Anne obit Mar 44

Goldwater, Barry M. May 55 Jun 78 obit Aug 98

Goldwater, S. S. obit Dec 42

Goldwyn, Samuel Jan 44 obit Mar 74

Golenor, John Anthony *see* Gavin, John

Goler, George Washington obit Nov 40

Golikov, Filip Apr 43 obit Sep 80

Gollancz, Victor Oct 63 obit Apr 67

Golschmann, Vladimir Apr 51 obit May 72

Golub, Leon Aug 84

Goma Y Tomas, Isidoro obit Oct 40

Gomez, Laureano May 50 obit Sep 65

Gomulka, Wladyslaw Jan 57 obit Oct 82

Gong Li May 97

Gonzales, Pancho Oct 49 obit Sep 95

Gonzales, Richard see Gonzales, Pancho

Gonzalez, Adolfo Suarez see Suárez González, Adolfo

González, César Oct 54

Gonzalez, Efren W. Jan 71

González, Felipe Jan 78

Gonzalez, Henry Jun 64 Feb 93

Gonzalez Videla, Gabriel Jun 50

Good, Robert A. Mar 72

Goodall, Jane Nov 67 Nov 91

Goode, Richard Nov 88

Goode, W. Wilson Oct 85

Goodell, Charles E. Dec 68 obit Mar 87

Gooden, Dwight Apr 86

Goodhart, Arthur Lehman Jul 64 obit Feb 79

Goodloe, John D. Apr 47

Goodman, Andrew Apr 75 obit Jun 93

Goodman, Benjamin David see Goodman, Benny

Goodman, Benny Jan 42 Oct 62 obit Aug 86

Goodman, Bertram May 54

Goodman, Julian Feb 67

Goodman, Paul Jun 68 obit Oct 72

Goodpaster, Andrew J. Jul 69

Goodrich, Arthur obit Aug 41

Goodrich, Frances Oct 56 [Goodrich, Frances; and Hackett, Albert] obit Apr 84

Goodrich, James Putnam obit Oct 40

Goodrich, Lloyd May 67 obit May 87

Goodrich, Marcus Apr 41 obit Jan 92

Goodson, Mark May 78 obit Feb 93

Goodspeed, Edgar Johnson Nov 46 obit Mar 62

Goodwin, Doris Kearns Nov 97

Goodwin, Harry obit Dec 42

Goodwin, Richard N. Dec 68

Goodwin, Robert C. May 51

Googe, George L. Jul 47 obit Dec 61

Goolagong, Evonne Nov 71

Goossens, Eugene May 45 obit Sep 62

Gorbach, Alfons Oct 61 obit Oct 72

Gorbachev, Mikhail Aug 85

Gorbachev, Raisa May 88 obit Nov 99

Gordimer, Nadine (WLB) Yrbk 59 Jun 80

Gordon, C. Henry obit Jan 41

Gordon, Crawford, Jr. Mar 58 obit Mar 67

Gordon, Cyrus H. May 63

Gordon, David Jun 94

Gordon, Donald Oct 50 obit Jun 69

Gordon, Dorothy Jan 55 obit Jul 70

Gordon, Godfrey Jervis see Gordon, Jan

Gordon, Janet see Woodham-Smith, Cecil Blanche Fitzgerald

Gordon, Jan obit Mar 44

Gordon, Jeff Aug 2000

Gordon, John Sloan obit Yrbk 40

Gordon, Kermit Jul 63 obit Aug 76

Gordon, Leon obit Feb 44

Gordon, Lincoln Feb 62

Gordon, Mary Nov 81

Gordon, Max Oct 43 obit Jan 79

Gordon, Odetta Felious see Odetta

Gordon, Ruth Apr 43 Apr 72 obit Oct 85

Gordon, Thomas S. Apr 57 obit Apr 59

Gordon Walker, Patrick Jan 66

Gordy, Berry, Jr. Jul 75

Gore, Al see Gore, Albert Jr.

Gore, Albert Jan 52 obit Feb 99

Gore, Albert Jr. Jun 87

Gore, Mary Elizabeth Aitcheson see Gore, Tipper

Gore, Tipper Oct 2000

Górecki, Henryk May 94

Gorelick, Kenny see G, Kenny

Goren, Charles H. Mar 59 obit Jul 91

Gorey, Edward Nov 76 obit Aug 2000

Gorin, Igor Jul 42 obit Jun 82

Göring, Hermann Wilhelm Aug 41 obit Nov 46

Görk, Haydar Oct 56

Gorman, Herbert Sherman Mar 40 obit Jan 55

Gorman, Mike see Gorman, Thomas F. X.

Gorman, Thomas F. X. Oct 56 obit Jul 89

Gorme, Eydie Feb 65

Gorrie, Jack Mar 52

Gorsuch, Anne Sep 82

Gort, Viscount Oct 40 obit May 46

Gorton, John G. Jul 68

Gorton, Slade Aug 93

Gosden, Freeman F. Dec 47 [Gosden, Freeman F.; and Correll, Charles J.] obit Feb 83

Goshorn, Clarence B. Mar 50 obit Jan 51

Goss, Albert S. Mar 45 obit Dec 50

Gossage, Goose see Gossage, Rich

Gossage, Rich Aug 84

Gossett, Louis, Jr. Nov 90

Gossett, William T. Jul 69 obit Oct 98

Gott, J. Richard III Oct 99

Gott, William Henry Ewart obit Oct 42

Gottlieb, Adolph Jan 59 obit Apr 74

Gottlieb, Melvin B. Jan 74

Gottlieb, Robert A. Sep 87

Gottwald, Klement Apr 48 obit Apr 53

Goudge, Elizabeth Sep 40 obit Aug 84

Goudsmit, Samuel A. Oct 54 obit Feb 79

Goudy, Frederic William Jun 41 obit Jun 47

Gough, Lewis K. Jan 53 obit Jan 68

Gouin, Felix Mar 46 obit Oct 79 (died Oct 77)

Goulart, Joao Sep 62 obit Feb 77

Gould, Arthur R. obit Sep 46

Gould, Beatrice Blackmar Nov 47 [Gould, Beatrice Blackmar; and Gould, Bruce] obit Apr 89

Gould, Bruce Nov 47 [Gould, Beatrice Blackmar; and Gould, Bruce] obit Oct 89

Gould, Chester Sep 71 obit Jul 85

Gould, Elliott Feb 71

Gould, Glenn Oct 60 obit Nov 82

Gould, Laurence M. Jan 78 obit Aug 95

Gould, Morton Sep 45 Jan 68 obit May 96

Gould, Ronald Nov 52

Gould, Samuel B. Jan 58 obit Sep 97

Gould, Stephen Jay Sep 82

Goulding, Ray Oct 57 [Elliott, Bob; and Goulding, Ray] obit May 90

Goulet, Robert Sep 62

Goulian, Mehran Jul 68

Gourielli, Helena Rubinstein *see* Rubinstein, Helena

Gove, Philip B. Oct 62 obit Jan 73

Gow, James Mar 44 [Gow, James; and d'Usseau, Arnaud] obit Mar 52

Gowdy, Curt May 67

Gower, Pauline Aug 43 obit Mar 47

Gowon, Yakubu Jun 70

Grace, Alonzo G. Jan 50 obit Dec 71

Grace, Eugene Gifford Apr 41 obit Oct 60

Grace, J. Peter, Jr. Mar 60 obit Jun 95

Grace, Princess of Monaco Mar 55 Oct 77 obit Nov 82

Grade, Lew Aug 79 obit Mar 99

Grady, Henry F. Jul 47 obit Nov 57

Graebner, Clark Feb 70

Graebner, Walter Aug 43

Graf, Herbert May 42 obit May 73

Graf, Steffi Feb 89

Graffman, Gary Jul 70

Grafton, Samuel Jan-Feb 40 obit Feb 98

Grafton, Sue Sep 95

Graham, Billy Apr 51 Jan 73

Graham, Bob Jul 86

Graham, Clarence R. Nov 50

Graham, Donald E. May 98

Graham, Elinor (WLB) Yrbk 52

Graham, Elizabeth N. *see* Arden, Elizabeth

Graham, Evarts A. Feb 52 obit May 57

Graham, Florence Nightingale *see* Arden, Elizabeth

Graham, Frank P. May 41 Jul 51 obit Apr 72

Graham, Gwethalyn Jan 45 obit Jan 66

Graham, Harry Chrysostom Apr 50

Graham, Horace F. obit Jan 42

Graham, John Oct 62 obit Apr 91

Graham, Jorie May 97

Graham, Katharine Jan 71

Graham, Martha Feb 44 Jun 61 obit May 91

Graham, Philip L. Feb 48 obit Oct 63

Graham, Robert *see* Graham, Bob

Graham, Sheilah Oct 69 obit Jan 89

Graham, Virginia Oct 56 obit Mar 99

Graham, Wallace H. Feb 47 obit Mar 96

Graham, William Franklin *see* Graham, Billy

Graham, Winston (WLB) Yrbk 55

Gramm, Donald Nov 75 obit Jul 83

Gramm, Phil May 86

Grammer, Kelsey May 96

Granahan, Kathryn E. Oct 59 obit Sep 79

Granato, Cammi Apr 98

Granato, Catherine Michelle *see* Granato, Cammi

Grand, Sarah obit Jul 43

Grandi, Dino Jul 43 obit Jul 88

Grandin, Temple Jul 94

Grandjany, Marcel May 43 obit Apr 75

Grandma Moses *see* Moses, Grandma

Granger, Lester B. Apr 46 obit Mar 76

Granger, Walter obit Oct 41

Granik, Theodore Dec 52 obit Nov 70

Grant, Cary Sep 41 Nov 65 obit Jan 87

Grant, Elihu obit Dec 42

Grant, Ethel Watts Mumford *see* Mumford, Ethel Watts

Grant, Gordon Jun 53 obit Jul 62

Grant, Heber J. obit Jun 45

Grant, Hilda Kay *see* Hilliard, Jan

Grant, Hugh Sep 95

Grant, Lee Mar 74

Grant, Margaret *see* Franken, Rose

Grant, Robert obit Jul 40

Grantham, Alexander May 54

Grantley, John Richard Brinsley Norton, 5th Baron obit Sep 43

Granville, William Spencer Leveson-Gower, 4th Earl *see* Leveson-Gower, William Spencer

Grappelli, Stéphane Aug 88 obit Feb 98

Graser, Earle W. obit Jun 41

Grass, Günter Oct 64 Jul 83

Grasso, Ella May 75 obit Mar 81

Grau, Shirley Ann (WLB) Yrbk 59

Grauer, Ben Feb 41 Jul 59 obit Jul 77

Grauer, Mrs. Ben *see* Kahane, Melanie

Grau San Martin, Ramón Oct 44 obit Oct 69

Gravel, Maurice Robert *see* Gravel, Mike

Gravel, Mike Jan 72

Graves, Alvin C. Dec 52 obit Oct 65

Graves, Bibb obit May 42

Graves, Earl G. Aug 97

Graves, Frederick Rogers obit Jul 40

Graves, Michael Jan 89

Graves, Morris Jul 56

Graves, Nancy May 81 obit Jan 96

Graves, Robert May 78 obit Feb 86

Graves, William Sidney obit Mar 40

Gray, C. Boyden Aug 89

Gray, Carl R., Jr. Mar 48 obit Feb 56

Gray, Elizabeth Janet Sep 43

Gray, Frizzell see Mfume, Kweisi

Gray, George, Kruger- see Kruger-Gray, George

Gray, Georgia Neese Clark see Clark, Georgia Neese

Gray, Gordon Sep 49 obit Feb 83

Gray, Hanna Holborn Mar 79

Gray, Harold E. Feb 69

Gray, L. Patrick, 3d Sep 72

Gray, Macy May 2000

Gray, Simon Jun 83

Gray, Spalding Sep 86

Gray, William H., 3d Feb 88

Grayson, C. Jackson, Jr. Sep 72

Grayson, David see Baker, Ray Stannard

Graziani, Rodolfo Apr 41 obit Mar 55

Grebe, John J. Oct 55

Grechko, Andrei A. Nov 68 obit Jun 76

Greco, José Mar 52

Gréco, Juliette Jan 92

Grede, William J. Feb 52 obit Aug 89

Greeley, Andrew M. Dec 72

Greeley, Dana McLean Mar 64 obit Aug 86

Green, Adolph Mar 45 [Comden, Betty; and Green, Adolph]

Green, Al Feb 96

Green, Constance McLaughlin Oct 63

Green, David see Ben-Gurion, David

Green, Dwight H. Apr 48 obit Apr 58

Green, Edith May 56 obit Jun 87

Green, Florence Topping obit Jun 45

Green, Howard Jan 60

Green, Julian Jan-Feb 40 obit Oct 98

Green, Mark J. Feb 88

Green, Martyn Jun 50 obit Apr 75

Green, Mrs. Howard see Green, Florence Topping

Green, Theodore Francis Feb 50 obit Jun 66

Green, Tim Aug 2000

Green, William Mar 42 obit Jan 53

Greenaway, Emerson Jul 58 obit Jun 90

Greenaway, Peter Feb 91

Greenbaum, Lucy see Freeman, Lucy

Greenberg, Hank see Greenberg, Maurice R. Jun 47 obit Oct 86

Greenberg, Maurice R. Nov 2000

Greenberg, Noah May 64 obit Feb 66

Greenbie, Sydney Sep 41 obit Sep 60

Greene, Balcomb Nov 65 obit Jan 91

Greene, Bob Jul 95

Greene, Brian Aug 2000

Greene, Frank Russell obit Jan 40

Greene, Graham Oct 69 obit May 91

Greene, Harold H. Aug 85 obit May 2000

Greene, Hugh Sep 63 obit Apr 87

Greene, Lorne Jan 67 obit Oct 87

Greene, Nancy Mar 69

Greene, Wallace M., Jr. Jun 65

Greenebaum, Leon C. Jan 62 obit May 68

Greenewalt, C. H. Jan 49

Greenfield, Abraham Lincoln obit Sep 41

Greenfield, Jerry Apr 94 [Cohen, Ben; and Greenfield, Jerry]

Greenough, Carroll obit Oct 41

Greenspan, Alan Dec 74 Jan 89

Greenstein, Jesse Leonard Sep 63

Greenstreet, Sydney May 43 obit Mar 54

Greenway, Walter Burton obit Feb 41

Greenwood, Allen obit Dec 42

Greenwood, Arthur Oct 40 obit Sep 54

Greenwood, Joan May 54 obit Apr 87

Greer, Germaine Nov 71 Oct 88

Gregg, Alan see Mallette, Gertrude E.

Gregg, Hugh Jan 54

Gregg, Milton F. Oct 55

Gregorian, Vartan Oct 85

Gregory, Cynthia May 77

Gregory, Dick Jun 62

Gregory, Edmund B. Sep 45 obit Mar 61

Gregory, J. Dennis see Williams, John A.

Gregory, Menas S. obit Jan 42

Gregory, Paul Apr 56

Grenfell, Joyce Mar 58 obit Feb 80

Grenfell, Wilfred Thomason obit Yrbk 40

Grennan, Jacqueline see Wexler, Jacqueline Grennan

Grès, Alix see Gres, Mme.

Gres, Mme. Jun 80 obit Feb 95

Gresley, Nigel obit May 41

Gretzky, Wayne Feb 82

Greuter, Helen Wright see Wright, Helen

Grew, Joseph Clark Feb 41 obit Jul 65

Grewe, Wilhelm Oct 58

Grey, Clifford obit Nov 41

Grey, J. D. Sep 52 obit Sep 85

Grey, Joel Jan 73

Gribble, Harry Wagstaff Sep 45 obit Apr 81

Grieder, Naomi Lane Babson see Babson, Naomi Lane

Grieff, Joseph Nicholas obit Aug 41

Grier, Pam Feb 98

Grier, Roosevelt Mar 75

Griffey, Ken, Jr. Aug 96

Griffies, Ethel Jan 68 obit Nov 75

Griffin, Bernard Oct 46 obit Oct 56

Griffin, John D. May 57

Griffin, John Howard Nov 60 obit Nov 80

Griffin, Marvin Jun 56 obit Aug 82

Griffin, Merv Sep 67

Griffin, R. Allen Feb 51

Griffin, Robert P. May 60

Griffis, Stanton Oct 44 obit Oct 74

Griffith, Andy May 60

Griffith, Clark Jun 50 obit Jan 56

Griffith, Ernest S. Oct 47 obit
Apr 97
Griffith, J. P. Crozer obit Sep
41
Griffith, Melanie Oct 90
Griffith, Nanci Feb 98
Griffith, Paul H. Jan 47 obit
Feb 75
Griffith Joyner, Florence Apr
89 obit Nov 98
Griffiths, Martha W. Oct 55
Griffiths, Mrs. Hicks G see
Griffiths, Martha W.
Grigg, James Apr 42 obit Jul
64
Grigg, John Oct 64
Grigg, Percy James see Grigg,
James
Grigorovich, Yuri Sep 75
Grillo, Frank Raúl see
Machito
Grimes, Tammy Jul 62
Grimes, W. H. Jun 47 obit Mar
72
Grimond, Jo Oct 63 obit Jan
94
Grimshaw, Robert obit Jun 41
Grisham, John Sep 93
Grissom, Virgil I. Nov 65 obit
Mar 67
Griswold, A. Whitney Apr 50
obit Jun 63
Griswold, Augustus H. obit
Mar 40
Griswold, Dwight P. Dec 47
obit Jun 54
Griswold, Erwin N. Oct 56
obit Jan 95
Griswold, Oscar W. Sep 43
obit Dec 59
Grivas, George Oct 64 obit
Mar 74
Grizodubova, Valentina S.
Dec 41 obit Jul 93
Grizzard, George Jun 76
Groat, Dick May 61
Groat, Richard M see Groat,
Dick
Grodin, Charles Nov 95
Groening, Matt Sep 90
Groenman, Frans Eyso Henri-
cus obit Aug 43
Grofé, Ferde Jul 40 obit May
72
Grogan, John Joseph Dec 51
Gromyko, Andrei A. Oct 43
Oct 58 obit Aug 89
Gronchi, Giovanni Oct 55
obit Jan 79

Groninger, Homer M. Aug 45
Gronouski, John A. Jan 66
obit Mar 96
Grooms, Charles Roger see
Grooms, Red
Grooms, Red Dec 72
Groot, Adriaan M. De obit
Mar 42
Gropius, Walter Nov 41 Mar
52 obit Sep 69
Gropper, William Mar 40 obit
Mar 77
Gros, Edmund L. obit Dec 42
Gross, Chaim Nov 41 Feb 66
obit Jul 91
Gross, Charles P. Mar 46 obit
Sep 75
Gross, Ernest A. Feb 51 obit
Jul 99
Gross, H. R. Jan 64 obit Oct 87
Gross, Hiam see Gross,
Chaim
Gross, Mason W. Jun 69 obit
Jan 78
Gross, Paul Magnus May 63
obit Jun 86
Gross, Robert E. Jan 56 obit
Nov 61
Grossberg, Yitzroch Loiza see
Rivers, Larry
Grossinger, Jennie Oct 56 obit
Jan 73
Grosvenor, Gilbert Dec 46
obit Mar 66
Grosvenor, Graham Bethune
obit Dec 43
Grosvenor, Melville Bell Apr
60 obit Jun 82
Grosz, George Apr 42 obit
Oct 59
Grosz, Karoly Sep 88 obit
Mar 96
Grotewohl, Otto Jul 50 obit
Nov 64
Groth, John Feb 43 obit Aug
88
Grotowski, Jerzy Dec 70 obit
Mar 99
Grouès, Henri Antoine see
Pierre, Abbé
Grove, Andrew S. Mar 98
Groves, Ernest R. Jun 43
[Groves, Ernest R; and
Groves, Gladys Hoagland]
obit Oct 46
Groves, Gladys Hoagland Jun
43 [Groves, Ernest R; and
Groves, Gladys Hoagland]
obit Sep 80

Groves, Leslie R. Aug 45 obit
Oct 70
Gruber, Frank Nov 41 obit
Feb 70
Gruber, Karl Feb 47
Gruber, L. Franklin obit Feb
42
Gruen, Victor Mar 59 obit
Apr 80
Gruenbaum, Victor David see
Gruen, Victor
Gruenberg, Sidonie Matsner
May 40 obit May 74
Gruening, Ernest Dec 46 Jul
66 obit Sep 74
Gruenther, Alfred M. Dec 50
obit Jul 83
Grumman, Leroy R. Aug 45
obit Jan 83
Gruppe, Charles Paul obit
Nov 40
Grzimek, Bernhard Mar 73
obit May 87
Guardia, Ernesto De La, Jr.
Jan 57
Guardia, Rafael Angel Cal-
deron see Calderón
Guardia, Rafael Ángel
Guardia, Ricardo Adolfo de
la see De La Guardia,
Ricardo Adolfo
Guare, John Aug 82
Gubaidulina, Sofia Oct 99
Gubelman, Minei Izrailevich
see Yaroslavsky, Emelyan
Gubitosi, Michael James
Vijencio see Blake, Robert
Guccione, Bob Aug 94
Guccione, Kathy Keeton see
Keeton, Kathy
Gudjonsson, Halldor see Lax-
ness, Halldór
Guedalla, Philip obit Feb 45
Gueden, Hilde Apr 55
Guerard, Albert J. (WLB)
Yrbk 46
Guerrero, José Gustavo Jan 47
obit Jan 59
Guertner, Franz obit Mar 41
Guest, Edgar A. Sep 41 obit
Nov 59
Guevara, Che see Guevara,
Ernesto
Guevara, Ernesto Jun 63 obit
Dec 67
Guffey, Joseph F. Mar 44 obit
May 59
Guggenheim, Florence see
Guggenheim, Mrs. Daniel

Guggenheim, Harry F. Oct 56 obit Mar 71

Guggenheim, Mrs. Daniel obit Jul 44 [Guggenheim, Florence]

Guggenheim, Mrs. Harry F. see Patterson, Alicia

Guggenheim, Peggy Oct 62 obit Feb 80

Guggenheimer, Minnie Oct 62 obit Jun 66

Guggenheimer, Mrs. Charles S. see Guggenheimer, Minnie

Guidry, Ron May 79

Guillaumat, Marie Louis Adolphe obit Jul 40

Guillaume, Augustin Jan 52

Guillaume, Robert Apr 2000

Guinan, Matthew Sep 74 obit May 95

Guinazu, Enrique Ruiz see Ruiz Guiñazú, Enrique

Guinness, Alec Oct 50 Mar 81 obit Oct 2000

Guinness, Arthur Jun 48

Guinness, Walter Edward obit Dec 44

Guinzburg, Harold K. Jul 57 obit Jan 62

Guion, Connie M. Feb 62

Guise, Jean Pierre Clement Marie, Duc De obit Oct 40

Guisewite, Cathy Feb 89

Guiterman, Arthur obit Mar 43

Gulick, Luther Halsey Jun 45 obit Mar 93

Gullander, W. P. Oct 63

Gullion, Allen W. Feb 43 obit Jul 46

Gumbel, Bryant Jul 86

Gumbel, Greg Sep 96

Gumm, Frances see Garland, Judy

Gumm, Harry see Von Tilzer, Harry

Gumpert, Martin Dec 51

Gundersen, Gunnar Feb 59 obit Aug 79

Gunn, Selskar Michael obit Sep 44

Gunn, Thom William Nov 88

Gunter, Julius Caldeen obit Yrbk 40

Gunter, Ray Jul 67 obit Jun 77

Gunther, Franklin Mott obit Feb 42

Gunther, John Nov 41 Feb 61 obit Jul 70

Guptill, Arthur L. Mar 55 obit May 56

Gurney, A. R. Jul 86

Gurney, Chan Oct 50

Gustaf V, King of Sweden Sep 42 obit Dec 50

Gustaf VI, King of Sweden Dec 50 obit Nov 73

Gustafsson, Greta Lovisa see Garbo, Greta

Gustavus V, King of Sweden see Gustaf V, King of Sweden

Gustavus VI, King of Sweden see Gustaf VI, King of Sweden

Guston, Philip Feb 71 obit Jul 80

Guth, Alan H. Sep 87

Guthman, Edwin O. Jun 50

Guthrie, A. B., Jr. Jul 50 obit Jul 91

Guthrie, Charles Ellsworth obit Sep 40

Guthrie, Janet Oct 78

Guthrie, Tyrone Jul 54 obit Jul 71

Guthrie, William Buck obit Yrbk 40

Guthrie, Woody May 63 obit Dec 67

Gutt, Camille Apr 48

Guttmacher, Alan F. Oct 65 obit May 74

Guy, Buddy Feb 2000

Guy, Raymond F. May 50

Guyer, Ulysses Samuel obit Jul 43

Guzman, Jacobo Arbenz see Arbenz Guzman, Jacobo

Guzy, Carol Feb 2000

Gwathmey, Charles Jan 88

Gwathmey, James T. obit Apr 44

Gwathmey, Robert Dec 43 obit Nov 88

Gwenn, Edmund Sep 43 obit Nov 59

Gwynn, Tony Oct 96

Gyalpo Wangchuk see Wangchuk, Jigme Dorji, Druk Gyalpo of Bhutan

Györgyi, Albert Szent- see Szent-Györgyi, Albert

Haack, Robert W. Mar 69 obit Aug 92

Haacke, Hans Jul 87

Haagen-Smit, A. J. Mar 66 obit May 77

Haakon VII, King of Norway May 40 obit Dec 57

Haas, Arthur E. obit Apr 41

Haas, Francis J. Aug 43 obit Oct 53

Habash, George Mar 88

Habe, Hans Feb 43 obit Nov 77

Haber, Heinz Dec 52

Habib, Philip Charles Sep 81 obit Jul 92

Habibie, Bacharuddin Jusuf Oct 98

Habré, Hissène Aug 87

Hacha, Emil Dec 42 obit Sep 45

Hacker

Hackett, Albert Oct 56 [Goodrich, Frances; and Hackett, Albert] obit May 95

Hackett, Buddy May 65

Hackett, Charles obit Feb 42

Hackett, Horatio B. obit Nov 41

Hackett, Walter obit Mar 44

Hackman, Gene Jul 72

Hackworth, Green H. Jan 58 obit Sep 73

Hadas, Moses Mar 60 obit Nov 66

Haddon, Alfred Cort obit May 40

Haddon, William, Jr. Feb 69 obit Apr 85

Hadfield, Robert Abbott obit Nov 40

Hadley, Jerry Nov 91

Hafstad, Lawrence R. Oct 56 obit Jan 94

Hagegard, Hakan May 85

Hagen, John P. Oct 57 obit Nov 90

Hagen, Uta May 44 [Ferrer, José; and Hagen, Uta] Oct 63

Hagen, Victor Wolfgang von see Von Hagen, Victor Wolfgang

Hagerty, James C. Mar 53 obit Jun 81

Haggard, Merle Jan 77

Haggard, William David obit Mar 40

Hagman, Larry Sep 80

Hagy, Ruth Geri Oct 57

Hahn, Emily Jul 42 obit Apr 97

Hahn, Otto Mar 51 obit Oct 68

Haig, Alexander Meigs, Jr. Jan 73 Sep 87

Haig-Brown, Roderick (WLB) Yrbk 50

Haile Selassie I Apr 41 Oct 54 obit Oct 75

Hailey, Arthur Feb 72

Hailsham, Quintin McGarel Hogg, 2d Viscount *see* Hogg, Quintin McGarel

Hainisch, Michael obit Mar 40

Hair, Jay D. Nov 93

Haitink, Bernard Nov 77

Halaby, Najeeb E. Oct 61

Halasz, Laszlo Jan 49

Halberstam, David Apr 73

Haldane, John Burdon Sanderson Nov 40 obit Jan 65

Haldeman, Bob *see* Haldeman, H. R.

Haldeman, H. R. Sep 78 obit Jan 94

Hale, Arthur obit Mar 40

Hale, Clara Jul 85 obit Feb 93

Hale, Richard W. obit Apr 43

Haley, Alex Jan 77 obit Mar 92

Haley, Andrew G. Oct 55 obit Nov 66

Haley, William J. Apr 48 obit Oct 87

Halfin, Diane Simone Michelle *see* Von Fürstenberg, Diane

Halifax, Edward Frederick Lindley Wood, 1st Earl of Sep 40 obit Feb 60

Halim, Mustafa Ben Sep 56

Hall, Arsenio Sep 89

Hall, Conrad L. Aug 2000

Hall, Donald May 84

Hall, Edward T. Feb 92

Hall, Florence Aug 43

Hall, Floyd D. Jun 70

Hall, Frank O. obit Dec 41

Hall, Fred Oct 55 obit May 70

Hall, George A. obit Nov 41

Hall, George W. obit Dec 41

Hall, Gus May 73

Hall, James obit Jul 40

Hall, Josef Washington *see* Close, Upton

Hall, Joyce Clyde May 53 obit Jan 83

Hall, Leonard W. Jul 53 obit Jul 79

Hall, Marjory (WLB) Yrbk 57

Hall, Paul Feb 66 obit Aug 80

Hall, Peter Feb 62

Hall, Radclyffe obit Nov 43

Hall, Raymond S. Oct 53

Hall, William Edwin Jan 54 obit Mar 61

Hallaren, Mary A. Mar 49

Halleck, Charles A. Mar 47 obit Apr 86

Halley, Rudolph Jun 53 obit Jan 57

Halligan, William J. Oct 57

Hallinan, Vincent Oct 52 obit Nov 92

Halloran, Roy D. obit Dec 43

Hallstein, Walter Oct 53 obit May 82

Halpert, Edith Gregor Jul 55 obit Nov 70

Halprin, Mrs. Samuel W. *see* Halprin, Rose Luria

Halprin, Rose Luria Jun 50

Halsey, Edwin A. obit Mar 45

Halsey, Margaret Nov 44 obit Apr 97

Halsey, William F., Jr. Dec 42 obit Nov 59

Halsman, Philippe Mar 60 obit Aug 79

Halston Dec 72 obit May 90

Hamblet, Julia E. Oct 53

Hambro, Carl Joachim May 40 obit Feb 65

Hamed, Prince Naseem Oct 98

Hamer, Dean H. Jun 97

Hamill, Dorothy Jun 76

Hamill, Pete Feb 98

Hamilton, Alice May 46 obit Nov 70

Hamilton, Charles Jul 76 obit Feb 97

Hamilton, Clayton obit Oct 46

Hamilton, Clive *see* Lewis, C. S.

Hamilton, Cosmo obit Dec 42

Hamilton, Edith Apr 63

Hamilton, George Livingston obit Nov 40

Hamilton, Hale obit Jul 42

Hamilton, Lee H. Mar 88

Hamilton, Margaret Apr 79 obit Jul 85

Hamilton, Scott Apr 85

Hamlin, Clarence Clark obit Yrbk 40

Hamlin, Talbot Oct 54 obit Dec 56 Yrbk 57

Hamlisch, Marvin May 76

Hamm, Mia Sep 99

Hammarskjöld, Dag May 53 obit Nov 61

Hammer, Armand Jun 73 obit Feb 91

Hammer Apr 91

Hammerstein, Oscar Feb 44 obit Nov 60

Hammerstein-Equord, Kurt Von obit Jun 43

Hammon, William McDowell Sep 57 obit Nov 89

Hammond, Aubrey Lindsay obit Apr 40

Hammond, Caleb D., Jr. Apr 56

Hammond, E. Cuyler Jun 57 obit Jan 87

Hammond, Godfrey Oct 53 obit Oct 69

Hammond, Graeme M. obit Dec 44

Hammond, John Hays, Jr. Jul 62 obit Apr 65

Hammond, John Jul 79 obit Aug 87

Hampden, Walter May 53 obit Sep 55

Hampshire, Susan Jan 74

Hampson, Thomas Mar 91

Hampton, Lionel Oct 71

Hancher, Virgil M. Feb 57 obit Mar 65

Hancock, Florence Nov 48

Hancock, John M. Apr 49 obit Dec 56 Yrbk 57

Hancock, Joy B. Feb 49 obit Oct 86

Hand, Learned Apr 50 obit Nov 61

Handke, Peter Apr 73

Handler, Philip Feb 64 obit Feb 82

Handley, Harold W. Jul 60 obit Nov 72

Handlin, Oscar Jul 52

Handy, Thomas T. Sep 51 obit Jun 82

Handy, W. C. Mar 41 obit Jun 58

Haney, Fred Jan 67

Hanfmann, George M. A. Oct 67 obit May 86

Hanks, Nancy Sep 71 obit Mar 83

Hanks, Tom Apr 89

Hanley, James obit Apr 42

Hanna, Edward Joseph obit Aug 44

Hanna, William Jul 83

Hannagan, Steve Aug 44 obit Mar 53

Hannah, Daryl May 90

Hannah, John A. Oct 52 obit Apr 91

Hannan, Philip M. Jul 68

Hannegan, Robert E. Jun 44 obit Nov 49

Hannikainen, Tauno Jul 55 obit Dec 68

Hansberry, Lorraine Sep 59 obit Feb 65

Hanschman, Nancy see Dickerson, Nancy Hanschman

Hansell, Haywood S. Jan 45 obit Jan 89

Hansen, Alvin H. Sep 45 obit Aug 75

Hansen, Carl F. Oct 62

Hansen, Fred Dec 65

Hansen, H. C. Mar 56 obit Apr 60

Hansen, Harry Dec 42 obit Yrbk 91 (died Jan 77)

Hansen, James E. May 96

Hansenne, Marcel Apr 46

Hanson, Duane Oct 83 obit Mar 96

Hanson, Howard Oct 41 Sep 66 obit Apr 81

Hanson, Ole obit Sep 40

Hansson, Per Albin Oct 42 obit Nov 46

Han Suyin (WLB) Yrbk 57

Hanus, Paul H. obit Feb 42

Harada, Tasuku obit Mar 40

Harbach, Otto Jul 50 obit Mar 63

Harber, W. Elmer Mar 51

Harberger, John, John Pico see Mr. John

Harbison, John Feb 93

Harbord, James G. Mar 45 obit Sep 47

Harburg, E. Y. Jul 80 obit Apr 81

Hard, Darlene Jul 64

Hardaway, Tim Jul 98

Harden, Arthur obit Aug 40

Harden, Cecil M. Feb 49 obit Feb 85

Harden, Mrs. Frost Revere see Harden, Cecil M.

Hardenbrook, Donald J. Jul 62 obit Aug 76

Hardie, S. J. L. Jul 51

Hardin, Clifford M. May 69

Hardin, Garrett Sep 74

Harding, Allan Francis see Harding, John

Harding, John Oct 52

Harding, Margaret S. Apr 47

Harding, Nelson obit Feb 45

Hardwick, Elizabeth Feb 81

Hardwicke, Cedric Oct 49 obit Oct 64

Hardy, Ashley Kingsley obit Sep 40

Hardy, Porter, Jr. May 57 obit Jun 95

Hare, David Aug 83

Hare, Raymond A. Jul 57 obit May 94

Harewood, George Henry Hubert Lascelles, 7th Earl of see Lascelles, George Henry Hubert

Hargis, Billy James Mar 72

Hargrave, Thomas J. Apr 49 obit Apr 62

Hargrove, Marion Jun 46

Hargrove, Roy Apr 2000

Häring, Bernard Jun 69 obit Sep 98

Haring, Keith Aug 86 obit Apr 90

Harington, Charles obit Yrbk 40

Harkin, Tom Jan 92

Harkins, Paul D. Apr 64

Harkness, Douglas S. Oct 61

Harkness, Edward Stephen Jan 40

Harkness, Georgia Nov 60

Harkness, Rebekah Apr 74 obit Sep 82

Harlan, John Marshall May 55 obit Feb 72

Harlan, Otis obit Jan 40

Harlech, William David Ormsby Gore see Ormsby-Gore, David

Harmon, Ernest N. Nov 46 obit Jan 80

Harmon, Millard F. Dec 42 obit Apr 45

Harmsworth, Esmond Cecil Dec 48 obit Sep 78

Harmsworth, Harold Sidney obit Jan 41

Harnoncourt, Nikolaus Jan 91

Harnoncourt, René d' see D'harnoncourt, René

Harnwell, Gaylord P. Jun 56

Haroutunian, Khoren Der see Der Harootian, Koren

Harp, Edward B. Jr. Oct 53

Harper, Alexander James obit Nov 40

Harper, Marion, Jr. Mar 61 obit Feb 90

Harper, Samuel Northrup obit Mar 43

Harper, Theodore Acland obit Jun 42

Harper, Valerie Feb 75

Harrar, J. George Jan 64 obit Jun 82

Harrell, Lynn Feb 83

Harrelson, Ken Apr 70

Harrelson, Walter May 59

Harrelson, Woody Jan 97

Harrer, Heinrich Oct 54

Harridge, Will Sep 49 obit Jun 71

Harriman, Averill see Harriman, W. Averell

Harriman, E. Roland Mar 51 obit Apr 78

Harriman, Florence Jaffray Hurst Mar 40 obit Nov 67

Harriman, Mrs. J. Borden see Harriman, Florence Jaffray Hurst

Harriman, W. Averell Apr 41 Nov 46 obit Sep 86

Harrington, David Nov 98

Harrington, Francis Clark obit Mar 40

Harrington, Michael Jan 69 Oct 88 obit Sep 89

Harrington, Russell C. Apr 56 obit Oct 71

Harris, Arthur Travers Sep 42 obit May 84

Harris, Barbara Apr 68

Harris, Barbara C. Jun 89

Harris, Bernice Kelly (WLB) Yrbk 49

Harris, Bucky Jun 48 obit Jan 78

Harris, Cyril M. Feb 77

Harris, E. Lynn Jun 96

Harris, Emmylou Oct 94

Harris, Franco Jun 76

Harris, Fred R. Jan 68

Harris, Harwell Hamilton Jan 62 obit Jan 91

Harris, James Rendel obit Apr 41

Harris, Judith Rich Apr 99

Harris, Julie Feb 56 Aug 77

Harris, Louis May 66

Harris, Mark (WLB) Yrbk 59

Harris, Mrs. Herbert Kavanaugh see Harris, Bernice Kelly

Harris, Mrs. Irving Drought see McCardell, Claire

Harris, Oren May 56

Harris, Patricia Roberts Dec 65 obit May 85

Harris, Richard May 64

Harris, Rosemary Sep 67

Harris, Roy Aug 40 obit Nov 79

Harris, Sam H. obit Aug 41

Harris, Seymour E. Feb 65 obit Dec 74

Harris, Stanley Raymond see Harris, Bucky

Harris, Walter Jun 55

Harris, William, Jr. obit Oct 46

Harrison, Earl G. Aug 43 obit Oct 55

Harrison, George M. Jan 49 obit Jan 69

Harrison, George Nov 66 Jan 89

Harrison, Gilbert A. Mar 49

Harrison, James L. Oct 62

Harrison, Jim Jul 92

Harrison, Joan May 44 obit Oct 94

Harrison, Pat obit Aug 41

Harrison, Rex Jan 47 Feb 86 obit Jul 90

Harrison, Shelby M. Jan 43

Harrison, Wallace K. Mar 47 obit Jan 82

Harrison, William H. Feb 49 obit Jul 56

Harrison, William K. Jul 52 obit Aug 87

Harron, Marion J. Dec 49

Harron, Mary Sep 2000

Harry, Debbie Nov 81

Harsanyi, Zsolt obit Apr 44

Harsch, Joseph C. Oct 44 obit Aug 98

Hart, Albert Bushnell obit Aug 43

Hart, Basil Henry Liddell see Liddell Hart, Basil Henry

Hart, Edward J. Feb 53 obit Jun 61

Hart, Gary May 76

Hart, Kitty Carlisle Oct 82

Hart, Lorenz May 40 [Rodgers, Richard; and Hart, Lorenz] obit Feb 44

Hart, Merwin K. Oct 41 obit Jan 63

Hart, Mickey Jan 94

Hart, Moss Jul 40 Nov 60 obit Feb 62

Hart, Philip A. Sep 59 obit Feb 77

Hart, Thomas C. Jan 42 obit Sep 71

Hart, William S. obit Jul 46

Hartford, Huntington, 2d Jun 59

Hartigan, Grace Sep 62

Hartke, Vance Mar 60

Hartle, Russell P. Jun 42 obit Jan 62

Hartley, Fred A., Jr. Jun 47 obit Jun 69

Hartley, Hal Aug 95

Hartley, Marsden obit Oct 43

Hartman, David Jun 81

Hartman, Grace Nov 42 [Hartman, Paul; and Hartman, Grace] obit Oct 55

Hartman, Louis F. Jan 53 obit Nov 70

Hartman, Paul Nov 42 [Hartman, Paul; and Hartman, Grace] obit Dec 73

Hartnell, Norman May 53 obit Aug 79

Hartnett, Robert C. Dec 49

Hartung, Hans Jul 58 obit Feb 90

Hartwell, John A. obit Jan 41

Hartwell, Lee see Hartwell, Leland H.

Hartwell, Leland H. Nov 99

Hartwig, Walter obit Mar 41

Harty, Hamilton obit Apr 41

Hartzog, George B., Jr. Jul 70

Harvard, Beverly Sep 97

Harvey, E. Newton May 52

Harvey, Laurence May 61 obit Jan 74

Harvey, Paul Mar 86

Hasek, Dominik May 98

Haseltine, William A. Nov 98

Hashimoto, Ryutaro Feb 98

Haskell, Molly Nov 98

Haskell, William N. Feb 47 obit Sep 52

Haskin, Frederic J. obit Jun 44

Haskins, Caryl P. Feb 58

Haslett, Caroline Oct 50 obit Mar 57

Hasluck, Paul Oct 46

Hass, Hans Feb 55

Hass, Henry B. Apr 56 obit Apr 87

Hassan II Sep 64 obit Oct 99

Hassan, Mahmoud Jul 47

Hassanal Bolkiah see Bolkiah, Muda Hassanal

Hassel, Kai-Uwe Von May 63

Hastert, Dennis Apr 99

Hastie, William H. Mar 44 obit Jun 76

Hatch, Carl A. Dec 44 obit Nov 63

Hatch, Orrin G. Aug 82

Hatcher, Harlan Oct 55 obit May 98

Hatcher, Richard G. Feb 72

Hatfield, Mark O. Nov 59 Mar 84

Hatoyama, Ichiro May 55 obit May 59

Hatta, Mohammad Dec 49 obit Yrbk 91 (died Mar 80)

Hauck, Louise Platt obit Feb 44

Hauge, Gabriel Oct 53 obit Sep 81

Haughey, Charles J. Feb 81

Haughton, Daniel J. Sep 74 obit Aug 87

Hauptmann, Gerhart obit Jul 46

Hauser, Conrad Augustine obit Apr 43

Hauser, Gayelord Jun 55 obit Feb 85

Hauser, Helmut Eugene Benjamin Gellert see Hauser, Gayelord

Hauser, Philip M. Jul 69 obit Feb 95

Haushofer, Karl Apr 42 obit Sep 46

Havel, Václav Mar 85 Aug 95

Havill, Edward (WLB) Yrbk 52

Hawass, Zahi Apr 2000

Hawes, Elizabeth Oct 40 obit Yrbk 91 (died Sep 71)

Hawk, Tony Jun 2000

Hawke, Bob Aug 83

Hawke, Ethan May 98

Hawkes, Anna L. Rose Oct 56

Hawkes, Herbert E. obit Jun 43

Hawking, Stephen W. May 84

Hawkins, Augustus Freeman Feb 83

Hawkins, Edler G. Jan 65

Hawkins, Erick Jan 74 obit Feb 95

Hawkins, Erskine Sep 41 obit Jan 94

Hawkins, Harry C. Apr 52

Hawkins, Jack Nov 59 obit Oct 73

Hawkins, Paula Sep 85

Hawks, Howard May 72 obit Mar 80 (died Dec 77)

Hawley, Cameron (WLB) Yrbk 57

Hawley, H. Dudley obit May 41

Hawley, Paul R. Apr 46 obit Jan 66

Hawley, Willis C. obit Sep 41

Hawn, Goldie Dec 71

Haworth, Leland J. Dec 50 obit May 79

Hay, Charles M. obit Mar 45

Hay, Mrs. Dudley C. see Hay, Regina Deem

Hay, Regina Deem Jul 48

Haya De La Torre, Víctor Raúl Jun 42 obit Sep 79

Hayakawa, S. I. Nov 59 Jan 77 obit Apr 92

Hayakawa, Sessue Sep 62 obit Jan 74

Hayashi, Senjuro obit Mar 43

Haycraft, Howard Nov 41 Feb 54 obit Jan 92

Haydée, Marcia Oct 77

Hayden, Carl T. Jul 51 obit Mar 72

Hayden, Melissa May 55

Hayden, Sterling May 78 obit Jul 86

Hayden, Tom Apr 76

Hayek, Friedrich A. Von Jun 45 obit May 92

Hayes, A. J. Oct 53

Hayes, Alfred Feb 66 obit Feb 90

Hayes, Anna Hansen Nov 49

Hayes, Bob Sep 66

Hayes, Carlton Joseph Huntley Jun 42 obit Nov 64

Hayes, David V. Apr 66

Hayes, Denis Oct 97

Hayes, Helen Jan 42 Oct 56 May 93

Hayes, Isaac Oct 72

Hayes, Mrs. John E. see Hayes, Anna Hansen

Hayes, Peter Lind Mar 59 obit Jul 98

Hayes, Robert M. Apr 89

Hayes, Roland May 42 obit Mar 77

Hayes, Samuel P., Jr. Sep 54

Hayes, Samuel P. Sep 54 obit Sep 58

Hayes, Wayne Woodrow see Hayes, Woody

Hayes, Woody Feb 75 obit May 87

Haynes, George Edmund Mar 46 obit Apr 60

Haynes, Roy Asa obit Yrbk 40

Hays, Arthur Garfield Sep 42 obit Feb 55

Hays, Brooks Jan 58 obit Jan 82

Hays, Wayne L. Nov 74 obit Apr 89

Hays, Will H. Jul 43 obit Apr 54

Hayter, Stanley William Dec 45 obit Jun 88

Hayward, Leland Feb 49 obit Apr 71

Hayward, Susan May 53 obit May 75

Haywood, Allan S. May 52 obit Apr 53

Hayworth, Rita May 60 obit Jul 87

Hazard, Paul Mar 41

Hazeltine, Alan Mar 48 obit Jul 64

Hazen, Charles D. obit Nov 41

Hazzard, Shirley Jan 91

Head, Edith May 45 obit Jan 82

Head, Henry obit Yrbk 40

Head, Matthew see Canaday, John

Head, Walter W. Apr 45 obit Jun 54

Headley, Elizabeth Cavanna see Cavanna, Betty

Heald, Henry Townley Feb 52 obit Jan 76

Healey, Denis Dec 71

Healy, Bernadine P. Nov 92

Healy, Timothy S. Jan 93 obit Jan 93

Heaney, Seamus Jan 82

Heard, Alexander Nov 66

Hearne, John J. Jul 50 obit May 69

Hearnes, Warren E. Jun 68

Hearns, Thomas Mar 83

Hearst, Patricia Aug 82

Hearst, William Randolph, Jr. Oct 55 obit Jul 93

Heath, Edward Oct 62

Heath, S. Burton Jan-Feb 40 obit Sep 49

Heathcoat-Amory, Derick see Amory, Derick Heathcoat

Heatter, Gabriel Apr 41 obit May 72

Hebert, F. Edward Nov 51 obit Feb 80

Heche, Anne Sep 98

Hecht, Anthony May 86

Hecht, Ben Feb 42 obit Jun 64

Hecht, George J. Oct 47 obit Jun 80

Heckart, Eileen Jun 58

Heckerling, Amy Jul 99

Heckler, Margaret M. Aug 83

Heckscher, August [financier] obit Jun 41

Heckscher, August [foundation executive] Oct 58 obit Jun 97

Hedden, Worth Tuttle (WLB) Yrbk 57 obit Jan 86

Hedin, Sven Anders May 40 obit Jan 53

Hedtoft, Hans Mar 49 obit Mar 55

Heeney, A. D. P. Jun 53

Hees, George Oct 59

Heffner, Richard D. Oct 64

Heflin, Van Jul 43 obit Sep 71

Hefner, Christie Oct 86

Hefner, Hugh Sep 68

Hegan, Alice Caldwell see Rice, Alice Caldwell Hegan

Heidegger, Martin Jun 72 obit Jul 76

Heiden, Eric Jun 80

Heiden, Konrad Mar 44 obit Sep 75 (died Jul 66)

Heidenstam, Rolf Von Oct 51 obit Oct 58

Heidenstam, Verner Von obit Jul 40

Heifetz, Jascha Feb 44 obit Feb 88

Height, Dorothy I. Sep 72

Heilbroner, Robert L. Jun 75

Heilbrun, Carolyn G. Jan 93

Heimlich, Henry J. Oct 86

Heineman, Ben W. Jan 62

Heinemann, Gustav Jun 69 obit Aug 76

Heinlein, Robert A. Mar 55 obit Jun 88

Heinrichs, April May 2000

Heintzleman, B. Frank Jun 53 obit Sep 65

Heinz, H. J. 2d Jun 47 obit Apr 87

Heinz, John Apr 81 obit May 91

Heisenberg, Werner Apr 57 obit Mar 76

Heiser, Victor G. Apr 42 obit May 72

Heiskell, Andrew Mar 66

Heiss, Carol E. Oct 59

Hektoen, Ludvig Dec 47 obit Sep 51

Helburn, Theresa Sep 44 [Langner, Lawrence; and Helburn, Theresa] obit Nov 59

Held, Al Jan 86

Helfgott, David Mar 97

Heliker, John Jan 69 obit Jul 2000

Hélion, Jean Nov 43 obit Jan 88

Heller, John R., Jr. Feb 49 obit Jul 89

Heller, Joseph Jan 73 obit Mar 2000

Heller, Walter Wolfgang Sep 61 obit Aug 87

Hellinger, Mark Sep 47 obit Jul 48

Hellman, Lillian May 41 Jun 60 obit Aug 84

Hellyer, Paul Sep 69

Helms, Jesse A. Jul 79

Helms, Richard M. Oct 67

Helmsley, Harry B. Jun 85 obit Mar 97

Heloise Jun 96

Helpern, Milton May 73 obit Jun 77

Helpmann, Robert Feb 50 obit Nov 86

Helprin, Mark Aug 91

Helstein, Ralph Jun 48 obit May 85

Heming, Arthur Henry Howard obit Yrbk 40

Hemingway, Margaux Mar 78 obit Sep 96

Hemingway, Mary Sep 68 obit Jan 87

Hench, Philip S. Dec 50 obit May 65

Henderson, E. L. Jun 50 obit Oct 53

Henderson, Florence Apr 71

Henderson, Joe Jun 96

Henderson, Lawrence J. obit Apr 42

Henderson, Leon Jul 40 obit Jan 87

Henderson, Loy W. Mar 48 obit May 86

Henderson, Nevile Apr 40 obit Feb 43

Henderson, Rickey Sep 90

Henderson, Skitch Jul 66

Hendl, Walter Jun 55

Hendricks, Barbara Mar 89

Hendrickson, Robert C. Nov 52 obit Feb 65

Henie, Sonja Sep 40 Jan 52 obit Nov 70

Henkle, Henrietta see Buckmaster, Henrietta

Henley, Beth Feb 83

Henner, Marilu Feb 99

Henning, Doug Aug 76 obit Apr 2000

Hennings, Thomas C., Jr. Oct 54 obit Nov 60

Hennock, Frieda B. Nov 48 obit Sep 60

Henreid, Paul Jul 43 obit Jun 92

Henriot, Philippe obit Aug 44

Henry, David D. Jun 66 obit Nov 95

Henry, E. William Feb 64

Henry, Jules obit Aug 41

Henry, Marguerite (WLB) Yrbk 47

Henry, Mellinger Edward obit Mar 46

Henry, Mrs. Sidney Crocker see Henry, Marguerite

Henry-Haye, Gaston Nov 40

Hensel, H. Struve Dec 48 obit Jul 91

Henson, Jim Mar 77 obit Jul 90

Hentoff, Nat Aug 86

Henze, Hans Werner Apr 66

Hepburn, Audrey Mar 54 Mar 93

Hepburn, Katharine May 42 Nov 69

Hepburn, Mitchell F. Dec 41 obit Feb 53

Heppner, Ben Jan 97

Hepworth, Barbara Feb 57 obit Aug 75

Herbert, Bob Oct 98

Herbert, Don Feb 56

Herbert, Elizabeth Sweeney Feb 54

Herbert, Mrs. Leo J. see Herbert, Elizabeth Sweeney

Herblock see Block, Herbert L.

Herbrand Arthur Russell obit Oct 40

Herbster, Ben M. Jul 62 obit Mar 85

Hering, Hermann S. obit Jul 40

Herlihy, James Leo Sep 61 obit Jan 94

Herlin, Emil obit Feb 43

Herman, Alexis M. Jan 98

Herman, Jerry Jan 65

Herman, Mildred see Hayden, Melissa

Herman, Pee Wee see Reubens, Paul

Herman, Woody Apr 73 obit Jan 88

Hernandez, Aileen C. Jul 71

Hernandez, Keith Feb 88

Hernández, Livan Mar 98

Hernandez, Orlando Apr 2000

Hernández Colón, Rafael May 73

Hernández Martínez, Maximiliano Jun 42 obit Jun 66

Herod, William Rogers Mar 51 obit Sep 74

Herold, J. Christopher (WLB) Yrbk 59 obit Feb 65

Herrera, Carolina Mar 96

Herrera, Felipe Mar 68

Herrera, Omar Torrijos see Torrijos Herrera, Omar

Herrera, Paloma Apr 2000

Herrera Campíns, Luis Jul 80

Herrick, Elinore Morehouse Apr 47 obit Jan 65

Herrick, Francis Hobart obit Nov 40

Herring, Clyde L. obit Nov 45

Herring, Pendleton Jul 50

Herriot, Edouard Feb 46 obit Jun 57

Hersey, John Feb 44 obit May 93

Hersh, Seymour Mar 84

Hershey, Alfred D. Jul 70 obit Aug 97

Hershey, Barbara Aug 89
Hershey, Lewis B. Jun 41 Jun 51 obit Jul 77
Hershey, Milton S. obit Nov 45
Hershiser, Orel Feb 90
Hersholt, Jean Dec 44 obit Sep 56
Herskovits, Melville J. Nov 48 obit Apr 63
Herskovitz, Marshall Sep 2000
Herter, Christian A. Dec 47 Mar 58 obit Feb 67
Hertz, Alfred obit Jun 42
Hertz, Emanuel obit Jul 40
Hertzberg, Arthur Jun 75
Hertzler, Arthur E. obit Oct 46
Hertzog, James Barry Munnik obit Jan 43
Herzberg, Gerhard Feb 73 obit Jul 99
Herzog, Chaim Apr 88 obit Jun 97
Herzog, Isaac Halevi Apr 59
Herzog, Maurice Jul 53
Herzog, Paul M. Jul 45 obit Jan 87
Herzog, Werner Aug 78
Hesburgh, Theodore M. Jan 55 Jul 82
Heschel, Abraham Joshua Apr 70 obit Mar 73
Heseltine, Michael Jun 85
Hess, Dean E. Sep 57
Hess, Elmer Jan 56 obit Jun 61
Hess, Max Oct 61 obit Nov 68
Hess, Myra Sep 43 obit Jan 66
Hess, Rudolf Mar 41 obit Oct 87
Hess, Victor Francis Oct 63 obit Feb 65
Hesse, Hermann Oct 62
Hesselgren, Kerstin Jan 41 obit Oct 62
Hester, James M. Jun 62
Heston, Charlton May 57 Jul 86
Hetfield, James Jan 2000
Heusen, Jimmy Van see Van Heusen, Jimmy
Heusinger, Adolf Feb 56
Heuss, Theodor Nov 49 obit Jan 64
Heuven Goedhart, G. J. Van Oct 52 obit Sep 56

Hevesy, George De Apr 59 obit Sep 66
Heward, Leslie H. obit Jun 43
Hewart, Gordon obit Jun 43
Hewitt, Don Jun 88
Hewitt, Henry K. Apr 43 obit Nov 72
Hewlett, J. Monroe obit Dec 41
Heydrich, Reinhard Jul 42 obit Jul 42
Heydt, Herman A. obit Oct 41
Heyerdahl, Thor Dec 47 Sep 72
Heym, Stefan Mar 43
Heyman, Mrs. Marcus A. see Komarovsky, Mirra
Heymann, Lida Gustava obit Sep 43
Heyns, Roger W. Dec 68 obit Nov 95
Heyrovsk, Jaroslav Jul 61 obit May 67
Heyward, Du Bose obit Jul 40
Hiaasen, Carl Apr 97
Hibbard, Edna obit Feb 43
Hibbard, Frederick P. obit Oct 43
Hibbard, Henry D. obit Dec 42
Hibbs, Ben Jul 46 obit May 75
Hickam, Homer H. Jr. Oct 2000
Hickel, Walter J. May 69
Hickenlooper, Bourke B. May 47 obit Oct 71
Hickerson, John D. May 50 obit Apr 89
Hickey, Margaret A. Dec 44 obit Feb 95
Hickey, Thomas F. obit Feb 41
Hickman, Emily Jun 45 obit Jul 47
Hickman, Herman Nov 51 obit Jul 58
Hicks, Beatrice A. Jan 57
Hicks, Clarence J. obit Feb 45
Hicks, Granville May 42 obit Aug 82
Hicks, Henry D. Oct 56
Hicks, Louise Day Mar 74
Higgins, Andrew J. May 43 obit Sep 52
Higgins, Daniel Paul Dec 50 obit Mar 54
Higgins, Frederick Robert obit Mar 41

Higgins, Marguerite Jun 51 obit Feb 66
Higginson, William obit Sep 43
Highet, Gilbert Sep 64 obit Mar 78
Highet, Mrs. Gilbert see Macinnes, Helen
Highsmith, Patricia Jan 90 obit Apr 95
Hightower, John B. Jul 70
Hightower, John M. Nov 52 obit Apr 87
Higinbotham, William A. Feb 47 obit Jan 95
Higley, Harvey V. Oct 56 obit Jan 87
Hilaly, Ahmed Naguib Jul 52 obit Mar 59
Hildebrand, Joel H. Feb 55 obit Jul 83
Hildegarde Nov 44
Hildred, William P. Apr 56
Hildreth, Horace A. Oct 48 obit Jul 88
Hilfiger, Tommy Apr 96
Hill, Abram Aug 45 obit Nov 86
Hill, Anita Sep 95
Hill, Arthur M. Oct 48 obit Nov 72
Hill, Arthur Mar 77
Hill, Benny Feb 83 obit Jun 92
Hill, Billy obit Feb 41
Hill, David G. Apr 60
Hill, Edwin C. Sep 40 obit Apr 57
Hill, Frank Pierce obit Oct 41
Hill, George Roy Apr 77
Hill, George Washington Jun 46
Hill, Graham Jul 73 obit Jan 76
Hill, Harry W. Jul 50 obit Sep 71
Hill, Helen obit May 42
Hill, Herbert Sep 70
Hill, Howard Copeland obit Aug 40
Hill, J. B. P. Clayton obit Jul 41
Hill, Julia "Butterfly" Apr 2000
Hill, Justina Hamilton Apr 41
Hill, Lister Oct 43 obit Feb 85
Hill, Mrs. Eben Clayton see Bailey, Carolyn Sherwin
Hill, Patty Smith obit Jun 46

Hofmann, Hans Oct 58 obit Mar 66

Hofmann, Klaus H. Apr 61

Hofstadter, Richard Oct 56 obit Dec 70

Hofstadter, Robert Oct 62 obit Jan 91

Hogan, Ben Oct 48 obit Oct 97

Hogan, Frank S. Sep 53 obit May 74

Hogan, Hulk Nov 98

Hogan, Paul Aug 87

Hogben, Lancelot Dec 41 obit Jan 84

Hoge, James F., Jr. Apr 98

Hogg, Quintin McGarel Sep 57

Hoggart, Richard Oct 63

Hogwood, Christopher Jul 85

Hohenlohe-Waldenburg, Stefanie Richter, Princess Jan-Feb 40

Hohenzollern, Friedrich Wilhelm Victor Albert obit Jul 41 [Wilhelm II]

Hoiby, Lee Mar 87

Holaday, William M. May 58

Holaday, William Perry obit Mar 46

Holberg, Mrs. Richard A. see Holberg, Ruth Langland

Holberg, Ruth Langland (WLB) Yrbk 49

Holbrook, Hal May 61

Holbrook, Sabra Nov 48

Holbrooke, Richard C. Oct 98

Holcomb, Thomas Jul 42 obit Jul 65

Holden, Louis Edward obit Jun 42

Holden, William Jun 54 obit Jan 82

Holder, Geoffrey Oct 57

Holenstein, Thomas May 58 obit Jan 63

Holifield, Chet Oct 55 obit Apr 95

Holladay, Billie see Holladay, Wilhelmina

Holladay, Wilhelmina Oct 87

Holland, Agnieszka Jan 98

Holland, Charles Thurstan obit Mar 41

Holland, Kenneth Mar 52 obit Feb 78

Holland, Sidney Jan 50 obit Nov 61

Holland, Spessard L. Feb 50 obit Dec 71

Hollander, Jacob Harry obit Sep 40

Hollander, John Sep 91

Hollenbeck, Don Feb 51 obit Sep 54

Holley, Edward G. Jun 74

Holley, Robert W. Jan 67 obit Apr 93

Holliday, Jennifer Jun 83

Holliday, Judy Apr 51 obit Jul 65

Holliger, Heinz Jan 87

Hollings, Ernest F. Jul 82

Hollister, John B. Oct 55

Hollomon, J. Herbert Mar 64 obit Aug 85

Holloway, James L., Jr. Jan 47

Holloway, Stanley Feb 63 obit Mar 82

Holm, Celeste Apr 44

Holm, Hanya Jul 54 obit Jan 93

Holman, Eugene May 48 obit Oct 62

Holmes, Burton May 44 obit Oct 58

Holmes, D. Brainerd Mar 63

Holmes, Jesse Herman obit Jul 42

Holmes, John Haynes Jan 41 obit May 64

Holmes, Julius C. Feb 45 obit Sep 68

Holmes, Larry Aug 81

Holmes, Phillips obit Oct 42

Holmes, Robert D. Jul 58

Holmgren, Mike Oct 2000

Holroyd, Michael Mar 89

Holsti, Rudolf obit Sep 45

Holt, Andrew David Nov 49 obit Sep 87

Holt, Arthur E. obit Mar 42

Holt, Cooper T. Jul 57

Holt, Hamilton Dec 47 obit May 51

Holt, Harold E. Oct 66 obit Feb 68

Holt, Isabella (WLB) Yrbk 56 obit May 62

Holt, John Jun 81 obit Nov 85

Holt, Rackham Apr 44

Holton, Linwood Feb 71

Holtz, Jackson J. Mar 50

Holtz, Lou Jun 89

Holtzman, Elizabeth Nov 73

Holyfield, Evander Aug 93

Holyoake, Keith Jacka Feb 63 obit Feb 84

Holzer, Jenny Jun 90

Home, Alexander Frederick Douglas-Home, 14th Earl of see Douglas-Home, Alexander Frederick

Homer, Arthur B. Jul 52 obit Sep 72

Honecker, Erich Apr 72 obit Jul 94

Honegger, Arthur Apr 41 obit Feb 56

Honeywell, Annette Jul 53

Honeywell, Harry E. obit Jan 40

Honjo, Shigeru, Baron obit Jan 46

Hoo, Victor Mar 47 obit Jul 72

Hood, Clifford F. Apr 53 obit Jan 79

Hook, Sidney Oct 52 Apr 88 obit Sep 89

Hooker, John Lee Nov 92

Hooks, Bell Apr 95

Hooks, Benjamin L. Apr 78

Hooks, Robert Mar 70

Hooper, C. E. Apr 47 obit Feb 55

Hooper, Franklin Henry obit Oct 40

Hoopes, Darlington Sep 52 obit Nov 89

Hooton, Earnest Albert Yrbk 40 obit Jun 54

Hoover, Herbert, Jr. Oct 54 obit Sep 69

Hoover, Herbert Mar 43 obit Jan 65

Hoover, J. Edgar Feb 40 May 50 obit Jun 72

Hoover, Lou Henry see Hoover, Mrs. Herbert

Hoover, Mrs. Herbert obit Feb 44

Hope, Bob Jun 41 Oct 53

Hope, Clifford R. May 53 obit Jul 70

Hope, Leslie Townes see Hope, Bob

Hope, Stanley C. May 59 obit Oct 82

Hope, Victor Alexander John Jan 42 obit Feb 52

Hope Namgyal, Maharani of Sikkim Feb 67

Hopkins, Alfred obit Jul 41

Hopkins, Arthur Jun 47 obit Apr 50

Hopkins, Ernest Martin Oct 44 obit Oct 64

Hopkins, Harry Lloyd Feb 41 obit Mar 46

Hopkins, John Jay Mar 54 obit Jul 57

Hopkins, Louis Bertram obit Sep 40

Hopkins, Nevil Monroe obit May 45

Hoppe, Willie Jun 47 obit Apr 59

Hoppenot, Henri Etienne Mar 44

Hopper, Dennis Aug 87

Hopper, Edward Dec 50 obit Jul 67

Hopper, Hedda Nov 42 obit Mar 66

Horder, Thomas J. Horder, 1st Baron Jul 44 obit Oct 55

Hore-Belisha, Leslie Horebelisha, 1st Baron Jul 41 obit May 57

Horgan, Paul Feb 71 obit May 95

Horgan, Stephen H. obit Oct 41

Horlick, William Jr. obit Apr 40

Hormel, James Oct 99

Hormel, Jay C. Jul 46 obit Oct 54

Horn, Carl Von Nov 67

Horn, Roy Uwe Ludwig see Roy

Hornblow, Arthur, Sr. obit Jun 42

Hornby, Leslie see Twiggy

Horne, Charles F. obit Nov 42

Horne, John E. Dec 52 obit Apr 85

Horne, Lena Jun 44 Nov 85

Horne, Marilyn Jul 67

Horner, H. Mansfield Oct 55 obit Jul 83

Horner, Henry obit Nov 40

Horner, James Mar 97

Horner, John R. Sep 92

Horner, Matina Souretis Jul 73

Horney, Karen Aug 41 obit Jan 53

Hornig, Donald F. May 64

Hornsby, Rogers Sep 52 obit Feb 63

Hornung, Paul Feb 63

Horowitz, Vladimir Sep 43 Mar 66 obit Jan 90

Horrocks, Brian Jan 45 obit Mar 85

Horsbrugh, Baroness Florence Feb 52 obit Mar 70

Horsfall, Frank L., Jr. Mar 41 Jan 61 obit Apr 71

Horst Jun 92 obit Mar 2000

Horthy, Stephen obit Oct 42

Horthy De Nagybánya, Nicholas Oct 40 obit Apr 57

Horton, Edward Everett Dec 46 obit Nov 70

Horton, Mildred McAfee see McAfee, Mildred H.

Horwich, Frances Oct 53

Horwich, Mrs. Harvey L. see Horwich, Frances

Horwood, William T. F. obit Feb 44

Hoshino, Naoki Nov 40

Hoskins, Bob Sep 90

Hoskins, Lewis M. Sep 50

Hosmer, Craig May 58 obit Mar 83

Hosokawa, Morihiro May 94

Hottel, Althea Kratz Oct 48

Hough, Henry Hughes obit Oct 43

Houghton, Alanson B. obit Nov 41

Houghton, Amory Jan 47 obit Apr 81

Houghton, Mrs. Hiram Cole Sep 50

Hou Hsiao-hsien Jul 99

Houk, Ralph Jul 62

Houle, Cyril O. May 62

Hounsfield, Godfrey Newbold Mar 80

Houphouët-Boigny, Félix Oct 58 Jul 91 obit Feb 94

Hours-Miédan, Magdeleine Apr 61

Houseman, John Jul 59 Apr 84 obit Jan 89

Houser, Theodore V. Mar 57 obit Feb 64

Houssay, Bernardo Alberto Jan 48 obit Nov 71

Houston, Andrew Jackson obit Aug 41

Houston, Charles H. Jul 48 obit Jun 50

Houston, David Franklin obit Oct 40

Houston, James A. Jul 87

Houston, Robert Griffith obit Mar 46

Houston, Whitney Nov 86

Houtte, Jean Van Mar 52

Hovde, Bryn J. Jan 46 obit Oct 54

Hovey, Otis Ellis obit Jun 41

Hoveyda, Amir Abbas Oct 71 obit Jun 79

Hovhaness, Alan Apr 65 obit Oct 2000 obit oct 2000

Hovick, Rose Louise see Lee, Gypsy Rose

Hoving, Jane Pickens Langley see Pickens, Jane

Hoving, Thomas Apr 67

Hoving, Walter Sep 46 obit Feb 90

Howar, Barbara Aug 89

Howard, Alice Sturtevant obit Nov 45

Howard, Bart B. Jan-Jun 40 obit Apr 41

Howard, Cordelia see Macdonald, Cordelia Howard

Howard, Elizabeth (WLB) Yrbk 51

Howard, Elston Apr 64 obit Feb 81

Howard, Frank Jan 72

Howard, John Mar 99

Howard, Katherine G. Jul 53

Howard, Leslie obit Jul 43

Howard, Mrs. Charles P. see Howard, Katherine G.

Howard, Mrs. Henry see Howard, Alice Sturtevant

Howard, Ron Jan 79 Aug 95

Howard, Roy Wilson Nov 40 obit Jan 65

Howard, Trevor Jul 64 obit Feb 88

Howe, C. D. Sep 45 obit Feb 61

Howe, Frederic Clemson obit Sep 40

Howe, Geoffrey Oct 80

Howe, Gordie Mar 62

Howe, Gordon see Howe, Gordie

Howe, Harold, 2d Nov 67

Howe, Harrison E. obit Feb 43

Howe, Helen (WLB) Yrbk 54 obit Mar 75

Howe, Irving Apr 78 obit Jul 93

Howe, James Wong Feb 43 obit Sep 76

Howe, Quincy Nov 40 obit Apr 77

Howe, Samuel B. obit Apr 41

Howe, Tina Jan 90

Howell, Charles R. Feb 54
obit Sep 73

Howell, Wallace E. Jul 50 obit
Sep 99

Howell, William H. obit Mar
45

Howley, Christine Wetherill
see Leser, Tina

Howorth, Lucy Somerville
Oct 51 obit Nov 97

Howorth, Mrs. Joseph Mar-
ion see Howorth, Lucy
Somerville

Howrey, Edward F. Jul 53

Hoxha, Enver Jan 50 obit Jun
85

Hoxie, Charles A. obit Dec 41

Ho Ying-Chin Oct 42 obit Jan
88

Hoyle, Fred Apr 60

Hoyt, Palmer Sep 43 obit Aug
79

Hrawi, Elias Feb 92

Hrdlicka, Ales Nov 41 obit
Oct 43

Hrdy, Sarah Blaffer Jun 2000

Hruska, Roman Lee Jul 56
obit Jul 99

Hsiao-ping, Teng see Deng
Xiaoping

Hsiung, S.-F Jul 42

Hsiung, Shih-hui see Hsiung,
S.-F

Hua Guofeng Mar 77

Hua Kuo-feng see Hua
Guofeng

Hubbard, Bernard Jul 43 obit
Jul 62

Hubbard, Margaret Ann
(WLB) Yrbk 58

Hubeny, Maximilian J. obit
Sep 42

Huberman, Bronislaw Jul 41
obit Jul 47

Huck, Arthur Feb 57 obit Mar
73

Huckel, Oliver, Rev. obit Jan
40

Huddleston, Trevor Oct 63
obit Jul 98

Hudleston, Edmund C. May
51

Hudlin, Reginald May 99

Hudlin, Warrington May 99

Hudson, C. W. obit Jun 43

Hudson, Charles L. Apr 67
obit Nov 92

Hudson, Harold W. obit Mar
43

Hudson, Henrietta obit May
42

Hudson, Jeffery see Crichton,
Michael

Hudson, Manley O. Jun 44
obit Jun 60

Hudson, Robert S. Nov 42
obit Apr 57

Hudson, Rock Oct 61 obit
Nov 85

Huebner, Clarence R. Oct 49
obit Nov 72

Huebner, Robert J. Sep 68
obit Nov 98

Huerta, Dolores Nov 97

Huffington, Arianna Stassi-
nopoulos Jul 98

Hufstedler, Shirley M. May
80

Huggins, Charles B. Feb 65
obit Mar 97

Huggins, Godfrey Nov 56 obit
Jun 71

Hughes, Barnard Sep 81

Hughes, Cathy Feb 2000

Hughes, Charles Evans Jul 41
obit Oct 48

Hughes, Edward Everett obit
Jan 40

Hughes, Edward James see
Hughes, Ted

Hughes, Emmet John Jan 64
obit Nov 82

Hughes, Harold E. Jun 63 obit
Jan 97

Hughes, Hatcher obit Nov 45

Hughes, Howard Apr 41 obit
May 76

Hughes, John Sep 91

Hughes, Langston Oct 40 obit
Jul 67

Hughes, Martha Groomes see
Hughes, Toni

Hughes, Paul Dec 43

Hughes, R. O. Oct 50

Hughes, Richard J. Jul 62 obit
Feb 93

Hughes, Robert May 87

Hughes, Rowland R. Feb 56
obit Jun 57

Hughes, Sarah T. Nov 50 obit
Jul 85

Hughes, Ted Jun 79 obit Jan
99

Hughes, Toni May 41

Hughley, D. L. Mar 2000

Huizenga, H. Wayne Jan 95

Hulcy, Dechard A. Sep 51

Hull, Bobby Oct 66

Hull, Brett Feb 92

Hull, Cordell Aug 40 obit Oct
55

Hull, Helen R. May 40 obit
Sep 71

Hull, John Adley obit Jun 44

Hull, John E. Apr 54

Hull, Josephine Oct 53 obit
May 57

Hull, William Edward obit
Jul 42

Humbard, Rex Sep 72

Humbert II, King of Italy see
Umberto II, King of Italy

Hume, Edgar Erskine Aug 44
obit Mar 52

Hume, T. C. obit Dec 43

Humphrey, Doris Apr 42
[Humphrey, Doris; and
Weidman, Charles] obit
Mar 59

Humphrey, George M. Feb 53
obit Mar 70

Humphrey, Helen F. Nov 52
obit Oct 63

Humphrey, Hubert H. Jul 49
Apr 66 obit Mar 78

Humphreys, Harry E., Jr. Nov
49 obit Nov 67

Humphry, Derek Mar 95

Hun, John Gale obit Nov 45

Hung-chun, Yu see Yui, O. K.

Hunsaker, Jerome C. Oct 42
obit Nov 84

Hun Sen Apr 90

Hunt, Bunker Aug 80

Hunt, H. L. Jan 70 obit Jan 75

Hunt, Helen Nov 96

Hunt, Herold C. May 56 obit
Jan 77

Hunt, James B., Jr. Jun 93

Hunt, John Oct 54 [Hunt,
John; Hillary, Edmund;
and Tenzing Norkey] obit
Jan 99

Hunt, Lester C. Mar 51 obit
Sep 54

Hunt, Linda Jan 88

Hunt, Mabel Leigh (WLB)
Yrbk 51

Hunter, Alberta May 79 obit
Jan 85

Hunter, Catfish May 75 obit
Nov 99

Hunter, Croil Jul 51 obit Oct
70

Hunter, Dard Sep 60 obit Mar 66

Hunter, Evan (WLB) Yrbk 56

Hunter, Glenn obit Mar 46

Hunter, Holly Jul 94

Hunter, Jim see Hunter, Catfish

Hunter, Kermit May 59

Hunter, Kim May 52

Hunter, Ross Dec 67 obit May 96

Hunter-Gault, Charlayne Apr 87

Hunthausen, Raymond G. Aug 87

Huntington, Anna Hyatt Oct 53 obit Dec 73

Huntley, Chester Robert see Huntley, Chet

Huntley, Chet Oct 56 obit May 74

Huntly, Frances E. see Mayne, Ethel C.

Huntziger, Charles Dec 41 obit Dec 41

Huppert, Isabelle Nov 81

Hurd, Douglas Feb 90

Hurd, Peter Oct 57 obit Sep 84

Hurley, Charles F. obit May 46

Hurley, Laurel Jun 57

Hurley, Patrick J. Nov 44 obit Sep 63

Hurley, Roy T. Jun 55 obit Dec 71

Hurok, Sol Sep 41 Apr 56 obit Apr 74

Hurston, Zora Neale May 42 obit Apr 60

Hurt, John Jan 82

Hurt, William May 86

Hurtado, Cesar Barros see Barros Hurtado, César

Hurtado, Miguel de la Madrid see De La Madrid, Miguel

Husak, Gustav Oct 71 obit Jan 92

Hu Shih Feb 42 obit Apr 62

Husing, Edward Britt see Husing, Ted

Husing, Ted Jun 42 obit Oct 62

Hussein, Ahmed Mar 56 obit Feb 85

Hussein, King of Jordan Jul 55 Apr 86 obit Apr 99

Hussein, Saddam Sep 81

Hussein, Taha Oct 53 obit Dec 73

Husseini, Faisal al- see Al-Husseini, Faisal

Hussein I, King of Hashemite Jordan see Hussein, King of Jordan

Hussein Ibn Talal see Hussein, King of Jordan

Husted, Marjorie Child Jun 49 obit Feb 87

Huston, Anjelica Jul 90

Huston, John Feb 49 Mar 81 obit Oct 87

Huston, Walter Feb 49 obit May 50

Hutcheson, William L. Sep 43 obit Jan 54

Hutchins, Robert Maynard Yrbk 40 Feb 54 obit Jul 77

Hutchinson, Paul Dec 49 obit Jun 56

Hutchinson, Ray Coryton Nov 40

Hutchison, Bruce Oct 56

Hutchison, Kay Bailey Sep 97

Hutchison, Miller Reese obit Apr 44

Hutton, Betty Jun 50

Hutton, Lauren Jul 94

Hutton, Maurice obit May 40

Hutton, Mrs. Lee W. Feb 48

Huxley, Julian Aug 42 Oct 63 obit Apr 75

Huxtable, Ada Louise Mar 73

Hu Yaobang Nov 83 obit Jun 89

Hwang, David Henry May 89

Hyatt, Anna see Huntington, Anna Hyatt

Hyde, H. Van Zile May 60

Hyde, Henry J. Oct 89

Hyderabad, Usman Ali, Nizam of see Usman Ali, Nizam of Hyderabad

Hylton-Foster, Harry Jan 61 obit Nov 65

Hymans, Paul obit Apr 41

Hynde, Chrissie Apr 93

Hynek, J. Allen Dec 68 obit Jun 86

Hyvernat, Henry, Mgr. obit Jul 41

Hy Yao-pang see Hu Yaobang

Iacocca, Lee A. Oct 71 Oct 88

Iakovos, Archbishop Jul 60

Ibáñez, Carlos Dec 52 obit Jul 60

Ibarra, Jose Maria Velasco see Velasco Ibarra, José María

Ibárruri, Dolores Jun 67 obit Jan 90

Ibn Saud, King of Saudi Arabia Feb 43 obit Jan 54

Icahn, Carl C. Apr 86

Ice-T Sep 94

Ickes, Harold L. Jul 41 obit Mar 52

Idei, Nobuyuki Mar 97

Idell, Albert E. Oct 43 obit Oct 58

Idleman, Finis Schuyler, Rev. obit May 41

Idol, Billy Jan 94

Idris al-Sanussi, Emir Muhammed see Idris I, King of Libya

Idris I, King of Libya Jan 56 obit Jul 83

Idris Senussi I see Idris I, King of Libya

Igleheart, Austin S. Oct 50

Iglesias, Enrique Apr 99

Iglesias, Julio Jun 84

Iglesias, Roberto Feb 60

Iglesias, Santiago Jan 40

Igoe, Herbert A. obit Apr 45

Ikeda, Hayato May 61 obit Oct 65

Ilg, Frances L. Sep 56 [Ilg, Frances L; and Ames, Louise] obit Sep 81

Iliescu, Ion Jun 90

Illia, Arturo Jan 65 obit Mar 83

Illich, Ivan Dec 69

Ilsley, J. L. Feb 48

Il Sung, Kim see Kim Il Sung

Iman Jun 95

Imlay, L. E. obit Aug 41

Impellitteri, Vincent R. Feb 51 obit Mar 87

Imus, Don Feb 96

Ince, Godfrey Sep 43

Indiana, Robert Mar 73

Indigo Girls Aug 98

Infeld, Leopold May 41 Jul 63 obit Mar 68

Ingalls, Jeremy (WLB) Yrbk 54 obit Jul 2000

Ingalls, Mildred Dodge Jeremy see Ingalls, Jeremy

Inge, William Jun 53 obit Jul 73

Ingersoll, Ralph Jul 40 obit
    May 85
Ingersoll, Raymond Vail obit
    Mar 40
Ingersoll, Royal E. Oct 42 obit
    Jul 76
Ingles, Harry C. Nov 47
Inglis, John J. obit Oct 46
Ingram, Jonas H. Apr 47 obit
    Oct 52
Innaurato, Albert Mar 88
Innes, Hammond (WLB)
    Yrbk 54
Innis, Roy May 69
Innocenti, Ferdinando Feb
    59 obit Jul 66
Inonu, Ismet Mar 41 Oct 64
    obit Feb 74
Inouye, Daniel K. May 60 Sep
    87
Inverchapel of Loch Eck,
    Archibald John Kerr Clark
    Kerr, 1st Baron see Kerr,
    Archibald Clark
Ionesco, Eugène Oct 59 obit
    Jun 94
Ireland, Patricia Jun 92
Irene Jun 46 obit Jan 63
Irons, Ernest E. Oct 49 obit
    Apr 59
Irons, Jeremy Aug 84
Ironside, Edmund May 40
Ironside, Henry Allan Feb 45
    obit Feb 51
Ironside, William Edmund
    Ironside, 1st Baron obit
    Nov 59
Irvan, Ernie Jul 98
Irvine, Alexander Fitzgerald,
    Rev. obit May 41
Irving, Frederick A. Mar 51
Irving, John Oct 79
Irving, Jules Jul 70 obit Sep
    79
Irwin, Bill Oct 87
Irwin, Elisabeth obit Dec 42
Irwin, Helen G. Oct 52
Irwin, Margaret (WLB) Yrbk
    46 obit Yrbk 91 (died Dec
    67)
Irwin, Robert B. Mar 48 obit
    Jan 52
Irwin, Robert Jan 93
Irwin, Steve Aug 2000
Isaacs, George Oct 45
Isaacs, Susan Oct 93
Isaak, Chris May 93
Iselin, Columbus O'D Nov 48
    obit Feb 71

Isham, Norman obit Feb 43
Isherwood, Christopher Oct
    72 obit Feb 86
Ishibashi, Tanzan Mar 57 obit
    Jun 73
Ishiguro, Kazuo Sep 90
Ishimoto, Tatsuo Apr 56
Ismay, Hastings Lionel Apr
    43 obit Feb 66
Isozaki, Arata Apr 88
Israel, Edward L., Rabbi obit
    Dec 41
Istomin, Eugene Oct 77
Italiaander, Rolf Jun 64
Italiano, Annemarie see Ban-
    croft, Anne
Itami, Juzo May 90 obit Mar
    98
Ittner, Martin H. Nov 42 obit
    May 45
Iturbi, José Sep 43 obit Aug
    80
Iverson, Kenneth R. Apr 51
Ives, Burl Jan 46 May 60 obit
    Jun 95
Ives, Charles Jun 47 obit Jul
    54
Ives, Irving M. Feb 48 obit
    Apr 62
Ives, James E. obit Feb 43
Ivey, John E., Jr. Jul 60 obit
    Aug 92
Ivey, Judith Jun 93
Ivins, Molly Jun 2000
Ivory, James Jul 81
Izac, Edouard V. M. Dec 45
    obit Mar 90
Izetbegovic, Alija Aug 93

J. S. of Dale see Stimson, Fre-
    deric Jesup
Jabbar, Kareem Abdul see
    Abdul-Jabbar, Kareem
Jabotinsky, Vladimir
    Evgenevich obit Sep 40
Jacinto, Domenich Felipe see
    Dali, Salvador
Jack, Homer A. Jul 61 obit
    Oct 93
Jack, William S. Mar 44
Jackson, Anne Sep 80
Jackson, Bo Jun 91
Jackson, C. D. Oct 51 obit
    Nov 64
Jackson, Charles May 44 obit
    Nov 68
Jackson, Chevalier Jul 40
Jackson, Daniel Dana obit Oct
    41

Jackson, Eugene B. Jun 61
Jackson, F. J. F. obit Jan 42
Jackson, Glenda Dec 71
Jackson, Henry M. Oct 53 Oct
    79 obit Oct 83
Jackson, Janet Jun 91
Jackson, Jesse Dec 70 Jan 86
Jackson, Jesse L., Jr. May 98
Jackson, Joe [comedian] obit
    Jul 42
Jackson, Joe [musician] Feb
    96
Jackson, Lady see Ward, Bar-
    bara
Jackson, Mahalia Oct 57 obit
    Mar 72
Jackson, Maynard Holbrook,
    Jr. Sep 76
Jackson, Michael Nov 83
Jackson, Phil Jul 92
Jackson, Reggie Jan 74
Jackson, Robert H. Mar 40
    Oct 50 obit Dec 54
Jackson, Samuel L. Nov 96
Jackson, Shirley Ann Jul 99
Jackson, William H. Mar 51
    obit Nov 71
Jackson, William K. Jul 46
    obit Dec 47
Jacob, François Dec 66
Jacob, John E. Feb 86
Jacobi, Derek May 81
Jacobi, Victor obit Nov 42
Jacobs, Amos see Thomas,
    Danny
Jacobs, Jane Mar 77
Jacobs, Joe obit Jan 40
Jacobs, Marc Feb 98
Jacobs, Philip Peter obit Aug
    40
Jacobs, Randall Aug 42 obit
    Oct 67
Jacobs, W. W. obit Oct 43
Jacobson, Leon Oct 62 obit
    Feb 93
Jacobsson, Per Oct 58 obit
    Jun 63
Jacopi, Giulio Jan 59
Jaden, Donna Mae see Paige,
    Janis
Jaffe, Harold W. Sep 92
Jaffe, Susan Sep 97
Jagan, Cheddi Apr 63 obit
    May 97
Jagendorf, Moritz Adolf
    (WLB) Yrbk 52
Jagger, Bianca Apr 87
Jagger, Mick Dec 72

Jagr, Jaromir Apr 97
Jahn, Helmut Feb 89
Jaipur, Maharani of Mar 68
Jakes, John Sep 88
Jakobovits, Immanuel Jun 88 obit Feb 2000
Jamali, Mohd F. Jan 54 obit Aug 97
James, Alexander R. obit Apr 46
James, Arthur Curtiss obit Jul 41
James, Arthur Horace Jul 40 obit Jun 73
James, Charles Jul 56
James, Clive Nov 84
James, Daniel, Jr. Mar 76 obit Apr 78
James, F. Cyril Oct 56
James, Harry Sep 43 obit Aug 83
James, P. D. Aug 80
James, W. Frank obit Jan 46
James, Will obit Nov 42
Jameson, William J. Jul 54
Jamieson, J. K. Jun 74
Jamieson, Leland obit Sep 41
Jamison, Judith Jan 73
Janas, Sigmund Apr 50
Janeway, Eliot Sep 70 obit Apr 93
Janeway, Elizabeth Mar 44
Janis, Byron Jun 66
Janis, Sidney Jul 70 obit Jan 90
Janney, Russell Mar 47 obit Sep 63
Janov, Arthur May 80
Janowitz, Tama Aug 89
Jansen, Dan Sep 94
Jansen, William Oct 51 obit Apr 68
Janson, Paul Emile obit Aug 44
Janssen, Charles L. obit Mar 41
Janssen, David Mar 67 obit Apr 80
Janssens, Jean Baptiste see Janssens, John Baptist
Janssens, John Baptist Sep 59 obit Dec 64
Jarman, Sanderford Sep 42 obit Dec 54 Yrbk 55
Jarmusch, Jim Apr 90
Jarreau, Al Oct 92
Jarrett, Keith May 85
Jarring, Gunnar V. Oct 57

Jaruzelski, Wojciech Mar 82
Järvi, Neeme Nov 93
Jarvik, Robert K. Jul 85
Jarvis, Howard Feb 79 obit Sep 86
Jarvis, Lucy Apr 72
Jarvis, Robert Y. obit Dec 43
Jastrow, Joseph obit Feb 44
Jastrow, Robert Jan 73
Javacheff, Christo Vladmirov see Christo
Javits, Jacob K. Jun 48 Oct 58 obit Apr 86
Jaworski, Leon Jun 74 obit Feb 83
Jay, Peter Oct 78
Jay, Ricky May 94
Jayewardene, J. R. Jan 84 obit Jan 97
Jayewardene, Junius Richard see Jayewardene, J. R.
Jaynes, Clare (WLB) Yrbk 54
Jazy, Michel Apr 67
Jeanmaire, Renée Nov 52
Jeanneret-Gris, Charles-Edouard see Le Corbusier
Jeans, James Hopwood Apr 41 obit Oct 46
Jebb, Gladwyn Dec 48
Jeffers, William M. Nov 42 obit Apr 53
Jefferson, Margo L. Jun 99
Jelliffe, Smith Ely obit Oct 45
Jellinek, Elvin M. May 47 obit Jan 64
Jemison, Mae C. Jul 93
Jencks, Christopher Apr 73
Jenkins, Hayes Alan May 56
Jenkins, Lew Jan 41 obit Yrbk 91 (died Oct 81)
Jenkins, Macgregor obit Apr 40
Jenkins, Ray H. Jun 54 obit Feb 81
Jenkins, Roy Mar 66 Oct 82
Jenkins, Sara (WLB) Yrbk 53
Jenks, Leon E. obit Mar 40
Jenner, Bruce Aug 77
Jenner, William E. Jun 51 obit May 85
Jennings, B. Brewster May 51 obit Dec 68
Jennings, John (WLB) Yrbk 49
Jennings, Paul Dec 69 obit Oct 87
Jennings, Peter Nov 83
Jennings, Waylon Apr 82

Jensen, Arthur R. Jan 73
Jensen, Ben F. Feb 60 obit Apr 70
Jensen, Jack Eugene see Jensen, Jackie
Jensen, Jackie Jun 59 obit Oct 82
Jensen, Mrs. Clyde R. see Bard, Mary
Jensen, Mrs. Oliver see Stafford, Jean
Jensen, Oliver O. May 45
Jernegan, John D. Nov 59
Jerusalem, Siegfried Sep 92
Jessel, George Mar 43 obit Jul 81
Jessup, Philip C. Apr 48 obit Mar 86
Jester, Beauford H. Jul 48 obit Sep 49
Jett, Joan Sep 93
Jewett, Frank B. Dec 46 obit Jan 50
Jewett, James R. obit May 43
Jewison, Norman Jun 79
Jhabvala, Ruth Prawer Mar 77
Jiang Qing see Chiang Ching-Kuo Jun 75 obit Jan 92
Jiang Zemin May 95
Jillette, Penn Jun 2000 [Penn and Teller]
Jiménez, Juan Ramón Feb 57 obit Sep 58
Jimenez, Marcos Perez see Pérez Jiménez, Marcos
Jimerson, Earl W. Sep 48 obit Dec 57 Yrbk 58
Jingsheng, Wei see Wei Jingsheng
Jinnah, Mohammed Ali May 42 obit Oct 48
Jobert, Michel Feb 75
Jobim, Antonio Carlos Jul 91 obit Feb 95
Jobs, Steven Mar 83 Sep 98
Jodl, Alfred obit Nov 46
Jodoin, Claude Mar 56
Joel, Billy Sep 79
Joesten, Joachim Jun 42
Joffrey, Robert Nov 67 obit Nov 88
Johannesen, Grant Jun 61
Johanson, Donald C. Feb 84
Johansson, Ingemar Nov 59
John XXIII, Pope Feb 59 obit Jul 63
John, Augustus Oct 41 obit Jan 62

John, Elton Mar 75
John, Tommy Oct 81
John Paul I, Pope Nov 78 obit Jan 79
John Paul II Nov 79 Mar 2000
Johns, Glynis Sep 73
Johns, Jasper May 67 May 87
Johnson, Alexander obit Jul 41
Johnson, Alvin Aug 42 obit Jul 71
Johnson, Amy obit Feb 41
Johnson, Arnold M. Oct 55 obit May 60
Johnson, Arthur Newhall obit Sep 40
Johnson, Ben Jun 88
Johnson, Bernice see Reagon, Bernice Johnson
Johnson, Betsey Jan 94
Johnson, Beverly Sep 94
Johnson, C. Oscar Feb 48 obit Jan 66
Johnson, Charles Sep 91
Johnson, Charles Spurgeon Nov 46 obit Jan 57
Johnson, Clarence L. Oct 68 obit Mar 91
Johnson, Claudia Alta Oct 64
Johnson, Clifton obit Jan 40
Johnson, Crockett Dec 43 obit Jan 84
Johnson, Daniel Nov 67 obit Nov 68
Johnson, Davey Sep 99
Johnson, David M. Jul 52
Johnson, Don Apr 86
Johnson, Douglas Wilson obit Apr 44
Johnson, Dwayne "The Rock" Jul 2000
Johnson, Earvin Jan 82
Johnson, Ed Dec 46 obit Jul 70
Johnson, Edward Mar 43 obit Jun 59
Johnson, F. Ross May 89
Johnson, Frank M. Aug 78 obit Oct 99
Johnson, Hall Jan 45 obit Jun 70
Johnson, Harold K. May 66 obit Nov 83
Johnson, Harold Ogden Sep 40 [Olsen, John Sigvard; and Johnson, Harold Ogden] obit Apr 62
Johnson, Herschel V. Jul 46

Johnson, Hewlett May 43 obit Dec 66
Johnson, Hiram Feb 41 obit Sep 45
Johnson, Holgar J. Mar 50
Johnson, Howard A. Apr 64 obit Sep 74
Johnson, Howard B. Sep 66
Johnson, Howard E. obit Jun 41
Johnson, Hugh S. Sep 40 obit Jun 42
Johnson, J. Monroe Feb 45 obit Sep 64
Johnson, Jack obit Jul 46
Johnson, Jimmy Jul 94
Johnson, John H. Oct 68
Johnson, Joseph B. Jul 56
Johnson, Joseph E. Nov 50 obit Jan 91
Johnson, Joseph T. Feb 52
Johnson, Kathie Lee see Gifford, Kathie Lee
Johnson, Keyshawn Oct 99
Johnson, Lady Bird see Johnson, Claudia Alta
Johnson, Leroy Sep 49 obit Jun 61
Johnson, Loren obit Feb 42
Johnson, Louis A. Jun 42 Apr 49 obit May 66
Johnson, Lyndon B. Jan 51 Mar 64 obit Mar 73
Johnson, Magic see Johnson, Earvin
Johnson, Malcolm Jun 49 obit Aug 76
Johnson, Marguerite Annie see Angelou, Maya
Johnson, Michael Jul 96
Johnson, Mordecai Wyatt Apr 41
Johnson, Nelson T. Jan-Feb 40 obit Feb 55
Johnson, Nicholas Mar 68
Johnson, Nunnally Aug 41 obit May 77
Johnson, Osa Apr 40 obit Feb 53
Johnson, Pamela Hansford (WLB) Yrbk 48 obit Aug 81
Johnson, Paul B. obit Feb 44
Johnson, Paul Sep 94
Johnson, Philip G. obit Nov 44
Johnson, Philip Oct 57 Nov 91
Johnson, Rafer Jun 61
Johnson, Randy Sep 2000

Johnson, Robert L. [publisher] Mar 48 obit Feb 66
Johnson, Robert L. [television executive] Apr 94
Johnson, Robert Wood Nov 43 obit Mar 68
Johnson, Roy W. May 58 obit Oct 65
Johnson, Sonia Feb 85
Johnson, Thomasina Walker Mar 47
Johnson, Thor Oct 49 obit Mar 75
Johnson, U. Alexis Oct 55 obit Jun 97
Johnson, Van Jul 45
Johnson, Virginia E. Apr 76
Johnson, Virginia May 85
Johnson, Walter Apr 57 obit Sep 85
Johnson, Wendell Apr 59 obit Nov 65
Johnson, William E. obit Mar 45
Johnston, Alvanley Jun 46 obit Nov 51
Johnston, Clem D. May 55 obit Jan 80
Johnston, Eric A. Apr 43 Oct 55 obit Oct 63
Johnston, Lynn Feb 98
Johnston, Olin D. Nov 51 obit Jun 65
Johnston, Victor Jul 49 obit May 67
Johnston, Wayne A. May 51 obit Feb 68
Johnstone, Margaret Blair, Rev. Jan 55
Johnstone-Wilson, Angus Frank see Wilson, Angus
Jolie, Angelina Oct 2000
Joliot-Curie, Frederic Oct 46 obit Oct 58
Joliot-Curie, Irène Apr 40 obit May 56
Jolson, Al Nov 40 obit Dec 50
Jónasson, Hermann Aug 41
Jones, Arthur Creech Jan 48 obit Jan 65
Jones, Barry Mar 58
Jones, Bill T. Jul 93
Jones, Billy obit Jan 41
Jones, Buck obit Jan 43
Jones, Candy Oct 61 obit Mar 90
Jones, Carolyn Mar 67 obit Sep 83
Jones, Cherry May 98

Jones, Chester Lloyd obit Mar 41

Jones, Chuck May 96

Jones, Clara Stanton Jul 76

Jones, David C. Jul 82

Jones, David Robert *see* Bowie, David

Jones, E. Stanley May 40 obit Mar 73

Jones, George Feb 95

Jones, Grace Sep 87

Jones, Grover obit Nov 40

Jones, Harold Spencer Mar 55 obit Jan 61

Jones, Howard P. Jul 63 obit Nov 73

Jones, Idwal (WLB) Yrbk 48 obit Jan 65

Jones, Jack *see* Jones, John Joseph May 76

Jones, James Earl Sep 69 Nov 94

Jones, James Larkin *see* Jones, Jack

Jones, James R. Oct 81

Jones, Jennifer May 44

Jones, Jerry May 96

Jones, Jesse H. Oct 40 obit Sep 56

Jones, Joe Oct 40 obit Jun 63

Jones, John Daniel obit Jun 42

Jones, John Joseph Nov 40 obit Jan 42

Jones, K. C. Feb 87

Jones, Kimberly Denise *see* Lil' Kim

Jones, Leroi May 70

Jones, Lewis Webster Oct 58

Jones, Marion Oct 98

Jones, Marvin Aug 43 obit Jan 84

Jones, Norman L. obit Jan 41

Jones, Preston Feb 77 obit Nov 79

Jones, Quincy Feb 77

Jones, Rickie Lee May 90

Jones, Robert Edmond Nov 46 obit Jan 55

Jones, Roger W. Nov 59 obit Aug 93

Jones, Roy Jr. Feb 99

Jones, Rufus Matthew Oct 41 obit Sep 48

Jones, Russell Oct 57 obit Aug 79

Jones, Sam Houston Mar 40 obit Yrbk 91 (died Feb 78)

Jones, Shirley Oct 61

Jones, Tom Apr 70

Jones, Tommy Lee Oct 95

Jong, Erica Jul 75 Apr 97

Jonsson, John Erik Jan 61 obit Nov 95

Jooss, Kurt Jul 76 obit Jul 79

Jooste, G. P. Apr 51

Joplin, Janis Mar 70 obit Mar 70

Jordan, B. Everett Nov 59 obit May 74

Jordan, Barbara C. Sep 74 Apr 93 obit Apr 96

Jordan, Frank C. obit Apr 41

Jordan, Hamilton Aug 77

Jordan, I. King Jan 91

Jordan, James Edward *see* Jordan, Jim

Jordan, Jim Nov 41 obit May 88

Jordan, Marian Nov 41 obit Jun 61

Jordan, Michael H. Feb 98

Jordan, Michael Sep 87 Feb 97

Jordan, Mildred (WLB) Yrbk 51

Jordan, Neil Aug 93

Jordan, Sara M. Mar 54 obit Jan 60

Jordan, Vernon E., Jr. Feb 72 Aug 93

Jordan, Virgil Oct 47 obit Jun 65

Jordan, W. K. Mar 55 obit Jul 80

Jordana, Francisco Gomez Mar 44

Jorgensen, Anker Sep 78

Joseph, Keith Feb 75 obit Feb 95

Joseph, Mrs. Robert H. *see* de Jong, Dola

Joseph, Sister Mary Dec 42

Joseph, Stephen C. Jan 89

Josephs, Devereux C. Jul 53 obit Mar 77

Josephson, Walter S. obit Mar 40

Jospin, Lionel Robert Jun 2000

Jouhaux, Léon Jan 48 obit Jul 54

Jourdan, Louis Jan 67

Jouvet, Louis Oct 49 obit Oct 51

Jowitt, William Allen Jowitt, 1st Earl Aug 41 obit Nov 57

Joxe, Louis Apr 61 obit Jun 91

Joy, C. Turner Jun 51 obit Sep 56

Joyce, J. Avery Mar 59

Joyce, James obit Mar 41

Joyner, Florence Griffith *see* Griffith Joyner, Florence

Joyner-Kersee, Jackie Jul 87

Juan Carlos, Count of Barcelona *see* Carlos, Juan

Juan Carlos, Prince of Spain *see* Carlos, Prince Juan

Juan Carlos I, King of Spain *see* Carlos, Prince Juan

Judd, Ashley Feb 2000

Judd, Charles Hubbard obit Sep 46

Judd, Nadine *see* Nerina, Nadia

Judd, Walter H. Sep 49 obit Apr 94

Judd, Wynonna *see* Wynonna

Judds *see* Wynonna

Judge, Mike May 97

Judson, Arthur Aug 45 obit Mar 75

Judson, Clara Ingram (WLB) Yrbk 48

Judson, Mrs. James McIntosh *see* Judson, Clara Ingram

Juin, Alphonse Aug 43 obit Mar 67

Jules-Bois, H. A. obit Aug 43

Julia, Raul Sep 82 obit Jan 95

Julian, Percy Lavon Sep 47 obit Jan 75

Juliana, Queen of The Netherlands Sep 44 Jan 55

Julia y Araelay, Raul Rafael Carlos *see* Julia, Raul

Jumblatt, Kamal Jan 77 obit Jan 77

Jung, Andrea May 2000

Jung, Carl Gustav Apr 43 Oct 53 obit Sep 61

Jurgensen, Sonny Jun 77

Just, Ward May 89

Justo, Agustin P. obit Mar 43

Kabakov, Ilya Apr 98

Kádár, János May 57 obit Aug 89

Kadare, Ismail Feb 92

Kael, Pauline Mar 74

Kaempffert, Waldemar B. Sep 43 obit Feb 57

Kagan, Henry Enoch Sep 65 obit Oct 69

Kaganovich, Lazar M. Apr 42 Oct 55 obit Sep 91

Kagawa, Toyohiko Sep 41
obit Jun 60
Kagey, Rudolf obit Jun 46
Kahal, Irving obit Apr 42
Kahane, Meir Oct 72 obit Jan
91
Kahane, Melanie Jul 59 obit
Feb 89
Kahmann, Chesley (WLB)
Yrbk 52
Kahn, Albert obit Sep 42
Kahn, Alfred E. Mar 79
Kahn, Ely Jacques Aug 45
obit Nov 72
Kahn, Gus obit Dec 41
Kahn, Herman Oct 62 obit
Aug 83
Kahn, Louis I. Oct 64 obit
May 74
Kahn, Madeline May 77 obit
Mar 2000
Kahn, Roger Jun 2000
Kaifu, Toshiki Jun 90
Kain, Karen May 80
Kainen, Jacob Feb 87
Kaiser, Edgar F. Sep 64 obit
Feb 82
Kaiser, Henry J. Oct 42 Mar
61 obit Nov 67
Kaiser, Jakob Feb 56 obit Jul
61
Kaiser, John B. May 43
Kaiser, Philip M. Oct 49
Kaiser Wilhelm II see Hohen-
zollern, Friedrich Wilhelm
Victor Albert
Kai-shek, Chiang see Chiang
Kai-Shek
Kalb, Marvin Jul 87
Kalich, Mrs. Jacob see Picon,
Molly
Kalikow, Peter S. Sep 88
Kaline, Al Dec 70
Kalinin, Mikhail Ivanovich
Jun 42 obit Jul 46
Kallay, Nicholas De Jun 42
obit May 67
Kallay de Nagy Kallo, Miklos
see Kallay, Nicholas De
Kallen, Horace M. Oct 53 obit
Apr 74
Kallio, Kyosti obit Feb 41
Kalmus, Herbert T. Feb 49
obit Sep 63
Kaltenborn, Hans Von Aug
40 obit Sep 65
Kaltenbrunner, Ernst Apr 43
obit Nov 46
Kamali, Norma Nov 98

Kamau, Johnstone see Ken-
yatta, Jomo
Kaminska, Ida Nov 69 obit
Jul 80
Kaminski, Janusz Mar 2000
Kaminsky, Mel see Brooks,
Mel
Kampelman, Max M. Jul 86
Kampmann, Viggo Jan 61 obit
Jul 76
Kamprad, Ingvar Jun 98
Kanawa, Kiri Te see Te
Kanawa, Kiri
Kander, Lizzie Black obit Sep
40
Kandinsky, Wassily obit Feb
45
Kane, Harnett T. (WLB) Yrbk
47 obit Yrbk 84
Kane, Joseph Nathan Nov 85
Kania, Stanislaw Jun 81
Kanin, Garson Jan 41 Oct 52
obit Jun 99
Kan-In, Prince Kotohito obit
Jun 45
Kanter, Albert L. Jul 53
Kanter, Rosabeth Moss Jun 96
Kantor, Michael see Kantor,
Mickey
Kantor, Mickey Mar 94
Kantrowitz, Adrian Oct 67
Kantrowitz, Arthur Oct 66
Kanzler, Ernest C. Apr 42 obit
Feb 68
Kapar, Karl obit Jun 41
Kapell, William May 48 obit
Jan 54
Kapitza, P. L. Oct 55 obit May
84
Kaplan, Joseph Oct 56 obit
Nov 91
Kaplan, Justin Jul 93
Kapp, Joe Sep 75
Kappel, Frederick R. Mar 57
obit Jan 95
Kapuscinski, Ryszard Sep 92
Karadic, Radovan Oct 95
Karajan, Herbert von Oct 56
Sep 86 obit Sep 89
Karamanlis, Constantine see
Caramanlis, Constantine
Karami, Rashid Nov 59 obit
Jul 87
Karan, Donna Aug 90
Kardelj, Edvard Dec 49 obit
Apr 79
Karelitz, George B. obit Mar
43

Karfiol, Bernard Nov 47 obit
Oct 52
Karinska, Barbara Jan 71
Karloff, Boris Mar 41 obit
Mar 69
Karmal, Babrak Mar 81 obit
Feb 97
Karman, Theodore von see
Von Kármán, Theodore
Karmazin, Mel May 2000
Karno, Fred obit Nov 41
Karolyi, Bela Oct 96
Karp, David (WLB) Yrbk 57
obit Feb 2000
Karpov, Anatoly Nov 78
Karsh, Yousuf Dec 52 Feb 80
Karsner, David obit Apr 41
Kartawidjaja, Djuanda see
Djuanda
Kasavubu, Joseph Mar 61
obit May 69
Kasdan, Lawrence May 92
Kase, Toshikazu Apr 57
Kasem, Casey Nov 97
Kasich, John R. Aug 98
Kasner, Edward Nov 43 obit
Mar 55
Kasparov, Gary Apr 86
Kassebaum, Nancy Landon
Feb 82
Kassem, Abdul Karim Nov 59
obit Mar 63
Kast, Ludwig W. obit Oct 41
Kasten, Bob see Kasten, Rob-
ert W.
Kasten, Robert W. Jun 89
Kastenmeier, Robert W. Jul
66
Kastler, Alfred Dec 67 obit
Mar 84
Kästner, Erich Jul 64 obit Oct
74
Kaszon, Hans Heinrich Thys-
sen-Bornemisza De see
Thyssen-Bornemisza De
Kaszon, Hans Heinrich
Katayama, Tetsu Jan 48
Katchalski, Ephraim see
Katzir, Ephraim
Katchor, Ben May 2000
Katsh, Abraham I. Mar 62
obit Oct 98
Katz, Alex Jul 75
Katz, Joel see Grey, Joel
Katz, Label A. Apr 60 obit
Jun 75
Katz, Lillian Vernon see Ver-
non, Lillian

Katz, Milton Oct 50 obit Oct 95

Katzen, Mollie Oct 96

Katzenbach, Nicholas Deb Jul 65

Katzenberg, Jeffrey May 95

Katzir, Ephraim Jan 75

Katz-Suchy, Juliusz Jun 51 obit Dec 71

Kauffmann, Henrik Apr 56 obit Jul 63

Kaufman, Cy see Coleman, Cy

Kaufman, George S. Aug 41 obit Sep 61

Kaufman, Henry Aug 81

Kaufman, Irving R. Apr 53 obit Apr 92

Kaunda, Kenneth Jul 66

Kaup, Felix F., Father obit Apr 40

Kaur, Rajkumari Amrit Oct 55 obit Mar 64

Kavanagh, Dan see Barnes, Julian

Kavner, Julie Oct 92

Kawabata, Yasunari Mar 69 obit Jun 72

Kawakami, Jotaro Mar 63 obit Jan 66

Kawakubo, Rei Aug 99

Kay, Beatrice Dec 42

Kay, Hershy Mar 62 obit Feb 82

Kaye, Danny Dec 41 Nov 52 obit Apr 87

Kaye, Nora Jan 53 obit Apr 87

Kay-Scott, Cyril see Wellman, Frederick Creighton

Kazan, Elia Jan 48 Oct 72

Kazanjian, Arlene Francis see Francis, Arlene

Kazantzakis, Nikos Jul 55 obit Jan 58

Kazin, Alfred May 66 obit Aug 98

Keach, Stacy Nov 71

Kean, Thomas H. Jul 85

Keane, Doris obit Jan 46

Kearns, Carroll D. Sep 56

Kearns, Doris see Goodwin, Doris Kearns

Kearns, Mrs. Carroll D see Kearns, Nora Lynch

Kearns, Nora Lynch Sep 56

Keating, Kenneth B. Oct 50 obit Jun 75

Keating, Paul May 92

Keaton, Diane Jun 78 May 96

Keaton, Michael Jun 92

Keck, George Fred Sep 45

Keck, Lucile L. Mar 54

Keck, Mrs. George Fred see Keck, Lucile L.

Kee, Elizabeth Jan 54

Kee, John Jun 50 obit Jun 51

Kee, Mrs. John see Kee, Elizabeth

Keech, Richmond B. Mar 50

Keegan, John Oct 89

Keeler, Ruby Dec 71 obit Apr 93

Keen, Sam Feb 95

Keenan, Joseph B. Sep 46 obit Feb 55

Keenan, Mike Mar 96

Keenan, Walter Francis Jr. obit Apr 40

Keene, Christopher Mar 90 obit Jan 96

Keene, Donald Jan 88

Keeney, Barnaby C. Mar 56 obit Aug 80

Keeny, Spurgeon M. Jan 58 obit Jan 89

Keeshan, Bob May 65

Keeton, Kathy Sep 93 obit Jan 98

Kefauver, Estes Jan 49 obit Oct 63

Keighley, William Nov 48 obit Aug 84

Keillor, Garrison Aug 85

Keino, Kipchoge Jun 67

Keita, Mobida Apr 60 obit Jul 77

Keitel, Harvey Mar 94

Keitel, Wilhelm Sep 40 obit Nov 46

Keith, Dora Wheeler obit Feb 41

Keith, Harold (WLB) Yrbk 58

Kekkonen, Urho K. Sep 50 obit Oct 86

Kelberine, Alexander obit Mar 40

Keldysh, Mstislav Feb 62 obit Aug 78

Kell, Joseph see Burgess, Anthony

Kellas, Eliza obit May 43

Kellems, Vivien Sep 48 obit Mar 75

Keller, Helen Dec 42 obit Jul 68

Keller, James Oct 51 obit Apr 77

Keller, K. T. May 47 obit Feb 66

Keller, Kasey Nov 98

Kelley, Augustine B. Apr 51 obit Feb 58

Kelley, Clarence M. May 74 obit Nov 97

Kelley, David E. May 98

Kelley, Edgar Stillman obit Jan 45

Kelley, Kitty Apr 92

Kellner, Erica see Anderson, Erica

Kellogg, John Harvey obit Feb 44

Kellogg, Remington Nov 49

Kellogg, Winthrop N. Apr 63

Kelly, E. Lowell Mar 55 obit Apr 86

Kelly, Edna F. Mar 50 obit Feb 98

Kelly, Ellsworth May 70

Kelly, Emmett Jul 54 obit May 79

Kelly, Eugene Curran see Kelly, Gene

Kelly, Florence Finch obit Jan 40

Kelly, Gene Dec 45 Feb 77 obit Apr 96

Kelly, Grace see Grace, Princess of Monaco

Kelly, Howard A. obit Mar 43

Kelly, Jim Nov 92

Kelly, Joe Jun 45 obit Jul 59

Kelly, John B., Jr. Jun 71 obit Apr 85

Kelly, Joseph William see Kelly, Joe

Kelly, Judith Oct 41 obit Jul 57

Kelly, Mervin J. Oct 56 obit May 71

Kelly, Mrs. Norman H. see Kelly, Regina Z.

Kelly, Nancy Jun 55 obit Mar 95

Kelly, Patrick Sep 89 obit Mar 90

Kelly, Petra Mar 84 obit Jan 93

Kelly, R. Jun 99

Kelly, Regina Z. (WLB) Yrbk 56

Kelly, Robert see Kelly, R.

Kelly, Sharon Pratt Nov 92

Kelly, Walt Oct 56 obit Dec 73

Kelman, Charles D. Jun 84

Kelsen, Hans Sep 57 obit Jun 73

Kelsey, Frances O. Apr 65

Kem, James P. Oct 50 obit Apr 65

Kemeny, John G. Feb 71 obit Feb 93

Kemmerer, E. W. Oct 41 obit Feb 46

Kemmis, Daniel Oct 96

Kemp, Hal obit Feb 41

Kemp, Jack Mar 80

Kemper, James S. Apr 41 obit Nov 81

Kempner, Robert M. W. May 43 obit Oct 93

Kempton, Murray Jun 73 obit Jul 97

Kemsley, James Gomer Berry, 1st Viscount see Berry, James Gomer

Kendall, Edward C. Dec 50 obit Jun 72

Kendall, William Mitchell obit Oct 41

Kendrew, John C. Oct 63 obit Nov 97

Kendrick, Baynard Feb 46 obit May 77

Keneally, Thomas Jun 87

Kennan, George F. Oct 47 Jan 59

Kennedy, Anthony M. Jul 88

Kennedy, Arthur Nov 61

Kennedy, Claudia J. Jan 2000

Kennedy, David M. Jun 69 obit Jul 96

Kennedy, Donald Jul 84

Kennedy, Edward Moore Sep 63 Oct 78

Kennedy, Jacqueline see Onassis, Jacqueline Kennedy

Kennedy, John B. Feb 44 obit Oct 61

Kennedy, John F., Jr. Jan 96 obit Sep 99

Kennedy, John F. Jun 50 Jul 61 obit Jan 64

Kennedy, Joseph P., 2d Jun 88

Kennedy, Joseph P. Nov 40 obit Jan 70

Kennedy, Nigel Jul 92

Kennedy, Paul Oct 93

Kennedy, Robert F. Feb 58 obit Jul 68

Kennedy, Rose Nov 70 obit Mar 95

Kennedy, Stephen P. Jun 56 obit Jan 79

Kennedy, Thomas Jun 60 obit Feb 63

Kennedy, William May 85

Kennedy, William P. Jan 50 obit Jul 68

Kennelly, Ardyth (WLB) Yrbk 53

Kennelly, Martin H. Dec 49 obit Jan 62

Kenney, George C. Jan 43 obit Oct 77

Kennon, Robert F. Oct 54 obit Apr 88

Kenny, Elizabeth Oct 42 obit Jan 53

Kenny G Nov 95

Kent, Allegra Mar 70

Kent, Corita Feb 69 obit Nov 86

Kent, George Edward Alexander Edmund, Duke of obit Oct 42

Kent, Raymond A. obit Apr 43

Kent, Rockwell Nov 42 obit Apr 71

Kenton, Stan Jun 79

Kenyatta, Jomo Oct 53 Apr 74 obit Oct 78

Kenyon, Dorothy Apr 47 obit Apr 72

Kenyon, Helen Oct 48

Kepes, György Mar 73

Kepler, Asher Raymond, Rev. obit Oct 42

Keppel, Francis May 63 obit Apr 90

Kerensky, Alexander Dec 66 obit Sep 70

Kerkorian, Kirk May 75 Mar 96

Kern, Jerome Jun 42 obit Dec 45

Kernan, W. F. Apr 42

Kerner, Otto Oct 61 obit Jul 76

Kerouac, Jack Nov 59 obit Dec 69

Kerr, Archibald Clark Dec 42 obit Sep 51 [Inverchapel of Loch Eck, Archibald John Kerr Clark Kerr, 1st Baron]

Kerr, Clark Apr 61

Kerr, Deborah Sep 47

Kerr, James W. Oct 59

Kerr, Jean Jul 58

Kerr, Mrs. Walter F see Kerr, Jean

Kerr, Robert Samuel May 50 obit Feb 63

Kerr, Steve Oct 98

Kerr, Walter Oct 53 obit Jan 97

Kerrey, Bob Feb 91

Kerrl, Hanns obit Feb 42

Kerry, John Jun 88

Kerst, Donald William Apr 50 obit Oct 93

Kersten, Charles J. Sep 52

Kertész, André Aug 79 obit Nov 85

Kesey, Ken May 76

Kesselring, Albert Nov 42 obit Oct 60

Kessing, O. O. Jun 49 obit Mar 63

Kessler, David A. Sep 91

Kessler, Henry H. Oct 57

Kestnbaum, Meyer May 53 obit Feb 61

Ketcham, Hank Jan 56

Kettering, Charles Franklin May 40 Dec 51 obit Feb 59

Kevorkian, Jack Sep 94

Key, Ben Witt obit Jul 40

Key, William S. Jul 43 obit Mar 59

Keyhoe, Donald Edward Jun 56 obit Feb 89

Keynes, John Maynard Jun 41 obit May 46

Keys, Ancel Jan 66

Keys, David A. Oct 58

Keyserling, Hermann, Count obit Jun 46

Keyserling, Leon H. Jan 47 obit Sep 87

Keyworth, George A., 2d Mar 86

Khachaturian, Aram Mar 48 obit Jun 78

Khalid, ibn Abul Aziz, King of Saudi Arabia see Khalid, King of Saudi Arabia

Khalid, King of Saudi Arabia Jan 76 obit Aug 82

Khama, Seretse May 67 obit Sep 80

Khamenei, Hojatoleslam Ali Nov 87

Khan, Aga see Aga Khan, The

Khan, Begum Liaquat Ali Jul 50

Khan, Chaka Jul 99

Khan, Liaquat Ali Jun 48 obit Dec 51

Khan, Michelle *see* Yeoh, Michelle

Khan, Mohammad Ayub *see* Ayub Khan, Mohammad

Khan, Taidje *see* Brynner, Yul

Khashoggi, Adnan Mar 86

Khatami, Mohammad Apr 98

Kheel, Theodore W. Sep 64

Khoman, Thanat Mar 58

Khomeini, Ayatollah Ruholla Nov 79 obit Jul 89

Khorana, Har Gobind Dec 70

Khouri, Faris El- Sep 48 obit Feb 62

Khoury, Bechara El- Dec 51 obit Feb 64

Khrushchev, Nikita S. Jul 54 obit Oct 71

Kiam, Omar Dec 45 obit May 54

Kiarostami, Abbas Jul 98

Kidd, Isaac Campbell obit Feb 42

Kidd, Michael Mar 60

Kidder, George W. Jul 49

Kidman, Nicole Mar 97

Kiefer, Anselm Jun 88

Kienholz, Edward Aug 89 obit Aug 94

Kiepura, Jan Nov 43 obit Nov 66

Kieran, John Apr 40 obit Feb 82

Kiesinger, Kurt Georg Apr 67 obit Apr 88

Kiesler, Frederick Jan 44 obit Feb 66

Kiéslowski, Krzysztof May 95 obit May 96

Kiewiet, Cornelis de *see* De Kiewiet, Cornelis W.

Kilday, Paul J. Oct 58 obit Dec 68

Kiley, Richard Apr 73 obit May 99

Kilgallen, Dorothy Feb 52 [Kilgallen, Dorothy; and Kollmar, Richard] obit Jan 66

Kilgore, Harley M. Jun 43 obit May 56

Killanin, Michael Morris Apr 73 obit Jul 99

Killebrew, Harmon Feb 66

Killian, James R. Feb 49 May 59 obit Mar 88

Killion, George Nov 52

Killy, Jean-Claude Jun 68

Kilmer, Aline obit Dec 41

Kilmer, Mrs. Joyce *see* Kilmer, Aline

Kilmer, Val Jan 96

Kilmuir, David Patrick Maxwell Fyfe, 1st Earl of *see* Maxwell, David

Kilpatrick, James J. Jul 80

Kilpatrick, John Reed Jul 48 obit Jul 60

Kimball, Abbott May 49 obit Nov 68

Kimball, Dan A. Sep 51 obit Oct 70

Kimball, James Henry obit Feb 44

Kimball, Lindsley F. Jul 51 obit Oct 92

Kimball, Spencer W. Feb 79 obit Jan 86

Kimball, Wilbur R. obit Sep 40

Kimble, George H. T. Oct 52

Kimbrel, M. Monroe Jun 63

Kimbrough, Emily Mar 44 obit Apr 89

Kim Dae Jung Sep 85

Kim Il Sung Sep 51 Yrbk 94 obit Yrbk 94

Kim Jong Il Oct 99

Kimmel, Husband E. Jan 42 obit Jul 68

Kimpton, Lawrence A. Jun 51 obit Jan 78

Kim Sung Ju *see* Kim Il Sung

Kim Young Sam Jun 95

Kincaid, Jamaica Mar 91

Kindelberger, J. H. Mar 51 obit Oct 62

Kinder, Katharine L. May 57

Kindler, Hans Sep 46 obit Oct 49

Kiner, Ralph May 54

King, Alan Jun 70

King, Annette *see* Reid, Charlotte T.

King, B. B. Jun 70

King, Billie Jean Dec 67

King, Carole Jan 74

King, Cecil R. Feb 52 obit May 74

King, Charles Glen Dec 67 obit Mar 88

King, Coretta Scott May 69

King, Don Jun 84

King, Ernest Joseph Feb 42 obit Sep 56

King, John W. May 64 obit Nov 96

King, Larry May 85

King, Leslie Lynch, Jr. *see* Ford, Gerald R.

King, Martin Luther, Jr. May 57 May 65 obit May 68

King, Mary-Claire Feb 95

King, Mrs. Martin Luther, Jr. *see* King, Coretta

King, Muriel Apr 43 obit May 77

King, Riley B. *see* King, B. B.

King, Samuel Wilder Oct 53 obit Jun 59

King, Stephen Oct 81

King, William Lyon Mackenzie Aug 40 obit Sep 50

Kingdon, Frank Jul 44 obit Apr 72

King Hussein *see* Hussein, King of Jordan

Kingman, Dave Mar 82

Kingman, Dong Oct 62 obit Yrbk 2000

Kingsland, Lawrence C. Jan 49

Kingsley, Ben Nov 83

Kingsley, J. Donald Feb 50

Kingsley, Myra Apr 43

Kingsley, Sidney Jun 43 obit May 95

Kingsolver, Barbara Jul 94

Kingston, Maxine Hong Mar 90

Kinkade, Thomas Jun 2000

Kinkaid, Thomas C. Dec 44 obit Jan 73

Kinnear, Helen Apr 57

Kinnell, Galway Aug 86

Kinnock, Neil Apr 84

Kinsey, Alfred C. Jan 54 obit Oct 56

Kinski, Nastassja Jun 84

Kinsley, Michael May 95

Kintner, Earl W. Apr 60 obit Mar 92

Kintner, Robert E. Oct 50 obit Feb 81

Kiphuth, Robert J. H. Jun 57 obit Mar 67

Kipling, Caroline Starr Balestier obit Jan 40

Kiplinger, Willard Monroe Mar 43 Jan 62 obit Oct 67

Kipnis, Alexander Dec 43 obit Jul 78

Kipping, Norman Dec 49

Kirbo, Charles H. Sep 77 obit Nov 96

Kirby, George May 77 obit Jan 96

Kirby, Robert E. Sep 79 obit Mar 99

Kirby, Rollin Dec 44 obit Jun 52

Kirchner, Leon Dec 67

Kirchwey, Freda Dec 42 obit Feb 76

Kirchwey, George W. obit Apr 42

Kiriyenko, Sergei Aug 98

Kirk, Alan Goodrich Jul 44 obit Dec 63

Kirk, Alexander C. Feb 45

Kirk, Claude R., Jr. Oct 67

Kirk, Grayson L. May 51 obit Jan 98

Kirk, Norman T. Feb 44 obit Nov 60

Kirk, Paul G., Jr. Aug 87

Kirk, Russell Sep 62 obit Jun 94

Kirk, William T. Feb 60 obit Mar 74

Kirkland, Gelsey Oct 75

Kirkland, Lane May 80 obit Oct 99

Kirkland, Winifred Margaretta obit Jul 43

Kirkpatrick, Chris see 'N Sync

Kirkpatrick, Helen May 41

Kirkpatrick, Ivone Jun 50 obit Jul 64

Kirkpatrick, Jeane Jul 81

Kirkpatrick, Miles W. Feb 72 obit Jul 98

Kirkpatrick, Ralph Sep 71 obit Aug 84

Kirkus, Virginia May 41 Jun 54 obit Nov 80

Kirshner, Sidney see Kingsley, Sidney

Kirstein, Lincoln Dec 52 Aug 90 obit Mar 96

Kirsten, Dorothy Feb 48 obit Jan 93

Kisevalter, George obit May 41

Kishi, Nobusuke Jun 57 obit Sep 87

Kiss Apr 99

Kissin, Evgeny Nov 97

Kissin, Yevgeny see Kissin, Evgeny

Kissinger, Henry Jun 58 Jun 72

Kistiakowsky, George B. Nov 60 obit Feb 83

Kistler, Darci Oct 91

Kitaj, R. B. Apr 82

Kitano, Takeshi Jul 98

Kitchell, Iva Dec 51 obit Jan 84

Kitson, Harry Dexter Apr 51 obit Nov 59

Kitt, Eartha Apr 55

Kittikachorn, Thanom Dec 69

Kittredge, George Lyman obit Sep 41

Klahre, Ethel S. May 62

Klass, Perri May 99

Klassen, Elmer T. May 73 obit Jun 90

Klaus, Josef Jan 65

Klaus, Václav Nov 97

Klee, Paul obit Aug 40

Kleffens, Eelco Van Oct 47

Kleiber, Carlos Jul 91

Klein, Calvin Jul 78

Klein, Edward E. Sep 66 obit Sep 85

Klein, Herbert G. Feb 71

Klein, Julius Jul 48 obit May 84

Klein, Robert Mar 77

Kleindienst, Richard G. Oct 72 obit Jun 2000

Kleinsmid, Rufus B. Von Jun 58 obit Sep 64

Kleist, Paul Ludwig Von Jul 43 obit Jan 55

Kleitman, Nathaniel Oct 57 obit Jan 2000

Klemperer, Otto Mar 65 obit Sep 73

Klenze, Camillo Von obit Apr 43

Kleppe, Thomas S. Aug 76

Klimecki, Tadeusz A. obit Aug 43

Kline, Allan B. Mar 48 obit Sep 68

Kline, Clarice May 61

Kline, Kevin Jul 86

Kline, Nathan S. Oct 65 obit May 83

Klopsteg, Paul E. May 59 obit Jul 91

Kluckhohn, Clyde Nov 51 obit Oct 60

Kluge, John Sep 93

Klumpp, Theodore G. Oct 58

Knabenshue, Paul obit Mar 42

Knappstein, Karl Heinrich Feb 65

Knatchbull-Hugessen, Hughe Mar 43 obit May 71

Knaths, Karl Jul 53 obit Apr 71

Knauer, Virginia H. Apr 70

Knickerbocker, Hubert Renfro Sep 40 obit Sep 49

Knievel, Evel Feb 72

Knievel, Robert Craig see Knievel, Evel

Knight, Bobby May 87

Knight, Douglas M. May 64

Knight, Eric Mowbray Jul 42 obit Mar 43

Knight, Frances G. Oct 55 obit Nov 99

Knight, Gladys Feb 87

Knight, Goodwin Jan 55 obit Jul 70

Knight, John S. Apr 45 obit Aug 81

Knight, O. A. Jun 52

Knight, Philip H. Aug 97

Knight, Ruth Adams Aug 43 (WLB) Yrbk 55

Knipling, E. F. May 75 obit Yrbk 2000

Knoblock, Edward obit Aug 45

Knoll, Hans G. May 55

Knopf, Alfred A. Jun 43 Nov 66 obit Oct 84

Knopf, Blanche Jul 57 [Knopf, Mrs. Alfred A.] obit Jul 66

Knopf, Mrs. Alfred A. see Knopf, Blanche

Knopf, Mrs. Hans see Vanderbilt, Amy

Knopf, Sigard Adolphus obit Sep 40

Knopfler, Mark Apr 95

Knorr, Nathan H. Feb 57 obit Aug 77

Knott, Sarah Gertrude Jul 47

Knowland, William Fife Apr 47 obit Apr 74

Knowles, John H. Dec 70 obit May 79

Knowlson, James S. Nov 42

Knox, Frank Aug 40 obit Jun 44

Knox, Jean Sep 42

Knox, Louise Chambers obit Mar 42

Knox, Mrs. Charles Briggs *see* Knox, Rose Markward

Knox, Ronald Arbuthnott Jul 50 obit Nov 57

Knox, Rose Markward May 49 obit Nov 50

Knudsen, Semon E. Jan 74 obit Sep 98

Knudsen, William S. Jul 40 obit Jun 48

Knussen, Oliver Feb 94

Knuth-Winterfeldt, Kield Gustav, Count Sep 59

Knutson, Coya Mar 56 obit Jan 97

Knutson, Harold Jan 47 obit Oct 53

Kobak, Edgar Apr 47 obit Jul 62

Koch, Bill Mar 99

Koch, Ed Sep 78

Koch, Frederick H. obit Oct 44

Koch, Fred Jr. Oct 53 obit Yrbk 2000

Koch, John May 65 obit Jun 78

Koch, Kenneth Feb 78

Koch, Theodore Wesley obit May 41

Koch, William I. *see* Koch, Bill

Kock, Karin Nov 48

Koenig, Joseph-Pierre *see* Koenig, Marie Pierre

Koenig, Marie Pierre Sep 44 obit Nov 70

Koestler, Arthur Apr 43 Jan 62 obit Apr 83

Koffka, Kurt obit Jan 42

Koga, Mineichi obit Oct 43

Kohl, Helmut Aug 77

Kohler, Foy D. Jan 50 obit Mar 91

Kohler, Walter J., Jr. Jan 53 obit May 76

Kohler, Walter Jodok obit May 40

Kohout, Pavel Feb 88

Kohoutek, Lubos Jun 74

Koivisto, Mauno Sep 82

Kokoschka, Oskar Oct 56 obit Apr 80

Kolár, Jirí Apr 86

Kolarov, Vassil Dec 49 obit Mar 50

Kolb-Danvin, Mrs. Charles Louis *see* Radziwill, Catherine, Princess

Kolbe, Parke Rexford obit Apr 42

Kolff, Willem Johan May 83

Kollek, Teddy Oct 74 Mar 93

Kollmar, Richard Feb 52 [Kilgallen, Dorothy; and Kollmar, Richard] obit Feb 71

Kollontay, Alexandra Oct 43 obit Apr 52

Kolodin, Irving Jul 47 obit Jun 88

Kolvenbach, Peter-Hans May 84

Komando, Kim Sep 2000

Komar, Vitali Oct 84 [Komar, Vitaly; and Melamid, Aleskandr]

Komarovsky, Mirra Oct 53 obit Apr 99

Kominski, David Daniel *see* Kaye, Danny

Koner, Pauline Oct 64

Konev, Ivan S. Oct 43 Jan 56 obit Jul 73

Konijnenburg, Willem Adriaan Van obit Apr 43

Konoye, Fumimaro, Prince Sep 40 obit Feb 46

Konstantinu, Mrs. Ilias *see* Clark, Eugenie

Konstanty, Casimer James *see* Konstanty, Jim

Konstanty, Jim Apr 51 obit Aug 76

Koo, V. K. Wellington Jul 41 obit Jan 86

Koogle, Tim Apr 2000

Koolhaas, Rem Nov 2000

Kooning, Elaine de *see* De Kooning, Elaine

Kooning, Willem de *see* De Kooning, Willem

Koons, Jeff May 90

Koontz, Elizabeth Duncan Jan 69 obit Apr 89

Koop, C. Everett Sep 83

Kopal, Zdenek Mar 69 obit Aug 93

Kopit, Arthur L. Dec 72

Koppel, Ted Jul 84

Kopple, Barbara Jul 98

Koprowski, Hilary Mar 68

Köprülü, Fuat Jan 53 obit Sep 66

Korbut, Olga Jul 73

Korda, Alexander Sep 46 obit Mar 56

Korda, Michael Aug 85

Koreff, Nora *see* Kaye, Nora

Korizis, Alexander Mar 41 obit Mar 41

Korman, Harvey Oct 79

Kornberg, Arthur Sep 68

Körner, Theodor Jul 51 obit Mar 57

Korngold, Erich Wolfgang Mar 43 obit Feb 58

Korngold, Julius obit Oct 45

Kors, Michael Jan 2000

Korth, Fred Jul 62 obit Jan 99

Kosaka, Zentaro Sep 61

Koscow, Sophia *see* Sidney, Sylvia

Kosinski, Jerzy Mar 74 obit Jul 91

Koslowski, Leon obit Jul 44

Kossak, Zofia Jun 44 obit Jun 68

Kostelanetz, André Jul 42 obit Mar 80

Kosygin, Aleksei N. Sep 65 obit Feb 81

Kotelawala, John Oct 55

Kotschnig, Walter M. Oct 52 obit Sep 85

Kott, Jan Apr 69

Kotto, Yaphet Mar 95

Kouchner, Bernard Aug 93

Koufax, Sandy Jan 64

Koussevitzky, Mrs. Serge *see* Koussevitzky, Natalya

Koussevitzky, Natalya obit Mar 42

Koussevitzky, Serge Nov 40 obit Jul 51

Kovacs, Ernie Feb 58 obit Mar 62

Kovic, Ron Aug 90

Kowalski, Frank Jr. Jul 60 obit Dec 74

Kozlenko, William Oct 41

Kozlov, Frol R. Nov 59 obit Mar 65

Kozol, Jonathan Jan 86

Kozyrev, Andrei V. Sep 92

Kozyrev, Nikolai A. Feb 70

Kraft, Christopher C., Jr. Feb 66

Kraft, Ole Björn Feb 53

Krag, Jens Otto Oct 62 obit Aug 78

Krainik, Ardis Nov 91 obit Mar 97

Kramer, Edward Adam obit Feb 42

Kramer, Jack *see* Kramer, Jake

Kramer, Jake May 47

Kramer, John Albert *see* Kramer, Jake

Kramer, Larry Mar 94

Kramer, Stanley May 51

Kramm, Joseph Jul 52

Krampe, Hugh J. *see* O'Brian, Hugh

Krantz, Judith May 82

Krasna, Norman May 52 obit Feb 85

Krasner, Lee Mar 74 obit Aug 84

Kratz, Althea Hallowell *see* Hottel, Althea Kratz

Kraus, Alfredo Jun 87 obit Nov 99

Kraus, Hans Peter Jul 60 obit Jan 89

Kraus, Lili Oct 75 obit Jan 87

Kraus, Rene Jul 41 obit Sep 47

Krause, Allen K. obit Jul 41

Kraushaar, Otto F. Nov 49 obit Nov 89

Krauss, Alison May 97

Krautter, Elisa Bialk *see* Bialk, Elisa

Kravchenko, Victor A. Jul 46 obit Mar 66

Kravchuk, Leonid M. Jan 93

Kravis, Henry R. Mar 89

Kravitz, Lenny Apr 96

Krebs, Hans Adolf Mar 54 obit Feb 82

Krebs, Richard Julius Herman *see* Valtin, Jan

Kreisky, Bruno Sep 60 obit Sep 90

Kreisler, Fritz Jul 44 obit Mar 62

Krekeler, Heinz L. Dec 51

Kremer, Gidon Mar 85

Krenek, Ernst Jul 42 obit Feb 92

Krens, Thomas Apr 89

Krenz, Egon Mar 90

Kreps, Juanita M. Jun 77

Kress, Samuel H. Oct 55

Krick, Irving P. Jul 50 obit Sep 96

Kriebel, Hermann obit Apr 41

Krim, Mathilde Aug 87

Krips, Josef Jun 65 obit Dec 74

Krishna Menon, V. K. Mar 53 obit Nov 74

Krishnamurti, Jiddu Oct 74 obit Apr 86

Kristiansen, Mrs. Erling *see* Selinko, Annemarie

Kristofferson, Kris Nov 74

Kristol, Irving Sep 74

Kristol, William May 97

Krivitsky, Walter G. obit Mar 41

Kroc, Ray Mar 73 obit Mar 84

Krock, Arthur Feb 43 obit Jun 74

Kroeber, A. L. Oct 58 obit Dec 60

Kroft, Steve Nov 96

Krohg, Per Nov 54

Krol, John Jan 69 obit May 96

Kroll, Jack Sep 46 obit Jul 71

Kroll, John Jacob *see* Kroll, Jack

Kroll, Jules B. Feb 99

Kroll, Leon Mar 43 obit Dec 74

Krone, Julie Oct 89

Kronenberger, Louis Aug 44 obit Jul 80

Kross, Anna M. Nov 45 obit Oct 79

Krueger, Maynard C. May 40

Krueger, Walter Apr 43 obit Oct 67

Krueger, Wilhelm obit Jun 43

Krug, J. A. Oct 44 obit May 70

Kruger, Barbara Jul 95

Kruger-Gray, George obit Jun 43

Kruif, Paul De *see* De Kruif, Paul

Krupa, Gene Sep 47 obit Dec 73

Krupp, Alfred May 55 obit Oct 67

Krupsak, Mary Anne Jul 75

Krutch, Joseph Wood Nov 59 obit Jul 70

Krzyzewski, Mike Jan 97

Kubelik, Jan obit Jan 41

Kubelik, Rafael Feb 51 obit Oct 96

Kubelsky, Benjamin *see* Benny, Jack

Kubitschek, Juscelino Apr 56 obit Nov 76

Kübler-Ross, Elisabeth Jun 80

Kubly, Herbert Feb 59 obit Oct 96

Kubrick, Stanley Feb 63 obit May 99

Kuchel, Thomas H. Feb 54 obit Feb 95

Küchler, Georg Von Sep 43

Kuchma, Leonid Oct 97

Kucinich, Dennis J. Mar 79

Kucuk, Fazil *see* Kutchuk, Fazil

Kudelka, James Mar 95

Kuekes, Edward D. Mar 54 obit Mar 87

Kuhlman, Kathryn Jul 74 obit Apr 76

Kuhlmann, Frederick obit Jun 41

Kuhn, Bowie Jan 70

Kuhn, Edward W. Jun 66

Kuhn, Irene Feb 46 obit Mar 96

Kuhn, Maggie Jul 78 obit Jul 95

Kuhn, Margaret E. *see* Kuhn, Maggie

Kuiper, Gerard P. Feb 59 obit Feb 74

Kukoc, Toni Jul 97

Kulik, Grigory Jul 42

Kullmer, Ann Feb 49

Kumaratunga, Chandrika Bandaranaike Jan 96

Kumm, Henry W. Jun 55 obit Mar 91

Kundera, Milan Mar 83

Kung, H. H. Mar 43 obit Oct 67

Küng, Hans Jul 63

Kunin, Madeleine Jul 87

Kunitz, Stanley Mar 43 Nov 59

Kuniyoshi, Yasuo Jun 41 obit Jun 53

Kunstler, William M. Apr 71 obit Nov 95

Kunz, Alfred A. Dec 41

Kunz, Stanley H. obit Jun 46

Kuok, Robert Jun 98

Kuo T'ai-ch'i *see* Quo Tai-Chi

Kuralt, Charles Jul 81 obit Sep 97

Kurchatov, Igor V. Nov 57 obit Apr 60

Kureishi, Hanif Feb 92

Kurenko, Maria Sep 44

Kurosawa, Akira Apr 65 Jul 91 obit Nov 98

Kurtz, Efrem Feb 46 obit Sep 95

Kurtz, Swoosie Oct 87

Kurusu, Sabro Jan 42 obit May 54

Kusch, Polykarp Mar 56 obit May 93

Kushner, Harold S. Apr 97

Kusner, Kathy Apr 73
Kutchuk, Fazil Feb 61 obit
  Mar 84
Kuter, Laurence S. Jul 48
Kutznetov, Vassili V. Jan 56
  obit Aug 90
Kuusinen, Hertta May 49 obit
  May 74
Kuwatly, Shukri Al May 56
  obit Oct 67
Kuzmin, Iosif I. Feb 59
Kuznets, Simon May 72 obit
  Sep 85
Kuznetsov, Nikolai G. Nov 42
  obit Jan 75
Ky, Nguyen Cao Dec 66
Kylian, Jiri Sep 82
Kyprianou, Spyros May 79
Kyser, Kay Apr 41 obit Sep
  85

L. L. Cool J Nov 97
Labelle, Patti Jul 86
Labouisse, Henry R. Oct 61
  obit May 87
La Cava, Gregory Dec 41 obit
  Apr 52
Lack, Pearl see Lang, Pearl
Lacoste, Robert Nov 57
Lacroix, Christian Apr 88
Lacy, Dan Nov 54
Ladd, Alan Sep 43 obit Mar
  64
Ladurie, Emmanuel Le Roy
  see Le Roy Ladurie,
  Emmanuel
Laeri, J. Howard Sep 68 obit
  Aug 86
Lafarge, John Nov 42 obit Jan
  64
La Farge, Oliver Jan 53 obit
  Oct 63
Laffer, Arthur Feb 82
Laffoon, Ruby obit Apr 41
Lafleur, Guy Mar 80
Lafollette, Charles M. Feb 50
La Follette, Robert M. May 44
  obit Apr 53
La Fontaine, Henri obit Jul 43
Lafontaine, Oskar Sep 90
Lagardère, Jean-Luc Aug 93
Lagasse, Emeril May 99
Lagerfeld, Karl Jan 82
Lagerkvist, Pär Jan 52 obit
  Sep 74
Lagerlöf, Selma Apr 40
La Gorce, John Oliver Nov 54
  obit Feb 60

La Guardia, Ernesto de, Jr. see
  Guardia, Ernesto De La, Jr.
La Guardia, Fiorello H. Oct
  40 obit Nov 47
La Guardia, Ricardo Adolfo
  de see De La Guardia,
  Ricardo Adolfo
Lahey, Frank H. Mar 41 obit
  Sep 53
Lahr, Bert Jan 52 obit Feb 68
Laich, Katherine Jun 72
Laidlaw, Patrick Playfair obit
  Apr 40
Laidler, Harry W. Feb 45 obit
  Oct 70
Laine, Cleo Feb 86
Laine, Frankie Nov 56
Laing, Hugh Nov 46 obit Jun
  88
Laing, R. D. Mar 73 obit Mar
  89
Laird, Donald A. Sep 46
Laird, Melvin R. Nov 64
Lake, Anthony Oct 94
Lake, Harriette see Sothern,
  Ann
Lake, Simon obit Jul 45
Laker, Frederick A. Jun 78
Lalanne, Jack Oct 94
Lall, Anand see Lall, Arthur
  S.
Lall, Arthur S. Nov 56 obit
  Jan 99
Lamarsh, Judy Apr 68 obit
  Jan 81
LaMarsh, Julia Verlyn see
  Lamarsh, Judy
Lamb, Brian Feb 95
Lamb, Willis E., Jr. Mar 56
Lambert, Janet (WLB) Yrbk
  54
Lambert, Sylvester M. Oct 41
  obit Feb 47
Lambert, W. V. Nov 55
Lamberton, Robert Eneas obit
  Oct 41
Lambsdorff, Otto May 80
Lamm, Norman Sep 78
Lamm, Richard D. May 85
Lamond, Felix obit Apr 40
Lamont, Corliss Jun 46 obit
  Jul 95
Lamont, Norman Aug 92
Lamont, Thomas William
  Oct 40 obit Feb 48
Lamorisse, Albert Jun 63 obit
  Jul 70
L'amour, Louis Feb 80 obit
  Jul 88

Lancaster, Burt Jul 53 Apr 86
  obit Jan 95
Lancaster, Osbert Oct 64 obit
  Sep 86
Lance, Bert Aug 77
Lanchester, Elsa May 50 obit
  Feb 87
Land, Edwin H. Nov 53 Mar
  81 obit May 91
Land, Emory S. Sep 41 obit
  Jan 72
Landau, Jacob Dec 65
Landau, Lev Jul 63 obit May
  68
Landers, Ann Nov 57
Landes, Bertha K. obit Jan 44
Landis, James M. Mar 42 obit
  Oct 64
Landis, Kenesaw Mountain
  May 44 obit Jan 45
Landon, Alf Feb 44 obit Nov
  87
Landon, Louise see Hauck,
  Louise Platt
Landon, Margaret Feb 45 obit
  Feb 94
Landon, Michael Jul 77 obit
  Sep 91
Landowska, Wanda Nov 45
  obit Nov 59
Landrieu, Maurice Edwin see
  Landrieu, Moon
Landrieu, Moon Jan 80
Landrum, Phil M. May 60
  obit Jan 91
Landry, Tom Jun 72 obit Apr
  2000
Landsbergis, Vytautas Jul 90
Landsteiner, Karl obit Aug 43
Lane, Allen May 54 obit Sep
  70
Lane, Arbuthnot obit Mar 43
Lane, Arthur Bliss Apr 48
  obit Oct 56
Lane, Burton Mar 67 obit Mar
  97
Lane, Carl D. (WLB) Yrbk 51
Lane, Gertrude B. obit Nov 41
Lane, Keith Westmacott see
  West, Keith
Lane, Nathan Aug 96
Lane, William Arbuthnot see
  Lane, Arbuthnot
Lane, William Preston, Jr. Jun
  49 obit Apr 67
Lang, Cosmo Gordon Aug 41
  obit Jan 46
Lang, David Feb 2000
Lang, Fritz Jun 43 obit Sep 76

Lang, Helmut Apr 97
Lang, Jack Aug 83
Lang, K. D. Sep 92
Lang, Pearl Jan 70
Langan, Dory see Previn, Dory
Langdon, Harry obit Feb 45
Lange, David Sep 85
Lange, Halvard M. Nov 47 obit Jul 70
Lange, Jessica May 83
Lange, John see Crichton, Michael
Lange, Oscar Apr 46 obit Dec 65
Langella, Frank Sep 80
Langer, Susanne Katherina Knauth Nov 63 obit Sep 85
Langer, William Feb 52 obit Jan 60
Langer, William L. Dec 68 obit Feb 78
Langham, Michael Sep 65
Langley, Adria Locke Aug 45
Langlie, Arthur B. Oct 50 obit Sep 66
Langlois, Henri Jan 73 obit Mar 77
Langmuir, Arthur Comings obit Jul 41
Langmuir, Irving Mar 40 Oct 50 obit Nov 57
Langner, Lawrence Sep 44 [Langner, Lawrence; and Helburn, Theresa] obit Feb 63
Lang of Lambeth, Cosmo Gordon Lang, 1st Baron see Lang, Cosmo Gordon
Laniel, Joseph Feb 54
Lanier, Jaron Jun 97
Lanman, Charles Rockwell obit Apr 41
Lannung, Hermod Dec 49
Lansbury, Angela Sep 67
Lansbury, George obit Jan 40
Lansdowne, J. Fenwick May 70
Lansing, Sherry May 81
Lansky, Aaron Jan 97
Lanting, Frans Nov 95
Lanusse, Alejandro Agustin Apr 73 obit Nov 96
Lanvin, Jeanne obit Sep 46
Lao She see Shaw, Lau
Lapchick, Joe Jun 65 obit Oct 70
Lapham, Lewis H. Mar 89

Lapham, Roger D. Jul 48 obit May 66
Lapidus, Morris Apr 66
Lapiere, Cherilyn see Cher
Lapointe, Ernest obit Jan 42
Lapp, Ralph E. Nov 55
Lardner, Ring Jr. Jul 87
Laredo, Jaime Sep 67
Laredo, Ruth Oct 87
Largent, Steve Jun 99
Largo Caballero, Francisco obit May 46
Larkin, Oliver W. Jul 50 obit Feb 71
Larkin, Philip Jan 85 obit Feb 86
La Rocque, François
La Roe, Wilbur, Jr. Mar 48 obit Jul 57
Larrick, George P. Jun 65 obit Oct 68
Larrocha, Alicia de Jul 68
Larsen, Roy E. Sep 50 obit Oct 79
Larson, Arthur Nov 56 obit May 93
Larson, Gary Feb 91
Larson, Jess Jun 51
Larson, Leonard W. May 62 obit Nov 74
Larssen, Pedar see Mallette, Gertrude E.
Lascelles, George Henry Hubert Jan 65
Lasch, Christopher Mar 85 obit Apr 94
Lash, Joseph P. Dec 72 obit Oct 87
Lasker, Emanuel obit Mar 41
Lasker, Mary Woodard see Lasker, Mrs. Albert D.
Lasker, Mrs. Albert D. Oct 59 obit May 94
Laski, Harold Joseph Sep 41 obit Apr 50
Laski, Marghanita (WLB) Yrbk 51 obit Apr 88
Lasky, Jesse L. Apr 47 obit Mar 58
Lasorda, Tommy Feb 89
Lassaw, Ibram Jan 57
Lasser, J. K. May 46 obit Jul 54
Lasser, Louise Oct 76
Lasseter, John Jun 97
Lasswell, Harold D. Jul 47 obit Feb 79
Latham, Dana Mar 59 obit Apr 74

Latham, Harold S. Jan 50 obit Apr 69
Latham, Jean Lee (WLB) Yrbk 56
Latifah, Queen see Queen Latifah
Latouche, John T. Jun 40 obit Oct 56
Latourette, Kenneth Scott Nov 53 obit Mar 69
Lattes, C. M. G. May 49
Lattimore, Owen Dec 45 July 64 obit Jul 89
Lattre De Tassigny, Jean Jan 45 obit Feb 52
Laubach, Frank C. Feb 50 obit Sep 70
Lauda, Niki Oct 80
Lauda, Nikolaus-Andreas see Lauda, Niki
Lauder, Estée Jul 86
Läuger, Paul Oct 45 [Läuger, Paul; and Müller, Paul]
Laughlin, Clara Elizabeth obit Apr 41
Laughlin, Irwin obit Jun 41
Laughlin, James May 82 obit Jan 98
Laughton, Charles Nov 48 obit Jan 63
Laugier, Henri Jul 48
Lauper, Cyndi Aug 85
Laurel, José P. Jun 53 obit Jan 60
Lauren, Ralph Oct 80
Laurence, William L. Oct 45 obit May 77
Laurent, Robert Jul 42 obit Jun 70
Laurents, Arthur Nov 84
Lauri, Lorenzo, Cardinal obit Dec 41
Lauritzen, Jonreed (WLB) Yrbk 52
Lausche, Frank J. Apr 46 Nov 58 obit Jun 90
Lautenberg, Frank Jan 91
Lauterbach, Jacob Zallel obit Jun 42
Laval, Pierre Sep 40 obit Nov 45
Laver, Rod Feb 63
Laverty, Maura (WLB) Yrbk 47
Lavery, Emmet Jul 47
Lavery, John obit Mar 41
Lavin, Linda Nov 87
Law, Richard K. Feb 44
Law, Vernon S. Apr 61

Lee, Willis A. obit Sep 45
Lee Bum Suk Jan 49
Leech, Margaret Jul 42 Nov 60 obit Apr 74
Leech, Paul Nicholas obit Mar 41
Leedom, Boyd May 56 obit Oct 69
Lee Kuan Yew Nov 59 Jan 95
Lee Kwan Yew see Lee Kuan Yew
Leese, Oliver Dec 44 obit Yrbk 91 (died Jan 78)
Lee Teng-Hui Mar 96
Lefaucheux, Marie-Helene Oct 47 obit Apr 64
Lefebvre, Marcel Mar 78 obit May 91
Lefévre, Théo Jun 62 obit Nov 73
Leffingwell, R. C. Mar 50 obit Dec 60
Lefrak, Samuel J. Jan 70
Le Gallienne, Eva Oct 42 Mar 55 obit Aug 91
Léger, Alexis Saint-Léger Apr 61 obit Nov 75
Léger, Fernand Jan 43 obit Oct 55
Léger, Jules Nov 76 obit Jan 81
Léger, Paul-Émile May 53 obit Jan 92
Le Guin, Ursula K. Jan 83
Leguizamo, John Apr 98
Lehman, Herbert Henry Jan 43 Jul 55 obit Jan 64
Lehman, John F., Jr. Nov 85
Lehmann, George obit Dec 41
Lehmann, Inge Nov 62
Lehmann, Lotte May 41 Jul 70 obit Oct 76
Lehmann-Haupt, Hellmut E. Apr 42 Mar 61 obit May 92
Lehrbas, Lloyd Jun 40 Apr 50 obit Jan 65
Lehrer, James see Lehrer, Jim
Lehrer, Jim Jan 87
Lehrer, Tom Jul 82
Leiber, Judith Sep 96
Leibovitz, Annie Oct 91
Leibowitz, Samuel S. Jan 53 obit Mar 78
Leigh, Douglas May 40 obit May 2000
Leigh, Jennifer Jason Aug 92
Leigh, Mike Jun 94
Leigh, Mrs. William Robinson see Traphagen, Ethel

Leigh, Robert D. Jun 47 obit Mar 61
Leigh, Vivien Jul 46 obit Oct 67
Leigh, W. Colston Jan 42 obit Sep 92
Leigh-Fermor, Patrick see Fermor, Patrick Leigh
Leigh-Mallory, Trafford L. Mar 44 obit Mar 45
Leighton, Margaret Carver (WLB) Yrbk 52
Leighton, Margaret Mar 57 obit Mar 76
Leighton, Robert B. Jul 66 obit May 97
Leinsdorf, Erich May 40 Oct 63 obit Nov 93
Leiper, Henry Smith Nov 48 obit Mar 75
Leiserson, William M. Feb 42 obit Apr 57
Leisk, David Johnson see Johnson, Crockett
Leith-Ross, Frederick Oct 42
Lejeune, John A. obit Jan 43
Lelong, Lucien Nov 55 obit Sep 58
Lelouch, Claude Nov 82
Lem, Stanislaw Oct 86
Lemass, Sean F. Mar 60 obit Jun 71
Lemay, Curtis E. Dec 44 Nov 54 obit Nov 90
Lemieux, Mario Aug 88
Lemkin, Raphael May 50 obit Nov 59
Lemmon, Jack Feb 61 Aug 88
Lemnitzer, Lyman L. Nov 55 obit Jan 89
Lemon, Ralph Feb 97
Lemond, Greg Oct 89
Lemonnier, André Nov 52 obit Jul 63
Lendl, Ivan Sep 84
L'engle, Madeleine Jan 97
Lengyel, Emil Feb 42 obit Apr 85
Lenhart, Jason Gregory see Gregory, Paul
Lennon, John Dec 65 obit Feb 81
Lennox, Annie May 88
Lennox-Boyd, Alan Tindal Jun 56 obit May 83
Leno, Jay Jun 88
Lenroot, Katharine F. May 40 Nov 50 obit Yrbk 91 (died Feb 82)

Lentaigne, Walter D. A. Jul 44 obit Oct 55
Lenya, Lotte Jun 59 obit Jan 82
Leonard see Hackett, Buddy
Leonard, Bill Nov 60 obit Feb 95
Leonard, Eddie obit Sep 41
Leonard, Edward F. obit Jan 41
Leonard, Elmore Sep 85
Leonard, Hugh Apr 83
Leonard, Lucille Putnam Feb 53 [Leonard, Mrs. Newton P.]
Leonard, Mrs. Newton P see Leonard, Lucille Putnam
Leonard, Sugar Ray Feb 81
Leonard, William A. see Leonard, Bill
Leone, Giovanni May 72
Leone, Lucile Petry see Petry, Lucile
Leoni, Raúl Oct 64 obit Sep 72
Leonid Danilovich Kuchma see Kuchma, Leonid
Leonidoff, Leon Jul 41 obit Oct 89
Leonov, Aleksei Jul 65
Leontief, Wassily Jan 67 obit Apr 99
Leopold, Alice K. Jan 55
Leopold III, King of The Belgians Dec 44 obit Nov 83
Lepage, Robert Apr 95
Le Pen, Jean-Marie Jan 88
Lepofsky, Manford see Lee, Manfred B.
Leppard, Raymond Mar 80
Lequerica Y Erquiza, José Félix De Jun 51 obit Jul 63
Lercaro, Giacomo Cardinal Sep 65 obit Jan 77
Lerch, Archer L. Nov 45 obit Oct 47
Lerman, Liz Nov 2000
Lerner, Alan Jay Jul 58 [Lerner, Alan Jay; and Loewe, Frederick] obit Aug 86
Lerner, Dorothy see Gordon, Dorothy
Lerner, Gerda Feb 98
Lerner, Max Oct 42 obit Aug 92
Le Roy Ladurie, Emmanuel Jul 84

Lesage, Jean Nov 61 obit Feb 81

Lescaze, William Apr 42 obit Apr 69

Lescot, Élie Jun 41 obit Dec 74

Leser, Tina Jun 57 obit Mar 86

Lesinski, John Sr. Jul 49 obit Jul 50

Lesinski, John Jr. Jun 57

Leslie, Lisa Jan 98

LeSourd, Catherine Marshall *see* Marshall, Catherine

L'esperance, Elise Nov 50 obit Apr 59

Lessing, Bruno obit Jan 40

Lessing, Doris Jan 76 Jan 95

Lester, Richard Apr 69

Lesueur, Larry Jun 43

Letourneau, Jean Oct 52

Letourneau, R. G. Apr 58 obit Jul 69

Letterman, David Nov 80

Lev, Ray Jan 49 obit Jul 68

Levant, Oscar Jan-Feb 40 Oct 52 obit Oct 72

Levay, Simon Oct 96

Levene, Phoebus Aaron Theodore obit Oct 40

Levenson, Sam Jul 59 obit Nov 80

Leverone, Nathaniel Nov 56 obit Jul 69

Levertov, Denise Aug 91 obit Mar 98

Leveson-Gower, William Spencer Sep 50 obit Sep 53

Lévesque, René Jan 75 obit Jan 88

Levi, Carlo Dec 52 obit Feb 75

Levi, Edward H. Jan 69 obit Jul 2000

Levi, Julian Apr 43 obit Apr 82

Levi, Primo Mar 87 obit Mar 87

Leviero, Anthony Sep 52 obit Nov 56

Levi-Montalcini, Rita Nov 89

Levin, Ira Aug 91

Levin, Meyer Apr 40 obit Sep 81

Levin, Yehuda Leib Sep 69 obit Jan 72

Levine, David Feb 73

Levine, Irving R. Jul 59

Levine, Jack Jun 56

Levine, James Apr 75

Levine, Joseph E. Oct 79 obit Sep 87

Levine, Philip May 47 obit Nov 87

Levinson, Barry Jul 90

Levinson, Salmon Oliver obit Mar 41

Lévi-Strauss, Claude Mar 72

Levi-Tanai, Sara May 58

Levitt, William J. Nov 56 obit Mar 94

Levitzki, Mischa obit Feb 41

Lévy, Bernard-Henri Nov 93

Levy, David H. Jan 95

Levy, David Mar 98

Levy, Marv Feb 98

Levy, William Auerbach- *see* Auerbach-Levy, William

Lewi, Mrs. Jack *see* Armstrong, Charlotte

Lewin, Murray obit Sep 43

Lewing, Adele obit Apr 43

Lewis, Albert Buell obit Yrbk 40

Lewis, C. S. Jan 44 obit Jan 64

Lewis, Carl Nov 84 Yrbk 96

Lewis, Cecil Day- *see* Day-Lewis, C.

Lewis, Chester M. May 56 obit Jun 90

Lewis, Claudius *see* Lewis, Lennox

Lewis, Clyde A. Feb 50

Lewis, Daniel Day- *see* Day-Lewis, Daniel

Lewis, David S. Jr. Aug 75

Lewis, Dean obit Dec 41

Lewis, Drew Feb 82

Lewis, Ethelreda obit Sep 46

Lewis, Flora Jan 89

Lewis, Francis Park obit Oct 40

Lewis, Fulton, Jr. Nov 42 obit Nov 66

Lewis, Henry Feb 73 obit Apr 96

Lewis, Jerry Nov 62

Lewis, John [civil rights] Sep 80

Lewis, John [musician] Jan 62

Lewis, John L. Mar 42 obit Jul 69

Lewis, Joseph Anthony Nov 55

Lewis, Juliette Feb 96

Lewis, Lawrence obit Jan 44

Lewis, Lennox Jan 99

Lewis, Loida Nicolas Apr 97

Lewis, Mary [opera singer] obit Feb 42

Lewis, Mary [executive] Sep 40

Lewis, Oscar Apr 68 obit Feb 71

Lewis, Ramsey Oct 96

Lewis, Richard Jul 93

Lewis, Roger Dec 73 obit Jan 88

Lewis, Shari Mar 58 obit Oct 98

Lewis, Willmott May 41 obit Feb 50

Lewis, Wilmarth Sheldon Jul 73 obit Jan 80

Lewitt, Sol Jul 86

Ley, Robert Sep 40 obit Dec 45

Ley, Willy Jun 41 Feb 53 obit Sep 69

Leyburn, James G. Apr 43

Leyland, Jim Nov 98

Lhevinne, Josef obit Jan 45

Lhevinne, Rosina Nov 61 obit Jan 77

Li, Choh-hao Apr 63 obit Jan 88

Li, Gong *see* Gong Li

Liaquat Ali Khan *see* Khan, Liaquat Ali

Liaquat Ali Khan, Begum *see* Khan, Begum Liaquat Ali

Libby, Frederick J. Apr 49 obit Sep 70

Libby, Willard F. Nov 54 obit Nov 80

Liberace Nov 54 Mar 86 obit Mar 87

Liberman, Alexander May 87 obit Mar 2000

Liberman, Evsei Jun 68 obit May 83

Lichtenberg, Bernard obit Nov 44

Lichtenberger, Andre obit Apr 40

Lichtenberger, Arthur Apr 61 obit Nov 68

Lichtenstein, Harvey May 87

Lichtenstein, Roy Feb 69 obit Jan 98

Lichtman, Joseph *see* Layton, Joe

Liddel, Urner May 51

Liddell Hart, Basil Henry Jan-Feb 40 obit Mar 70

Liddy, G. Gordon Oct 80

Lie, Jonas Jan 40

Lie, Trygve Mar 46 obit Feb 69

Liebenow, Robert C. May 56

Lieberman, Joseph I. Jul 94

Liebermann, Rolf Sep 73 obit Mar 99

Lieberson, Goddard Mar 76 obit Jul 77

Liebes, Dorothy Apr 48 obit Dec 72

Liebler, Theodore A. obit Jun 41

Liebling, Leonard obit Dec 45

Liebman, Joshua Loth Oct 46 obit Jul 48

Liebman, Max Apr 53 obit Sep 81

Lifshitz, Ralph see Lauren, Ralph

Lifton, Robert Jay Nov 73

Ligachev, Yegor K. Aug 90

Liggett, Louis Kroh obit Jul 46

Lightfoot, Gordon Aug 78

Lightner, Milton C. Nov 58 obit May 68

Li Lieh-Chun obit Apr 46

Li Lieh-hsun see Li Lieh-Chun

Lilienthal, David E. Jun 44 obit Mar 81

Lil' Kim Oct 2000

Lillard, George W. obit Yrbk 40

Lillehei, C. Walton May 69 obit Nov 99

Lillie, Beatrice Feb 45 Sep 64 obit Mar 89

Lilly, John C. Nov 62

Lima, Sigrid de see De Lima, Sigrid

Liman, Arthur L. Jan 88 obit Oct 97

Limann, Hilla Jun 81 obit Apr 98

Limb, Ben C. Jan 51

Limbaugh, Rush Mar 93

Limón, José Jun 53 Apr 68 obit Jan 73

Lin, Maya Apr 93

Lin, Yutang May 40 obit May 76

Lin Ch'ang-jen see Lin Sen

Lincoln, Joseph C. obit Apr 44

Lincoln, Leroy A. Jun 46 obit Jun 57

Lincoln, Murray D. Mar 53 obit Jan 67

Lind, Joseph Conrad see Hayes, Peter Lind

Lindbergh, Anne Morrow Nov 40 Jun 76

Lindbergh, Charles A. Jul 41 Jan 54 obit Oct 74

Lindemann, Frederick Alexander Mar 52 obit Sep 57

Linden, Hal Jan 87

Lindenberg, Hedda see Sterne, Hedda

Lindfors, Viveca Apr 55 obit Jan 96

Lindgren, Astrid Oct 96

Lindley, Ernest Hiram obit Oct 40

Lindley, Ernest K. Jun 43 obit Yrbk 91 (died Jun 79)

Lindros, Eric Apr 98

Lindsay, Howard Apr 42 [Lindsay, Howard; and Stickney, Dorothy] obit Apr 68

Lindsay, John V. Nov 62

Lindsay, Ronald obit Sep 45

Lindsey, Ben B. obit May 43

Lindsley, Thayer Jan 57 obit Jul 76

Lindt, Auguste R. Nov 59 obit Yrbk 2000

Ling, James J. Apr 70

Link, Edwin Jan 74 obit Yrbk 83 (died Sep 81)

Link, O. Winston Jun 95

Linkletter, Art Nov 53

Linlithgow, Victor Alexander John Hope, 2d Marquess of see Hope, Victor Alexander John

Linnell, John see They Might Be Giants

Linowitz, Sol M. Mar 67

Lin Piao May 67 obit Oct 72

Lin Sen obit Sep 43

Linton, Frank B. A. obit Jan 44

Lionni, Leo Sep 97 obit Feb 2000

Lion of Kashmir see Abdullah, Mohammad

Liotta, Ray May 94

Li-pai see Tsung-Jen Li and Tsung-Hsi Pai

Lipchitz, Chaim Jacob see Lipchitz, Jacques

Lipchitz, Jacques Nov 48 Apr 62 obit Jul 73

Li Peng Nov 88

Lipinski, Tara Apr 98

Lipmann, Fritz Mar 54 obit Sep 86

Lippincott, Joseph Wharton May 55 obit Jan 77

Lippincott, Joshua Bertram obit Jan 40

Lippmann, Walter Sep 40 Nov 62 obit Jan 75

Lippold, Richard Nov 56

Lipschitz, Chaim U. Dec 66

Lipsky, Eleazar (WLB) Yrbk 59 obit Apr 93

Lipton, Seymour Nov 64 obit Feb 87

Litchfield, Edward H. Nov 53 obit May 68

Litchfield, P. W. Dec 50 obit May 59

Lithgow, John Nov 96

Li Tsung-Jen Nov 42 [Li Tsung-Jen; and Pai Tsung-Hsi] obit Mar 69

Littell, Philip obit Dec 43

Little, Clarence C. Dec 44 obit Feb 72

Little, Lou Nov 45 obit Jul 79

Little, Philip obit May 42

Little, Rich Nov 75

Little, William Lawson Jr. Aug 40

Littledale, Clara Savage Oct 46 obit Mar 56

Littlejohn, Robert McG Sep 46 obit Jul 82

Littler, Gene Jul 56

Little Richard Sep 86

Litton, Andrew Sep 98

Littrell, Brian see Backstreet Boys

Litvinov, Maxim Dec 41 obit Feb 52

Liu Shao-ch'i Oct 57 obit Dec 74

Liu Shaoqi see Liu Shao-ch'i

Lively, Penelope Apr 94

Livingston, Homer J. Sep 55 obit Jul 70

Livingston, John W. Jul 59 obit Aug 97

Livingston, M. Stanley Feb 55 obit Nov 86

Livingston, Mrs. Leon J. see Parnis, Mollie

Lizhi, Fang see Fang Lizhi

Ljungberg, Ernst Carl Mar 55

Lleo, Manuel Urrutia see Urrutia Lleo, Manuel

Lleras Camargo, Alberto Sep 47 Jun 65 obit Mar 90

Lord Irwin *see* Halifax, Edward Frederick Lindley Wood, 1st Earl of

Loren, Sophia Mar 59

Lorentz, Pare Apr 40 obit May 92

Lorenz, John G. Sep 66

Lorenz, Konrad Jul 55 Oct 77 obit Apr 89

Lorenzo, Frank Feb 87

Lorge, Irving Jul 59 obit Apr 61

Loring, Eugene Mar 72 obit Oct 82

Loring, Jules *see* Mackaye, Julia Gunther

Loring, Peter *see* Shellabarger, Samuel

Lortel, Lucille Feb 85 obit Jul 99

Los Angeles, Victoria de *see* Angeles, Victoria de los

Losch, Tilly Jul 44 obit Feb 76

Losey, Joseph Dec 69 obit Aug 84

Lothar, Ernst (WLB) Yrbk 47

Lothian, Philip Henry Kerr, 11th Marquis of obit Yrbk 40

Lott, Ronnie Feb 94

Lott, Trent Sep 96

Lou, Liza Jan 2000

Louchheim, Aline B. *see* Saarinen, Aline B.

Louchheim, Katie Jun 56 obit Apr 91

Louchheim, Mrs. Walter C., Jr. *see* Louchheim, Katie

Loud, Pat Jul 74

Loudon, Alexander Jul 42 obit Mar 53

Loudon, Dorothy Jun 84

Louganis, Greg Oct 84

Lougheed, Peter Aug 79

Loughlin, Anne Feb 50

Louis, Joe Oct 40 obit Jun 81

Louis, Murray Oct 68

Louis-Dreyfus, Julia Oct 95

Louise Caroline Alberta, Duchess of Argyll, Princess obit Jan 40

Loutfi, Omar Jan 57 obit Jul 63

Louw, Eric H. Mar 62 obit Sep 68

Lovano, Joe Mar 98

Love, Courtney Jun 96

Love, George H. Mar 50 obit Sep 91

Love, Iris Aug 82

Love, J. Spencer Nov 57 obit Mar 62

Love, John A. Nov 63

Love, Susan M. Oct 94

LoVecchio, Frank Paul *see* Laine, Frankie

Loveless, Herschel C. Jul 58 obit Jul 89

Lovell, Bernard Oct 59

Lovell, James A., Jr. Mar 69

Lovelock, James Nov 92

Loveman, Amy Jun 43 obit Feb 56

Lovett, Lyle Sep 97

Lovett, Robert A. Aug 42 Nov 51 obit Jun 86

Lovett, Robert Morss Aug 43 obit Apr 56

Lovins, Amory B. Jun 97

Low, David Jan-Feb 40 obit Nov 63

Lowden, Frank O. obit May 43

Lowdermilk, W. C. Feb 49 obit Jul 74

Lowe, Jack Jan 54 [Whittemore, Arthur; and Lowe, Jack] obit Aug 96

Lowe, Rob Jul 2000

Lowell, A. Lawrence obit Feb 43

Lowell, Robert Jul 47 Jan 72 obit Nov 77

Lowenstein, Allard K. Sep 71 obit May 80

Lowery, Joseph E. Nov 82

Lowey, Nita M. Sep 97

Lownsbery, Eloise (WLB) Yrbk 47

Lowrie, Jean E. Jun 73

Lowry, Edward G. obit Sep 43

Loy, Myrna Oct 50 obit Feb 94

Loynd, Harry, J. Feb 52

Lozovsky, S. A. Nov 41

Lozowick, Louis Apr 42 obit Nov 73

Lubbers, Ruud May 88

Lubell, Samuel Nov 56 obit Oct 87

Lubic, Ruth Watson Sep 96

Lubin, Isador Oct 41 Jan 53 obit Sep 78

Lübke, Heinrich Jan 60 obit May 72

Lubovitch, Lar Mar 92

Luca, Giuseppe De *see* De Luca, Giuseppe

Lucas, Craig Sep 91

Lucas, George Apr 78

Lucas, Jerry Jun 72

Lucas, John Oct 95

Lucas, Martha B. *see* Pate, Martha B.

Lucas, Scott W. Dec 47 obit Apr 68

Lucci, Susan Oct 89

Luccock, Halford E. Jun 60 obit Jan 61

Luce, Charles F. Dec 68

Luce, Clare Boothe Nov 42 Apr 53 obit Nov 87

Luce, Henry R. Jul 41 Jan 61 obit Apr 67

Luce, Robert obit May 46

Lucet, Charles Dec 67

Lucioni, Luigi Oct 43 obit Sep 88

Luckman, Charles Oct 47 obit Apr 99

Luckstone, Isidore obit May 41

Ludington, Flora B. Nov 53

Ludlam, Charles Aug 86 obit Jul 87

Ludlum, Robert Nov 82

Ludwig, Christa Mar 71

Ludwig, Daniel Keith May 79 obit Oct 92

Lugar, Richard G. Oct 77

Luhan, Mabel Dodge Jan-Feb 40 obit Oct 62

Luhring, Oscar Raymond obit Oct 44

Lujack, Johnny Dec 47

Lujan, Manuel, Jr. Sep 89

Lukas, J. Anthony Jan 87 obit Aug 97

Lukas, Paul Feb 42 obit Oct 71

Lumet, Sidney Sep 67

Lumley, Roger Jan 58 obit Sep 69

Lumpkin, Alva M. obit Sep 41

Lumumba, Patrice Nov 60 obit Apr 61

Lund, Wendell L. Sep 42

Lundeberg, Harry Nov 52 obit Mar 57

Lundeen, Ernest obit Oct 40

Lunden, Joan May 89

Lunn, Katharine Fowler *see* Fowler-Billings, Katharine

L.; and MacKaye, Julia
Gunther]

Mackaye, Julia Gunther
(WLB) Yrbk 49 [MacKaye,
David L.; and MacKaye,
Julia Gunther]

MacKaye, Loring *see* Mackaye, David L.; Mackaye,
Julia Gunther

Mackenzie, C. J. Jun 52

Mackenzie, Clinton obit Mar
40

Mackenzie, Gisele Nov 55

MacKenzie, Marie Marguer-
ite Louise Gisele La Fleche
see Mackenzie, Gisele

Mackenzie, Warren Sep 94

Mackenzie, William Warrender, 1st Baron *see* Amulree, William Warrender
Mackenzie, 1st Baron of
Strathbraan

Mackie, Bob Oct 88

Mackinnon, Catharine A. Jun
94

Mackintosh, Cameron Mar 91

Maclachlan, Kyle Aug 93

Maclaine, Shirley Dec 59 Jul
78

Maclean, Basil C. May 57 obit
Apr 63

Maclean, Malcolm Shaw Jul
40

Macleish, Archibald Oct 40
Nov 59 obit Jun 82

Maclennan, Hugh (WLB)
Yrbk 46 obit Jan 91

MacLeod, Dorothy Shaw Apr
49

Macleod, Iain Apr 56 obit Oct
70

Macleod, Mrs. W. Murdoch
see MacLeod, Dorothy
Shaw

Macmahon, Arthur W. Apr
58 obit Apr 80

Macmillan, Donald Baxter
Sep 48 obit Nov 70

Macmillan, Ernest Mar 55
obit Jun 73

Macmillan, Harold Mar 43
Jan 55 obit Feb 87

MacMitchell, Leslie Apr 46

Macmurray, Fred Feb 67 obit
Feb 92

Macneil, Cornell Jan 76

Macneil, Neil May 40

Macneil, Robert Feb 80

Macphail, Larry Mar 45 obit
Nov 75

Macrae, John obit Apr 44

Macrossie, Allan, Rev. obit
Mar 40

Macveagh, Lincoln Nov 41
Jun 52 obit Mar 72

Macy, Edith Dewing Dec 52
obit Oct 67

Macy, George Nov 54 obit
Sep 56

Macy, John W., Jr. Jan 62 obit
Apr 87

Macy, Mrs. Edward W. *see*
Macy, Edith Dewing

Madariaga, Salvador De Jan
64 obit Feb 79

Madden, John Aug 85

Madden, Ray J. Apr 53 obit
Nov 87

Maddox, Lester G. Dec 67

Maddox, William P. Nov 47
obit Dec 72

Maddux, Greg Feb 96

Maddy, Joseph E. Apr 46 obit
May 66

Madeira, Jean Oct 63 obit Sep
72

Madeleva, Sister Mary Feb 42
obit Oct 64

Madigan, Edward R. Nov 92
obit Feb 95

Madonna May 86

Madrid, Miguel de la *see* De
La Madrid, Miguel

Maenner, T. H. Nov 49 obit
Mar 58

Magallanes, Nicholas May 55
obit Jul 77

Magaziner, Ira C. Apr 95

Magee, Elizabeth S. Oct 50

Magee, James C. May 43

Maggiolo, Walter A. Jul 52
obit Yrbk 2000

Magill, Roswell Mar 48 obit
Feb 64

Maglie, Sal Jun 53 obit Feb 93

Maglione, Luigi, Cardinal
obit Oct 44

Magloire, Paul E. Feb 52

Magnani, Anna Apr 56 obit
Nov 73

Magner, Thomas F. obit Feb
46

Magnuson, Paul B. Jun 48
obit Jan 69

Magnuson, Warren G. Oct 45
obit Jul 89

Magoffin, Ralph Van Deman
obit Jul 42

Magritte, René Sep 66 obit
Oct 67

Magruder, William M. Mar
72 obit Nov 77

Magsaysay, Ramón Dec 52
obit May 57

Maguiness, William Edward
see Mack, Ted

Mahady, Henry J. Jul 54

Mahan, John W. Jul 59

Maharaj Ji, Guru Dec 74

Mahathir Bin Mohamad Aug
88

Mahendra, King of Nepal Jul
56 obit Mar 72

Maher, Ahmed, Pasha obit
Apr 45

Maher, Aly Mar 52 obit Nov
60

Maher, Bill Jul 97

Mahesh Yogi, Maharishi Dec
72

Mahfouz, Naguib May 89

Mahmoud Hassan *see* Has-
san, Mahmoud

Mahon, George H. Mar 58
obit Jan 86

Mahoney, John Aug 99

Maier, Walter A. May 47 obit
Feb 50

Maile, Boniface R. Feb 51

Mailer, Norman Oct 48 Feb
70

Mailhouse, Max obit Dec 41

Maillol, Aristide May 42 obit
Nov 44

Main, Charles Thomas obit
Apr 43

Main, Marjorie Oct 51 obit
Jun 75

Mainbocher Feb 42 obit Mar
77

Maines, Natalie *see* Dixie
Chicks

Maisky, Ivan Sep 41 obit Oct
75

Major, John Oct 90 Apr 97

Makarios III May 56 obit Sep
77

Makarova, Natalia Feb 72

Makeba, Miriam Jun 65

Makemson, Maud W. Jun 41

Makin, Norman J. O. Mar 46

Makins, Roger Jan 53 obit Jan
97

Makonnen, Tafari *see* Haile
Selassie I

Malamud, Bernard (WLB)
Yrbk 58 Jul 78 obit May 86

Malan, Daniel François

Malbin, Elaine Feb 59

Malcolm, George A. Nov 54

Malden, Karl Apr 57

Malenkov, Georgi M. Jun 52 obit Mar 88

Malick, Terrence Jun 99

Malik, Adam Nov 70 obit Nov 84

Malik, Charles H. Apr 48 obit Feb 88

Malik, Jacob Apr 49 obit Apr 80

Malin, Patrick Murphy Mar 50 obit Feb 65

Malinovsky, Rodion Y. Mar 44 Nov 60 obit May 67

Malinowski, Bronislaw Jun 41 obit Jul 42

Malkovich, John May 88

Mallakh, Kamal, El see El Mallakh, Kamal

Malle, Louis Feb 76 obit Feb 96

Mallette, Gertrude E. (WLB) Yrbk 50

Mallory, C. C. Feb 56 obit Mar 59

Mallory, F. B. obit Nov 41

Mallory, L. D. Sep 60 obit Sep 94

Malone, George W. Dec 50 obit Jul 61

Malone, John C. Aug 95

Malone, Karl Jan 93

Malone, Moses Jun 86

Malone, Ross L. Mar 59 obit Oct 74

Maloney, Francis T. obit Mar 45

Maloney, Walter E. Oct 52

Malott, Deane W. Mar 51 obit Nov 96

Malraux, André Mar 59 obit Feb 77

Maltz, Albert Jan-Feb 40 obit Jul 85

Malvern, Godfrey Huggins, 1st Viscount see Huggins, Godfrey

Mamet, David Aug 78 Mar 98

Mamlok, Hans J. obit Yrbk 40

Mamoulian, Rouben Mar 49 obit Jan 88

Manchester, William Nov 67

Mancini, Henry Jul 64 obit Aug 94

Mandel, Georges Yrbk 40

Mandela, Nelson Jan 84 Nov 95

Mandela, Winnie Jan 86

Mandelbrot, Benoit Jun 87

Mandlikova, Hana Jan 86

Mandrell, Barbara Aug 82

Manessier, Alfred May 57 obit Oct 93

Maney, Richard Jul 64 obit Sep 68

Mangione, Chuck May 80

Mangione, Jerre Mar 43 obit Nov 98

Mangrum, Lloyd Sep 51 obit Jan 74

Manilow, Barry Jul 78

Mankiewicz, Joseph L. Sep 49 obit Apr 93

Mankiller, Wilma P. Nov 88

Mankin, Helen Douglas Apr 46

Mankowitz, Wolf (WLB) Yrbk 56 obit Aug 98

Manley, Michael Jan 76 obit May 97

Manley, Norman W. Nov 59 obit Nov 69

Manly, John Matthews obit May 40

Mann, Erica see Jong, Erica

Mann, Erika Yrbk 40 obit Nov 69

Mann, Klaus Yrbk 40 obit Jul 49

Mann, Marty Jun 49 obit Sep 80

Mann, Michael Jan 93

Mann, Thomas C. Apr 64 obit Apr 99

Mann, Thomas May 42 obit Oct 55

Mann, Tom obit May 41

Manna, Charlie Jan 65 obit Dec 71

Mannerheim, Carl Gustaf Emil von Apr 40 obit Feb 51

Mannes, Marya Apr 59

Manning, Ernest Dec 59 obit May 96

Manning, Harry May 52 obit Oct 74

Manning, Marie see Fairfax, Beatrice

Manning, Peyton Sep 98

Manning, Reg Jun 51

Manning, William Thomas, Bishop Apr 40 obit Jan 50

Mansbridge, Albert Jun 42

Mansfield, Michael J. Apr 52 Jan 78

Mansfield, Mike see Mansfield, Michael J.

Manship, Paul May 40 obit Mar 66

Mansholt, Sicco L. May 66

Manson, John T. obit Apr 44

Manson, Marilyn May 99

Mansouri, Lotfi Apr 90

Manstein, Fritz Erich Von Oct 42 obit Sep 73

Mantle, Burns Nov 44 obit Mar 48

Mantle, Mickey Jul 53 obit Oct 95

Manuilsky, Dmitri Z. Dec 48 obit May 59

Manzù, Giacomo Mar 61 obit Mar 91

Mao Tse-Tung see Mao Zedong

Mao Zedong Feb 43 May 62 obit Oct 76

Mapes, Victor obit Jan 44

Mapplethorpe, Robert May 89 obit May 89

Maradona, Diego Nov 90

Marais, Jean Apr 62 obit Jan 99

Marble, Alice Nov 40 obit Mar 91

Marburg, Theodore obit Apr 46

Marcantonio, Vito Feb 49 obit Oct 54

Marca-Relli, Conrad Sep 70 obit Nov 2000

Marceau, Marcel Feb 57

March, Charles Hoyt obit Sep 45

March, Fredric Mar 43 [March, Fredric; and Eldridge, Florence] obit Jun 75

Marchais, Georges Jun 76 obit Jan 98

Marchal, Léon Sep 43 obit Dec 56 Yrbk 57

Marcial-Dorado, Carolina obit Sep 41

Marciano, Rocky Sep 52 obit Nov 69

Marcos, Ferdinand E. Feb 67 obit Nov 89

Marcus, Greil Oct 99

Marcus, Jacob R. May 60 obit Jan 96

Marcus, Stanley Jun 49

Marcuse, Herbert Mar 69 obit Sep 79

Marden, Brice Aug 90

Marden, Orison S. Jul 67 obit Oct 75

Mardikian, George M. Nov 47

Marek, Kurt W. Jan 57 obit Jun 72

Marella, Paolo, Cardinal Oct 64

Marett, Robert R. obit Apr 43

Margai, Milton Feb 62 obit Jun 64

Margaret, Princess of Great Britain Nov 53

Marge see Damerel, Donna

Margesson, Henry David Reginald Margesson, 1st Viscount Feb 41 obit Feb 66

Margoliouth, David Samuel obit Apr 40

Margret, Ann see Ann-Margret

Margrethe II, Queen of Denmark Nov 72

Margueritte, Victor obit May 42

Margulis, Lynn Jul 92

Marías, Julián Feb 72

Maria Theresa, Archduchess of Austria obit Apr 44

Marie, Andre Sep 48 obit Sep 74

Marin, John Jul 49 obit Dec 53

Marín, Luis Muñoz see Munoz Marin, Luis

Marini, Marino Jan 54 obit Oct 80

Marino, Dan Jan 89

Marion, George obit Jan 46

Maris, Roger Nov 61 obit Feb 86

Marisol Apr 68

Maritain, Jacques May 42 obit Jun 73

Marius, Emilie Alexander obit Apr 40

Marjolin, Robert Dec 48 obit Jun 86

Mark, Herman F. May 61 obit Jun 92

Mark, Louis obit May 42

Mark, Mary Ellen Sep 99

Mark, Rebecca May 99

Markel, Lester Dec 52 obit Jan 78

Marker, Laurie Feb 2000

Marker-Kraus, Laurie see Marker, Laurie

Markey, Edward J. Nov 97

Markham, Beryl Nov 42 obit Oct 86

Markham, Edwin Mar 40

Markova, Alicia Sep 43

Markovic, Ante Nov 91

Marks, Leonard H. Jun 66

Marks, Simon Marks, 1st Baron Nov 62 obit Feb 65

Marland, Sidney P., Jr. Apr 72 obit Jul 92

Marland, William C. Apr 56 obit Jan 66

Marples, Ernest May 60

Marquand, Hilary A. Apr 51

Marquand, John Apr 42 obit Oct 60

Marquardt, Alexandria obit Jun 43

Marquis, Albert Nelson obit Feb 44

Marquis, Frederick James Marquis, 1st Baron Woolton see Woolton, Frederick James Marquis, 1st Earl

Marriner, Neville Aug 78

Marriott, Alice Lee (WLB) Yrbk 50 obit May 92

Marriott, J. Willard Jun 72 obit Oct 85

Marriott, John obit Jul 45

Marrow, Tracy see Ice-T

Marsalis, Branford Sep 91

Marsalis, Ellis Aug 2000

Marsh, Ernest Sterling Feb 60

Marsh, Jean Nov 77

Marsh, John, Rev. Dr. Mar 60

Marsh, Reginald Sep 41 obit Sep 54

Marshak, Robert E. Jul 73 obit Feb 93

Marshall, Barry J. Sep 96

Marshall, Burke Feb 65

Marshall, C. Herbert, Jr. Oct 49

Marshall, Catherine Jan 55 obit May 83

Marshall, David Jul 56 obit Feb 96

Marshall, E. G. Jun 86 obit Nov 98

Marshall, Garry Nov 92

Marshall, George C. Oct 40 Mar 47 obit Dec 59

Marshall, Lois Jun 60 obit May 97

Marshall, M. Lee Sep 48 obit Oct 50

Marshall, Penny Mar 80 May 92

Marshall, Peter, Rev. Apr 48 obit Feb 49

Marshall, Ray Nov 77

Marshall, Rosamond Aug 42 obit Feb 58

Marshall, S. L. A. Nov 53 obit Mar 78

Marshall, Susan Jul 99

Marshall, Thurgood Nov 54 Sep 89 obit Mar 93

Marshall, Tully obit Apr 43

Marshall, Verne Feb 41 obit May 65

Marshall, Walter P. Apr 50 obit Jun 69

Marsten, Richard see Hunter, Evan

Martel, Giffard Le Quesne Jul 43 obit Nov 58

Martell, Edward Nov 64

Martens, Wilfried Feb 87

Martin, Agnes Sep 89

Martin, Alfred Manuel see Martin, Billy

Martin, Allie Beth Jun 75 obit Jun 76

Martin, Archer John Porter Nov 53

Martin, Billy Oct 76 obit Feb 90

Martin, Charles H. obit Nov 46

Martin, Christy Oct 97

Martin, Collier Ford obit May 41

Martin, Dean Nov 64 obit Mar 96

Martin, Dick Sep 69

Martin, Edgar Stanley Jr. obit Sep 40

Martin, Edmund F. Jan 62 obit Mar 93

Martin, Edward Oct 45 obit May 67

Martin, Fletcher Feb 58 obit Jul 79

Martin, Frank L. obit Sep 41

Martin, George Brown obit Dec 45

Martin, Glenn L. Feb 43 obit Feb 56

Martin, Harry Jun 48 obit Mar 59

Martin, Helen see Rood, Helen Martin

Martin, Jackie Apr 43
Martin, James S., Jr. Mar 77
Martin, John Bartlow (WLB) Yrbk 56 obit Mar 87
Martin, Joseph W., Jr. Oct 40 May 48 obit Apr 68
Martin, Judith Jun 86
Martin, Lillien J. Apr 42 obit May 43
Martin, Lynn Oct 89
Martin, Mary Jan 44 obit Jan 91
Martin, Paul Dec 51 obit Nov 92
Martin, Percy Alvin obit Apr 42
Martin, Ricky Sep 99
Martin, Steve Aug 78 Nov 2000
Martin, Thomas E. Mar 56 obit Sep 71
Martin, Walter B. Nov 54 obit May 66
Martin, William C., Bishop Apr 53
Martin, William McChesney, Jr. May 51 obit Oct 98
Martin Artajo, Alberto Nov 49
Martinelli, Giovanni Jan 45 obit Mar 69
Martinez, Alicia see Alonso, Alicia
Martínez, Maximiliano Hernández see Hernández Martínez, Maximiliano
Martínez Trueba, Andrés Nov 54 obit Feb 60
Martini, Helen Jul 55
Martini, Mrs. Fred see Martini, Helen
Martino, Gaetano May 56 obit Oct 67
Martins, Peter Jun 78
Martinu, Bohuslav Nov 44 obit Nov 59
Martland, Harrison Stanford Nov 40 obit Jun 54
Marton, Eva Apr 85
Martos, Rafael see Raphael
Marty, Martin E. Jun 68
Marvel, Elizabeth Newell Apr 62 [Marval, Mrs. Archie D.]
Marvin, Charles F. obit Jul 43
Marvin, Cloyd H. Dec 49 obit Jun 69
Marvin, Dwight Edwards, Rev. obit Mar 40

Marvin, Harry obit Jan 40
Marvin, Lee Sep 66 obit Oct 87
Marx, Chico May 48 [Marx, Chico; Marx, Groucho; and Marx, Harpo] obit Dec 61
Marx, Elizabeth Lisl Weil see Weil, Lisl
Marx, Groucho Mar 48 [Marx, Chico; Marx, Groucho; and Marx, Harpo] Feb 73 obit Oct 77
Marx, Harpo Mar 48 [Marx, Chico; Marx, Groucho; and Marx, Harpo] obit Nov 64
Mary Alice Nov 95
Mary Joseph Butler, Mother obit Jan 40
Mary Kay see Ash, Mary Kay
Marzotto, Gaetano, Count Jul 53
Masaryk, Jan May 44 obit Apr 48
Mascagni, Pietro obit Sep 45
Masekela, Hugh Mar 93
Masina, Giulietta Apr 58 obit Jun 94
Masina, Guilia Anna see Masina, Giulietta
Masliansky, Zvei Hirsch, Rev. obit Mar 43
Mason, Bobbie Ann Sep 89
Mason, Jackie Jul 87
Mason, James May 47 obit Sep 84
Mason, Joseph Warren Teets obit Jul 41
Mason, Lowell B. Jun 49
Mason, Marsha Apr 81
Mason, Noah M. Nov 57 obit May 65
Mason, Norman P. Jun 59
Massee, W. Wellington obit Oct 42
Masserman, Jules H. Jul 80 obit Jan 95
Massevitch, Alla G. Jan 64
Massey, Raymond Feb 46 obit Sep 83
Massey, Vincent Oct 51 obit Feb 68
Massey, Walter E. Jun 97
Massigli, René May 56
Massine, Leonide Apr 40 obit May 79
Masson, André Nov 74 obit Jan 88
Masters, Kelly Ray see Ball, Zachary

Masters, William H. Nov 68
Mastroianni, Marcello Jun 63 obit Feb 97
Mastroianni, Umberto Sep 60
Masursky, Harold Aug 86 obit Oct 90
Matalin, Mary Sep 96
Mateos, Adolfo López see López Mateos, Adolfo
Mates, Leo Nov 56
Mather, Kirtley F. Jan 51
Matheson, Samuel Pritchard, Archbishop obit Jul 42
Mathews, David Jan 76
Mathews, Shailer, Rev. obit Dec 41
Mathewson, Lemuel Dec 52 obit Apr 70
Mathias, Charles McC., Jr. Dec 72
Mathias, Robert Bruce Sep 52
Mathis, Johnny Jul 65 Feb 93
Matisse, Henri May 43 Jun 53 obit Jan 55
Matlin, Marlee May 92
Matola, Sharon Jun 93
Matskevich, Vladimir V. Nov 55
Matson, Randy Sep 68
Matsudaira, Koto Nov 58
Matsui, Keishiro, Baron obit Jul 46
Matsui, Robert T. Oct 94
Matsuoka, Yosuke Mar 41 obit Jul 46
Matta Echauren, Roberto Antonio Sebastian see Matta
Matta Nov 57
Mattei, Enrico Apr 59 obit Jan 63
Matthau, Walter Jun 66 obit Sep 2000
Matthews, Burnita Shelton Apr 50 obit Jun 88
Matthews, Francis P. Sep 49 obit Dec 52
Matthews, H. Freeman Mar 45 obit Jan 87
Matthews, Herbert L. Nov 43 obit Sep 77
Matthews, J. B. May 43
Matthews, T. S. Apr 50 obit Mar 91
Matthews, W. Donald Sep 52
Matthiessen, Peter Oct 75
Mattingly, Don Oct 88
Mattingly, Garrett Nov 60 obit Feb 63

Mattson, Henry Jan 56 obit Nov 71

Mature, Victor Dec 51 obit Oct 99

Matzinger, Polly Oct 98

Mauch, Gene Dec 74

Maudling, Reginald May 60 obit Apr 79

Maugham, W. Somerset Jan 63 obit Jan 66

Mauldin, Bill May 45 Nov 64

Mauldin, William Henry see Mauldin, Bill

Maunoury, Maurice Bourgès see Bourgès-Maunoury, Maurice

Maura, Carmen Apr 92

Maurer, Ion Gheorghe Sep 71 obit Jul 2000

Mauriac, Claude Sep 93 obit Jun 99

Maurier, Daphne du see Du Maurier, Daphne

Mauroy, Pierre Jun 82

Maverick, Maury, Sr. Mar 44 obit Sep 54

Maw, Herbert B. Oct 48 obit Jan 91

Max, Adolphe obit Jan 40

Max, Peter May 71

Maximos, Demetrios Mar 48 obit Dec 55

Maxon, Lou R. Aug 43 obit Jul 71

Maxton, James obit Sep 46

Maxtone Graham, Joyce see Struther, Jan

Maxwell, David Dec 51 obit Mar 67 [Kilmuir, David Patrick Maxwell Fyfe, 1st Earl of]

Maxwell, David F. Jun 57

Maxwell, Elsa Mar 43 obit Jan 64

Maxwell, Robert Sep 88 obit Feb 92

Maxwell, Russell L. Nov 42 obit Jan 69

Maxwell, Vera Jul 77 obit Mar 95

Maxwell, William (WLB) Yrbk 49 obit Oct 2000

Maxwell Davies, Peter see Davies, Peter Maxwell

May, Andrew Jackson Apr 41 obit Nov 59

May, Catherine Jan 60

May, Charles H. obit Jan 44

May, Elaine Mar 61

May, Geraldine P. Feb 49

May, Henry John obit Jan 40

May, John L. Jan 91 obit Jun 94

May, Rollo Jun 73 obit Jan 95

Maybank, Burnet R. Apr 49 obit Nov 54

Mayer, Daniel Nov 49

Mayer, Jane see Jaynes, Clare

Mayer, Jean Sep 70 obit Feb 93

Mayer, Louis B. Jun 43 obit Jan 58

Mayer, Maria Goeppert Jun 64 obit Apr 72

Mayer, René May 48 obit Feb 73

Mayes, Mrs. Gilford see Mayes, Rose Gorr

Mayes, Rose Gorr May 50

Mayle, Peter Oct 92

Maynard, John A. F., Rev. Oct 43

Maynard, Joyce Jan 99

Maynard, Robert C. Jun 86 obit Oct 93

Mayne, Ethel C. obit Jun 41

Maynor, Dorothy Jan-Feb 40 Dec 51 obit May 96

Mayo, Charles W. Nov 41 Nov 54 obit Oct 68

Mayo, Katherine obit Yrbk 40

Mayo, Robert P. Feb 70

Mayr, Ernst Nov 84

Mays, Benjamin E. May 45 obit May 84

Mays, Ewing W. Jan 52

Mays, Willie May 55 Dec 66

Maza, José Nov 55 obit Jul 64

Mazen, Abu see Abbas, Mahmoud

Mazey, Emil Jan 48 obit Nov 83

Mazowiecki, Tadeusz Feb 90

Mazursky, Paul May 80

Mazzo, Kay Jul 71

Mbeki, Thabo Aug 98

M'bow, Amadou-Mahtar May 87

Mboya, Tom Jun 59 obit Sep 69

McAdie, Alexander George obit Dec 43

McAdoo, William Gibbs obit Mar 41

McAfee, Mildred H. Sep 42 obit Jan 95

McAlary, Michael obit Mar 99

McAuliffe, Anthony C. Feb 50 obit Oct 75

McBain, Ed see Hunter, Evan

McBride, Christian Jan 2000

McBride, Katharine E. Feb 42 obit Jul 76

McBride, Lloyd Feb 78 obit Jan 84

McBride, Mary Margaret Apr 41 Mar 54 obit Jun 76

McBride, Patricia Jul 66

McCabe, Gibson Feb 63 obit Yrbk 2000

McCabe, Thomas B. Sep 48 obit Jul 82

McCaffrey, Barry R. Jul 97

McCaffrey, John L. Nov 50

McCain, John S., Jr. Jun 70 obit Jun 81

McCain, John S. Sr. Oct 43 obit Oct 45

McCain, John S. 3d. Feb 89

McCall, Duke K. Nov 59

McCall, Tom Jun 74 obit Mar 83

McCambridge, Mercedes Jun 64

McCardell, Claire Nov 54 obit Jun 58

McCarey, Leo Jul 46 obit Sep 69

McCarl, John Raymond obit Sep 40

McCarran, Patrick A. Jul 47 obit Dec 54

McCarrens, John S. obit Sep 43

McCarthy, Carolyn Mar 98

McCarthy, Clem Oct 41 obit Jul 62

McCarthy, Eugene J. Nov 55

McCarthy, Frank Sep 45 obit Feb 87

McCarthy, Joe May 48 obit Mar 78

McCarthy, Joseph R. Jan 50 obit Jul 57

McCarthy, Joseph Vincent see McCarthy, Joe

McCarthy, Kenneth C. Nov 53

McCarthy, Leighton Oct 42 obit Nov 52

McCarthy, Mary (WLB) Yrbk 55 Feb 69 obit Jan 90

McCartney, Paul Nov 66 Jan 86

McCarty, Dan Jul 53

McCarver, Tim May 2000

McClanahan, Rue May 89

McCleery, Albert Feb 55 obit Jul 72

McClellan, Harold C. Oct 54 obit Sep 79

McClellan, John L. Apr 50 obit Feb 78

McClintic, Guthrie May 43 obit Jan 62

McClintock, Barbara Mar 84 obit Nov 92

McClintock, Robert Mills Apr 55

McClinton, Katharine Morrison Mar 58 obit Mar 93

McClinton, Mrs. Harold L. *see* McClinton, Katharine Morrison

McCloskey, John Robert *see* McCloskey, Robert

McCloskey, Mark A. Nov 55 obit Jan 78

McCloskey, Paul N., Jr. Nov 71

McCloskey, Robert Sep 42

McCloy, John J. Apr 47 Nov 61 obit May 89

McCobb, Paul Nov 58 obit Apr 69

McColough, C. Peter Jan 81

McComas, O. Parker Nov 55 obit Feb 58

McConachie, G. W. Grant Nov 58 obit Sep 65

McCone, John A. Jan 59 obit Apr 91

McConnell, F. B. Jul 52 obit Feb 62

McConnell, Joseph H. Nov 50 obit May 97

McConnell, Samuel K., Jr. Nov 56

McCormack, Arthur Thomas obit Sep 43

McCormack, Emmet J. Jul 53 obit Apr 65

McCormack, John obit Oct 45

McCormack, John W. Jun 43 Apr 62 obit Jan 81

McCormick, Anne O'Hare Mar 40 obit Jul 54

McCormick, Edward J. Nov 53 obit Feb 75

McCormick, Edward T. May 51 obit Oct 91

McCormick, Fowler Jun 47 obit Feb 73

McCormick, Jay Apr 43

McCormick, Lynde D. Feb 52 obit Oct 56

McCormick, Myron Jan 54 obit Oct 62

McCormick, Robert R. Aug 42 obit May 55

McCormick, William Patrick Glyn, Rev. obit Yrbk 40

McCourt, Frank Feb 98

McCovey, Willie Nov 70

McCowen, Alec Oct 69

McCoy, Charles B. Jul 70 obit Mar 95

McCoy, Frank R. Nov 45 obit Sep 54

McCracken, Harold (WLB) Yrbk 49

McCracken, James Nov 63 obit Jun 88

McCracken, Joan Jun 45 obit Jan 62

McCracken, Paul W. Dec 69

McCracken, Robert James Jul 49 obit Apr 73

McCrady, Edward Jan 57

McCrary, Jinx Jul 53 [McCrary, Tex; and McCrary, Jinx]

McCrary, Tex Jul 53 [McCrary, Tex; and McCrary, Jink]

McCreery, Richard L. May 45 obit Dec 67

McCullers, Carson Sep 40 obit Dec 67

McCullough, Colleen Apr 82

McCullough, David Jan 93

McCune, Charles Andrew obit Yrbk 40

McCune, Francis K. Mar 61

McCune, George S. obit Feb 42

McCurdy, William Albert, Rev. obit Feb 42

McCurry, Michael D. Nov 96

McDaniel, Glen May 52

McDaniel, Hattie Sep 40 obit Dec 52

McDaniel, James Feb 2000

McDermott, Alice Sep 92

McDermott, Michael J. Feb 51 obit Oct 55

McDevitt, James L. Mar 59 obit May 63

McDiarmid, E. W. Dec 48

McDivitt, James A. Nov 65

McDonagh, Martin Aug 98

McDonald, Audra Apr 99

McDonald, David J. Jun 53 obit Oct 79

McDonald, David L. Nov 63 obit Mar 98

McDonald, Erroll Oct 99

McDonald, Eugene F., Jr. Oct 49 obit Oct 58

McDonald, James G. Apr 49 obit Dec 64

McDonnell, Mary May 97

McDonnell, William A. Feb 59

McDonough, Roger H. Jun 68

McDormand, Frances Sep 97

McDowall, Roddy Apr 61 obit Jan 99

McDowell, Malcolm Dec 73

McElroy, Neil H. Apr 51 obit Jan 73

McEnroe, John Feb 80

McEntee, Gerald W. Oct 2000

McEntire, Reba Oct 94

McEwan, Ian Jul 93

McEwen, Terence A. Jul 85 obit Jan 99

McFadden, Mary Apr 83

McFarland, Ernest W. Jan 51 obit Aug 84

McFarlane, Robert C. May 84

McFarlane, Todd Feb 99

McGannon, Donald H. Feb 71 obit Jul 84

McGarry, William J. obit Nov 41

McGeachy, Mary Craig Apr 44

McGee, Fibber *see* Jordan, Jim

McGee, Frank Jun 64 obit Jun 74

McGee, Gale Nov 61 obit Jun 92

McGee, Molly *see* Jordan, Marian

McGhee, George C. Sep 50

McGill, Ralph Jun 47 obit Mar 69

McGill, William J. Jun 71 obit Jan 98

McGillicuddy, Cornelius *see* Mack, Connie

McGinley, Laurence J. Jun 49 obit Oct 92

McGinley, Phyllis Feb 41 Nov 61 obit Apr 78

McGinnis, Patrick B. Nov 55 obit Apr 73

McGinniss, Joe Jan 84

McGovern, Francis Edward obit Jun 46

McGovern, George S. Mar 67

McGovern, John W. Nov 61 obit Jun 75

McGovern, Maureen Feb 90

McGranery, James P. May 52 obit Feb 63

McGrath, Earl James Apr 49 obit Apr 93

McGrath, J. Howard Jan 48 obit Nov 66

McGraw, Curtis W. Jun 50 obit Nov 53

McGraw, Eloise Jarvis (WLB) Yrbk 55

McGreal, Mrs. William see Yates, Elizabeth

McGregor, G. R. Mar 54 obit Apr 71

McGregor, J. Harry Oct 58

McGroarty, John Steven obit Sep 44

McGuane, Thomas Nov 87

McGuigan, James Sep 50 obit Jun 74

McGuire, Dorothy Sep 41

McGuire, William Anthony obit Nov 40

McGurn, Barrett Apr 65

McGwire, Mark Jul 98

McHale, Kathryn Jan 47 obit Dec 56 Yrbk 57

McHenry, Donald F. Sep 80

McInerney, Jay Nov 87

McIntire, Carl Oct 71

McIntire, Ross T. Oct 45 obit Feb 60

McIntosh, Millicent Carey Jul 47

McIntyre, James Francis Feb 53 obit Sep 79

McIntyre, James T., Jr. Jan 79

McIntyre, Marvin H. obit Feb 44

McIntyre, Natalie see Gray, Macy

McIntyre, Thomas J. Nov 63 obit Oct 92

McIver, Pearl Mar 49

McKay, David O. Jun 51 obit Mar 70

McKay, Douglas May 49 obit Oct 59

McKay, Jim Oct 73

McKayle, Donald Jun 71

McKeen, John E. Jun 61 obit Apr 78

McKeever, Ed Nov 45

McKeldin, Theodore R. Oct 52 obit Oct 74

McKellar, K. D. Jan 46 obit Jan 58

McKellen, Ian Jan 84

McKelway, B. M. Jan 58 obit Oct 76

McKenna, F. E. May 66 obit Feb 79

McKenna, Reginald obit Oct 43

McKenna, Siobhan Nov 56 obit Jan 87

McKenney, Eileen see West, Nathanael

McKenney, Ruth Aug 42 obit Oct 72

McKenzie, Kevin Jan 2000

McKenzie, Roderick Duncan obit Jan 40

McKenzie, Vashti Murphy Nov 2000

McKenzie, William P. obit Oct 42

McKinley, Chuck Nov 63 obit Sep 86

McKinney, Cynthia A. Aug 96

McKinney, Frank E. Jan 52 obit Mar 74

McKinney, Robert Jan 57

McKissick, Floyd B. Jan 68 obit Jun 91

McKittrick, Thomas H. Jul 44 obit Mar 70

McKneally, Martin B. Mar 60 obit Aug 92

McKuen, Rod Feb 70

McLain, Dennis Jan 69

McLaren, Malcolm Aug 97

McLaughlin, Ann Dore Nov 88

McLaughlin, Audrey Jul 90

McLaughlin, John Jul 87

McLaughlin, Leo May 70 obit Nov 96

McLean, A. J. see Backstreet Boys

McLean, Alice T. Jul 45 obit Dec 68

McLean, Don May 73

McLean, Evalyn Walsh May 43 obit May 47

McLean, Robert Nov 51 obit Feb 81

McLennan, Isabel Stewart see McMeekin, Isabel McLennan

McLintock, Gordon Nov 53 obit Jun 90

McLuhan, Marshall Jun 67 obit Feb 81

McMahon, Brien Dec 45 obit Sep 52

McMahon, Ed Apr 77

McMahon, Vince Feb 99

McMahon, William Sep 71 obit May 88

McManamy, Frank obit Nov 44

McManus, James Kenneth see McKay, Jim

McMath, Sid Mar 49

McMeekin, Clark see Clark, Dorothy Park; McMeekin, Isabel McLennan

McMeekin, Isabel McLennan Sep 42 (WLB) Yrbk 57 [McMeekin, Isabel McLennan; and Clark, Dorothy Park]

McMein, Neysa Feb 41 obit Jun 49

McMillan, Edwin M. Feb 52 obit Nov 91

McMillan, John L. Nov 56

McMillan, Terry Feb 93

McMillen, Tom Jan 93

McMinnies, Mary (WLB) Yrbk 59

McMurrin, Sterling M. Jun 61 obit Jun 96

McMurtrie, Douglas C. Jul 44

McMurtry, Larry Jun 84

McNair, Arnold D. Feb 55

McNair, Barbara Nov 71

McNair, Lesley J. Nov 42 obit Sep 44

McNair, Sylvia Nov 97

McNally, Andrew, 3d Nov 56

McNally, Terrence Mar 88

McNamara, James Barnabas obit Apr 41

McNamara, Patrick V. Nov 55 obit Jun 66

McNamara, Robert S. Sep 61 Mar 87

McNamee, Graham obit Jul 42

McNarney, Joseph T. Nov 44 obit Mar 72

McNary, Charles L. Aug 40 obit Apr 44

McNaughton, Andrew Nov 42 obit Nov 66

McNealy, Scott Apr 96

Menshikov, Mikhail A. May 58 obit Sep 76

Menthon, Francois De Mar 44

Menuhin, Yehudi Feb 41 May 73 obit Jun 99

Menzel, Donald H. Apr 56 obit Mar 77

Menzies, Robert G. Feb 41 Jan 50 obit Jul 78

Mercer, Johnny Jun 48 obit Aug 76

Mercer, Mabel Feb 73 obit Jun 84

Mercer, Samuel A. B. Feb 53

Merchant, Ismail Mar 93

Merchant, Livingston T. Nov 56 obit Jul 76

Merck, George W. Dec 46 obit Jan 58

Mercouri, Melina Jul 65 Mar 88 obit May 94

Meredith, Burgess Jul 40 obit Nov 97

Mérida, Carlos Jan 60

Merivale, Philip obit Apr 46

Meriwether, John Mar 99

Meriwether, W. Delano Jan 78

Merle-Smith, Van Santvoord obit Dec 43

Merman, Ethel Oct 41 May 55 obit Apr 84

Merriam, C. Hart obit May 42

Merriam, Charles Edward Feb 47 obit Feb 53

Merriam, George Ernest, Rev. obit May 41

Merriam, John Campbell obit Dec 45

Merrick, David Jan 61 obit Jul 2000

Merrick, Elliott (WLB) Yrbk 50 obit Jul 97

Merrifield, R. Bruce Mar 85

Merrill, Charles E. Apr 56

Merrill, Frank Jul 44 obit Feb 56

Merrill, James Aug 81 obit Apr 95

Merrill, John Douglas obit Jan 40

Merrill, Linda see Ashley, Merrill

Merrill, Robert Mar 52

Merritt, Matthew J. obit Nov 46

Merry Del Val, Alfonso, 2d Marquis De Nov 65

Merton, Robert K. Sep 65

Merwin, W. S. May 88

Merz, Charles Nov 54 obit Nov 77

Meservey, Robert Preston see Preston, Robert

Meskill, Thomas J. Mar 74

Messer, Thomas M. Nov 61

Messerschmitt, Willy Apr 40 obit Nov 78

Messersmith, George S. Oct 42 obit Apr 60

Messiaen, Olivier Feb 74 obit Jun 92

Messick, Dale Jul 61

Messier, Mark Jul 95

Messmer, Pierre Nov 63

Messner, Reinhold Mar 80

Mesta, Perle Sep 49 obit May 75

Metaxas, John Yrbk 40 obit Mar 41

Metcalf, Jesse H. obit Dec 42

Metcalf, Lee Feb 70 obit Mar 78

Metheny, Pat May 96

Metrovic, Ivan Oct 40 obit Mar 62

Metzelthin, Pearl V. Nov 42 obit Jan 48

Metzenbaum, Howard M. Jul 80

Metzman, G. Jul 46 obit Jun 60

Meyer, Agnes E. Jan 49 obit Nov 70

Meyer, Albert Jan 60 obit May 65

Meyer, Cord Jr. Mar 48

Meyer, Debbie May 69

Meyer, Eugene Sep 41 obit Oct 59

Meyer, Jean Nov 55

Meyer, K. F. Mar 52 obit Jun 74

Meyer, Mrs. Eugene see Meyer, Agnes E.

Meyer, Ron Mar 97

Meyerowitz, William May 42

Meyers, George Julian obit Jan 40

Meyerson, Golda see Meir, Golda

Meyner, Robert B. Apr 55 obit Jul 90

Mfume, Kweisi Jan 96

Michael, George Nov 88

Michael, Moina obit Jun 44

Michaels, Lorne Aug 99

Michael V, King of Rumania Oct 44

Michals, Duane Apr 81

Michel, Robert H. Sep 81

Michelin, Edouard obit Oct 40

Michelman, Kate Nov 2000

Michelson, Charles Aug 40 obit Jan 48

Michener, Daniel Roland Jan 68 obit Nov 91

Michener, James A. Jun 48 Aug 75 obit Jan 98

Michie, Allan A. Nov 42 obit Jan 74

Michnik, Adam Jul 90

Middlecoff, Cary Jul 52 obit Nov 98

Middleton, Arthur see O'Brien, Edward J.

Middleton, Drew Sep 43 obit Mar 90

Midgley, Thomas, Jr. obit Dec 44

Midler, Bette Jun 73 Nov 97

Midori Jun 90

Mielziner, Jo Mar 46 obit May 76

Miers, Earl Schenck (WLB) Yrbk 49 Sep 67 obit Jan 73

Mies Van Der Rohe, Ludwig Oct 51 obit Oct 69

Mifune, Toshiro Jun 81 obit Mar 98

Mignone, Francisco Jun 42

Mihajlov, Mihajlo Jan 79

Mihajlovic, Dragoliub see Mikhailovitch, Draja

Mikell, Henry Judah, Bishop obit Apr 42

Mikhailov, Nikolai A. Nov 58

Mikhailovitch, Draja Mar 42 obit Sep 46

Mikhalkov, Nikita Oct 95

Miki, Takeo Apr 75 obit Jan 89

Mikita, Stan Oct 70

Mikolajczyk, Stanislaw Mar 44 obit Feb 67

Mikoyan, Anastas I. May 55 obit Jan 79

Mikulski, Barbara A. Nov 85

Mikva, Abner J. Jul 80

Milam, Carl H. Jun 45 obit Oct 63

Milanov, Zinka Jul 44 obit Jul 89

Milchan, Arnon Oct 2000

Miles, Mary Nov 42

Milgram, Stanley Aug 79 obit Mar 85

Milhaud, Darius Jun 41 May 61 obit Sep 74

Milland, Ray Feb 46 obit Apr 86

Millar, Alexander Copeland, Rev. obit Yrbk 40

Millar, George (WLB) Yrbk 49

Millar, Kenneth see Macdonald, Ross

Millar, Margaret (WLB) Yrbk 46 obit Jun 94

Millar, Mrs. Kenneth see De Mille, Agnes; Millar, Margaret

Millard, Bailey obit May 41

Mille, Cecil B. de see De Mille, Cecil B.

Miller, Alice Duer Sep 41 obit Oct 42

Miller, Ann Apr 80

Miller, Arjay Jan 67

Miller, Arnold Nov 74 obit Sep 85

Miller, Arthur Oct 47 Feb 73

Miller, Bebe Apr 99

Miller, Benjamin Meek obit Mar 44

Miller, Dayton C. obit Apr 41

Miller, Douglas Nov 41

Miller, Edward G., Jr. Jun 51 obit Jun 68

Miller, Frieda S. Feb 45 obit Oct 73

Miller, G. William Jun 78

Miller, George P. Feb 64

Miller, Gilbert Apr 58 obit Feb 69

Miller, Glenn Feb 42 obit Yrbk 91 (died Dec 44)

Miller, Harry W. Mar 62 obit Mar 77

Miller, Henry Nov 70 obit Jul 80

Miller, Irving Nov 52 obit Feb 81

Miller, J. Cloyd Dec 51

Miller, J. Irwin Nov 61

Miller, James C., 3d May 86

Miller, Jason Jan 74

Miller, John see Miller, Jason

Miller, Johnny Sep 74

Miller, Jonathan Oct 70 Nov 86

Miller, Justin Jan 47 obit Mar 73

Miller, Lee P. Jul 59

Miller, Marshall E. Oct 53

Miller, Marvin May 73

Miller, Max May 40 obit Feb 68

Miller, Merle (WLB) Yrbk 50 obit Jul 86

Miller, Mildred Jun 57

Miller, Mitch Jul 56

Miller, Neal E. Jul 74

Miller, Nicole Mar 95

Miller, Reggie Mar 96

Miller, Roger Sep 86 obit Jan 93

Miller, Shannon Jul 96

Miller, Watson B. Sep 47 obit Apr 61

Miller, Webb obit Jan 40

Miller, William E. Feb 62 obit Aug 83

Miller, William Lash obit Oct 40

Miller, Zell Jul 96

Millerand, Alexander obit May 43

Milles, Carl Yrbk 40 Dec 52 obit Nov 55

Millett, John D. Feb 53 obit Jan 94

Millett, Kate Jan 71 Jun 95

Milligan, Mary Louise May 57

Millikan, Robert A. Jun 40 Jun 52 obit Feb 54

Millikin, Eugene D. Apr 48 obit Oct 58

Million, J. W. obit Nov 41

Millis, Harry Alvin Nov 40 obit Sep 48

Millo, Aprile Apr 88

Mills, Frederick C. Nov 48 obit Apr 64

Mills, Hayley Apr 63

Mills, John May 63

Mills, Wilbur D. Nov 56 obit Jul 92

Milnes, Sherrill Nov 70

Milosevic, Slobodan Apr 90

Milosz, Czeslaw Oct 81

Milstein, Nathan Mar 50 obit Feb 93

Minard, George Cann obit Aug 40

Mindszenty, József Jan 57 obit Jun 75

Miner, Tony see Miner, Worthington C.

Miner, Worthington C. Feb 53 obit Mar 83

Mingus, Charles Feb 71 obit Mar 79

Mink, Patsy Takemoto Sep 68

Minnelli, Liza Oct 70 Jul 88

Minnelli, Vincente May 75 obit Sep 86

Minor, Halsey Oct 98

Minor, Robert Apr 41 obit Jan 53

Minow, Newton N. Oct 61

Minsky, Marvin Sep 88

Mintoff, Dom Mar 84

Minton, Sherman Mar 41 Dec 49 obit May 65

Mirabella, Grace Oct 91

Miranda, Carmen Jun 41 obit Oct 55

Miró, Joan May 40 Nov 73 obit Feb 84

Miró Cardona, José Nov 61 obit Oct 74

Mirren, Helen Jul 95

Mirvish, Edwin Apr 89

Mirvish, Robert F. (WLB) Yrbk 57

Mirza, Iskander May 56 obit Jan 70

Mistral, Gabriela Feb 46 obit Mar 57

Mitchell, Arthur Oct 66

Mitchell, George J. Apr 89

Mitchell, H. L. Jan 47

Mitchell, Howard May 52 obit Aug 88

Mitchell, James P. Sep 55 obit Dec 64

Mitchell, Joan Mar 86 obit Jan 93

Mitchell, John Newton Jun 69 obit Jan 89

Mitchell, Joni Oct 76

Mitchell, Stephen A. Oct 52 obit Jun 74

Mitchell, William D. Jan 46 obit Nov 55

Mitchell, William L. Nov 59

Mitchum, Robert Sep 70 obit Sep 97

Mitford, Jessica Sep 74 obit Oct 96

Mitropoulos, Dimitri Mar 41 Mar 52 obit Jan 61

Mitscher, Marc A. Aug 44 obit Mar 47

Mitsotakis, Constantine Nov 90

Mittell, Philip obit Mar 43

Mittermeier, Russell A. Oct 92

Mitterrand, François Dec 68 Oct 82 obit Mar 96

Mix, Tom obit Yrbk 40

Miyake, Issey Nov 97

Miyazawa, Kiichi Feb 92

Mizner, Elizabeth Howard *see* Howard, Elizabeth

Mizrahi, Isaac Jan 91

Mnouchkine, Ariane Mar 93

Moats, Alice-Leone May 43 obit Jul 89

Mobutu, Joseph Désiré *see* Mobutu Sese Seko

Mobutu Sese Seko Sep 66 [Mobutu, Joseph D.] May 97

Moch, Jules Oct 50 obit Nov 85

Modjeski, Ralph obit Aug 40

Moën, Lars May 41

Moffat, J. Pierrepont obit Mar 43

Moffatt, James obit Aug 44

Moffo, Anna May 61

Mohammad, Bakshi Ghulam *see* Bakshi, Ghulam Mohammad

Mohammed, Ghulam Jul 54 obit Nov 56

Mohammed Riza Shah Pahlevi Jan 50 Sep 77 obit Sep 80

Mohammed V, King of Morocco Oct 51 [Sidi Mohammed, Sultan of Morocco] obit Apr 61

Mohammed Zahir Shah Mar 56

Mohrhardt, Foster E. Jun 67

Moi, Daniel Arap May 79

Moir, Phyllis Apr 42

Moiseev, Igor *see* Moiseyev, Igor

Moiseiwitsch, Tanya Nov 55

Moiseyev, Igor Nov 58

Moisseiff, Leon S. obit Oct 43

Moley, Raymond Jul 45 obit Apr 75

Molina, Rafael L. Trujillo *see* Trujillo Molina, Rafael Leónidas

Molinari, Susan Mar 96

Mollenhoff, Clark R. Nov 58 obit May 91

Mollet, Guy Sep 50 obit Nov 75

Mollison, Amy *see* Johnson, Amy

Molloy, Daniel M. obit Mar 44

Molloy, Robert (WLB) Yrbk 48 obit Mar 77

Molotov, Viacheslav M. Jan-Feb 40 Jun 54 obit Jan 87

Molyneux, Edward H. Jun 42 obit May 74

Momaday, N. Scott Apr 75

Momsen, C. B. Jul 46 obit Jul 67

Monaco, Mario del *see* Del Monaco, Mario

Monaghan, Francis Joseph obit Jan 43

Monaghan, Frank Nov 43 obit Sep 69

Monaghan, Thomas Jun 90

Monckton, Walter Turner *see* Monckton of Brenchley, Walter Turner Monckton, 1st Viscount

Monckton of Brenchley, Walter Turner Monckton, 1st Viscount Dec 51 obit Feb 65

Mondale, Joan Jan 80

Mondale, Walter F. Jan 69 May 78

Mondavi, Robert Apr 99

Mondriaan, Piet obit Mar 44

Monk, Art Apr 95

Monk, Meredith Feb 85

Monk, Thelonious Oct 64 obit Apr 82

Monnet, Jean Sep 47 obit May 79

Monod, Jacques Jul 71 obit Jul 76

Monroe, Anne S. obit Dec 42

Monroe, Earl May 78

Monroe, Lucy Aug 42 obit Nov 87

Monroe, Marilyn Jul 59 obit Oct 62

Monroe, Vaughn Jul 42 obit Jul 73

Monroney, A. S. Mike Nov 51 obit Apr 80

Monsarrat, Nicholas (WLB) Yrbk 50 obit Oct 79

Monsky, Henry Nov 41 obit Jun 47

Montagnier, Luc Aug 88

Montagu, Ashley Feb 67 obit Mar 2000

Montagu, Ewen Jun 56 obit Sep 85

Montague, James J. obit Feb 42

Montale, Eugenio Apr 76 obit Nov 81

Montana, Claude Jan 92

Montana, Joe Sep 83

Montanari, A. J. Feb 68

Montand, Yves Jul 60 Sep 88 obit Jan 92

Montebello, Philippe de *see* De Montebello, Philippe

Montenegro, Fernanda Oct 99

Montessori, Maria Nov 40 obit Jun 52

Monteux, Pierre Apr 46 obit Sep 64

Montgomery, Bernard Law Dec 42 obit May 76 [Montgomery of Alamein, Bernard Law Montgomery, 1st Viscount]

Montgomery, Deane Nov 57 obit May 92

Montgomery, Elizabeth Rider (WLB) Yrbk 52

Montgomery, James Shera Apr 48 obit Sep 52

Montgomery, L. M. obit Jun 42

Montgomery, Robert Bruce *see* Crispin, Edmund

Montgomery, Robert Jan 48 obit Nov 81

Montgomery, Ruth Feb 57

Montgomery of Alamein, Bernard Law Montgomery, 1st Viscount *see* Montgomery, Bernard Law

Montini, Giovanni Battista *see* Paul VI, Pope

Montoya, Carlos Mar 68 obit May 93

Montoya, Joseph M. Mar 75 obit Jul 78

Montresor, Beni Dec 67

Moody, Blair Sep 51 obit Oct 54

Moody, Joseph E. Dec 48 obit Jul 84

Moody, Ralph (WLB) Yrbk 55

Moon, Bucklin (WLB) Yrbk 50

Moon, Sun Myung Mar 83

Moon, Warren Nov 91

Mooney, Edward Apr 46 obit Jan 59

Mooney, Thomas J. obit Apr 42

Mooney, Tom *see* Mooney, Thomas J.

Moore, Archie Nov 60 obit Feb 99

Moore, Brian Jan 86 obit Mar 99

Moore, Bryant E. Feb 49 obit Mar 51

Moore, Charlotte Emma see Sitterly, Charlotte Moore

Moore, Demi Sep 93

Moore, Douglas Nov 47 obit Oct 69

Moore, Dudley Jun 82

Moore, Edward Caldwell obit May 43

Moore, Elisabeth Luce Oct 60

Moore, Garry Nov 54 obit Jan 94

Moore, George E. Jan 68

Moore, George S. May 70 obit Yrbk 2000

Moore, Gerald Oct 67 obit May 87

Moore, Grace Apr 44 obit Mar 47

Moore, Henry Feb 54 Feb 78 obit Oct 86

Moore, Henry R. Sep 43 obit May 78

Moore, Julianne Oct 98

Moore, Marianne Dec 52 Apr 68 obit Mar 72

Moore, Mary Tyler Feb 71

Moore, Melba Jan 73

Moore, Michael C. Aug 97

Moore, Michael May 97

Moore, Mike see Moore, Michael C.

Moore, Mrs. Maurice T. see Moore, Elisabeth Luce

Moore, Paul, Jr. Jan 67

Moore, Preston J. Apr 59

Moore, R. Walton obit Apr 41

Moore, Raymond obit Mar 40

Moore, Robert Webber obit Jan 43

Moore, Roger Feb 75

Moore, Ruth (WLB) Yrbk 54

Moore, T. Albert obit Apr 40

Moore, Thomas W. Sep 67

Moore-Brabazon, J. C. T. May 41

Moorehead, Agnes Jun 52 obit Jun 74

Moorer, Thomas H. Apr 71

Moorland, Jesse Edward obit Jan 40

Moos, Malcolm C. Nov 68

Mora, Francis Luis obit Jul 40

Mora, José A. Nov 56 obit Mar 75

Moraes, Frank Nov 57 obit Jul 74

Moran, Léon obit Oct 41

Moran Cho see Cho, Margaret

Morano, Albert P. Mar 52 obit Feb 88

Morath, Max Nov 63

Moravia, Alberto Apr 70 obit Nov 90

Mordkin, Mikhail obit Sep 44

More, Adelyne see Ogden, C. K.

Moreau, Jeanne Dec 66

Moreell, Ben Jun 46 obit Sep 78

Morehead, Albert H. Mar 55 obit Dec 66

Morehead, John H. obit Jul 42

Morehouse, Daniel Walter obit Mar 41

Morehouse, Ward Jan-Feb 40 obit Feb 67

Morell, Parker obit Apr 43

Moreno, Mario see Cantinflas

Moreno, Rita Sep 85

Morfit, Thomas Garrison see Moore, Garry

Morgan, Anne Jan 46 obit Mar 52

Morgan, Arthur E. Jul 56 obit Jan 76

Morgan, Edward P. [government official] May 51

Morgan, Edward P. [journalist] Apr 64 obit Mar 93

Morgan, Frederick Feb 46 obit May 67

Morgan, Henry Mar 47 obit Jul 94

Morgan, J. Pierpont obit Apr 43

Morgan, Joe Sep 84

Morgan, Joy Elmer Jan 46

Morgan, Lorrie Apr 99

Morgan, Lucy Mar 59

Morgan, Thomas A. Mar 50 obit Jan 68

Morgan, Thomas E. Jun 59 obit Oct 95

Morgan, Thomas Hunt obit Feb 46

Morganfield, McKinley see Waters, Muddy

Morgenstierne, Wilhelm Munthe De May 49 obit Sep 63

Morgenthau, Hans J. Mar 63 obit Sep 80

Morgenthau, Henry, Jr. Sep 40 obit Apr 67

Morgenthau, Robert M. Jan 86

Moriarty, Michael Jul 76

Morin, Relman Nov 58 obit Oct 73

Morini, Erica Apr 46 obit Jan 96

Morínigo, Higinio Jun 42

Morison, Samuel Eliot Oct 51 Sep 62 obit Jul 76

Morissette, Alanis May 97

Morita, Akio Feb 72 obit Feb 2000

Morley, Malcolm Jun 84

Morley, Robert Nov 63 obit Aug 92

Moro, Aldo Jun 64 obit Jun 78

Morón, Alonzo G. Oct 49 obit Dec 71

Morricone, Ennio Oct 2000

Morrill, J. L. Feb 51

Morris, Dave Hennen obit Jun 44

Morris, Desmond Nov 74

Morris, Earl Jun 68 obit Jul 92

Morris, Edmund Jul 89

Morris, James, [Journalist] see Morris, Jan

Morris, James Jul 86

Morris, Jan Jan 64 Jun 86

Morris, Mark Aug 88

Morris, Newbold Mar 52 obit Apr 66

Morris, Robert Apr 71

Morris, Roland Sletor obit Jan 46

Morris, Steveland Judkins see Wonder, Stevie

Morris, William Richard Apr 41 [Nuffield, William Richard Morris, 1st Viscount] obit Oct 63

Morris, Willie Jan 76 obit Oct 99

Morris, Wright May 82 obit Jul 98

Morrison, Adrienne obit Jan 41

Morrison, Delesseps S. Nov 49 obit Jul 64

Morrison, Frank see Spillane, Mickey

Morrison, Frank B. May 64

Morrison, Henry Clinton obit May 45

Morrison, Herbert Jul 40 Feb 51 obit Apr 65 [Morrison of Lambeth, 1st Baron]

Morrison, Margaret Mackie see Cost, March

Morrison, Marion Michael see Wayne, John

Morrison, Peggy see Cost, March

Morrison, Philip Jul 81

Morrison, Toni May 79

Morrison, Van Sep 96

Morrison, William Shepherd Jan 52 obit Apr 61 [Dunrossil, William Shepherd Morrison, 1st Viscount]

Morrison of Lambeth, 1st Baron see Morrison, Herbert

Morrow, Elizabeth Cutter Apr 43 obit Mar 55

Morrow, Honore Willsie obit May 40

Morrow, Mrs. Dwight Whitney see Morrow, Elizabeth Cutter

Morsch, Lucile M. Jun 57 obit Nov 72

Morse, Carol see Hall, Marjory

Morse, Clarence G. Nov 57

Morse, David A. Mar 49 obit Mar 91

Morse, John Lovett obit May 40

Morse, Marston Mar 57 obit Aug 77

Morse, Philip M. Jun 48 obit Nov 85

Morse, Robert Nov 62

Morse, True D. Nov 59 obit Sep 98

Morse, Wayne Apr 42 Nov 54 obit Sep 74

Mortenson, Norma Jean see Monroe, Marilyn

Mortier, Gérard Jul 91

Mortimer, Charles G. Nov 55 obit Feb 79

Mortimer, John Apr 83

Morton, Craig Jun 78

Morton, Elizabeth Homer Jul 61

Morton, Florrinell F. Jul 61

Morton, Henry Holdich obit Jul 40

Morton, James F. obit Dec 41

Morton, James Madison Jr. obit Aug 40

Morton, James obit Oct 43

Morton, Joe Feb 99

Morton, John Jamieson, Jr. Mar 55

Morton, Rogers C. B. Nov 71 obit Jun 79

Morton, Thruston B. Nov 57 obit Oct 82

Mosbacher, Emil, Jr. Mar 63 obit Nov 97

Mosbacher, Robert Jun 89

Mosca, Gaetano obit Jan 42

Moschen, Michael Jul 2000

Moscicki, Ignace obit Nov 46

Mosconi, Willie Jun 63 obit Nov 93

Moscoso, Teodoro Oct 63 obit Aug 92

Moscovitch, Maurice obit Aug 40

Mosel, Tad Nov 61

Moseley-Braun, Carol Jun 94

Moser, Annemarie see Proell, Annemarie

Moser, Fritz Jun 55

Moses, Edwin Nov 86

Moses, George Higgins obit Feb 45

Moses, Grandma Jan 49 obit Feb 62

Moses, Harry M. Oct 49 obit Jun 56

Moses, John obit Apr 45

Moses, Robert Nov 40 Feb 54 obit Sep 81

Mosher, A. R. Dec 50 obit Dec 59

Mosher, Gouverneur Frank obit Sep 41

Mosher, Ira Feb 45 obit May 68

Mosley, J. Brooke Sep 70 obit Apr 88

Mosley, Oswald Jul 40 obit Feb 81

Mosley, Walter Sep 94

Moss, Cynthia May 93

Moss, Frank E. Dec 71

Moss, John E., Jr. Nov 56 obit Feb 98

Mossadegh, Mohammed May 51 obit May 67

Mössbauer, Rudolf L. May 62

Mostel, Zero Apr 43 Nov 63 obit Nov 77

Motherwell, Hiram obit Jan 46

Motherwell, Robert Nov 62 obit Sep 91

Motley, Arthur H. Jan 61 obit Jul 84

Motley, Constance Baker May 64

Moton, Robert Russa obit Jul 40

Motrico, José María de Areilza, Count of see Areilza, José Maria de, Count of Motrico

Mott, C. S. Sep 69 obit Apr 73

Mott, Frank Luther Oct 41 obit Dec 64

Mott, James W. obit Dec 45

Mott, John R. Jan 47 obit Mar 55

Mott, Lewis F. obit Jan 42

Mott, Stewart R. Apr 75

Motta, Giuseppe obit Jan 40

Moulton, F. R. Jan 46 obit Jan 53

Moulton, Harold G. Nov 44 obit Feb 66

Mountbatten, Louis Jun 42 obit Oct 79 [Mountbatten of Burma, 1st Earl]

Mountbatten, Philip Oct 47 [Edinburgh, Philip, 3d Duke of]

Mountbatten of Burma, 1st Earl see Mountbatten, Louis

Mountevans, Edward R. G. R. Evans, 1st Baron see Evans, Edward R. G. R.

Mouskos, Michael Christedoulos see Makarios III

Moutet, Marius Jul 47 obit Dec 68

Mowat, Farley Feb 86

Mowat, Robert B. obit Nov 41

Mowery, Edward J. Nov 53 obit Feb 71

Mowinckel, Johan Ludwig obit Nov 43

Mowrer, Edgar Ansel Oct 41 Jul 62 obit May 77

Mowrer, Lilian Thomson May 40 obit Jan 91

Mowrey, Corma Nov 50

Moya, Manuel A. De Nov 57

Moyers, Bill Jan 66 Feb 76

Moylan, Mary Ellen Feb 57

Moyne, Walter Edward Guinness, 1st Baron see Guinness, Walter Edward

Moynihan, Daniel Patrick Feb 68 Feb 86
Mr. John Oct 56 obit Sep 93
Mubarak Hosni Apr 82
Muccio, John J. Jan 51 obit Jul 89
Muck, Karl Mar 40
Mudd, Emily Nov 56 obit Jul 98
Mudd, Roger Jan 81
Mueller, Frederick H. Dec 59 obit Oct 76
Mueller, George E. Nov 64
Mueller, Mildred *see* Miller, Mildred
Mueller, R. H. Apr 64 obit Sep 82
Muench, Aloisius Apr 60 obit Apr 62
Mugabe, Robert Apr 79
Muggeridge, Malcolm Apr 55 Jul 75 obit Jan 91
Muhammad, Elijah Jan 71 obit Apr 75
Muir, James May 50 obit Jan 60
Muir, Malcolm Apr 53 obit Mar 79
Muir, P. H. Apr 63
Muir, Percy *see* Muir, P. H.
Muir, Ramsay obit Jun 41
Mujibur Rahman Jan 73 obit Oct 75
Mukherjee, Bharati Apr 92
Muldoon, Robert D. Feb 78 obit Sep 92
Muldowney, Shirley Oct 97
Muller, H. J. Feb 47 obit Jun 67
Müller, Paul Oct 45 [Läuger, Paul; and Müller, Paul] obit Dec 65
Mulligan, Gerry Dec 60 obit Mar 96
Mulliken, Robert S. Sep 67 obit Jan 87
Mullis, Kary B. Feb 96
Mulloy, Gardnar Nov 57
Mulroney, Brian Apr 84
Mumford, Ethel Watts obit Jan 40
Mumford, L. Quincy Jun 54 obit Jan 83
Mumford, Lewis Nov 40 Mar 63 obit Mar 90
Münch, Charles Dec 47 obit Dec 68
Munch, Edvard Yrbk 40 obit Mar 44

Mundt, Karl E. Jul 48 obit Oct 74
Mundy, Talbot Chetwynd obit Sep 40
Muni, Paul Jan 44 obit Nov 67
Muniz, João Carlos Sep 52 obit Sep 60
Munk, Kaj obit Feb 44
Munn, Biggie *see* Munn, Clarence L.
Munn, Clarence L. Nov 53
Munn, Frank May 44 obit Dec 53
Münnich, Ferenc May 59 obit Jan 68
Munoz Marin, Luis Oct 42 Nov 53 obit Jun 80
Munro, Alice Sep 90
Munro, Leslie Knox Nov 53 obit Apr 74
Munsel, Patrice Mar 45
Munson, Thurman Nov 77 obit Sep 79
Murakami Harakui Sep 97
Murayama, Makio Oct 74
Murch, Walter Apr 2000
Murdoch, Iris (WLB) Yrbk 58 Aug 80 obit Apr 99
Murdoch, Rupert May 77
Murdock, George J. obit Sep 42
Murdock, George Peter Mar 57
Murdock, Victor obit Aug 45
Muren, Dennis Mar 97
Murphree, Eger V. Sep 56 obit Jan 63
Murphy, Charles S. Apr 50 obit Oct 83
Murphy, Eddie Nov 83
Murphy, Frank Jul 40 obit Sep 49
Murphy, Franklin D. Mar 71 obit Aug 94
Murphy, Franklin W. obit Jan 41
Murphy, Frederick E. obit Mar 40
Murphy, Gardner May 60 obit May 79
Murphy, George Dec 65 obit Jul 92
Murphy, Patricia Apr 62
Murphy, Patrick V. Nov 72
Murphy, Robert D. Feb 43 Nov 58 obit Mar 78
Murphy, Thomas A. Oct 79

Murphy, Thomas F. Mar 51 obit Jan 96
Murphy, W. B. Nov 55 obit Aug 94
Murray, Albert May 94
Murray, Anne Jan 82
Murray, Arthur Apr 43 obit May 91
Murray, Augustus Taber obit Mar 40
Murray, Bill Jan 85
Murray, Charles A. Jul 86
Murray, Charlie obit Sep 41
Murray, Don Sep 59
Murray, Dwight H. May 57 obit Nov 74
Murray, Elizabeth Apr 95
Murray, J. Harold obit Feb 41
Murray, James E. Aug 45 obit May 61
Murray, John Courtney May 61 obit Oct 67
Murray, Patty Aug 94
Murray, Philip Jan 41 Feb 49 obit Dec 52
Murray, Thomas E. Sep 50 obit Sep 61
Murray, Tom Nov 56 obit Jan 72
Murray, William S. obit Mar 42
Murrell, Ethel Ernest Oct 51
Murrell, Mrs. John Moore *see* Murrell, Ethel Ernest
Murrow, Edward R. Feb 42 Nov 53 obit Jun 65
Murtaugh, Daniel Feb 61 obit Feb 77
Murville, Maurice Couve de *see* Couve de Murville, Maurice
Museveni, Yoweri Aug 90
Musgrave, Thea May 78
Musial, Stan Dec 48
Muskie, Edmund S. Feb 55 Dec 68 obit Jun 96
Musmanno, Michael A. Jun 67 obit Dec 68
Mussert, Anton Nov 42
Mussolini, Benito Mar 42 obit May 45
Mussolini, Bruno obit Oct 41
Muste, Abraham Johannes Oct 65 obit Apr 67
Muster, Thomas May 97
Muti, Ettore obit Oct 43
Muti, Riccardo Jul 80
Mutombo, Dikembe Feb 2000
Mutter, Anne-Sophie Jan 90

Muzorewa, Abel T. Mar 79

Mwinyi, Ali Hassan Jun 95

Mydans, Carl M. May 45 [Mydans, Carl M.; and Mydans, Shelley Smith]

Mydans, Shelley Smith May 45 [Mydans, Carl M.; and Mydans, Shelley Smith]

Myer, Dillon S. Jul 47 obit Jan 83

Myers, C. Kilmer Feb 60

Myers, Dee Dee Aug 94

Myers, Francis J. Apr 49 obit Sep 56

Myers, Gustavus obit Jan 43

Myers, Jerome obit Aug 40

Myers, Margaret Jane see Myers, Dee Dee

Myers, Mike Aug 97

Myers, Norman May 93

Myhrvold, Nathan Sep 97

Myrdal, Alva Dec 50 obit Mar 86

Myrdal, Gunnar Sep 46 Mar 75 obit Jul 87

Mysore, Maharaja of see Wadiyar, Sri Krishnaraja, Bahadur Maharaja of Mysore

'N Sync Nov 2000

Nabarro, Gerald Nov 63 obit Jan 74

Nabokov, Vladimir May 66 obit Aug 77

Nabors, Jim Nov 69

Nabrit, James M., Jr. Jan 61 obit Mar 98

Nabrit, S. M. Jan 63

Nabulsi, Suleiman Mar 57

Nader, Ralph Nov 68 Apr 86

Nadler, Marcus May 55 obit Jun 65

Nagano, Osami Jul 42 obit Feb 47

Naguib, Mohammed Oct 52

Nagy, Ivan May 77

Nahas, Mustafa Jul 51 obit Nov 65

Naidu, Sarojini May 43 obit Mar 49

Naifeh, Steven Mar 98 [Naifeh, Steven; and Smith, Gregory White]

Naipaul, V. S. Jul 77

Nair, Mira Nov 93

Naisbitt, John Nov 84

Naish, J. Carrol Jan 57 obit Mar 73

Nájera, Francisco Castillo see Castillo Nájera, Francisco

Najib Ahmadzi see Najibullah, Mohammed

Najibullah, Mohammed Jun 88 obit Jan 97

Nakasone, Yasuhiro Jun 83

Nakian, Reuben Feb 85 obit Feb 87

Namath, Joe Dec 66

Namboodiripad, E. M. S. Nov 76

Nam Il Sep 51 obit Apr 76

Namphy, Henri Sep 88

Narasimha Rao, P. V. see Rao, P. V. Narasimha

Narayan, Jaya Prakash May 58 obit Nov 79

Narayan, R. K. Sep 87

Narelle, Marie obit Mar 41

Narendra Shiromani, Maharajah of Bikaner see Shiromani, Narendra

Nares, Owen obit Sep 43

Nash, Ogden Apr 41 obit Jul 71

Nash, Paul obit Sep 46

Nash, Philleo Nov 62 obit Jan 88

Nash, Walter Oct 42 Mar 58 obit Jul 68

Nason, John W. Jul 53

Nasser, Gamal Abdel Nov 54 obit Nov 70

Nast, Condé obit Nov 42

Nastase, Ilie Oct 74

Nathan, Daniel see Dannay, Frederic

Nathan, George Jean Apr 45 obit Jun 58

Nathan, Robert R. Sep 41

Natta, Giulio Nov 64

Nauman, Bruce Nov 90

Navarre, Henri Nov 53

Navarro, Mary De obit Jul 40

Navasky, Victor S. May 86

Navon, Yitzhak May 82

Navratilova, Martina Sep 77

Naylor, Gloria Apr 93

Nazarbayev, Nursultan Oct 2000

Nazimova, Alla obit Aug 45

Nazimuddin, Khwaja Mar 49 obit Dec 64

N'dour, Youssou Jan 96

Neagle, Anna Nov 45 [Neagle, Anna; and Wilcox, Herbert] obit Jul 86

Neal, Herbert Vincent obit Mar 40

Neal, Patricia Sep 64

Nearing, Scott Oct 71 obit Oct 83

Nederlander, James Morton Apr 91

Neel, Alice Aug 76 obit Jan 85

Neely, Matthew M. Jan 50 obit Mar 58

Neeson, Liam Nov 94

Neghelli, Marchese di see Graziani, Rodolfo

Negrín, Juan Sep 45 obit Jan 57

Nehru, B. K. Feb 63

Nehru, Jawaharlal Jan 41 Apr 48 obit Jul 64

Neier, Aryeh Nov 78

Neill, A. S. Apr 61 obit Nov 73

Neill, Charles Patrick obit Nov 42

Neill, Stephen Charles Mar 60

Neilson, Frances Fullerton (WLB) Yrbk 55

Neilson, Mrs. Winthrop see Neilson, Frances Fullerton

Neilson, William Allan obit Mar 46

Neiman, Leroy Jul 96

Nelles, Percy Walker Feb 44

Nelligan, Kate Jul 83

Nelson, Byron Mar 45

Nelson, Donald M. Mar 41 obit Dec 59

Nelson, Gaylord May 60

Nelson, Harriet May 49 [Nelson, Ozzie; and Nelson, Harriet] obit Jan 95

Nelson, Ozzie May 49 [Nelson, Ozzie; and Nelson, Harriet] obit Aug 75

Nelson, Willie Feb 79

Nemerov, Howard Oct 64 obit Sep 91

Nemirovich-Dantchenko, Vladimir obit Jun 43

Nenni, Pietro Mar 47 obit Feb 80

Nerina, Nadia Nov 57

Nernst, Walter H. obit Jan 42

Neruda, Pablo Dec 70 obit Nov 73

Nervi, Pier Luigi Jan 58 obit Mar 79

Nervo, Luis Padilla *see* Padilla Nervo, Luis

Nesbitt, Cathleen Nov 56 obit Sep 82

Nesmeianov, Aleksandr N. Nov 58

Nessen, Ron Jan 76

Nestingen, Ivan A. Mar 62 obit Jun 78

Netanyahu, Benjamin Jun 96

Netherwood, Douglas B. obit Oct 43

Nettles, Graig Jul 84

Neuberger, Maurine B. Oct 61 obit Jul 2000

Neuberger, Richard L. Feb 55 obit May 60

Neuharth, Allen H. Apr 86

Neuhaus, Richard John Jun 88

Neuman, Leo Handel obit May 41

Neumann, Emanuel Mar 67 obit Jan 81

Neumann, Heinrich obit Jan 40

Neumann, John Von *see* Von Neumann, John

Neumeier, John Jul 91

Neurath, Otto obit Feb 46

Neustadt, Richard E. Nov 68

Neutra, Richard J. May 47 Jul 61 obit Jun 70

Neuwirth, Bebe Nov 97

Nevelson, Louise Oct 67 obit May 88

Neville, John Jan 59

Neville, Robert A. R. Nov 53

Nevins, Allan Oct 68 obit Apr 71

Nevinson, Christopher R. W. obit Nov 46

Newall, Cyril Louis Norton Aug 40

Newberry, Truman H. obit Nov 45

Newbolt, Francis George obit Jan 41

Newby, P. H. (WLB) Yrbk 53

Newcombe, Don Feb 57

Newcombe, John Oct 77

Newcomer, Francis K. Mar 50 obit Oct 67

Newcomer, Mabel Sep 44

Newell, Edward Theodore obit Apr 41

Newell, Homer E., Jr. Nov 54 obit Sep 83

Newell, Horatio B. obit Oct 43

Newhall, Arthur B. Oct 42

Newhart, Bob Mar 62

Newhouse, Maggi *see* McNellis, Maggi

Newhouse, Samuel I. Mar 61 obit Oct 79

Ne Win Apr 71

Newley, Anthony Oct 66 obit Jul 99

Newlon, Jesse H. obit Oct 41

Newman, Alfred Jul 43 obit Apr 70

Newman, Arnold Oct 80

Newman, Barnett Sep 69 obit Sep 70

Newman, Bernard Apr 59 obit Apr 68

Newman, Edwin Sep 67

Newman, J. Wilson Apr 55

Newman, Paul Nov 59 May 85

Newman, Randy Oct 82

Newsom, Carroll Vincent Apr 57 obit Apr 90

Newsom, Herschel D. Apr 51 obit Sep 70

Newton, Alfred Edward obit Nov 40

Newton, Christopher Feb 95

Newton, Cleveland Alexander obit Oct 45

Newton, Eric Feb 56 obit Apr 65

Newton, Helmut Nov 91

Newton, Huey P. Feb 73 obit Oct 89

Newton, Wayne Feb 90

Newton-John, Olivia Nov 78

Ney, Hubert Nov 56

Ngawang Lobsang Yishey Tenzing Gyatso *see* Dalai Lama

Ngo Dinh Diem Mar 55 obit Jan 64

Nguyen Cao Ky *see* Ky, Nguyen Cao

Nguyen Tat Thanh *see* Ho Chi Minh

Nguyen Thi Binh Jul 76

Nguyen Van Thieu *see* Thieu, Nguyen Van

Niall, Michael *see* Breslin, Howard

Niarchos, Stavros May 58 obit Jun 96

Nice, Harry obit Apr 41

Nichols, Dudley Sep 41 obit Mar 60

Nichols, Herbert B. Sep 47

Nichols, Kenneth D. Nov 48 obit Sep 2000

Nichols, Mike Mar 61 Jan 92

Nichols, Roy Franklin Jul 49 obit Mar 73

Nichols, William I. Jun 58

Nichols, William T. Oct 53

Nicholson, Ben Jan 58 obit Apr 82

Nicholson, Jack *see* Steen, Marguerite Oct 74 Apr 95

Nicholson, Margaret Nov 57

Nickerson, Albert L. Nov 59 obit Nov 94

Nicklaus, Jack Nov 62

Nicolet, Marcel Nov 58

Nicolson, Harold George May 67 obit Jun 68

Nicolson, Marjorie Hope Apr 40 obit Jun 81

Nidetch, Jean Dec 73

Niebuhr, Reinhold Mar 41 Nov 51 obit Jul 71

Niederland, William G. Oct 80 obit Oct 93

Nielsen, A. C. Dec 51 obit Jul 80

Nielsen, Alice obit Apr 43

Niemeyer, Oscar Feb 60

Niemöller, Martin Mar 43 Mar 65 obit May 84

Niggli, Josephina (WLB) Yrbk 49

Nijinsky, Waslaw Oct 40 obit May 50

Nikolais, Alwin Feb 68 obit Jul 93

Nikolayev, Andrian Nov 64

Nikolayevna-Tereshkova, Valentina *see* Tereshkova, Valentina

Niles, John Jacob Nov 59 obit Apr 80

Nilsson, Birgit May 60

Nimeiry, Gaafar Muhammad Al- Nov 77

Nimitz, Chester W. Feb 42 obit Mar 66

Nimoy, Leonard Feb 77

Nin, Anaïs Feb 44 Sep 75 obit Mar 77

Nipkow, Paul Gottlieb obit Oct 40

Nirenberg, Marshall W. Apr 65

Nitze, Paul H. Feb 62

Niven, David Mar 57 obit Sep 83

Nixon, Lewis obit Nov 40

Nixon, Patricia Jan 70 obit Aug 93

Nixon, Richard M. Jul 48 Jun 58 Dec 69 Yrbk 94 obit Jun 94

Nizer, Louis Nov 55 obit Jan 95

Nkomo, Joshua Apr 76 obit Sep 99

Nkrumah, Kwame Jul 53 obit Jun 72

Noah, Yannick Aug 87

Noble, Adrian Aug 99

Noble, Allan May 57

Noble, Edward J. Jan 44 obit Mar 59

Noble, Gladwyn Kingsley obit Jan 41

Nobs, Ernst Sep 49 obit Jun 57

Nock, Albert Jay May 44 obit Sep 45

Noel-Baker, Philip John Feb 46 obit Mar 83

Nofziger, Lyn Jan 83

Noguchi, Isamu Sep 43 obit Feb 89

Noguès, Auguste Feb 43 obit Jun 71

Noguès, Charles see Noguès, Auguste

Nolan, Christopher Sep 88

Nolan, Lloyd Nov 56 obit Nov 85

Nolan, W. I. obit Sep 43

Noland, Kenneth Sep 72

Nolde, O. Frederick Feb 47 obit Sep 72

Nolte, Nick Nov 80

Nomura, Kichisaburo Apr 41 obit Jul 64

No Name see Senarens, Luis Philip

Noon, Malik Firoz Khan Jun 57

Noonan, Peggy Jul 90

Noor al-Hussein Apr 91

Norden, Carl L. Jan 45 obit Sep 65

Nordhoff, Heinz Nov 56 obit Jun 68

Nordmann, Charles obit Yrbk 40

Norell, Norman Nov 64 obit Dec 72

Norford, Thomasina Johnson see Johnson, Thomasina Walker

Norgay, Tenzing see Tenzing Norgay

Noriega, Manuel Antonio Mar 88

Norkey, Tenzing see Tenzing Norkey

Norman, Greg Aug 89

Norman, Jessye Feb 76

Norman, Marsha May 84

Norman, Montagu Yrbk 40 obit Mar 50

Norodom Sihanouk Mar 54 Aug 93

Norrington, Roger Jan 90

Norris, Charles G. obit Aug 45

Norris, Chuck Jan 89

Norris, George W. obit Oct 44

Norris, Henry Hutchinson obit May 40

Norris, James Flack obit Sep 40

Norstad, Lauris May 48 Feb 59 obit Oct 88

North, Andrew see Norton, Andre

North, John Ringling Jun 51 obit Jul 85

North, Oliver L. Mar 92

North, Sterling Nov 43 obit Feb 75

Northrop, John H. Jun 47 obit Sep 87

Northrop, John K. Mar 49 obit Apr 81

Northrup, Edwin Fitch obit Jan 40

Norton, Alice Mary see Norton, Andre

Norton, Andre Jan 57

Norton, Edward Jun 2000

Norton, Eleanor Holmes Nov 76

Norton, Howard M. Jun 47

Norton, John Richard Brinsley, 5th Baron of Grantley see Grantley, John Richard Brinsley Norton, 5th Baron

Norton, Mary T. Nov 44 obit Nov 59

Norton, Thomas obit Jan 42

Norton, W. W. obit Dec 45

Norville, Deborah Apr 90

Norway, Nevil Shute see Shute, Nevil

Norwich, Alfred Duff Cooper, 1st Viscount see Cooper, Alfred Duff

Notman, J. Geoffrey Jan 58

Noue, Jehan De, Comte Jan 47

Nourse, Edwin G. Oct 46 obit Jun 74

Novaës, Guiomar Jun 53 obit May 79

Novak, Joseph see Kosinski, Jerzy

Novak, Kim Apr 57

Novak, Marilyn Pauline see Novak, Kim

Novak, Michael Feb 85

Novello, Antonia May 92

Novikov, Nikolai V. Feb 47

Novotn, Antonín May 58 obit Mar 75

Novotna, Jarmila Mar 40 obit Apr 94

Noyes, W. Albert, Jr. Oct 47

Noyes, William A. obit Dec 41

Nozick, Robert Jun 82

Nu, Thakin Dec 51 obit Apr 95

Nuckols, William P. May 52

Nufer, Albert F. Mar 55 obit Jan 57

Nuffield, William Richard Morris, 1st Viscount see Morris, William Richard

Nugent, Elliott Jul 44 obit Oct 80

Nujoma, Sam Feb 90

Nuñez Portuondo, Emilio Apr 57

Nunn, Sam Jan 80

Nunn, Trevor Nov 80

Nur el Hussein see Noor al-Hussein

Nureyev, Rudolf Jul 63 obit Feb 93

Nuri As-Said Jun 55 obit Oct 58

Nuridsany, Claude Jun 97 [Nuridsany, Claude; and Pérennou, Marie]

Nutting, Anthony Feb 55 obit May 99

Nutting, Wallace obit Sep 41

Nyad, Diana Aug 79

Nyborg, Victor H. Feb 54

Nye, Archibald E. Feb 42 obit Jan 68

Nye, Bill Jul 98

Nye, Gerald Prentice Nov 41 obit Sep 71

Nye, Russell Blaine Jul 45 obit Nov 93

Nyerere, Julius K. Apr 63 obit Jan 2000

Nykvist, Sven Jun 89

Nylander, Olof O. obit Sep 43

Nyrop, Donald W. Jun 52

Nystrom, Paul H. Mar 51 obit Oct 69

Oakes, Grant W. Jan 50

Oaksey, Geoffrey Lawrence see Lawrence, Geoffrey

Oates, Joyce Carol Sep 70 Jun 94

Obando Y Bravo, Miguel Mar 88

Obasanjo, Olusegun Jul 99

Oberlin, Russell Jul 60

Oberon, Merle Nov 41 obit Jan 80

Oberteuffer, George obit Jan 40

Oberth, Hermann Apr 57 obit Mar 90

Obolensky, Serge Oct 59 obit Nov 78

Oboler, Arch Mar 40 obit May 87

Obote, Milton Apr 81

O'Boyle, Patrick Jul 73 obit Sep 87

Obraztsov, Sergei Nov 64

Obraztsova, Elena Feb 83

O'Brian, Hugh Jul 58

O'Brian, Patrick Jun 95 obit Mar 2000

O'Brien, Conan May 96

O'Brien, Conor Cruise Apr 67

O'Brien, Dan Jul 96

O'Brien, Edna Sep 80

O'Brien, Edward J. obit Apr 41

O'Brien, Lawrence F. Nov 61 Apr 77 obit Nov 90

O'Brien, Leo W. Jun 59 obit Jul 82

O'Brien, Pat Mar 66 obit Jan 84

O'Brien, Tim Aug 95

Obst, Lynda Oct 2000

Obuchi, Keizo May 99 obit Aug 2000

O'Byrne, Mrs. Roscoe C. Nov 48

O'Casey, Sean Nov 62 obit Nov 64

Ochoa, Severo Jun 62 obit Jan 94

Ochsner, Alton Oct 66 obit Nov 81

Ocker, William C. obit Nov 42

O'Connell, Hugh obit Mar 43

O'Connell, William Jun 41 obit Jun 44

O'Connor, Andrew obit Aug 41

O'Connor, Basil Sep 44 obit May 72

O'Connor, Carroll Jul 72

O'Connor, Donald May 55

O'Connor, Edwin Nov 63 obit May 68

O'Connor, Flannery (WLB) Yrbk 58 obit Sep 65

O'Connor, James Francis obit Mar 45

O'Connor, John J. Jun 84 obit Jul 2000

O'Connor, Sandra Day Jan 82

O'Connor, Sinéad Jun 91

O'Conor, Herbert R. Feb 50 obit May 60

O'Daniel, W. Lee Oct 47 obit Jun 69

O'Day, Anita Jun 90

O'Day, Caroline Goodwin obit Feb 43

Odell, George C. D. Dec 44 obit Dec 49

Odets, Clifford Nov 41 obit Nov 63

Odetta Dec 60

Odishaw, Hugh Feb 71 obit Jun 84

Odlin, Reno Jul 65

Odlum, Floyd B. Nov 41 obit Aug 76

Odlum, Mrs. Floyd B. see Cochran, Jacqueline

O'Donnell, Donat see O'Brien, Conor Cruise

O'Donnell, Edwin P. obit Jun 43

O'Donnell, Emmett, Jr. Jul 48 obit Feb 72

O'Donnell, Rosie Aug 95

O'Dowd, George A. see Boy George

Odria, Manuel A. Nov 54 obit Apr 74

Oduber, Daniel Jul 77

O'Dwyer, Paul Sep 69 obit Sep 98

O'Dwyer, William Sep 41 May 47 obit Jan 65

Oe, Hikari May 99

Oe, Kenzaburo May 96

Oechsner, Frederick Cable Mar 43 obit Jun 92

Oenslager, Donald Sep 46 obit Aug 75

Oettinger, Katherine Brownell Nov 57 obit Jan 98

O'Faoláin, Séan Apr 90 obit Jun 91

O'Flanagan, Michael obit Sep 42

Ogata, Sadako Oct 97

Ogburn, Charlton Feb 55 obit Apr 62

Ogburn, William F. Feb 55 obit Jul 59

Ogden, C. K. Jan 44 obit Jun 57

Ogilvie, Elisabeth (WLB) Yrbk 51

Ogilvy, David M. Jul 61 obit Oct 99

O'Gorman, James A. obit Jul 43

O'Gorman, Juan Nov 56

O'Gorman, Patrick F. obit Apr 40

O'Hair, Madalyn Murray Jan 77 obit Jun 2001

O'Hara, John Feb 41 obit Jun 70

O'Hara, Mary Jan 44 obit Jan 81

O'Hara, Maureen Feb 53

Ohga, Norio Jun 98

Ohira, Masayoshi Mar 64 obit Aug 80

Ohlin, Lloyd E. Apr 63

Ohlsson, Garrick Jun 75

O'Horgan, Tom Apr 70

Oistrakh, David Mar 56 obit Dec 74

Ojike, Mbonu Jul 47

Ojukwu, Chukuemeka Odumegwu Feb 69

O'Keeffe, Georgia Jun 41 Feb 64 obit Apr 86

O'Kelly, Sean T. Jul 48 obit Jan 67

O'Konski, Alvin E. Nov 55 obit Aug 87

Okun, Arthur M. Feb 70 obit May 80

Olaf V, King of Norway see Olav V, King of Norway

Olajuwon, Hakeem Nov 93

Olav V, King of Norway Jan 62 obit Mar 91

Oldenbroek, Jacobus H. Mar 50

Oldenburg, Claes Feb 70

Oldfield, Barney obit Nov 46

Oldman, Gary Jan 96

Olds, Irving S. Oct 48 obit Apr 63

O'Leary, Hazel R. Jan 94

O'Leary, James A. obit May 44

Oleson, Lloyd F. Jun 47

Oliphant, Marcus L. Dec 51 obit Oct 2000

Oliphant, Pat Jul 91

Olitski, Jules Oct 69

Oliveira Salazar, Antonio de see Salazar, Antonio De Oliveira

Oliver, Edna May obit Jan 43

Oliver, James A. Jan 66 obit May 82

Oliver, Lunsford E. Sep 47

Olivero, Magda Apr 80

Olivetti, Adriano Jan 59 obit Apr 60

Olivier, Lady see Plowright, Joan

Olivier, Laurence Jun 46 Jan 79 obit Sep 89

Ollenhauer, Erich Jan 53 obit Feb 64

Olmedo, Alex Dec 59

Olmedo y Rodriguez Alejandro see Olmedo, Alex

Olmos, Edward James Aug 92

Olmstead, Albert Ten Eyck obit May 45

Olmsted, Frederick Law Jun 49 obit Mar 58

Olsen, John Sep 40 [Olsen, John Sigvard; and Johnson, Harold Ogden] obit Mar 63

Olsen, Kenneth H. Mar 87

Olson, Harry F. Nov 55 obit Jun 82

Olsson, Ann-Margret see Ann-Margret

Oltman, Florine May 70

O'Mahoney, Joseph C. Oct 45 obit Jan 63

O'Malley, Walter F. Mar 54 obit Oct 79

O'Meara, Walter (WLB) Yrbk 58 obit Nov 89

O'Melveny, Henry W. obit Jun 41

Onassis, Aristotle Socrates Mar 63 obit May 75

Onassis, Christina Feb 76 obit Jan 89

Onassis, Jacqueline Kennedy Oct 61 [Kennedy, Jacqueline] obit Jul 94

Ondaatje, Michael Oct 93

O'Neal, A. Daniel Jun 79

O'Neal, Edward A. Sep 46 obit May 58

O'Neal, Frederick Nov 46 obit Oct 92

O'Neal, Ryan Feb 73

O'Neal, Shaquille Jul 96

O'Neil, George obit Jul 40

O'Neil, James F. Nov 47 obit Sep 81

O'Neil, Thomas F. Nov 55 obit Jun 98

O'Neill, C. William Jul 58

O'Neill, Eugene F. Apr 63

O'Neill, Francis A., Jr. Dec 60 obit Mar 92

O'Neill, Gerard K. Feb 79 obit Jun 92

O'Neill, J. E. Jun 52

O'Neill, Terence Sep 68 obit Sep 90

O'Neill, Thomas P., Jr. Apr 74 obit Mar 94

O'Neill, Tip see O'Neill, Thomas P., Jr.

O'Neill, William A. Feb 85

Ongania, Juan Carlos Oct 68 obit Aug 95

Onís, Harriet De see De Onís, Harriet

Ono, Yoko Nov 72

Onsager, Lars Apr 58 obit Jan 77

Oort, Jan Hendrik Jun 69 obit Jan 93

Oosterbaan, Benjamin Gaylord see Oosterbaan, Bennie

Oosterbaan, Bennie Dec 49 obit Jan 91

Opel, John R. Mar 86

Ophuls, Marcel Jun 77

Oppenheim, E. Phillips obit Mar 46

Oppenheimer, Eric see Newton, Eric

Oppenheimer, Franz obit Nov 43

Oppenheimer, Harry Frederick Feb 61 obit Nov 2000

Oppenheimer, J. Robert Nov 45 Apr 64 obit Apr 67

Orbach, Jerry May 70

Orff, Carl Aug 76 obit May 82

Orlando, Vittorio Emanuele Feb 44 obit Jan 53

Orlebar, Augustus H. obit Sep 43

Orlemanski, Stanislaus, Rev. Jun 44

Ormandy, Eugene Jan 41 obit May 85

Ormond, Julia Mar 99

Ormsby-Gore, David Mar 61 obit Mar 85

Ornish, Dean Apr 94

Orowitz, Eugene Maurice see Landon, Michael

Orozco, Jose Clemente Sep 40 obit Oct 49

Orr, Bobby Nov 69

Orr, H. Winnett Oct 41

Orr, John Boyd see Boyd-Orr, John Boyd Orr

Orr, Louis M. Apr 60 obit Jul 61

Orsborn, Albert Nov 46 obit Apr 67

Ortega, Daniel Oct 84

Ortega Saavedra, Daniel see Ortega, Daniel

Ortiz, Roberto M. obit Sep 42

Orton, Helen Fuller Jan 41 obit Apr 55

Orville, Howard T. May 56 obit Jul 60

Osato, Sono Oct 45

Osborn, Fairfield Sep 49 obit Nov 69

Osborn, Frederick Nov 41 obit Mar 81

Osborn, Robert C. Jun 59 obit Feb 95

Osborne, John Jun 59 obit Feb 95

Osborne, Oliver Thomas obit Yrbk 40

Osborne, Tom Mar 98

Osborne, William Hamilton obit Feb 43

Osbourne, Ozzy Nov 98

Oscar of the Waldorf see Tschirky, Oscar

Osgood, Charles E. Apr 62

O'Shea, Milo Jun 82

O'Shea, William F. obit Apr 45

Osmeña, Sergio Sep 44 obit Dec 61

Osmond, Donny Feb 98

Ospina Perez, Mariano Feb 50 obit Jun 76

Osterberg, James Newell *see* Pop, Iggy

Osumi, Mineo Osumi, Baron obit Apr 41

Otero, Miguel Antonio obit Sep 44

O'Toole, Peter Sep 68

Ott, Mel Jul 41 obit Jan 59

Ottaviani, Alfredo Dec 66 obit Sep 79

Otter, Anne Sofie von Sep 95

Ottinger, Nathan obit Jan 41

Ottley, Roi Oct 43 obit Dec 60

Otto, Frei Oct 71

Otto of Austria, Archduke Jun 41

Ötüken, Adnan Jun 54

Ouédraogo, Idrissa May 93

Oumansky, Constantine Feb 41 obit Mar 45

Oursler, Fulton Oct 42 obit Jul 52

Ousmane, Sembène *see* Sembène, Ousmane

Ovanda Candia, Alfredo Mar 70 obit Mar 82

Overholser, Winfred Nov 53 obit Dec 64

Overman, Lynne obit Apr 43

Overstreet, Harry A. Sep 50 obit Oct 70

Ovitz, Michael S. Oct 95

Owen, A. David K. May 46 obit Sep 70

Owen, David Sep 77

Owen, Ruth Bryan *see* Rohde, Ruth Bryan Owen

Owen, Steve Dec 46 obit Jul 64

Owens, Clarence Julian obit Apr 41

Owens, Dana *see* Queen Latifah

Owens, James Cleveland *see* Owens, Jesse

Owens, Jesse Nov 56 obit May 80

Owens, Robert Bowie obit Yrbk 40

Owings, Nathaniel A. May 71 obit Aug 84

Oxenham, John obit Mar 41

Oxford And Asquith, Margot Asquith, Countess of *see* Asquith, Margot

Oxnam, G. Bromley Nov 44 obit Apr 63

Oz, Amos Jul 83

Oz, Frank Oct 99

Özal, Turgut Jun 85 obit Jun 93

Ozawa, Seiji Feb 68 Jul 98

Ozbirn, Catharine Freeman Jan 62 [Ozbirn, Mrs. E. Lee] obit Mar 74

Ozick, Cynthia Aug 83

Oznowicz, Frank *see* Oz, Frank

Paar, Jack Apr 59

Paasikivi, Juho Kusti May 44 obit Feb 57

Pacciardi, Randolfo Mar 44 obit Jul 91

Pace, Charles Ashford obit Feb 41

Pace, Frank, Jr. Feb 50 obit Feb 88

Pacelli, Eugenio Maria Giuseppe Giovanni *see* Pius XII, Pope

Pacheco E Chaves, João Nov 54

Pacino, Al Jul 74

Packard, David Jun 69 obit Jun 96

Packard, Eleanor Apr 41 obit Jun 72

Packard, Frank L. obit Apr 42

Packard, Vance Apr 58 obit Feb 97

Packard, Winthrop obit May 43

Packer, Fred L. obit Feb 57

Packwood, Bob Jan 81

Padover, Saul K. Oct 52 obit Apr 81

Paepcke, Walter P. Apr 60

Page, Geraldine Nov 53 obit Aug 87

Page, Irvine H. Jun 66 obit Aug 91

Page, Joe Apr 50 obit Jun 80

Page, Patti Sep 65

Page, Robert Morris Nov 64 obit Jul 92

Page, Ruth Jun 62 obit Jul 91

Pagels, Elaine Hiesey Feb 96

Paglia, Camille Aug 92

Pagnanelli, George *see* Carlson, John Roy

Pagnol, Marcel Mar 56 obit Jun 74

Pahlevi, Farah Diba *see* Farah Diba Pahlevi

Pahlevi, Mohammed Riza *see* Mohammed Zahir Shah

Pahlmann, William C. Oct 64 obit Jan 88

Paicovitch, Yigal *see* Allon, Yigal

Paige, Janis Jan 59

Paige, Leroy Sep 52 obit Aug 82

Paige, Satchel *see* Paige, Leroy

Paik, Nam June Mar 83

Paine, Thomas Otten Mar 70 obit Jul 92

Pais, Abraham Jan 94 obit Oct 2000

Paisley, Ian Jan 71 Jun 86

Pai Tsung-Hsi Nov 42 [Li Tsung-Jen; and Pai Tsung-Hsi] obit Feb 67

Pak, Chong-Hui *see* Park, Chung Hee

Pak, Jung Hi *see* Park, Chung Hee

Pak, Se Ri Jan 99

Pakenham, Antonia *see* Fraser, Antonia

Pakula, Alan J. Jun 80 obit Feb 99

Palade, George E. Jul 67

Palance, Jack Aug 92

Palethorpe-Todd, Richard Andrew *see* Todd, Richard

Paley, Grace Mar 86

Paley, William S. Oct 40 Dec 51 obit Jan 91

Palin, Michael Feb 2000

Palinurus *see* Connolly, Cyril

Palme, Olof May 70 obit Apr 86

Palmer, Arnold Sep 60

Palmer, Jim May 80

Palmer, John Leslie obit Sep 44

Palmer, Lilli May 51 obit Mar 86

Palmieri, Eddie Jun 92

Pandit, Mrs. Ranjit *see* Pandit, Vijaya Lakshmi

Pandit, Vijaya Lakshmi Jan 46 obit Feb 91

Panetta, Leon E. Jun 93

Panic, Milan Jun 93

Panofsky, Wolfgang K. H. Jun 70

Panov, Valery Oct 74

Pant, Govind Ballabh Jan 59 obit May 61

Pantaleoni, Helenka A. Nov 56 obit Mar 87

Pantaleoni, Mrs. Guido *see* Pantaleoni, Helenka A.

Pantani, Marco Feb 99

Papaleo, Anthony *see* Franciosa, Anthony

Papandreou, Andreas May 70 Apr 83 obit Sep 96

Papandreou, George Dec 44 obit Dec 68

Papashvily, George Mar 45 [Papashvily, George; and Papashvily, Helen] obit May 78

Papashvily, Helen Mar 45 [Papashvily, George; and Papashvily, Helen]

Papen, Franz Von Jun 41 obit Jun 69

Papp, Joseph May 65 obit Jan 92

Parcells, Bill Apr 91

Paretsky, Sara May 92

Parizeau, Jacques Jul 93

Park, Chung Hee Jan 69 obit Jan 80

Park, Dorothy Dowden *see* Clark, Dorothy Park

Park, Thomas Jan 63 obit Jun 92

Parkening, Christopher Apr 87

Parker, Alan Mar 94

Parker, John J. Dec 55 obit May 58

Parker, Mrs. James C. *see* Parker, Karla V.

Parker, Raymond K. *see* Parker, Buddy

Parker, Robert B. Nov 93

Parker, Sarah Jessica Sep 98

Parker, Trey May 98 [Parker, Trey; and Stone, Matt]

Parkes, Henry Bamford Mar 54

Parkinson, C. Northcote Dec 60 obit May 93

Parks, Bert Feb 73 obit Apr 92

Parks, Gordon Oct 68 Oct 92

Parks, Rosa May 89

Parks, Suzan-Lori Apr 99

Parmoor, Charles Alfred Cripps, 1st Baron *see* Cripps, Charles Alfred

Parnis, Mollie May 56 obit Sep 92

Parodi, Alexandre Jun 46

Parr, Albert Eide Jul 42 obit Sep 91

Parran, Thomas Aug 40 obit Apr 68

Parrish, Maxfield Nov 65 obit Apr 66

Parrish, Mrs. Wayne William *see* Knight, Frances G.

Parry, Albert Apr 61 obit Jul 92

Parseghian, Ara Feb 68

Parsons, Estelle Oct 75

Parsons, Harriet Jan 53 obit Mar 83

Parsons, Louella Oct 40 obit Oct 73

Parsons, Mrs. William Barclay *see* Parsons, Rose Peabody

Parsons, Rose Peabody Dec 59 obit Jun 85

Parsons, Talcott Jan 61 obit Jul 79

Pärt, Arvo Feb 95

Partch, Harry Sep 65 obit Oct 74

Partch, Virgil Franklin Jul 46 obit Oct 84

Parton, Dolly Aug 77

Partridge, Deborah *see* Wolfe, Deborah Partridge

Partridge, Eric Jan 63 obit Jul 79

Pasionaria, La *see* Ibárruri, Dolores

Pasolini, Pier Paolo Jul 70 obit Jan 76

Passman, Otto, E. Oct 60 obit Sep 88

Passos, John Dos *see* Dos Passos, John

Pasternak, Boris Leonidovich Feb 59 obit Jul 60

Pastora Gómez, Edén Jul 86

Pastore, John O. Apr 53 obit Yrbk 2000

Pastrana Borrero, Misael Jul 71 obit Nov 97

Pataki, George E. Apr 96

Patch, Alexander M. May 43 obit Jan 46

Pate, Martha B. May 47 obit Jul 83

Patel, Vallabhbhai Mar 48 obit Jan 51

Paterno, Joe Feb 84

Paterson, Chat Mar 48 obit May 92

Paterson, Katherine Nov 97

Patinkin, Mandy Jan 99

Patino, Simon I. Oct 42 obit May 47

Patman, Wright Feb 46 obit Apr 76

Paton, Alan Jun 52 obit May 88

Patri, Angelo Nov 40 obit Nov 65

Patten, Chris Jul 93

Patten, Gilbert obit Mar 45

Patterson, Alicia Nov 55 obit Sep 63

Patterson, Eleanor Medill Nov 40 obit Sep 48

Patterson, Floyd Oct 60

Patterson, Francine Nov 2000

Patterson, Frederick Douglas Jun 47 obit Jun 88

Patterson, Joseph M. Jan 42 obit Jun 46

Patterson, P. J. Feb 95

Patterson, Penny *see* Patterson, Francine

Patterson, Percival J. *see* Patterson, P. J.

Patton, Frances Gray (WLB) Yrbk 55 obit Sep 2000

Patton, George S., Jr. Jan 43 obit Feb 46

Patton, James G. Jan 45 Feb 66

Patton, Marguerite Courtright *see* Patton, Mrs. James B.

Patton, Mrs. Lewis *see* Patton, Frances Gray

Pauker, Ana Mar 48

Paul VI, Pope Jan 56 [Montini, Giovanni Battista] Nov 63 obit Sep 78

Paul, Alice Sep 47 obit Sep 77

Paul, Elliot Feb 40 obit Jun 58

Paul, Les Aug 87

Paul-Boncour, Joseph Jun 45 obit May 72

Pauley, Jane May 80

Pauli, Wolfgang Jun 46 obit Mar 59

Pauling, Linus C. May 49 Feb 64 Jun 94 obit Oct 94

Pavarotti, Luciano Jun 73

Pavelic, Ante Aug 42 obit Feb 60

Paxton, Tom Sep 82

Payne, Robert (WLB) Yrbk 47 obit Apr 83

Payne, Roger S. Jun 95

Peterson, Esther Dec 61 obit Mar 98

Peterson, Oscar Oct 83

Peterson, Peter G. Jun 72

Peterson, Roger Tory Apr 59 obit Oct 96

Petherbridge, Margaret *see* Farrar, Margaret

Pethick-Lawrence, Frederick William Jun 46 obit Nov 61

Petiot, Henry Jules Charles *see* Daniel-Rops, Henry

Petit, Philippe Sep 88

Petit, Roland Apr 52

Petitpierre, Max Dec 53 obit Jun 94

Petri, Egon Nov 42 obit Jul 62

Petrillo, James C. Yrbk 40 obit Jan 85

Petronio, Stephen Mar 98

Petry, Ann Mar 46 obit Jul 97

Pettit, Robert Oct 61

Petty, Richard Aug 80

Petty, Tom Nov 91

Peurifoy, John E. Jan 49 obit Oct 55

Pevsner, Antoine Mar 59 obit Jun 62

Pfeiffer, Eckhard Jun 98

Pfeiffer, Michelle Mar 90

Pflimlin, Pierre Nov 55 obit Oct 2000

Pfost, Gracie May 55 obit Oct 65

Pham Van Dong Feb 75 obit Sep 2000

Phan Dinh Khai *see* Le Duc Tho

Phelps, William Lyon Jan 43

Philbin, Regis Oct 94

Philbrick, Herbert A. Mar 53 obit Oct 93

Philip, André Aug 43 obit Sep 70

Phillips, Caryl Jul 94

Phillips, H. I. Sep 43 obit Apr 65

Phillips, Irna Apr 43 obit Feb 74

Phillips, Kevin Sep 94

Phillips, Morgan Sep 49 obit Feb 63

Phillips, Pauline Esther Friedman *see* Van Buren, Abigail

Phillips, Thomas Hal (WLB) Yrbk 56

Phillips, William [editor] Oct 84

Phillips, William [diplomat] Jul 40 obit Apr 68

Phipps, Joyce Irene *see* Grenfell, Joyce

Phoui Sananikone *see* Sananikone, Phoui

Phouma, Souvanna *see* Souvanna Phouma

Phumiphon Aduldet *see* Rama IX, King of Thailand

Piaf, Edith Dec 50 obit Nov 63

Piaget, Jean Dec 58 obit Nov 80

Piatigorsky, Gregor Oct 45 obit Sep 76

Piazza, Mike Jul 99

Picasso, Pablo Jan 43 Nov 62 obit May 73

Picasso, Paloma Apr 86

Piccard, Auguste Sep 47 [Piccard, Auguste; and Piccard, Jean Felix] obit May 62

Piccard, Jacques Dec 65

Piccard, Jean Felix Sept 47 [Piccard, Auguste; and Piccard, Jean Felix] obit Mar 63

Pickens, Jane Dec 49 obit Apr 92

Pickens, T. Boone Jul 85

Pickering, William H. Nov 58

Pickersgill, J. W. Mar 68

Pickford, Mary Apr 45 obit Jul 79

Picon, Molly Jun 51 obit Jun 92

Pidgeon, Walter Sep 42 obit Nov 84

Piëch, Ferdinand Sep 99

Piel, Gerard Jun 59

Pierce, Bob Dec 61

Pierce, J. R. Feb 61

Pierce, Lorne Nov 56

Pierce, Samuel R. Jr. Nov 82

Piercy, Marge Nov 94

Pierlot, Hubert, Count May 43 obit Feb 64

Pifer, Alan Apr 69

Pike, James A. May 57 obit Nov 69

Pile, Frederick Alfred Feb 42 obit Yrbk 91 (died Nov 76)

Pileggi, Nicholas Jan 99

Pilgrim, David *see* Saunders, Hilary Aidan St. George

Pinay, Antoine Apr 52 obit Feb 95

Pincherle, Alberto *see* Moravia, Alberto

Pincus, Gregory May 66 obit Oct 67

Pindling, Lynden Oscar May 68 obit Yrbk 2000

Pineau, Christian Jul 56 obit Jun 95

Piñero, Miguel Nov 83 obit Aug 88

Piñero Jesús T. Oct 46 obit Jan 53

P'ing, Lan *see* Jiang Qing

Piniella, Lou Aug 86

Pinilla, Gustavo Rojas *see* Rojas Pinilla, Gustavo

Pinker, Steven A. Sep 98

Pinnock, Trevor Sep 89

Pinochet Ugarte, Augusto Dec 74

Pinsky, Robert Feb 99

Pinter, Harold Nov 63

Pinza, Ezio Feb 41 Dec 53 obit Jul 57

Piper, John Apr 64 obit Aug 92

Pipher, Mary Aug 99

Pippen, Scottie Mar 94

Pippin, Horace Aug 45 obit Yrbk 47

Pire, Georges May 59 obit Mar 69

Piscator, Erwin Oct 42 obit Apr 66

Piston, Walter Jun 48 Dec 61 obit Jan 77

Pitino, Rick Jan 98

Pitt, Brad Mar 96

Pittman, Robert Jul 2000

Pius XII, Pope Apr 41 Mar 50 obit Dec 58

Pivot, Bernard Oct 90

Plain, Belva Feb 99

Plant, Robert Oct 98

Plavsic, Biljana Feb 98

Player, Gary Nov 61

Plaza Lasso, Galo Oct 51 Apr 69 obit Mar 87

Pleasence, Donald Jun 69 obit Apr 95

Pleven, René Jun 50 obit Mar 93

Plimpton, George Feb 69

Plisetskaya, Maya Jun 63

Plotkin, Mark J. Jun 97

Plowden, David Feb 96

Plowden, Edwin Noel Jul 47

Plowright, Joan Feb 64

Plummer, Christopher Jul 56 Aug 88

Plunkett, Jim Sep 71 Feb 82

Poage, W. R. Dec 69 obit Mar 87

Podgorny, Nikolai V. May 66 obit Mar 83

Podhoretz, Norman Oct 68

Pogorelich, Ivo Sep 88

Pogrebin, Letty Cottin Nov 97

Poindexter, John M. Nov 87

Poinso-Chapuis, Germaine Jun 48

Poitier, Sidney May 59 Sep 2000

Polanski, Roman Jun 69

Polese, Kim Jul 97

Poletti, Charles Sep 43

Poling, Daniel Nov 43 obit Mar 68

Pollack, Jack H. Dec 57 obit Feb 85

Pollack, Sydney Sep 86

Pollini, Maurizio Nov 80

Pollitt, Harry May 48 obit Sep 60

Pollock, Jackson Apr 56

Pol Pot Apr 80 obit Jun 98

Pomeroy, Wardell B. Jul 74

Pompidou, Georges Nov 62 obit May 74

Poncins, Gontran, Vicomte De Jun 41

Ponnamperuma, Cyril Apr 84 obit Mar 95

Ponnelle, Jean-Pierre Mar 83 obit Sep 88

Pons, Lily Jan 44 obit Apr 76

Poole, Elijah see Muhammad, Elijah

Poor, Henry Varnum Apr 42 obit Jan 71

Poorten, Hein Ter see Ter Poorten, Hein

Pop, Iggy Jan 95

Popcorn, Faith Feb 93

Pope, Liston Apr 56 obit Jun 74

Pope John XXIII see John XXIII, Pope

Pope John Paul I see John Paul I, Pope

Pope John Paul II see John Paul II

Popenoe, Paul Dec 46

Pope Paul VI see Paul VI, Pope

Pope Pius XII see Pius Xii, Pope

Popham, Robert Brooke- see Brooke-Popham, Robert

Popkin, Zelda (WLB) Yrbk 51 obit Jul 83

Popov, Oleg Mar 64

Popovic, Koca Jan 57 obit Jan 93

Popper, Karl Raimund Jan 63 obit Nov 94

Portal, Charles Mar 41 obit Jun 71 [Portal of Hungerford, Charles Frederick Algernon Portal, 1st Viscount]

Portal of Hungerford, Charles Frederick Algernon Portal, 1st Viscount see Portal, Charles

Porter, Cole Jul 40 obit Dec 64

Porter, Eliot Nov 76 obit Jan 91

Porter, Katherine Anne May 40 Mar 63 obit Nov 80

Porter, Mrs. Eugene Vandergrift see Porter, Elizabeth K.

Porter, Richard William Nov 58 obit Jan 97

Porter, Sylvia Oct 41 Apr 80 obit Aug 91

Porter, William J. Mar 74 obit May 88

Portinari, Candido Yrbk 40 obit Mar 62

Posner, Richard A. Jan 93

Post, Emily Mar 41 obit Nov 60

Poston, Tom Apr 61

Pot, Pol see Pol Pot

Potok, Chaim May 83

Potter, Beatrix obit Mar 44

Potter, Dan M. Feb 64

Potter, Dennis Jul 94 obit Jul 94

Potter, William E. Dec 57 obit Feb 89

Potvin, Denis Oct 86

Poujade, Pierre Apr 56

Pound, Ezra Nov 42 May 63 obit Dec 72

Pound, Roscoe May 47 obit Sep 64

Pousette-Dart, Richard Mar 76 obit Jan 93

Poussaint, Alvin F. Jul 73

Powdermaker, Hortense Feb 61 obit Sep 70

Powell, Adam Clayton Apr 42 obit May 72

Powell, Anthony Sep 77 obit Aug 2000

Powell, Benjamin E. Jun 59

Powell, Colin L. Jun 88

Powell, Dick Feb 48 obit Feb 63

Powell, J. Enoch Nov 64 obit Jun 99

Powell, Jane Dec 74

Powell, Jody Jul 77

Powell, Lawrence Clark Jun 60

Powell, Lewis F., Jr. Feb 65 obit Nov 98

Powell, Michael Aug 87 obit Apr 90

Powell, Mike Oct 93

Powell, Richard Stillman see Barbour, Ralph Henry

Powell, Robert Stephenson Smyth Baden-, 1st Baron Baden-Powell of Gilwe see Robert Stephenson Smyth Baden-Powell

Powell, Sandy Jun 2000

Powell, William Oct 47 obit May 84

Power, Tyrone Dec 50 obit Jan 59

Powers, J. F. Jan 89 obit Sep 99

Powys, Llewelyn Jan 40

Pozner, Vladimir May 43

Pozsgay, Imre Mar 90

Prado Ugarteche, Manuel Jun 42 obit Oct 67

Praeger, Frederick A. Sep 59 obit Aug 94

Prasad, Rajendra Apr 50 obit Apr 63

Pratt, E. J. Oct 46 obit Jun 64

Pratt, Fletcher May 42 obit Sep 56

Pratt, J. Gaither Nov 64

Pratt, Jane Jun 99

Pratt, Mrs. Harry Rogers see Rothery, Agnes

Pratt, William Veazie Jun 43 obit Feb 58

Prebisch, Raúl Dec 69 obit Jul 86

Preminger, Otto Jul 59 obit Jun 86

Prentis, Henning Webb, Jr. Sep 40 obit Feb 60

Prescott, Orville Mar 57 obit Jul 96

Presley, Elvis Sep 59 obit Oct 77

Presley, Priscilla Beaulieu Sep 90

Press, Frank Jul 66

Presser, Jackie Sep 83 obit Aug 88

Pressler, Larry Oct 83

Pressman, Lee May 47 obit Jan 70

Preston, Robert Dec 58 obit May 87

Prestopino, Gregorio Jun 64 obit Apr 85

Preus, Jacob A. O. May 75 obit Oct 94

Previn, André May 72

Previn, Dory Sep 75

Prey, Hermann Feb 75 obit Oct 98

Pribichevich, Stoyan Aug 44 obit Jul 76

Price, Byron Feb 42 obit Sep 81

Price, Charles C. Dec 57

Price, Don K. Feb 67 obit Sep 95

Price, Dorothy Reeder *see* Carnegie, Dorothy

Price, George Aug 84

Price, Gwilym A. May 49 obit Aug 85

Price, Leontyne May 61 Oct 78

Price, Margaret Aug 86

Price, Nick Jun 96

Price, Reynolds Apr 87

Price, Richard Jan 94

Price, Vincent Nov 56 obit Jan 94

Priceman, James *see* Kirkland, Winifred Margaretta

Pride, Alfred M. Nov 54 obit Feb 89

Pride, Charley Apr 75

Priest, Mrs. Roy F. *see* Priest, Ivy Baker

Priestley, J. B. May 76 obit Oct 84

Prigogine, Ilya Feb 87

Priley, Mrs. Joseph Carl *see* Hubbard, Margaret Ann

Primakov, Yevgeny Feb 99

Primrose, William Dec 46 obit Jul 82

Primus, Pearl Apr 44 obit Jan 95

Prince, Harold Apr 71

Prince Andrew *see* Andrew, Duke of York

Prince Charles of Belgium *see* Charles, Prince of Belgium

Prince Feb 86

Princess Diana *see* Diana, Princess of Wales

Princess Stephanie *see* Stephanie, Princess of Monaco

Prinz, Joachim Feb 63 obit Nov 88

Prinze, Freddie Jun 75 obit Mar 77

Prío Socarrás, Carlos May 49 obit Jun 77

Pritchett, V. S. Jan 74 obit Jun 97

Procopé, Hjalmar Johan Apr 40 obit Apr 54

Proell, Annemarie Sep 76

Profet, Margie Nov 98

Profumo, John D. Oct 59

Prokofiev, Sergey Nov 41 obit Apr 53

Protess, David Oct 99

Proulx, E. Annie Apr 95

Proxmire, William Jun 58 Aug 78

Pruden, Edward Hughes Sep 50

Prusiner, Stanley Jun 97

Pryor, Richard Feb 76

Pu, Cheng-his *see* Park, Chung Hee

Pucci, Emilio Feb 61 obit Jan 93

Puck, Wolfgang Jan 98

Puente, Ernest Anthony, Jr. *see* Puente, Tito

Puente, Tito Nov 77 obit Aug 2000

Puff Daddy Apr 98

Puig, Manuel Jan 88 obit Sep 90

Pulitzer, Joseph, 2d Dec 54 obit May 55

Pumarejo, Alfonso López *see* López, Alfonso

Purcell, Edward M. Sep 54 obit May 97

Puryear, Martin Aug 99

Pusey, Merlo J. Jul 52 obit Jan 86

Putin, Vladimir Apr 2000

Putnam, Roger L. Jan 52

Puttnam, David Feb 89

Puzo, Mario Mar 75 obit Sep 99

Pyle, Ernest Taylor *see* Pyle, Ernie

Pyle, Ernie Apr 41 obit May 45

Pym, Francis Sep 82

Pynchon, Thomas Oct 87

Qabus Bin Said Aug 78

Qaddafi, Muammar Al- Sep 73 Mar 92

Qing, Jiang *see* Jiang Qing

Quadros, Jânio da Silva Jun 61 obit Apr 92

Quaison-Sackey, Alex Mar 66 obit Feb 93

Quant, Mary Jan 68

Quasimodo, Salvatore Mar 60 obit Sep 68

Quay, Jan Eduard de May 63 obit Aug 85

Quayle, Anthony Dec 71 obit Jan 90

Quayle, Dan Jun 89

Queen, Ellery *see* Dannay, Frederic; Lee, Manfred B.

Queen Latifah Feb 97

Queen Noor *see* Noor al-Hussein

Quennell, Peter May 84 obit Jan 94

Quesada, Elwood Richard Apr 50 Jan 60 obit Apr 93

Queuille, Henri Oct 48 obit Sep 70

Quezon, Manuel L. Aug 41 obit Sep 44

Quigley, Jane *see* Alexander, Jane

Quill, Michael J. Aug 41 Mar 53 obit Mar 66

Quimby, Edith H. Jul 49 obit Mar 83

Quimby, Mrs. Shirley L. *see* Quimby, Edith H.

Quindlen, Anna Apr 93

Quine, W. V. Nov 99

Quine, Willard van Orman *see* Quine, W. V.

Quinn, Anthony Dec 57

Quinn, Sally Oct 88

Quintanilla, Luis Nov 40

Quintero, Joaquin Alvarez *see* Alvarez Quintero, Joaquin

Quintero, José Apr 54 obit May 99

Quirino, Elpidio Sep 48 obit May 56

Quisling, Vidkun Nov 40 obit Yrbk 46

Quoirez, Françoise *see* Sagan, Françoise

Quo Tai-Chi May 46 obit Apr 52

Raab, Julius Apr 54 obit Feb 64

Rabe, David Jul 73

Rabi, I. I. Apr 48 obit Mar 88

Rabi, Isidor Isaac *see* Rabi, I. I.

Rabin, Yitzhak Sep 74 Jan 95 obit Jan 96

Raborn, William Francis Jul 58 obit Jun 90

Rackmil, Milton R. Nov 52 obit Jan 92

Radcliffe, Cyril John Jun 63 obit May 77

Raddall, Thomas (WLB) Yrbk 51

Radhakrishnan, Sarvepalli Jun 52 obit Jun 75

Radner, Gilda Feb 80 obit Jul 89

Radvanyi, Netty *see* Seghers, Anna

Radziwill, Catherine, Princess obit Jul 41

Radziwill, Lee Apr 77

Rae, Bob Feb 91

Rae, Edna *see* Burstyn, Ellen

Raeder, Erich Apr 41 obit Jan 61

Raedler, Dorothy Dec 54 obit Feb 94

Rafferty, Max Jan 69 obit Aug 82

Rafsanjani, Hashemi Nov 89

Rafshoon, Gerald Jul 79

Ragland, Rags obit Oct 46

Ragon, Heartsill obit Nov 40

Rahman, Abdul, Paramount Ruler of Malaya Dec 57 obit May 60

Rahman, Abdul Dec 57 obit Mar 91

Rahman, Sheik Mujibur *see* Mujibur Rahman

Rahman, Ziaur Jun 81

Rahner, Karl Jul 70 obit May 84

Raimu, Jules obit Nov 46

Raines, Franklin D. Oct 2000

Rainey, Froelich G. Feb 67 obit Jan 93

Rainey, Homer P. Nov 46 obit Feb 86

Rainier III, Prince of Monaco Nov 55

Rains, Albert McKinley Sep 59 obit May 91

Rains, Claude Nov 49 obit Jul 67

Rainwater, Richard Apr 99

Rajagopalachari, Chakravarti Jul 42 obit Feb 73

Rakosi, Matyas Mar 49 obit Mar 71

Rakowski, Mieczyslaw Apr 89

Ralls, Charles C. Jan 51

Ralston, Dennis Oct 65

Ram, Jagjivan Oct 78 obit Aug 86

Rama IX, King of Thailand Jul 50

Ramadier, Paul Jun 47 obit Dec 61

Raman, Chandrasekhara Venkata Nov 48 obit Jan 71

Ramaphosa, Cyril Sep 95

Rama Rau, Benegal *see* Rau, Benegal Rama

Rama Rau, Dhanvanthi Apr 54 obit Sep 87

Rama Rau, Santha Aug 45 (WLB) Yrbk 59

Rambam, Cyvia *see* Rambert, Marie

Rambert, Marie Feb 81 obit Aug 82

Rameau, Jean obit Apr 42

Ramey, Howard K. obit May 43

Ramey, Samuel Jul 81

Ramírez, Pedro P. Aug 43 obit Sep 62

Ramm, Fredrik obit Jan 44

Ramo, Simon Apr 58 [Ramo, Simon; and Wooldridge, Dean E.]

Ramos, Fidel Mar 94

Rampal, Jean-Pierre Mar 70 obit Aug 2000

Rampersad, Arnold Sep 98

Ramphele, Mamphela Jul 97

Rampling, Anne *see* Rice, Anne

Ramsay, Bertram Mar 44 obit Feb 45

Ramsey, Arthur Michael Apr 60 obit Jun 88

Ramsey, Dewitt C. Jan 53 obit Nov 61

Ramsey, Norman F. Dec 63

Ramspeck, Robert Jun 51 obit Dec 72

Rance, Hubert Elvin Dec 53 obit Mar 74

Rand, Ayn May 82

Rand, Ellen obit Feb 42

Rand, James Henry, Sr. obit Nov 44

Rand, William M. May 53

Randall, Clarence B. Jun 52 obit Oct 67

Randall, Jean *see* Hauck, Louise Platt

Randall, John D. May 60

Randall, Mrs. J. G. *see* Randall, Ruth Painter

Randall, Ruth Painter (WLB) Yrbk 57

Randall, Tony Jan 61

Randers, Gunnar Jan 57

Randi, James May 87

Randi, The Amazing *see* Randi, James

Randolph, Asa Philip May 40 Oct 51 obit Jul 79

Randolph, Jennings Jan 62 obit Jul 98

Randolph, Woodruff May 48 obit Jan 67

Ranganathan, S. R. Sep 65 obit Dec 72

Rangel, Charles B. Mar 84

Rank, J. Arthur Nov 45 obit May 72 [Rank, Joseph, Arthur Rank, 1st Baron]

Rank, Joseph obit Jan 44

Rankin, J. Lee Feb 59 obit Sep 96

Rankin, John E. Feb 44 obit Jan 61

Rankin, Karl Lott Apr 55 obit Apr 91

Ransom, John Crowe Jul 64 obit Sep 74

Ranson, S. Walter obit Oct 42

Rao, P. V. Narasimha Jan 92

Rao, Shanta Dec 57

Rapacki, Adam Jul 58 obit Dec 70

Raphael, Chaim Dec 63 obit Jan 95

Raphaël, Sally Jessy Feb 90

Raphael Aug 91

Rapp, William J. obit Oct 42

Rappard, William E. Oct 51 obit Jul 58

Raskin, A. H. May 78 obit Feb 94

Raskin, Abraham Henry *see* Raskin, A. H.

Raskin, Judith Apr 64 obit Feb 85

Rasminsky, Louis Dec 61

Rasmussen, Gustav Dec 47 obit Nov 53

Rassweiler, Clifford F. Oct 58

Rathbone, Basil Mar 51 obit Oct 67

Rathbone, Eleanor Jun 43 obit Feb 46

Rathbone, Josephine Adams obit Jul 41

Rathbone, Monroe J. Mar 57 obit Sep 76

Rather, Dan May 75

Ratoff, Gregory Aug 43 obit Feb 61

Rattigan, Terence Dec 56 obit Feb 78

Rattle, Simon Feb 88

Rattner, Abraham Mar 48 obit Apr 78

Ratushinskaya, Irina Jul 88

Ratzinger, Cardinal *see* Ratzinger, Joseph

Ratzinger, Joseph Apr 86

Rau, Benegal Narsing Dec 51 obit Feb 54

Rau, Benegal Rama Feb 49 obit Feb 70

Rau, Dhanvanthi Rama *see* Rama Rau, Dhanvanthi

Rau, Johannes Mar 87

Rau, Santha Rama *see* Rama Rau, Santha

Rauh, Joseph L., Jr. Apr 65 obit Nov 92

Rauschenberg, Robert Oct 65 Oct 87

Rauschning, Hermann May 41 obit Apr 83

Rautenberg, Robert Mar 40

Ravdin, I. S. Apr 68 obit Oct 72

Raven, Peter H. Feb 94

Raver, Paul J. Sep 41

Rawalt, Marguerite Mar 56

Rawl, Lawrence G. Feb 92

Rawlings, Bernard Aug 45 obit Dec 62

Rawlings, Jerry Jun 82

Rawlings, Marjorie Kinnan Jul 42 obit Feb 54

Rawls, Lou Mar 84

Ray, Amy *see* Indigo Girls

Ray, Charles obit Jan 44

Ray, Dixy Lee Jun 73 obit Mar 94

Ray, Gordon Norton Mar 68 obit Feb 87

Ray, Man Dec 65 obit Jan 77

Ray, Randolph Apr 45 obit Jul 63

Ray, Robert D. Jan 77

Ray, Satyajit Mar 61 obit Jun 92

Ray, Ted obit Oct 43

Rayburn, Sam Oct 40 Mar 49 obit Jan 62

Raye, Martha Jul 63 obit Jan 95

Raymond, Lee Nov 99

Razmara, Ali Oct 50 obit Mar 51

Rea, Gardner May 46 obit Feb 67

Read, Herbert Mar 62 obit Sep 68

Reading, Stella, Marchioness of Apr 48 obit Jul 71

Reagan, Nancy May 82

Reagan, Patricia Ann *see* Davis, Patti

Reagan, Ronald Dec 49 Feb 67 Nov 82

Reagan, Ron Feb 92

Reagon, Bernice Johnson Aug 99

Reardon, John Nov 74 obit Jun 88

Reasoner, Harry Feb 66 obit Oct 91

Reavey, Mrs. George *see* Pereira, I. Rice

Reavis, Smith Freeman obit Mar 40

Reba *see* McEntire, Reba

Reber, Samuel Sep 49 obit Feb 72

Reckord, Milton A. Mar 45

Redding, J. Saunders Apr 69 obit Apr 88

Reddy, Helen Apr 75

Reddy, N. Sanjiva Mar 81 obit Aug 96

Redfield, Robert Dec 53 obit Jan 59

Redford, Robert Apr 71 Mar 82

Redgrave, Lynn Sep 69

Redgrave, Michael Feb 50 obit May 85

Redgrave, Steven Jan 2000

Redgrave, Vanessa Dec 66

Redman, Joshua Jan 97

Redpath, Anne Jan 57 obit Mar 65

Redpath, Jean Feb 84

Redstone, Sumner Jan 96

Redway, Jacques Wardlaw obit Jan 43

Reece, B. Carroll May 46 obit May 61

Reed, Carol Mar 50 obit Jun 76

Reed, Daniel A. May 53 obit Apr 59

Reed, Edward Bliss obit Mar 40

Reed, Herbert Calhoun obit Sep 40

Reed, Ishmael Oct 86

Reed, James, Sr. obit Sep 41

Reed, James A. obit Oct 44

Reed, John Howard obit Mar 40

Reed, John S. Jan 85

Reed, Lou Jul 89

Reed, Margie Yvonne *see* Raye, Martha

Reed, Philip D. Jan 49 obit May 89

Reed, Ralph Mar 96

Reed, Ralph T. Apr 51 obit Mar 68

Reed, Rex Jan 72

Reed, Stanley F. Feb 42 obit May 80

Reed, Willis Jan 73

Rees, Edward H. Jan 58 obit Dec 69

Rees, Mina S. Nov 57 obit Jan 98

Reese, Della Sep 71

Reese, Everett D. Mar 54

Reese, Harold Jun 50 obit Oct 99

Reese, Pee Wee *see* Reese, Harold

Reeve, Christopher May 82

Reeve, Sidney A. obit Aug 41

Reeves, Jesse S. obit Aug 42

Reeves, Keanu May 95

Regan, Donald T. Nov 81

Regan, Judith Sep 2000

Reggio, Godfrey Jul 95

Régine Apr 80

Rehnquist, William H. Apr 72

Reich, Charles A. Jun 72

Reich, Nathaniel Julius obit Nov 43

Reich, Robert B. Apr 93

Reich, Steve Apr 86

Rich, Daniel Catton Dec 55 obit Feb 77

Rich, Frank Apr 99

Rich, Louise Dickinson May 43 obit Jul 91

Richard, Louis obit Sep 40

Richard, Maurice Dec 58 obit Yrbk 2000

Richards, A. N. Sep 50 obit Apr 66

Richards, Ann W. Feb 91

Richards, C. R. obit Jan 41

Richards, Dickinson W. Mar 57 obit Apr 73

Richards, I. A. Dec 72 obit Oct 79

Richards, James P. Sep 51 obit Apr 79

Richards, John G. obit Dec 41

Richards, John S. Jun 55

Richards, Keith Feb 89

Richards, Laura E. obit May 43

Richards, Lloyd Oct 87

Richards, Michael Nov 97

Richards, Robert E. Jun 57

Richards, Vincent Jul 47 obit Dec 59

Richards, Wayne E. Jul 54

Richardson, Bill Apr 96

Richardson, Bobby May 66

Richardson, Elliot L. Mar 71 obit Mar 2000

Richardson, Henrietta see Richardson, Henry Handel

Richardson, Henry Handel obit May 46

Richardson, Kevin see Backstreet Boys

Richardson, Miranda Feb 94

Richardson, Norval obit Yrbk 40

Richardson, Ralph Nov 50 obit Nov 83

Richardson, Robert Clinton, Jr. see Richardson, Bobby

Richardson, Seth Feb 48 obit May 53

Richardson, Tony Dec 63 obit Feb 92

Richberg, Donald R. Dec 49 obit Jan 61

Richie, Lionel Jul 84

Richler, Mordecai May 75

Richman, Charles J. obit Jan 41

Richmond, Charles Alexander obit Sep 40

Richmond, Mitch Jun 99

Richter, Burton Sep 77

Richter, Charles Francis May 75 obit Nov 85

Richter, Conrad Jun 51 obit Dec 68

Richter, George Martin obit Jul 42

Richter, Sviatoslav Feb 61 obit Oct 97

Rickenbacker, Eddie see Rickenbacker, Edward Vernon

Rickenbacker, Edward Vernon Nov 40 Feb 52 obit Oct 73

Ricketts, Louis Davidson obit Mar 40

Rickey, Branch Oct 45 obit Jan 66

Rickey, George Feb 80

Rickey, James W. obit Jun 43

Rickover, Hyman G. May 53 obit Aug 86

Riddell, R. Gerald Sep 50 obit Apr 51

Riddleberger, James W. May 57 obit Jan 83

Ride, Sally K. Oct 83

Ridenour, Nina Apr 51

Ridge, Lola obit Jul 41

Ridgway, Matthew B. Jul 47 obit Sep 93

Riebel, John P. Jan 57

Riecken, Henry W. Dec 61

Riefenstahl, Berta Helene Amalia see Riefenstahl, Leni

Riefenstahl, Leni May 75

Riefler, Winfield W. May 48 obit Jun 74

Riegle, Donald W., Jr. Oct 86

Riesenberg, Felix, Jr. (WLB) Yrbk 57

Riesman, David [educator] obit Jul 40

Riesman, David [social scientist] Jan 55

Rieve, Emil Jul 46 obit Mar 75

Rifkin, Jeremy Feb 86

Rifkind, Simon H. May 46 obit Jan 96

Rigg, Diana Oct 74

Rigg, Edgar T. Jun 61

Riggio, Leonard Jun 98

Riggio, Vincent Jul 49 obit Nov 60

Riggs, Austen Fox obit Mar 40

Riggs, Bobby see Riggs, Robert Larimore

Riggs, Robert Larimore Sep 49 obit Jan 96

Riggs, T. L. obit Jun 43

Righter, Carroll Oct 72 obit Jun 88

Rigling, Alfred obit Jan 41

Riiser-Larsen, Hjalmar Nov 51 obit Jul 65

Riklis, Meshulam Dec 71

Riles, Wilson Dec 71

Riley, Bridget Sep 81

Riley, Pat Aug 88

Riley, Richard W. Oct 93

Riley, Susan B. Feb 53

Riley, William E. Nov 51

Rimes, Leann May 98

Rincón de Gautier, Felisa see Gautier, Felisa Rincón De

Rinehart, Stanley M., Jr. Dec 54 obit Jun 69

Rinfret, Pierre A. Jul 72

Ring, Barbara T. obit Nov 41

Ringgold, Faith Feb 96

Ringling, Robert E. May 45 obit Feb 50

Ringwald, Molly May 87

Rio, Carlos Alberto Arroyo del see Arroyo Del Río, Carlos Alberto

Riopelle, Jean-Paul Oct 89

Riordan, Richard May 2000

Rios, Juan Antonio Apr 42 obit Jul 46

Ríos Montt, José Efraín May 83

Ripken, Cal, Jr. Jun 92

Ripley, Alexandra Mar 92

Ripley, Elizabeth (WLB) Yrbk 58

Ripley, Joseph obit Nov 40

Ripley, Robert L. Jul 45 obit Jul 49

Ripley, S. Dillon Oct 66

Ripley, William Z. obit Oct 41

Ritchard, Cyril Jan 57 obit Feb 78

Ritchie, Dennis Mar 99

Ritchie, Jean Oct 59

Riter, Henry G., 3d Oct 55 obit Sep 58

Ritner, Ann (WLB) Yrbk 53

Ritt, Martin Nov 79 obit Feb 91

Rittenhouse, Constance Mar 48 [Rittenhouse, Mrs. Paul]

Rittenhouse, Mrs. Paul *see* Rittenhouse, Constance

Ritter, Bruce Jun 83 obit Feb 2000

Ritter, John Jun 80

Ritter, Joseph Elmer Dec 64 obit Oct 67

Ritter, Thelma Dec 57 obit Feb 74 (died Feb 69)

Rivera, Chita Oct 84

Rivera, Diego Jul 48 obit Feb 58

Rivera, Geraldo May 75

Rivero, Jose Ignacio obit May 44

Rivers, Joan Jan 70 Mar 87

Rivers, L. Mendel Oct 60 obit Feb 71

Rivers, Larry Apr 69

Rivers, Thomas M. Jul 60 obit Jul 62

Rives, Amelie *see* Troubetzkoy, Amelie

Rives, Hallie Erminie (WLB) Yrbk 56

Rivkin, Dorothy Carnegie *see* Carnegie, Dorothy

Rivlin, Alice M. Oct 82

Riza Shah Pahlavi obit Sep 44

Rizzo, Frank L. Mar 73 obit Sep 91

Rizzuto, Phil Jul 50

Roa, Raúl Nov 73 obit Sep 82

Robards, Jason Jr. Oct 59

Robarts, John P. Dec 62 obit Jan 83

Robb, Charles S. Apr 89

Robb, Hunter obit Jan 40

Robb, Inez Dec 58 obit Jun 79

Robbe-Grillet, Alain Dec 74

Robbins, Frederick C. Jun 55 [Enders, John F; Robbins, Frederick C; and Weller, Thomas H.]

Robbins, Harold May 70 obit Jan 98

Robbins, Jerome May 47 May 69 obit Oct 98

Robbins, Tim Jul 94

Robbins, Tom Jun 93

Robbins, William J. Feb 56

Robens, Alfred Jun 56

Robert, Georges Jun 43

Roberts, Albert H. obit Jul 46

Roberts, C. Wesley Apr 53 obit Jun 75

Roberts, Charles G. D. obit Jan 44

Roberts, Cokie May 94

Roberts, Dennis J. Dec 56 obit Sep 94

Roberts, Dorothy James (WLB) Yrbk 56 obit Jun 90

Roberts, Elizabeth Madox obit May 41

Roberts, Florence obit Jul 40

Roberts, George Lucas obit Apr 41

Roberts, Goodridge May 55

Roberts, Julia May 91

Roberts, Kate L. obit Oct 41

Roberts, Marcus Mar 94

Roberts, Oral Nov 60

Roberts, Owen J. Oct 41 obit Jul 55

Roberts, Robin Dec 53

Roberts, Walter Orr Dec 60 obit May 90

Robertson, A. Willis Dec 49 obit Dec 71

Robertson, Anna Mary *see* Moses, Grandma

Robertson, Ben, Jr. Nov 42

Robertson, Brian Sep 48 obit Jun 74

Robertson, Cliff Dec 69

Robertson, Constance (WLB) Yrbk 46

Robertson, D. B. May 50 obit Dec 61

Robertson, Ethel Florence Lindesay *see* Richardson, Henry Handel

Robertson, Marion Gordon *see* Robertson, Pat

Robertson, Mrs. Miles E. *see* Robertson, Constance

Robertson, Norman A. Dec 57 obit Sep 68

Robertson, Oscar Jan 66

Robertson, Pat Sep 87

Robertson, R. B. May 57

Robertson, Reuben B., Jr. Dec 55 obit May 60

Robertson, Walter S. Dec 53 obit May 70

Robert Stephenson Smyth Baden-Powell obit Mar 41

Robeson, Eslanda Goode Sep 45 obit Yrbk 91 (died Dec 65)

Robeson, Mrs. Paul *see* Robeson, Eslanda Goode

Robeson, Paul Mar 41 Mar 76

Robey, Ralph W. May 41 obit Sep 72

Robichaud, Louis J. May 68

Robins, Edward obit Jul 43

Robins, Margaret Dreier obit Apr 45

Robins, Mrs. Raymond *see* Robins, Margaret Dreier

Robinson, Arthur H. Mar 96

Robinson, Bill Feb 41 obit Jan 50

Robinson, Boardman Dec 41 obit Oct 52

Robinson, Brooks Sep 73

Robinson, David Jul 93

Robinson, Eddie Jun 88

Robinson, Edward G. Jan 50 obit Mar 73

Robinson, Elmer E. Nov 55

Robinson, Frank Jun 71

Robinson, Frederick B. obit Dec 41

Robinson, Henry Morton Jul 50 obit Mar 61

Robinson, Holton D. obit Jun 45

Robinson, Jackie Feb 47 obit Dec 72

Robinson, Jack Roosevelt *see* Robinson, Jackie

Robinson, John Feb 65 obit Feb 84

Robinson, Kim Stanley Nov 98

Robinson, M. R. Dec 56 obit May 82

Robinson, Mary Apr 91

Robinson, Randall Sep 98

Robinson, Ray *see* Robinson, Sugar Ray

Robinson, Samuel M. Feb 42

Robinson, Smokey Jul 80

Robinson, Spottswood W. Mar 62 obit Jan 99

Robinson, Sugar Ray Mar 51 obit Jun 89

Robinson, William, Jr. *see* Robinson, Smokey

Robinson, William E. Feb 58 obit Jul 69

Robinson, William Heath obit Nov 44

Robison, Emily *see* Dixie Chicks

Robison, Paula May 82

Robitzek, Edward H. Dec 53 obit May 84

Robles, Marco A. Jun 68 obit Jun 90

Robsjohn-Gibbings, T. H. Sep 65 obit Feb 77

Robson, Flora Jan 51 obit Sep 84

Robson, May obit Dec 42

Robus, Hugo Dec 62 obit Feb 64

Roca, Julio A. obit Nov 42

Rocard, Michel Oct 88

Rochberg, George Sep 85

Roche, James M. Feb 67

Roche, Josephine Aug 41 obit Sep 76

Roche, Kevin Nov 70

Roche, Margaret Eleanor see McNellis, Maggi

Rock, John Dec 64 obit Jan 85

Rockefeller, David Mar 59

Rockefeller, John D., 3d Jun 53 obit Sep 78

Rockefeller, John D., Jr. Jul 41 obit Jul 60

Rockefeller, John D. 4th Mar 78

Rockefeller, Laurance S. Jun 59

Rockefeller, Nelson A. Mar 41 Mar 51 obit Mar 79

Rockefeller, Winthrop Sep 59 obit Apr 73

Rockley, Alicia-Margaret Amherst, Baroness see Amherst, Alicia-Margaret

Rockwell, Norman Jun 45 obit Jan 79

Rodahl, Kaare Feb 56

Roddick, Anita Sep 92

Roderick, David M. Apr 87

Rodgers, Bill Aug 82

Rodgers, Richard May 40 [Rodgers, Richard; and Hart, Lorenz] Apr 51 obit Feb 80

Rodgers and Hart see Rodgers, Richard; Hart, Lorenz

Rodin, Judith Jun 99

Rodino, Peter W., Jr. Oct 54

Rodman, Dennis Sep 96

Rodriguez, Andrés Sep 91 obit Jun 97

Rodriguez, Cecilia May 99

Rodriguez, Chi Chi Oct 69

Rodriguez, Eloy May 2000

Rodriguez, Jorge Alessandri see Alessandri, Jorge

Rodriguez, Juan see Rodriguez, Chi Chi

Rodriguez, Nicolas obit Sep 40

Rodriguez, Robert Aug 96

Rodzinski, Artur Aug 40 obit Feb 59

Roebling, Mary G. Oct 60 obit Jan 95

Roeg, Nicolas Jan 96

Roehm, Carolyne Feb 92

Roelofs, Henrietta obit Mar 42

Roemer, Buddy Nov 90

Roemer, Charles Elson, 3d see Roemer, Buddy

Rogers, Bernard W. Oct 84

Rogers, Bruce Dec 46 obit Jul 57

Rogers, Carl R. Dec 62 obit Mar 87

Rogers, Dale Evans Sep 56

Rogers, Edith Nourse Apr 42 obit Nov 60

Rogers, Frank B. Jun 62

Rogers, Fred M. Jul 71

Rogers, Ginger Apr 41 Dec 67 obit Jul 95

Rogers, Kenny Jan 81

Rogers, Lynn L. Oct 94

Rogers, Mark Homer obit Nov 41

Rogers, Norman McLeod obit Jul 40

Rogers, Paul Mar 60

Rogers, Robert Emmons obit Jul 41

Rogers, Roy Mar 48 Oct 83 obit Sep 98

Rogers, Rutherford David Jun 62

Rogers, Will, Jr. Dec 53 obit Sep 93

Rogers, William P. Feb 58 Sep 69

Rogge, O. John Feb 48 obit Jun 81

Rohatyn, Felix G. May 78

Rohde, Ruth Bryan Owen Dec 44 obit Oct 54

Rohe, Vera-Ellen see Vera-Ellen

Rohmer, Eric Apr 77

Roh Tae Woo Feb 88

Rojas Pinilla, Gustavo Jun 56 obit Mar 75

Rokossovsky, Konstantin Jan 44 obit Oct 68

Rolland, Romain obit Feb 45

Rollin, Betty Aug 94

Rollins, Carl Purington Sep 48 obit Jan 61

Rollins, Sonny Apr 76

Rolvaag, Karl F. Feb 64 obit Mar 91

Roman, Nancy G. Dec 60

Romano, Emanuel Mar 40 obit Feb 85

Romano, Umberto Mar 54 obit Nov 82

Romanoff, Alexis L. Dec 53

Rombauer, Irma S. Dec 53 obit Dec 62

Romberg, Sigmund Mar 45 obit Dec 51

Rome, Harold Apr 42 obit Jan 94

Romero Barceló, Carlos Oct 77

Rommel, Erwin Aug 42 obit Dec 44

Romnes, H. I. Feb 68 obit Jan 74

Romney, George Jun 58 obit Oct 95

Romulo, Carlos P. Mar 43 Apr 57 obit Feb 86

Ronaldo Aug 98

Ronan, William J. Oct 69

Roncalli, Angelo Giuseppe see John XXIII, Pope

Roney, Marianne May 57 [Cohen, Barbara; and Roney, Marianne]

Ronne, Finn Feb 48 obit Mar 80

Ronstadt, Linda Jan 78

Rood, Helen Martin obit Mar 43

Rooks, Lowell W. Apr 47

Roome, Mrs. Charles O. see Goertz, Arthémise

Rooney, Andy Jul 82

Rooney, John J. Dec 64 obit Jan 76

Rooney, Mickey Feb 42 Sep 65

Roosa, Robert V. Dec 62 obit Mar 94

Roosevelt, Alice Lee see Longworth, Alice Roosevelt

Roosevelt, Anna C. Jun 97

Roosevelt, Eleanor Nov 40 Jan 49 obit Jan 63

Roosevelt, Elliott Dec 46 obit Jan 91

Roosevelt, Franklin D., Jr. Jan 50 obit Sep 88

Roosevelt, Franklin D. Mar 42 obit Apr 45

Rountree, William M. Jun 59 obit Jan 96

Rourke, Constance Mayfield obit May 41

Rourke, Mickey Oct 91

Rous, Peyton Mar 67 obit Apr 70

Rouse, James W. Feb 82 obit Jun 96

Rouse, Milford O. Jun 68

Roussy de Sales, Raoul de *see* De Roussy De Sales, Raoul

Routley, T. Clarence Jan 56 obit Jun 63

Rove, Karl Oct 2000

Rovere, Richard H. Apr 77 obit Jan 80

Rowan, Andrew S. obit Mar 43

Rowan, Carl T. Jan 58

Rowan, Chad *see* Akebono

Rowan, Dan Sep 69 obit Nov 87

Rowans, Virginia *see* Tanner, Edward Everett, 3d

Rowe, L. S. Aug 45 obit Jan 47

Rowell, Chester H. Yrbk 40 obit May 48

Rowland, John G. Oct 97

Rowlands, Gena Nov 75

Rowlands, Virginia Cathryn *see* Rowlands, Gena

Rowley, James J. Jan 63 obit Jan 93

Rowntree, Cecil obit Dec 43

Rowse, A. L. Jul 79 obit Jan 98

Roxas, Manuel May 46 obit May 48

Roy Jan 98 [Siegfried and Roy]

Roy, Maurice Feb 58 obit Jan 86

Roy, Patrick Nov 99

Royal, Forrest B. obit Jul 45

Royall, Kenneth C. Jan 47 obit Sep 71

Royden, Maude Apr 42 obit Oct 56

Royen, Jan Herman Van Dec 53

Royko, Mike Jun 94 obit Jul 97

Royle, Edwin Milton obit Apr 42

Royster, Vermont C. Dec 53 obit Oct 96

Rozelle, Pete Jun 64 obit Feb 97

Rózsa, Miklós Feb 92 obit Oct 95

Rubattel, Rodolphe Dec 54 obit Dec 61

Rubbia, Carlo Jun 85

Rubicam, Raymond Dec 43 obit Jul 78

Rubik, Erno Feb 87

Rubin, Barbara Jo Dec 69

Rubin, Reuven Apr 43 obit Jan 75

Rubin, Robert E. Jul 97

Rubin, Theodore Isaac Feb 80

Rubin, William Nov 86

Rubín De La Borbolla, Daniel F. Feb 60

Rubinstein, Artur Dec 45 Feb 66 obit Mar 83

Rubinstein, Helena Jun 43 obit May 65

Rubottom, R. R., Jr. May 59

Ruckelshaus, William D. Jul 71

Ruckstull, F. Wellington obit Jul 42

Rudd, Paul Sep 77

Rudel, Julius Jul 65

Ruder, David S. Nov 88

Rudkin, Margaret Sep 59 obit Oct 67

Rudkin, Mrs. Henry Albert *see* Rudkin, Margaret

Rudman, Warren B. Nov 89

Rudolph, Paul Feb 72 obit Nov 97

Rudolph, Wilma Sep 61 obit Jan 95

Rueff, Jacques Feb 69 obit Jun 78

Ruffin, William H. Feb 51

Ruffing, Charles Nov 41 obit Apr 86

Ruffing, Red *see* Ruffing, Charles

Rugambwa, Laurean Cardinal Sep 60 obit Feb 98

Rugg, Harold Ordway May 41 obit Jul 60

Ruiz Cortines, Adolfo Sep 52 obit Jan 74

Ruiz Guiñazú, Enrique Apr 42 obit Jan 68

Ruiz Soler, Antonio Jun 68

Rukeyser, Louis Feb 83

Rukeyser, Muriel Mar 43 obit Apr 80

Rule, Ann Sep 2000

Ruml, Beardsley May 43 obit Jun 60

Rummel, Joseph F. Jun 59 obit Jan 65

Rumor, Mariano Jul 69 obit Mar 90

Rumpler, Edmund obit Oct 40

Rumsfeld, Donald Apr 70

Runbeck, Margaret Lee (WLB) Yrbk 52 obit Dec 56

Runcie, Robert Nov 80 obit Oct 2000

Rundstedt, Gerd von *see* Rundstedt, Karl Von

Rundstedt, Karl Von Nov 41 obit Apr 53

Runkle, Erwin W. obit Apr 41

Runyon, Damon Nov 42 obit Jan 47

Runyon, Mefford R. May 49

Rupertus, William H. obit May 45

Rusby, Henry H. obit Jan 41

Ruscha, Edward Oct 89

Rush, Kenneth May 75 obit Feb 95

Rushdi, Tevfik Bey *see* Aras, Tevfik Rüstü

Rushdie, Salman Nov 86

Rushing, Matthew Jul 2000

Rushmore, David Barker obit Jul 40

Rusk, Dean Jun 49 Jul 61 obit Feb 95

Rusk, Howard A. Mar 46 May 67 obit Jan 90

Ruslander, Mark *see* Russell, Mark

Russell, Anna Apr 54

Russell, Bertrand Apr 40 Jan 51 obit Mar 70

Russell, Bill *see* Russell, William F. Jul 75 [Russell, William F.]

Russell, Charles Ellsworth *see* Russell, Pee Wee

Russell, Charles H. Dec 55 obit Nov 89

Russell, Charles obit Jun 41

Russell, Donald J. May 62 obit Feb 86

Russell, Harold Jan 50 Jan 66

Russell, Herbrand Arthur, 11th Duke of Bedford *see* Herbrand Arthur Russell

Russell, James Earl obit Dec 45

Russell, James S. Jan 62

Russell, Ken Oct 75

Russell, Mark Mar 81

Russell, Mary Annette Russell obit Mar 41

Russell, Pee Wee Aug 44 obit Apr 69

Russell, Richard B. Nov 49 obit Mar 71

Russell, Rosalind Jan 43 obit Feb 77

Russell, William F. Apr 47 obit Jun 56

Russell, William Felton *see* Russell, Bill

Russert, Tim Oct 97

Russo, Rene Jul 97

Rust, Bernhard Jul 42

Rustin, Bayard Jun 67 obit Oct 87

Rutenberg, Pinhas obit Mar 42

Rutenborn, Günter, Rev. Oct 60

Ruth, Babe Aug 44 obit Oct 48

Ruth, George Herman *see* Ruth, Babe

Rutherford, Joseph Franklin Nov 40 obit Mar 42

Rutherford, Margaret Jan 64 obit Jul 72

Rutledge, Brett *see* Paul, Elliot

Rutledge, Wiley May 43 obit Oct 49

Ryan, John obit Oct 45

Ryan, Joseph P. Jan 49 obit Sep 63

Ryan, Meg May 99

Ryan, Nolan Oct 70

Ryan, Patrick J. May 55

Ryan, Robert Dec 63 obit Sep 73

Ryan, T. Claude Jan 43 obit Nov 82

Ryan, Thelma Catherine *see* Nixon, Patricia

Ryan, William F. May 67 obit Dec 72

Ryder, Winona Jun 94

Rykiel, Sonia May 90

Ryle, Martin Sep 73 obit Jan 85

Rysanek, Leonie Mar 66 obit May 98

Ryti, Risto Feb 41 obit Jan 57

Ryun, Jim May 68

Saarinen, Aline B. Dec 56 obit Sep 72

Saarinen, Eero Oct 49 obit Nov 61

Saarinen, Eliel Oct 42 obit Sep 50

Saatchi, Maurice Jan 89

Sabah, Jaber Al-Ahmad Al-Jaber Al-, Sheik Aug 88

Sabath, Adolph J. Jul 46 obit Dec 52

Sabatier, Paul obit Oct 41

Sabatini, Gabriela Jun 92

Sabato, Ernesto Oct 85

Sabin, Albert B. Feb 58 obit Apr 93

Sabin, Florence R. Apr 45 obit Dec 53

Sabry, Hassan, Pasha obit Yrbk 40

Sachar, Abram Leon Nov 49 obit Sep 93

Sachs, Bernard obit Mar 44

Sachs, Curt Aug 44 obit Apr 59

Sachs, Jeffrey D. Nov 93

Sachs, Nelly Mar 67 obit Jul 70

Sackett, Frederic M., Jr. obit Jul 41

Sacks, Oliver Feb 85

Sadak, Necmeddin Jan 50 obit Dec 53

Sadat, Anwar Mar 71 obit Nov 81

Sadat, Jihan Aug 86

Saddler, Donald Jan 63

Sade Sep 86

Sadik, Nafis Feb 96

Sadler, Michael obit Dec 43

Saerchinger, Cesar Apr 40

Safdie, Moshe Sep 68

Safer, Morley Jul 80

Safire, William Dec 73

Sagan, Carl Apr 70 obit Feb 97

Sagan, Françoise Sep 60

Sage, Dean obit Aug 43

Sagendorph, Robb Dec 56 obit Sep 70

Sager, Ruth Jul 67 obit Jun 97

Sahl, Mort Dec 60

Said, Edward W. Nov 89

Said, Nuri as- *see* Nuri As-Said

Said Bin Taimur Oct 57 obit Aug 78 (died Oct 72)

Saillant, Louis Jul 48 obit Jan 75

Saint, Eva Marie Jun 55

Sainte-Marie, Buffy Jul 69

Saint Exupery, Antoine De Jan-Feb 40 obit May 45

Saint-Gaudens, Homer Oct 41 obit Feb 59

Saionji, Kimmochi, Prince obit Jan 41

Sajak, Pat Jul 89

Sakel, Manfred Jan 41 obit Feb 58

Sakharov, Andrei Dmitrievich Jul 71 obit Feb 90

Salam, Abdus Apr 88 obit Jan 97

Salant, Richard S. Nov 61 obit Apr 93

Salazar, Alberto May 83

Salazar, Antonio De Oliveira May 41 May 52 obit Oct 70

Sale, Rhys M. Dec 57

Saleh, Allah-Yar Feb 53

Salerno-Sonnenberg, Nadja Nov 87

Sales, Nykesha Jun 99

Sales, Soupy Jan 67

Saliers, Emily *see* Indigo Girls

Salinas De Gortari, Carlos Mar 89

Salinger, Pierre Jul 61 Mar 87

Salisbury, Harrison E. Jul 55 Jan 82 obit Sep 93

Salit, Norman, Rabbi Mar 55 obit Oct 60

Salk, Jonas May 54 obit Aug 95

Salk, Lee Sep 79 obit Jul 92

Salle, David Sep 86

Salomon, Henry, Jr. Dec 56 obit Apr 58

Salote Tupou, Queen of Tonga Dec 53 obit Feb 66

Salten, Felix obit Nov 45

Salter, Alfred obit Sep 45

Salter, Andrew May 44 obit Jan 97

Salter, Arthur Mar 44

Saltonstall, Leverett Jun 44 Apr 56 obit Sep 79

Saltzman, Charles E. Oct 47 obit Aug 94

Salvemini, Gaetano Dec 43 obit Nov 57

Salverson, Laura Goodman (WLB) Yrbk 57

Salzmann, Siegfried *see* Salten, Felix

Samaranch, Juan Antonio Feb 94

Samaras, Lucas Nov 72

Samaroff, Olga Mar 46 obit Jun 48

Sammartino, Peter Dec 58 obit May 92

Sampras, Pete May 94

Sampson, Edith S. Dec 50 obit Jan 80

Samuel, Bernard Sep 49 obit Mar 54

Samuel, Herbert 1st Viscount Apr 55 obit Mar 63

Samuel, Sealhenry *see* Seal

Samuelson, Joan Aug 96

Samuelson, Paul Anthony May 65

Sananikone, Phoui Sep 59 obit Feb 84

Sanborn, David Aug 92

Sanborn, Pitts obit Apr 41

Sánchez Vicario, Arantxa Aug 98

Sandage, Allan Jan 99

Sandberg, Ryne Nov 94

Sandburg, Carl Jun 40 Dec 63 obit Oct 67

Sandefer, Jefferson Davis obit Apr 40

Sander, Jil Oct 97

Sanders, Barry Sep 93

Sanders, Bernard Jun 91

Sanders, Carl E. Dec 64

Sanders, Colonel *see* Sanders, Harland

Sanders, Deion Jan 95

Sanders, George Jun 43 obit Jun 72

Sanders, Harland Apr 73 obit Feb 81

Sanders, Jared Young obit May 44

Sanders, Lawrence Apr 89 obit May 98

Sanders, Marlene Feb 81

Sanderson, Derek Apr 75

Sandler, Adam May 98

Sandor, Gyorgy Jul 47

Sandström, Emil Jan 51 obit Sep 62

Sandys, Duncan May 52

Sanford, John Elroy *see* Foxx, Redd

Sanford, Terry Nov 61 obit Jul 98

Sanger, Frederick Jul 81

Sanger, Margaret Aug 44 obit Nov 66

San Martin, Ramon Grau *see* Grau San Martin, Ramón

Santa Cruz, Hernan Dec 49

Santana, Manuel Sep 67

Santayana, George Apr 44 obit Nov 52

Santelmann, William F. Apr 53

Santmyer, Helen Hooven Feb 85 obit Apr 86

Santolalla, Irene Silva De Dec 56 obit Sep 92

Santos, José Edwardo Dos May 94

Santos, Rufino J. Dec 60 obit Nov 73

Sapieha, Princess *see* Peterson, Virgilia

Saposs, David Nov 40 obit Jan 69

Sar, Saloth *see* Pol Pot

Saracoglu, Sükrü Jun 42 obit Mar 54

Saragat, Giuseppe Dec 56 Jul 65 obit Jul 88

Sarah, Duchess of York Mar 87

Sarajoglu Shukri, Bey *see* Saracoglu, Sükrü

Saralegui, Cristina Jan 99

Sarandon, Susan Sep 89

Sarasin, Pote Dec 55

Sarbanes, Paul S. Jan 97

Sardauna of Sokoto *see* Ahmadu, Alhaji, Sardauna of Sokoto

Sardi, Melchiorre Pio Vincenzo *see* Sardi, Vincent, Sr.

Sardi, Vincent, Jr. May 57 [Sardi, Vincent, Sr.; and Sardi, Vincent, Jr.]

Sardi, Vincent, Sr. May 57 [Sardi, Vincent, Sr.; and Sardi, Vincent, Jr.] obit Jan 70

Sardina, Adolfo *see* Adolfo

Sarg, Tony obit Apr 42

Sargeant, Howland H. Dec 52 obit Apr 84

Sargent, Francis W. Jun 71 obit Jan 99

Sargent, Malcolm Watts Dec 45 obit Jan 68

Sargent, Porter Jul 41 obit May 51

Sarkis, Elias Mar 79 obit Aug 85

Sarney, José Mar 86

Sarnoff, David Nov 40 Oct 51 obit Feb 72

Sarnoff, Robert W. Dec 56 obit May 97

Sarojini Nayadu *see* Naidu, Sarojini

Saroyan, William Jul 40 Nov 72 obit Jul 81

Sarraute, Nathalie Jun 66 obit Jan 2000

Sarton, George Jul 42 obit May 56

Sarton, May May 82 obit Sep 95

Sartre, Jean Paul Mar 47 May 71 obit Jun 80

Sassa, Scott Jan 2000

Sasser, James R. Jul 93

Sassoon, Vidal Apr 99

Sastroamidjojo, Ali Jun 50 obit May 75

Satcher, David Feb 97

Sato, Eisaku Dec 65 obit Aug 75

Satterfield, John C. Jul 62

Sauckel, Fritz obit Nov 46

Saud, King of Saudi Arabia Apr 54 obit Apr 69

Sauer, Emil Von obit Jun 42

Sauer, George Nov 48 obit Apr 94

Saul, Ralph S. Feb 71

Saulnier, Raymond J. Dec 57

Saund, Dalip S. Jun 60 obit Jun 73

Saunders, Carl M. Jun 50 obit Nov 74

Saunders, Hilary Aidan St. George Jun 43 obit Feb 52

Saunders, John Monk obit Apr 40

Saunders, Robert Dec 51 obit Mar 55

Saunders, Stuart T. Apr 66 obit Mar 87

Saura, Carlos Sep 78

Sauvé, Jeanne Aug 84 obit Mar 93

Savage, Augusta Jan 41 obit May 62

Savage, John Lucian Apr 43 obit Feb 68

Savage, Michael Joseph obit Apr 40

Savalas, Aristoteles *see* Savalas, Telly

Savalas, Telly Feb 76 obit Mar 94

Savery, Constance (WLB) Yrbk 48

Saville, Curtis Jan 86 [Saville, Curtis; and Saville, Kathleen]

Saville, Kathleen Jan 86 [Saville, Curtis; and Saville, Kathleen]

Savimbi, Jonas Aug 86

Savitch, Jessica Jan 83 obit Mar 84

Savitt, Dick see Savitt, Richard

Savitt, Richard Jun 52

Sawhill, John C. Apr 79 obit Yrbk 2000

Sawyer, Charles Jul 48 obit Jun 79

Sawyer, Diane Oct 85

Sawyer, Eddie Nov 50 obit Jan 98

Sawyer, Edwin Milby see Sawyer, Eddie

Sawyer, Helen Oct 54

Sawyer, John E. Jul 61 obit Apr 95

Saxbe, William B. Jul 74

Saxon, James J. Dec 63 obit Apr 80

Saxon, Lyle obit May 46

Saxton, Alexander Nov 43

Sayão, Bidú Feb 42 obit Jun 99

Sayegh, Fayez A. Jul 57

Sayles, John Feb 84

Sayles, R. W. obit Dec 42

Saylor, Michael Sep 2000

Sayre, Francis B., Jr. Dec 56

Sayre, Francis B. Jan-Feb 40 obit May 72

Sayre, Morris Jan 48 obit Apr 53

Sayre, Mrs. Raymond May 49 [Sayre, Ruth Buxton]

Sayre, Ruth Buxton see Sayre, Mrs. Raymond

Scali, John Sep 73 obit Jan 96

Scalia, Antonin Nov 86

Scammon, Richard M. Mar 71

Scarbrough, Roger Lumley, 11th Earl of see Lumley, Roger

Scardino, Marjorie Apr 2000

Scargill, Arthur Jan 85

Scavullo, Francesco May 85

Scelba, Mario May 53 obit Feb 92

Schacht, Al May 46 obit Sep 84

Schacht, Hjalmar Oct 44 obit Sep 70

Schachter, Mrs. Jules see Edwards, Joan

Schaefer, George Feb 70 obit Jan 98

Schaefer, Vincent J. Jan 48 obit Sep 93

Schaefer, William Donald Jul 88

Schäffer, Fritz Mar 53 obit May 67

Schain, Josephine Jul 45

Schaller, George B. Aug 85

Schama, Simon Nov 91

Schanberg, Sydney H. Aug 90

Schapiro, Meyer Jul 84 obit May 96

Schapiro, Miriam Aug 2000

Schärf, Adolf Oct 57 obit Apr 65

Schary, Dore May 48 obit Sep 80

Schaufuss, Peter May 82

Schechter, A. A. May 41 obit Aug 89

Scheck, Barry Mar 98

Scheel, Walter Feb 71

Scheele, Leonard A. May 48 obit Mar 93

Scheer, Alan Austin Jan 64

Scheffer, Victor B. Apr 94

Scheiberling, Edward N. Dec 44 obit Jan 68

Schell, Jonathan Jul 92

Schell, Maria Jun 61

Schell, Maximilian Dec 62

Schelling, Ernest Jan-Feb 40

Schemm, Mrs. Ferdinard Ripley see Walker, Mildred

Scherbo, Vitaly see Shcherbo, Vitaly

Scherer, Jean-Marie Maurice see Rohmer, Eric

Scherer, Paul May 41 obit May 69

Scherer, Roy Jr. see Hudson, Rock

Schereschewsky, Joseph Williams obit Sep 40

Scherman, Harry Sep 43 Jul 63 obit Jan 70

Scherman, Thomas Dec 54 obit Jul 79

Schertz, Ruth Louise see Phillips, Ruth

Schertzinger, Victor obit Dec 41

Scheuer, James Apr 68

Schiaparelli, Elsa Jan-Feb 40 Nov 51 obit Jan 74

Schick, Bela Jul 44 obit Feb 68

Schickele, Peter May 79

Schiff, Dorothy Jul 45 Jan 65 obit Oct 89

Schiffrin, André Jan 2000

Schilder, Paul Ferdinand obit Jan 41

Schildkraut, Joseph Apr 56 obit Mar 64

Schillebeeckx, Edward Jun 83

Schiller, Karl Dec 71 obit Mar 95

Schillinger, Joseph obit May 43

Schindler, Alexander M. Sep 87

Schindler, John A. Mar 56 obit Jan 58

Schiotz, Aksel Mar 49 obit Jun 75

Schiotz, Fredrik Axel Apr 72 obit May 89

Schippers, Thomas Apr 70 obit Feb 78

Schirra, Walter M., Jr. Jun 66

Schisgal, Murray Jan 68

Schlafly, Phyllis Jun 78

Schlamme, Martha Feb 64 obit Jan 86

Schlauch, Margaret Dec 42 obit Sep 86

Schlee, Mrs. George Matthias see Valentina

Schleich, Michel obit Jun 45

Schlein, Miriam (WLB) Yrbk 59

Schlesinger, Arthur M. Oct 46 Jan 79

Schlesinger, Bruno see Walter, Bruno

Schlesinger, Frank obit Aug 43

Schlesinger, James R. Oct 73

Schlesinger, John Nov 70

Schlessinger, Laura Sep 97

Schlink, Frederick John Mar 41 obit Mar 95

Schlöndorff, Volker Aug 83

Schlosser, Alex L. obit Mar 43

Schmelkes, Franz C. obit Feb 43

Schmid, Carlo Feb 65 obit Apr 80

Schmidt, Benno C., Jr. Aug 86

Schmidt, Fritz obit Aug 43

Schmidt, Helmut Oct 74

Schmidt, Maarten Sep 66

Schmitt, Bernadotte E. Dec 42 obit May 69

Schmitt, Gladys Mar 43 obit Dec 72

Schmitt, Harrison H. Jul 74

Schmoke, Kurt L. Feb 95

Schnabel, Artur Jul 42 obit Sep 51

Schnabel, Julian Nov 83

Schneerson, Menachem M. Sep 83 obit Aug 94

Schneider, Alan Dec 69 obit Jun 84

Schneider, Alexander Mar 76 obit Mar 93

Schneider, Alma K. Dec 54

Schneider, Eugene obit Jan 43

Schneider, Hannes Mar 41 obit Jun 55

Schneider, Mrs. Daniel Jacob see Schneider, Alma K.

Schneider, Romy Jan 65 obit Jul 82

Schneiderman, Rose Feb 46 obit Oct 72

Schneirla, T. C. Dec 55 obit Nov 68

Schnittke, Alfred Jul 92 obit Oct 98

Schnitzler, William F. Apr 65

Schnurer, Carolyn Mar 55

Schnurer, Mrs. Harold T. see Schnurer, Carolyn

Schoenberg, Arnold Apr 42 obit Sep 51

Schoenbrun, David Jan 60 obit Jul 88

Schoendienst, Albert Fred see Schoendienst, Red

Schoendienst, Red Dec 64

Schoeneman, George J. Nov 47

Schoen-René, Anna Eugénie obit Jan 43

Schoeppel, Andrew F. Mar 52 obit Mar 62

Schoff, Hannah Kent obit Feb 41

Schofield, Frank H. obit Apr 42

Scholder, Fritz Apr 85

Schollander, Don Sep 65

Schomburg, August Nov 60

Schoonmaker, Edwin Davies obit Jan 40

Schoonmaker, Thelma Mar 97

Schoonmaker-Powell, Thelma see Schoonmaker, Thelma

Schoonover, Lawrence (WLB) Yrbk 57 obit Mar 80

Schopf, J. William May 95

Schorr, Daniel Sep 59 Feb 78

Schorr, Friedrich Jul 42 obit Jun 54

Schott, Marge Aug 99

Schottland, Charles I. Dec 56 obit Sep 95

Schrader, Paul Aug 81

Schram, Emil Oct 41 May 53 obit Nov 87

Schranz, Karl Jan 71

Schratt, Katharina obit May 40

Schreiber, Georges May 43

Schreiber, J.-J. Servan- see Servan-Schreiber, J.-J

Schreiber, Walther Feb 54 obit Sep 58

Schrembs, Joseph obit Dec 45

Schrempp, Juergen Oct 99

Schreyer, Edward Richard Feb 81

Schricker, Henry F. Sep 50 obit Feb 67

Schriever, Bernard A. Oct 57

Schrift, Shirley see Winters, Shelley

Schröder, Gerhard Dec 62 Nov 98 obit Mar 90

Schroeder, Frederick R., Jr. Oct 49

Schroeder, Patricia Oct 78

Schroeder, R. W. Jul 41

Schroeder, Ted see Schroeder, Frederick R., Jr.

Schuchert, Charles obit Jan 43

Schuck, Arthur A. Apr 50 obit Apr 63

Schulberg, Budd Jun 41 May 51

Schuller, Gunther Apr 64

Schuller, Mary Craig see McGeachy, Mary Craig

Schuller, Robert H. Jun 79

Schulte, Karl Joseph, Cardinal obit May 41

Schultes, Richard Mar 95

Schulthess, Edmund obit Jun 44

Schultz, Howard M. May 97

Schultz, Richard D. Jul 96

Schultz, Sigrid Apr 44

Schultze, Charles L. Jan 70

Schulz, Charles M. Dec 60 obit Apr 2000

Schulz, Leo obit Oct 44

Schumacher, Kurt Feb 48 obit Oct 52

Schuman, Robert Jan 48 obit Nov 63

Schuman, William Jun 42 Dec 62 obit Apr 92

Schumann, Maurice Apr 70 obit Apr 98

Schumer, Charles E. Jul 95

Schurman, Jacob G. obit Oct 42

Schuster, M. Lincoln Jul 41 [Simon, Richard L; and Schuster, M. Lincoln] obit Feb 71

Schwartz, Arthur Nov 79 obit Oct 84

Schwartz, Bernard see Curtis, Tony

Schwartz, Delmore Jun 60 obit Nov 66

Schwartz, Felice N. May 93 obit Apr 96

Schwartz, Maurice Feb 56 obit Jul 60

Schwartz, Tony Jul 85

Schwarz, Gerard Apr 86

Schwarzenegger, Arnold Apr 79 Oct 91

Schwarzhaupt, Elisabeth Jan 67 obit Jan 87

Schwarzkopf, Elisabeth Dec 55

Schwarzkopf, H. Norman May 91

Schwarzschild, Martin Feb 67 obit Jun 99

Schwebel, Stephen M. Jul 52

Schweiker, Richard S. Feb 77

Schweitzer, Albert Jan 48 Jul 65

Schweitzer, Pierre-Paul Dec 63 obit Mar 94

Schwellenbach, Lewis B. Jun 45 obit Jul 48

Schwidetzky, Oscar Dec 43 obit Nov 63

Schwinger, Julian Oct 67 obit Sep 94

Schygulla, Hanna Jul 84

Scicolone, Sophia *see* Loren, Sophia

Scobie, Ronald M. Feb 45

Scofield, Paul Mar 62

Scoggin, Margaret C. Jul 52 obit Sep 68

Scorsese, Martin Feb 79

Scott, Arthur Carroll obit Yrbk 40

Scott, Barbara Ann Jul 48

Scott, C. Kay- *see* Wellman, Frederick Creighton

Scott, David R. Oct 71

Scott, George C. Apr 71 obit Nov 99

Scott, Harold Dec 50

Scott, Hazel Aug 43 obit Nov 81

Scott, Henry L. Jun 49

Scott, Hugh Sep 48 obit Sep 94

Scott, James B. obit Aug 43

Scott, John R. K. obit Feb 46

Scott, K. Frances Nov 48

Scott, Michael Apr 53 obit Apr 85

Scott, Peter Markham May 68 obit Nov 89

Scott, Raymond Jul 41 obit May 94

Scott, Ridley Oct 91

Scott, Robert L., Jr. Oct 43

Scott, Sheila Nov 74 obit Jan 89

Scott, Tom Nov 46

Scott, W. Kerr Apr 56 obit Jul 58

Scott, Willard Jul 89

Scotto, Renata Sep 78

Scourby, Alexander Jul 65 obit Apr 85

Scowcroft, Brent Jul 87

Scranton, William W. Jan 64

Scribner, Fred C., Jr. Dec 58 obit Apr 94

Scrugham, James Graves obit Jul 45

Scudder, Janet obit Jul 40

Scull, Robert C. Apr 74 obit Feb 86

Sculley, John Aug 88

Seaborg, Glenn T. Jul 48 Dec 61 obit May 99

Seabrook, William B. Nov 40 obit Oct 45

Seabury, David Sep 41 obit May 60

Seaga, Edward Apr 81

Seagrave, Gordon S. Nov 43 obit May 65

Seagren, Bob Jun 74

Seal Feb 97

Seamans, Robert C., Jr. Dec 66

Searing, Annie E. P. obit Jun 42

Sears, Paul B. Jul 60

Sears, Robert Richardson Jul 52 obit Aug 89

Sears, William Joseph, Sr. obit May 44

Seaton, Fred A. Nov 56 obit Mar 74

Seaver, George Thomas *see* Seaver, Tom

Seaver, Tom Mar 70

Sebald, William J. Oct 51

Seberg, Jean Apr 66 obit Oct 79

Sebrell, W. H., Jr. May 51 obit Nov 92

Sec *see* Mannes, Marya

Secondari, John H. Apr 67 obit Apr 75

Sedaka, Neil Oct 78

Sedaris, David Jul 97

Sedgman, Francis Arthur *see* Sedgman, Frank

Sedgman, Frank Nov 51

Seefried, Irmgard Feb 56 obit Jan 89

Seeger, Pete Dec 63

Seferis, George *see* Sepheriades, Georgios S.

Segal, Bernard G. Jun 70 obit Aug 97

Segal, Erich Apr 71

Segal, George [artist] Jan 72 obit Sep 2000

Segal, George [actor] Nov 75

Seger, George N. obit Oct 40

Seghers, Anna Dec 42 obit Jul 83

Segni, Antonio Dec 55 obit Jan 73

Segovia, Andrés May 48 Jun 64 obit Jul 87

Segré, Emilio Apr 60 obit Jul 89

Segura, Francisco Sep 51

Seibert, Florence B. Nov 42 obit Oct 91

Seibold, Louis obit Jun 45

Seid, Ruth *see* Sinclair, Jo

Seidel, Martie *see* Dixie Chicks

Seidelman, Susan May 90

Seidman, L. William Sep 76

Seifert, Elizabeth (WLB) Yrbk 51 obit Oct 83

Seifert, Shirley (WLB) Yrbk 51

Seif-Ul-Islam Abdullah, Prince Dec 47 obit Sep 55

Seinfeld, Jerry Aug 92

Seitz, Frederick Apr 56

Seitz, George B. obit Aug 44

Seixas, E. Victor, Jr. Jul 52

Sekulovich, Mladen *see* Malden, Karl

Selassie, Haile *see* Haile Selassie I

Selden, David Jul 74 obit Aug 98

Seldes, George Sep 41 obit Sep 95

Seles, Monica Nov 92

Self, Henry Oct 42

Selfridge, H. Gordon Mar 41 obit Jun 47

Selig, Allan H. *see* Selig, Bud

Selig, Bud Jan 99

Selincourt, Ernest de *see* De Selincourt, Ernest

Selinko, Annemarie Jan 55

Sell, Hildegarde Loretta *see* Hildegarde

Sellars, Peter Jan 86

Selleck, Tom Nov 83

Sellers, Peter Dec 60 obit Sep 80

Seltzer, Louis B. Dec 56 obit Jun 80

Selwyn, Edgar obit Apr 44

Selwyn-Lloyd, Baron Apr 52 obit Jul 78

Selye, Hans Jun 53 Jan 81 obit Jan 83

Selzer, Richard Apr 93

Selznick, David O. Jun 41 obit Sep 65

Selznick, Myron obit May 44

Sembène, Ousmane Apr 94

Semenov, Nikolay Nikolaevich Mar 57

Semon, Waldo Lonsbury Yrbk 40 obit Aug 99

Sen, Binay Ranjan Dec 52 obit Aug 93

Sen, Hun *see* Hun Sen

Senanayake, Don Stephen Apr 50 obit May 52

Senanayake, Dudley Dec 52 obit Jun 73

Senarens, Luis Philip obit Jan 40

Sendak, Maurice Jun 68 Jun 89

Sender, Toni May 50

Senghor, Léopold Sédar Mar 62 Jul 94

Sengstacke, John H. Nov 49 obit Aug 97

Senior, Clarence Dec 61 obit Nov 74

Senn, Milton J. E. Jun 50 obit Aug 90

Sensenich, Roscoe L. Jun 49 obit Feb 63

Sepheriades, Georgios S. May 64 obit Nov 71

Serban, Andrei Feb 78

Seredy, Kate May 40 obit May 75

Sereno, Paul C. Jun 97

Sergio, Lisa Jun 44 obit Aug 89

Sergius, Metropolitan obit Jul 44

Serkin, Peter Jun 86

Serkin, Rudolf Jul 40 Jun 90 obit Jul 91

Serlin, Oscar Mar 43 obit Apr 71

Serling, Rod Dec 59 obit Aug 75

Serov, Ivan A. Dec 56

Serra, Richard Jan 85

Serrano Suner, Ramon Nov 40

Serratosa Cibils, Joaquin Feb 54

Sert, José Luis Apr 74 obit May 83

Sert, Jose Maria obit Jan 46

Sert, Josep Lluis see Sert, José Luis

Servan-Schreiber, J.-J. Jan 55

Sessions, Roger Jan 75 obit May 85

Sessions, William S. Jul 88

Seton, Anya (WLB) Yrbk 53 obit Jan 91

Seton, Ernest Thompson May 43 obit Dec 46

Settle, Mary Lee (WLB) Yrbk 59

Seuss, Dr. see Geisel, Theodor Seuss

Sevareid, Eric Jul 42 Oct 66 obit Aug 92

Severance, H. Craig obit Nov 41

Seversky, Alexander de see De Seversky, Alexander

Sevier, Henry Hulme obit Mar 40

Sevigny, Chloë Aug 2000

Sevitzky, Fabien Jul 46 obit Apr 67

Sewell, James Luther see Sewell, Luke

Sewell, Luke Nov 44

Sewell, Winifred Jun 60

Sexton, W. R. obit Oct 43

Seyferth, O. A. Jul 50

Seymour, Charles May 41 obit Nov 63

Seymour, Flora Warren Jun 42

Seymour, Harriet Ayer obit Sep 44

Seymour, Lynn Nov 79

Seymour, Whitney North May 61 obit Jul 83

Seyss-Inquart, Artur Von May 41 obit Nov 46

Sforza, Carlo, Count Jun 42 obit Oct 52

Shabandar, Moussa Feb 56

Shafer, Paul W. Jul 52 obit Oct 54

Shaffer, Peter May 67 Nov 88

Shafik, Doria May 55

Shagari, Alhaji Shehu Aug 80

Shah, Idries Jun 76 obit Feb 97

Shaham, Gil Apr 97

Shahn, Ben Dec 54 obit May 69

Shah of Iran see Mohammed Riza Shah Pahlevi

Shakespeare, Frank Sep 70

Shalala, Donna Mar 91

Shalikashvili, John Nov 95

Shambaugh, Benjamin Franklin obit May 40

Shamir, Yitzhak Feb 83 Yrbk 96

Shandling, Garry Apr 89

Shang Chen Jul 44

Shange, Ntozake Sep 78

Shankar, Ravi Apr 68

Shanker, Albert Apr 69 obit May 97

Shannon, James A. Jan 65 obit Jul 94

Shannon, Peggy obit Jul 41

Shannon, William V. Jan 79 obit Nov 88

Shantz, Bobby see Shantz, Robert Clayton

Shantz, Robert Clayton Apr 53

Shaoqi, Liu see Liu Shao-ch'i

Shapiro, Harry Lionel Dec 52 obit Mar 90

Shapiro, Irving S. Nov 76

Shapiro, Karl Oct 44 obit Aug 2000

Shapley, Harlow Jan 41 Dec 52 Dec 72

Shaposhnikov, Boris Mar 42 obit May 45

Shapp, Milton J. Jul 73 obit Feb 95

Sharansky, Natan see Shcharansky, Anatoly

Sharett, Moshe see Shertok, Moshe

Sharif, Mohammad Nawaz Sep 98

Sharif, Omar May 70

Sharon, Ariel Apr 81

Sharp, Harry Clay obit Yrbk 40

Sharp, Mitchell Jul 66

Sharpton, Al, Jr. Nov 95

Shastri, Lal Bahadur Dec 64 obit Feb 66

Shatner, William Jul 87

Shaver, Dorothy Jan 46 obit Sep 59

Shaver, Erwin L., Rev. Mar 49

Shaver, Mary obit Mar 42

Shaw, Artie May 41

Shaw, Bernard Feb 95

Shaw, George Bernard Jun 44 obit Dec 50

Shaw, Henry obit May 41

Shaw, Irwin Oct 42 obit Jul 84

Shaw, Lau Oct 45

Shaw, Lloyd Sep 43

Shaw, Louis Agassiz obit Oct 40

Shaw, Patricia Hearst see Hearst, Patricia

Shaw, Ralph R. Jun 56 obit Dec 72

Shaw, Robert [actor] May 68 obit Oct 78

Shaw, Robert [conductor] Sep 49 Jul 66 obit Jul 66

Shawcross, Hartley Dec 45

Shawkey, Morris Purdy obit Apr 41

Shawn, Ted Oct 49 obit Feb 72

Shawn, Wallace Jun 86

Shay, Edith (WLB) Yrbk 52 [Shay, Edith; and Shay, Frank]

Shay, Frank (WLB) Yrbk 52 [Shay, Edith; and Shay, Frank] obit Mar 54

Shazar, Zalman Feb 64 obit Nov 74

Shcharansky, Anatoly Feb 87

Shcherbo, Vitaly Jul 96

Shea, Andrew B. Jan 57 obit Jan 73

Shea, William A. Oct 65 obit Nov 91

Shear, T. Leslie obit Aug 45

Shearer, Augustus H. obit Jul 41

Shearer, Moira Jan 50

Shearer, George Apr 58

Sheckell, Thomas O. obit Apr 43

Sheean, Vincent Aug 41 obit May 75

Sheed, Frank Sep 81 obit Jan 82

Sheed, Wilfrid Aug 81

Sheehan, Neil Aug 89

Sheehan, Winfield R. obit Aug 45

Sheehy, Gail Jun 93

Sheeler, Charles Nov 50 obit Jun 65

Sheen, Fulton J., Archbishop Nov 41 Jan 51 obit Feb 80

Sheen, Martin Jun 77

Shehan, Cardinal see Shehan, Lawrence

Shehan, Lawrence Oct 65 obit Oct 84

Shehu, Mehmet Feb 58 obit Feb 82

Sheil, Bernard J. Dec 68 obit Nov 69

Sheindlin, Judith Sep 98

Shelby, Carroll Nov 93

Sheldon, Charles M. obit Apr 46

Sheldon, Edward obit May 46

Sheldon, Sidney Oct 80

Shelepin, Aleksandr Feb 71 obit Jan 95

Shellabarger, Samuel May 45 obit May 54

Shelly, Mary Jo Oct 51 obit Sep 76

Shelly, Warner S. Feb 52

Shelton, Henry H. Aug 98

Shelton, James E. Feb 51

Shepard, Alan B. Dec 61 obit Sep 98

Shepard, E. H. Dec 63 obit May 76

Shepard, Sam Apr 79

Shepherd, Cybill Mar 87

Shepherd, Jean Apr 84 obit Jan 2000

Shepherd, Lemuel C., Jr. Feb 52 obit Oct 90

Shepherd, Michael see Ludlum, Robert

Shepilov, Dmitri Trofimovitch Dec 55

Sheppard, Morris obit Jun 41

Shera, Jesse H. Jun 64 obit Jun 82

Sherard, Robert Harborough obit Mar 43

Sherley, Swagar obit Apr 41

Sherman, Allan Sep 66 obit Jan 74

Sherman, Cindy Oct 90

Sherman, Forrest P. Mar 48 obit Sep 51

Sherman, Frederic Fairchild obit Yrbk 40

Sherman, Henry C. Jan 49 obit Dec 55

Sherrill, Henry Knox Mar 47 obit Jun 80

Sherrod, Robert Jun 44 Dec 62 obit May 94

Shertok, Moshe Apr 48 obit Sep 65

Sherwood, Robert E. Jun 40 obit Jan 56

Shevardnadze, Eduard Feb 86

Shevchenko, Arkady N. Sep 85 obit May 98

Shiber, Etta Dec 43 obit Jan 49

Shidehara, Kijuro Apr 46 obit Apr 51

Shield, Lansing P. Jun 51 obit Mar 60

Shields, Brooke Oct 82

Shields, James P. Mar 51 obit Sep 53

Shifrin, Aleksandr Mikhailovich see Werner, Max

Shigemitsu, Mamoru Jun 43 obit Mar 57

Shih, Hu see Hu Shih

Shikler, Aaron Dec 71

Shillard-Smith, Christine Wetherill see Leser, Tina

Shilts, Randy Oct 93 obit May 94

Shimazaki, Tôson obit Oct 43

Shimkin, Leon May 54

Shine, F. W. obit Nov 41

Shinn, Everett May 51 obit Jun 53

Shinn, Florence Scovel obit Yrbk 40

Shinn, Milicent Washburn obit Oct 40

Shinwell, Emanuel Jan 43 obit Jun 86

Shipley, Jenny Mar 2000

Shipley, Ruth B. Dec 47 obit Jan 67

Shippen, Katherine B. (WLB) Yrbk 54

Shiras, George obit May 42

Shirer, William L. Jul 41 May 62 obit Feb 94

Shirley, Donna Aug 98

Shiromani, Narendra obit Mar 43

Shivers, Allan Oct 51 obit Mar 85

Shockley, William Dec 53 obit Oct 89

Shoemaker, Bill see Shoemaker, Willie

Shoemaker, Eugene M. Jun 67 obit Oct 97

Shoemaker, Samuel M. Apr 55 obit Dec 63

Shoemaker, Willie Jul 66

Sholokhov, Mikhail Aleksandrovich Jan 42 Feb 60 obit Apr 84

Shone, Terence Allen Nov 46 obit Dec 65

Shope, Richard E. Dec 63 obit Dec 66

Shore, Dinah Jun 42 Dec 66 obit May 94

Shoriki, Matsutaro Feb 58

Short, Bobby Jul 72

Short, Dewey Dec 51 obit Feb 80

Short, Hassard Nov 48 obit Dec 56

Short, Joseph Feb 51 obit Nov 52

Short, Martin Sep 92

Short, Walter C. Jan 46 obit Oct 49

Shorter, Wayne Apr 96

Shortz, Will Apr 96

Shostakovich, Dmitrii Dmitrievich May 41 obit Oct 75

Shotton, Burt Jun 49 obit Oct 62

Shotwell, James T. Oct 44 obit Sep 65
Shoulders, Harrison H. Nov 46 obit Jan 64
Shoup, Carl Feb 49 obit Sep 2000
Shoup, David M. Jan 60 obit Mar 83
Shoup, Oliver Henry obit Nov 40
Shreeve, Herbert Edward obit Jun 42
Shreve, Earl Owen Oct 47
Shreve, R. H. Nov 45 obit Oct 46
Shridharani, Krishnalal Jan 42 obit Oct 60
Shriver, Eunice Kennedy Jul 96
Shriver, Maria Nov 91
Shriver, R. Sargent Dec 61
Shu, Ch'ing-ch'un see Shaw, Lau
Shula, Don Mar 74
Shull, Martha A. Apr 57
Shulman, Harry Apr 52 obit May 55
Shulman, Irving (WLB) Yrbk 56 obit Jun 95
Shulman, Max Oct 59 obit Oct 88
Shultz, George P. May 69 Apr 88
Shuman, Charles B. Feb 56
Shu-meng, Luan see Jiang Qing
Shumlin, Herman Mar 41 obit Aug 79
Shumway, Norman E. Apr 71
Shurlock, Geoffery M. Jan 62 obit Jun 76
Shuster, George Nauman Jan 41 Oct 60 obit Mar 77
Shute, Nevil Jul 42 obit Mar 60
Shvernik, Nikolai Oct 51 obit Feb 71
Sibley, Antoinette Dec 70
Sickert, Walter Richard obit Mar 42
Sides, John H. Jan 61 obit Jun 78
Sidi Mohammed, Sultan of Morocco see Mohammed V, King of Morocco
Sidney, Sylvia Oct 81 obit Sep 99
Siebert, Mickie see Siebert, Muriel

Siebert, Muriel Aug 97
Siegel, Bernie S. Jun 93
Siegfried Jan 98 [Siegfried and Roy]
Siemiller, P. L. Nov 66
Siepi, Cesare Dec 55
Sigerist, Henry Ernest Sep 40 obit Jun 57
Signoret, Simone Dec 60 obit Nov 85
Sihanouk, Norodom see Norodom Sihanouk
Sikorski, Wladyslaw Jan-Feb 40 obit Aug 43
Sikorsky, Igor I. Oct 40 Dec 56 obit Dec 72
Silber, John R. Feb 84
Silberman, Charles E. Jul 79
Siles, Hernando obit Jan 43
Siles Zuazo, Hernán Sep 58 Jun 85 obit Oct 96
Sillanpää, Frans Eemil Jan-Feb 40 obit Jul 64
Sillcox, Lewis Ketcham Dec 54 obit May 89
Sills, Beverly Nov 69 Feb 82
Silva, Maria Helena Vieira da see Vieira Da Silva, Maria Helena
Silva de Santolalla, Irene see Santolalla, Irene Silva De
Silver, Abba Hillel Dec 41 May 63 obit Jan 64
Silverman, Fred Nov 78
Silvers, Phil Dec 57 obit Jan 86
Silzer, George Sebastian obit Yrbk 40
Simenon, Georges Apr 70 obit Nov 89
Simionato, Giulietta Apr 60
Simkhovitch, Mary Melinda Kingsbury Mar 43 obit Dec 51
Simkin, William E. Jan 67 obit May 92
Simmons, Adele Smith May 91
Simmons, Furnifold McLendell obit Jan 40
Simmons, Gene see Kiss
Simmons, Jean Feb 52
Simmons, Richard May 82
Simmons, Russell Jun 98
Simmons, Ruth J. Jan 96
Simms, Hilda Nov 44 obit May 94
Simms, John F. Sep 56 obit Jun 75

Simms, Phil Oct 94
Simms, Ruth Hanna McCormick obit Feb 45
Simon, Carly Aug 76
Simon, Charlie May (WLB) Yrbk 46
Simon, Claude May 92
Simon, Edith (WLB) Yrbk 54
Simon, Herbert A. Jun 79
Simon, John Allsebrook Simon, 1st Viscount Jul 40 obit Mar 54
Simon, Mrs. Howard see Simon, Charlie May
Simon, Neil Feb 68 Mar 89
Simon, Norton Mar 68 obit Aug 93
Simon, Paul [musician] Mar 75
Simon, Paul [senator] Jan 88
Simon, Richard L. Jul 41 [Simon, Richard L; and Schuster, M. Lincoln] obit Oct 60
Simon, William E. Apr 74 obit Aug 2000
Simon and Schuster see Simon, Richard L.; Schuster, Lincoln M.
Simonds, Frederic W. obit May 41
Simonds, G. G. Oct 43 obit Jul 74
Simone, Nina Apr 68
Simonetta Dec 55
Simons, David G. Dec 57
Simons, Elwyn L. Jun 94
Simons, Hans Mar 57 obit May 72
Simonson, Lee Nov 47 obit Mar 67
Simpson, Adele Nov 70 obit Oct 95
Simpson, Alan Feb 64 obit Jul 98
Simpson, Alan K. Oct 90
Simpson, Carole Nov 99
Simpson, George Gaylord Dec 64 obit Jan 85
Simpson, Harriette Louisa see Arnow, Harriette Simpson
Simpson, Helen De Guerry obit Yrbk 40
Simpson, Howard E. May 58 obit Apr 85
Simpson, Kenneth F. obit Mar 41
Simpson, Louis Dec 64

Simpson, Milward L. Jan 57 obit Aug 93

Simpson, Mona Feb 93

Simpson, O. J. Apr 69

Simpson, Richard M. Dec 53 obit Mar 60

Simpson, Valerie Apr 97 [Ashford, Nickolas; and Simpson, Valerie]

Simpson, Wallis Warfield *see* Windsor, Wallis Warfield

Simpson, William H. Feb 45 obit Oct 80

Sims, Hugo S., Jr. Oct 49

Sims, William L., 2d Dec 56

Sin, Jaime L. Sep 95

Sinatra, Frank Jun 43 Oct 60 obit Jul 98

Sinbad Feb 97

Sinclair, Adelaide Helen Grant Macdonald *see* Sinclair, D. B.

Sinclair, April Sep 99

Sinclair, Archibald Sep 40 obit Oct 70 [Thurso, Archibald Henry Sinclair Macdonald, 1st Viscount]

Sinclair, D. B. obit Jan 83

Sinclair, D. B. Apr 51 [Sinclair, Adelaide Helen Grant Macdonald]

Sinclair, Jo Mar 46 obit Jun 95

Sinclair, May obit Dec 46

Sinclair, Upton Dec 62 obit Jan 69

Sinclair-Cowan, Bertha Muzzy *see* Bower, Bertha Muzzy

Sinding, Christian obit Jan 42

Singer, Adam *see* Karp, David

Singer, Isaac Bashevis Jan 69 Sep 91

Singer, Israel J. obit Mar 44

Singer, Kurt D. Dec 54

Singer, Peter Mar 91

Singer, Richard obit Mar 40

Singer, S. Fred Dec 55

Singh, Giani Zail Sep 87 obit Mar 95

Singh, Swaran Mar 71 obit Jan 95

Singh, Vishwanath Pratap May 90

Singher, Martial Feb 47 obit May 90

Singletary, Mike Mar 93

Singleton, John Feb 97

Sinise, Gary Apr 97

Sink, M. Virginia Mar 64

Sinnott, Edmund W. Oct 48 obit Mar 68

Sinopoli, Giuseppe Mar 91

Sinsheimer, Robert L. Jun 68

Sinyavsky, Andrei D. Jul 75 obit May 97

Siple, Paul A. Feb 57 obit Jan 69

Siqueiros, David Alfaro Jun 59 obit Feb 74

Sirica, John J. May 74 obit Oct 92

Sirikit Kitiyakara, Consort of Bhumibol Adulyadej, King of Thailand *see* Sirikit Kitiyakara, Consort of Rama IX, King of Thailand

Sirikit Kitiyakara, Consort of Rama IX, King of Thailand Dec 60

Sirin *see* Nabokov, Vladimir

Siroky, Viliam Apr 57 obit Nov 71

Sisavang Vong, King of Laos Apr 54 obit Jan 60

Sisco, Joseph J. Jan 72

Sister Wendy *see* Beckett, Wendy

Sitgreaves, Beverley obit Sep 43

Sitterly, Charlotte Moore Jan 62 obit Jun 90

Sitwell, Osbert Sep 65 obit Jun 69

Six, Robert F. Oct 70 obit Nov 86

Siza, Alvaro Feb 2000

Sizoo, Joseph R. Dec 64 obit Nov 66

Skelton, Red Nov 47 obit Nov 97

Skelton, Richard Bernard *see* Skelton, Red

Skidmore, Hubert Standish obit Mar 46

Skidmore, Louis Dec 51 obit Dec 62

Skillin, Edward S. May 49 obit Yrbk 2000

Skilton, Charles Sanford obit May 41

Skinner, B. F. Jan 64 Nov 79 obit Oct 90

Skinner, Cornelia Otis Jan 42 Dec 64 obit Sep 79

Skinner, Eleanor Oakes *see* Skinner, Mrs. James M., Jr.

Skinner, Mrs. James M., Jr. May 51 [Skinner, Eleanor Oakes]

Skinner, Otis obit Feb 42

Skinner, Samuel K. Aug 89

Skira, Albert Apr 67 obit Jun 90

Skocpol, Theda Aug 2000

Skolnick, Mark H. Jun 97

Skouras, Spyros P. Jun 43 obit Nov 71

Skrowaczewski, Stanislaw Dec 64

Skutt, V. J. Dec 59 obit Apr 93

Slade, Roy Jun 85

Slaney, Mary Decker *see* Decker, Mary

Slater, John E. Nov 51

Slater, Rodney Jan 99

Slatkin, Leonard Feb 86

Slaughter, Frank G. Oct 42

Slaughter, Louise M. Apr 99

Slavenska, Mia Feb 54

Slayton, Donald K. Feb 76 obit Aug 93

Sleeper, Ruth Oct 52 obit Feb 93

Slemon, C. Roy Dec 56

Slezak, Walter Mar 55 obit Jun 83

Slichter, Sumner H. Jun 47 obit Dec 59

Slick, Grace Apr 82

Sligh, Charles R., Jr. Apr 53

Slim, Mongi Mar 58 obit Dec 69

Slim, William Joseph Slim, Viscount Jun 45 obit Feb 71

Sliwa, Curtis Feb 83

Sloan, Alfred Pritchard, Jr. Nov 40 obit Mar 66

Sloan, George A. Jan 52 obit Jul 55

Sloan, Samuel obit May 45

Sloane, Eric Sep 72 obit May 85

Sloane, Everett Jan 57 obit Oct 65

Slobodkin, Louis Apr 57 obit Aug 75

Slocum, Harvey Feb 57 obit Jan 62

Slonimsky, Nicolas Apr 55 Feb 91 obit Mar 96

Slye, Maud Yrbk 40 obit Nov 54

Smadel, Joseph E. May 63

Small, John D. Feb 46 obit Mar 63

Small, John Humphrey obit Sep 46

Smallens, Alexander May 47 obit Jan 73

Smallpeice, Basil Oct 69

Smallwood, Joseph R. Feb 53 obit Mar 92

Smallwood, Robert B. Mar 56 obit Sep 74

Smart, David A. Jun 44

Smathers, George A. Apr 54

Smeal, Eleanor Cutri Mar 80

Smedberg, William Renwick, 3d Dec 57

Smedley, Agnes Jan 44 obit Jun 50

Smedley, Constance obit Apr 41

Smetona, Antanas obit Feb 44

Smiley, Jane Apr 90

Smith, Albert W. obit Oct 42

Smith, Alfred E. Sep 44

Smith, Anna Deavere Sep 94

Smith, Austin E. Mar 50 obit Jan 94

Smith, Barbara Jul 98

Smith, Ben Oct 45 obit Jul 64

Smith, Betty Nov 43 obit Mar 72

Smith, Bruce [police administrator] Feb 53 obit Nov 55

Smith, Bruce [football player] Mar 95

Smith, C. Aubrey Sep 44 obit Jan 49

Smith, C. R. Sep 45 obit Jun 90

Smith, Carleton Apr 61 obit Jul 84

Smith, Carleton Sprague Dec 60 obit Nov 94

Smith, Cecil Woodham- see Woodham-Smith, Cecil Blanche Fitzgerald

Smith, Chesterfield H. Nov 74

Smith, Clara E. obit Jul 43

Smith, Clyde Harold obit May 40

Smith, Courtney Dec 59 obit Mar 69

Smith, Cyril Stanley Jul 48 obit Oct 92

Smith, David T. Oct 50

Smith, Dean Apr 94

Smith, Dick Mar 59

Smith, E. Durant obit Jan 45

Smith, Elizabeth Rudel Dec 61

Smith, Emmitt Nov 94

Smith, Ernest Bramah see Bramah, Ernest

Smith, Frances Octavia see Rogers, Dale Evans

Smith, Frederick W. Jun 2000

Smith, George Adam obit Apr 42

Smith, George Albert Nov 47 obit May 51

Smith, Gerald L. K. Aug 43 obit Jun 76

Smith, Gerard C. Oct 70 obit Sep 94

Smith, Gregory White Mar 98 [Naifeh, Steven; and Smith, Gregory White]

Smith, H. Alexander Apr 48 obit Jan 67

Smith, H. Allen May 42 obit May 76

Smith, Harold D. Jul 43 obit Mar 47

Smith, Harrison Dec 54 obit Feb 71

Smith, Hazel Brannon Sep 73 obit Jul 94

Smith, Hedrick Jun 91

Smith, Holland M. Apr 45 obit Mar 67

Smith, Howard K. Mar 43 Jul 76

Smith, Howard W. Feb 41 obit Nov 76

Smith, Ian Douglas May 66

Smith, Ida B. Wise Feb 43 obit Apr 52

Smith, James H., Jr. Jan 58 obit Feb 83

Smith, James Todd see L. L. Cool J

Smith, Jeff Aug 91

Smith, Jim see Dale, Jim

Smith, John L. Jun 52 obit Dec 58

Smith, Kate Yrbk 40 Nov 65 obit Aug 86

Smith, Kevin Feb 98

Smith, Lady Eleanor obit Nov 45

Smith, Lillian May 44 obit Dec 66

Smith, Liz May 87

Smith, Logan Pearsall obit Apr 46

Smith, Maggie Jun 70

Smith, Margaret Chase Feb 45 Mar 62 obit Aug 95

Smith, Margaret Nicholson see Nicholson, Margaret

Smith, Martin Cruz Nov 90

Smith, Mary Alice see Mary Alice

Smith, Mary Carter Feb 96

Smith, Mary Elizabeth see Smith, Liz

Smith, Mary Louise Oct 76 obit Nov 97

Smith, Merriman Dec 64 obit Nov 93 (died Apr 70)

Smith, Oliver Sep 61 obit Mar 94

Smith, Ozzie Feb 97

Smith, Page Sep 90 obit Nov 95

Smith, Patti Apr 89

Smith, Paul C. Apr 43 obit Sep 76

Smith, Red see Smith, Walter Wellesley

Smith, Rex Jan 42

Smith, Richard Emerson see Smith, Dick

Smith, Robert Paul Dec 58

Smith, Robert Sep 2000

Smith, Robyn Nov 76

Smith, Roger B. May 86

Smith, Rosamund see Oates, Joyce Carol

Smith, Roy Burnett obit Feb 41

Smith, Sidney Jan 55 obit May 59

Smith, Sylvester C., Jr. Jul 63

Smith, T. V. Feb 56 obit Jul 64

Smith, Thomas R. obit Jun 42

Smith, Virginia B. Jun 78

Smith, Walter Bedell Apr 44 Dec 53 obit Nov 61

Smith, Walter Wellesley Apr 59 obit Feb 82

Smith, Wilbur Fisk obit Sep 40

Smith, William French Jan 82 obit Jan 91

Smith, William Jay Mar 74

Smith, William Ward Feb 48 obit Jul 66

Smith, Will Sep 96

Smith, Zadie Aug 2000

Smithdas, Robert J. Dec 66

Smoot, George Apr 94

Smoot, Reed obit Mar 41

Smothers, Dick Dec 68

Smothers, Tom Dec 68

Smuin, Michael Oct 84

Smuts, Jan Christiaan Aug 41 obit Oct 50

Smylie, Robert E. Feb 56

Smyslov, Vassily Jul 67

Smyth, Ethel Mary obit Jun 44

Smyth, H. D. *see* Smyth, Henry Dewolf

Smyth, Henry Dewolf Dec 48 obit Nov 86

Snavely, Guy E. Apr 51

Snead, Sammy Jun 49

Snead, Samuel Jackson *see* Snead, Sammy

Sneider, Vern (WLB) Yrbk 56 obit Jun 81

Snell, Foster Dee Jan 43

Snell, George D. May 86 obit Aug 96

Snell, Henry Bayley obit Mar 43

Snell, Henry Snell, 1st Baron May 41

Snell, Peter Dec 62

Snider, Duke May 56

Snider, Edwin Donald *see* Snider, Duke

Snipes, Wesley Sep 93

Snodgrass, W. D. Nov 60

Snook, H. Clyde obit Nov 42

Snow, C. P. (WLB) Yrbk 54 Dec 61 obit Aug 80

Snow, Clyde Collins Apr 97

Snow, Edgar Jun 41 obit Apr 72

Snow, Edward Rowe (WLB) Yrbk 58

Snow, Glenn E. Nov 47

Snowdon, Lord *see* Armstrong-Jones, Antony

Snowe, Olympia J. May 95

Snow of Leicester, Baron *see* Snow, C. P.

Snyder, Alice D. obit Apr 43

Snyder, Gary Nov 78

Snyder, Howard McC Feb 55 obit Nov 70

Snyder, J. Buell obit Apr 46

Snyder, Janet *see* Lambert, Janet

Snyder, John W. Jul 45 obit Jan 86

Snyder, Peggy Lou *see* Nelson, Harriet

Snyder, Solomon H. Apr 96

Snyder, Tom Jun 80

Soames, Christopher, Baron of Fletching Aug 81 obit Oct 87

Soares, Mário Oct 75

Sobchak, Anatoly A. Jul 92 obit Jul 2000

Sobeloff, Simon E. Mar 55 obit Sep 73

Sobhuza II, King of Swaziland Mar 82 obit Mar 82

Sobolev, Arkady A. Apr 55 obit Jan 65

Socarras, Carlos Prio *see* Prío Socarrás, Carlos

Sockman, Ralph W. Jun 46 obit Nov 70

Soderberg, C. Richard Feb 58 obit Jan 80

Soderbergh, Steven Oct 98

Sodero, Cesare Mar 43 obit Jan 48

Söderström, Elisabeth Nov 85

Soeharto Jun 67 Oct 92

Soekarno *see* Sukarno

Soglow, Otto Sep 40 obit May 75

Soheily, Ali Sep 43 obit Jul 58

Sokolovsky, Vassily D. Dec 53 obit Jul 68

Sokolow, Anna Feb 69 obit Sep 2000

Sokolsky, George E. May 41 obit Jan 63

Solandt, Omond M. Mar 74

Solarz, Stephen J. Nov 86

Solberg, Thorvald A. Dec 48

Soldati, Mario Apr 58 obit Nov 99

Soler, Antonio Ruiz *see* Ruiz Soler, Antonio

Soleri, Paolo Feb 72

Solh, Sami Feb 58 obit Jan 69

Solti, Georg Mar 64 obit Nov 97

Solzhenitsyn, Aleksandr Feb 69 Jul 88

Somers, Jane *see* Lessing, Doris

Somervell, Brehon Aug 42 obit Apr 55

Somerville, James Apr 43 obit Apr 49

Somes, Michael Dec 55 obit Feb 95

Sommerfeld, A. Apr 50 obit May 51

Somoza, Anastasio [1896–1956] Jun 42 obit Dec 56

Somoza, Anastasio [1925–1980] Mar 78 obit Nov 80

Sondheim, Stephen Nov 73

Songgram, Luang Pibul *see* Pibul Songgram, Luang

Sonnenfeld, Barry Nov 98

Sontag, Susan Jun 69 Feb 92

Soong, Chingling *see* Sun Yat-Sen

Soong, T.V. Mar 41 obit Jun 71

Sophoulis, Themistocles Nov 47 obit Sep 49

Sordoni, Andrew J. Jul 56 obit Apr 63

Sorel, Edward Mar 94

Sorensen, Theodore Dec 61

Sorensen, Virginia (WLB) Yrbk 50

Sorkin, Aaron Jun 2000

Sorokin, Pitirim Alexandrovich Jul 42 obit Apr 68

Soros, George Apr 97

Sorvino, Mira Aug 98

Sosa, Sammy May 99

Soss, Wilma Porter Mar 65 obit Jan 87

Soth, Lauren K. Dec 56 obit Jun 98

Sothern, Ann Dec 56

Souers, Sidney W. Feb 49 obit Mar 73

Soukup, Frantisek obit Yrbk 40

Soulages, Pierre Apr 58

Soule, George Henry Dec 45 obit Jun 70

Soustelle, Jacques Dec 58 obit Oct 90

Souter, David H. Jan 91

Southworth, Billy Nov 44 obit Jan 70

Southworth, James L. Jun 43 [Hingson, Robert A.; Edwards, Waldo B.; and Southworth, James L.]

Southworth, William H. *see* Southworth, Billy

Souvanna Phouma Nov 62 obit Mar 84

Souzay, Gérard Jan 66

Sovern, Michael I. Feb 81

Sowell, Thomas Jul 81

Soyer, Isaac Mar 41 [Soyer, Isaac; Soyer, Moses; and Soyer, Raphael] obit Sep 81

Soyer, Moses Mar 41 [Soyer, Isaac; Soyer, Moses; and Soyer, Raphael] obit Oct 74

Soyer, Raphael Mar 41 [Soyer, Isaac; Soyer, Moses; and Soyer, Raphael] obit Jan 88

Soyinka, Wole Dec 74

Soyinka Akinwande Oluwole see Soyinka, Wole

Spaak, Paul-Henri May 45 Apr 58 obit Oct 72

Spaatz, Carl Sep 42 obit Sep 74

Spacek, Sissy Jan 78

Spacey, Kevin Apr 97

Spaeth, Sigmund Jul 42 obit Jan 66

Spahn, Warren May 62

Spain, Frances Lander Jun 60

Spalding, Albert Jan 44 obit Jul 53

Spang, J. P., Jr. Jun 49 obit Feb 70

Spangler, Harrison E. Aug 43 obit Oct 65

Spark, Muriel Nov 75

Sparkman, John J. Mar 50 obit Jan 86

Sparling, Edward J. Jul 48

Spassky, Boris Nov 72

Spaulding, Rolland H. obit May 42

Speakes, Larry Mar 85

Speaks, John Charles obit Dec 45

Speare, Elizabeth George (WLB) Yrbk 59 obit Jan 95

Spearman, Charles E. obit Oct 45

Spears, Britney Apr 2000

Specter, Arlen Aug 88

Spector, Phil Jul 89

Spectorsky, A. C. Jan 60 obit Mar 72

Speer, Albert Oct 76 obit Oct 81

Speicher, Eugene Oct 47 obit Jul 62

Speidel, Hans Apr 52 obit Feb 85

Spelling, Aaron May 86

Spellman, Francis Apr 40 Apr 47 obit Jan 68

Spence, Brent Sep 52 obit Jan 68

Spence, Hartzell Oct 42

Spencer, Lady Diana see Diana, Princess of Wales

Spencer, P. C. Jul 51 obit Jan 70

Spencer-Churchill, Clementine Ogilvy Hozier Jul 53 [Churchill, Lady] obit Mar 78

Spender, J. Alfred obit Aug 42

Spender, Percy C. Mar 50

Spender, Stephen Jan 40 Mar 77 obit Sep 95

Sperry, Armstrong Oct 41

Sperry, Roger W. Jan 86 obit Jun 94

Sperry, Willard L., Rev. Dr. May 52 obit Sep 54

Sperti, George Speri Jan 40 obit Jul 91

Spiegel, Clara see Jaynes, Clare

Spiegelman, Sol Nov 80 obit Mar 83

Spielberg, Steven Jul 78 Feb 96

Spilhaus, Athelstan Jun 65 obit Jun 98

Spillane, Mickey Sep 81

Spiller, William Gibson obit Apr 40

Spingarn, Arthur B. Jan 65 obit Jan 72

Spinola, Antonio De Sep 74 obit Nov 96

Spitalny, Phil Oct 40 obit Dec 70

Spitz, Mark Oct 72

Spitzer, Lyman, Jr. Jan 60 obit Jun 97

Spivak, Lawrence E. May 56 obit May 94

Spivakov, Vladimir Feb 96

Spock, Benjamin Dec 56 Nov 69 obit Jun 98

Spofford, Charles M. Feb 51 obit May 91

Sporborg, Constance Amberg see Sporborg, Mrs. William Dick

Sporborg, Constance Nov 47 [Sporborg, Mrs. William Dick] obit Feb 61 [Sporborg, Mrs. William Dick]

Sporn, Philip Nov 66

Spottswood, James obit Yrbk 40

Spottswood, Stephen Gill Apr 62 obit Jan 75

Sprague, Embert Hiram obit Mar 40

Sprague, Robert Chapman Jan 51 obit Nov 91

Spring, Howard Jan 41 obit Jun 65

Springer, Adele I. Apr 47

Springer, Axel Dec 68 obit Nov 85

Springsteen, Bruce Apr 78 Aug 92

Sprinkel, Beryl Jul 87

Sproul, Allan Dec 50 obit Jun 78

Sproul, Robert Gordon Jul 45 obit Nov 75

Spruance, Raymond Ames Apr 44 obit Mar 70

Spry, Constance May 40 obit Mar 60

Spurgeon, Caroline F. E. obit Dec 42

Spyrou, Aristocles Matthew see Athenagoras I, Patriarch

Squires, Richard Anderson obit May 40

St. Clair Sinclair, Mary Amelia see Sinclair, May

St. Denis, Ruth Oct 49 obit Oct 68

St. George, Katharine Dec 47 obit Jul 83

St. George, Mrs. George B. see St. George, Katharine

St. George, Thomas R. Jan 44

St. John, Robert Jun 42

St. Johns, Adela Rogers Aug 76 obit Sep 88

St. Laurent, Louis S. Mar 48 obit Oct 73

St. Laurent, Yves Dec 64

Staats, Elmer B. Jun 67

Stabler, Ken Oct 79

Stace, W. T. Apr 61 obit Oct 67

Stack, Andy see Rule, Ann

Stacy, Walter P. Jan 46 obit Oct 51

Stade, Frederica Von see Von Stade, Frederica

Stader, Maria Jul 58 obit Aug 99

Stafford, Jean (WLB) Yrbk 51 obit May 79

Stafford, Robert T. Sep 60

Stafford, Thomas P. Jan 77

Stagg, Alonzo Mar 44 obit Apr 65

Staggers, Harley O. Mar 71 obit Nov 91

Stahl, Lesley Jun 96
Stahle, Nils K. Apr 56
Stahr, Elvis J., Jr. Sep 61 obit Feb 99
Stainback, Ingram Macklin Dec 47 obit Jun 61
Stakman, E. C. Dec 49 obit Mar 79
Staley, Oren Lee Sep 65 obit Nov 88
Stalin, Joseph Mar 42 obit Apr 53
Stalina, Svetlana Iosifovna see Alliluyeva, Svetlana
Stallone, Sylvester Oct 77 Feb 94
Stalnaker, John M. Jul 58 obit Oct 90
Stamm, John S. Feb 49 obit May 56
Stamos, Theodoros Jan 59 obit Apr 97
Stamp, Josiah Charles Stamp, 1st Baron obit Jun 41
Standish, Burt L. see Patten, Gilbert
Standley, W. H. May 42 obit Dec 63
Stanfield, Robert L. Dec 58
Stanfield, Robert Nelson obit Jun 45
Stanford, Otis Binet see Whyte, William H. Jr.
Stankiewicz, Richard Jun 67 obit May 83
Stanky, Eddie Jun 51 obit Aug 99
Stanky, Edward Raymond see Stanky, Eddie
Stanley, Freelan O. obit Nov 40
Stanley, Kim May 55
Stanley, Oliver Apr 43 obit Jan 51
Stanley, Paul see Kiss
Stanley, Thomas B. Dec 55 obit Oct 70
Stanley, Wendell Meredith Apr 47 obit Sep 71
Stanley, Winifred Jun 43
Stans, Maurice H. Dec 58 obit Jun 98
Stanton, Frank Nov 45 Oct 65
Stanwyck, Barbara Jul 47 obit Mar 90
Staples, Brent May 2000
Stapleton, Jean Dec 72
Stapleton, Maureen May 59

Stapp, John Paul Dec 59 obit May 2000
Starch, Daniel Jan 63
Stargell, Willie Jun 80
Stark, Harold Raynsford May 40 obit Oct 72
Stark, Louis Jun 45 obit Sep 54
Starkenborgh Stachouwer, A. W. L., Tjarda Van Feb 42
Starker, Janos May 63
Starkie, Walter Fitzwilliam May 64 obit Feb 77
Starr, Bart Jan 68
Starr, Cecile Mar 55
Starr, Chauncey Apr 54
Starr, Kenneth W. May 98
Starr, Louis E. Jun 47
Starr, Mark Jul 46 obit Jul 85
Starr, Ringo Dec 65
Starzl, Thomas E. Mar 93
Stassen, Harold E. May 40 Mar 48
Statz, Hermann Jan 58
Staubach, Roger Apr 72
Staudinger, Hermann Apr 54 obit Nov 65
Stauning, Thorvald obit Jun 42
Stauss, Emil Georg Von obit Feb 43
Stavropoulos, George Mar 85 obit Feb 91
Steacie, E. W. R. Jan 53 obit Nov 62
Steadman, Ralph May 99
Steagall, Henry Bascom obit Jan 44
Stearns, Harold E. obit Oct 43
Stebbins, George Coles obit Nov 45
Steber, Eleanor Mar 43 obit Jan 91
Steel, Danielle Jul 89
Steel, David Jul 78
Steel, Johannes Jun 41 obit Feb 89
Steel, Kurt see Kagey, Rudolf
Steele, Frederic Dorr obit Aug 44
Steele, Shelby Feb 93
Steell, Willis obit Mar 41
Steelman, John R. May 41 Nov 52 obit Nov 99
Steen, Marguerite Oct 41 obit Sep 75
Stefan, Paul obit Jan 44
Stefánsson, Vilhjalmur Oct 42 obit Nov 62

Stegner, Wallace Apr 77 obit Jun 93
Steichen, Edward Oct 42 Dec 64 obit May 73
Steig, William Jul 44
Steiger, Rod Jun 65
Stein, Gertrude obit Sep 46
Stein, Herbert Mar 73 obit Feb 2000
Stein, Jules May 67 obit Jun 81
Steinbeck, John Feb 40 May 63 obit Feb 69
Steinberg, Hans Wilhelm see Steinberg, William Sep 40
Steinberg, Milton Mar 40 obit Apr 50
Steinberg, Saul Mar 57 obit Jul 99
Steinberg, William Mar 58 obit Jul 78
Steinbrenner, George Michael 3d Feb 79
Steincrohn, Peter J. Mar 57
Steinem, Gloria Mar 72 Mar 88
Steiner, George Oct 83
Steiner, Max Sep 43 obit Feb 72
Steiner, Walter Ralph obit Jan 43
Steinfeld, Jesse L. Apr 74
Steinhardt, Laurence A. Jul 41 obit Apr 50
Steinhaus, Edward A. Dec 55
Steinkraus, Herman W. Nov 49 obit Jul 74
Steinman, D. B. Dec 57 obit Nov 60
Steinman, Mrs. John F. see Watkins, Shirley
Stekel, Wilhelm obit Aug 40
Stella, Antonietta Dec 59
Stella, Frank Apr 71 Apr 88
Stella, Joseph obit Dec 46
Stelle, John Jan 46 obit Sep 62
Steloff, Frances Nov 65 obit Jun 89
Stengel, Casey Jun 49 obit Nov 75
Stengel, Charles Dillon see Stengel, Casey
Stenmark, Ingemar Apr 82
Stennis, John C. Jan 53 obit Jul 95
Stephanie, Princess of Monaco Aug 86

Stephanopoulos, George Jan 95

Stephanopoulos, Stephanos Jul 55

Stephens, Hubert D. obit Apr 46

Stephens, John A. Dec 56

Stephens, Ward obit Nov 40

Stephens, William D. obit Jun 44

Stephenson, James obit Sep 41

Stepinac, Alojzije Feb 53 obit Apr 60

Stepovich, Michael A. Nov 58

Steptoe, Patrick Mar 79 obit Jun 88

Sterling, J. E. Wallace Jan 51 obit Aug 85

Stern, Arthur Cecil Apr 56 obit Jul 92

Stern, Bill Jun 41 obit Jan 72

Stern, David Apr 91

Stern, Howard Jan 96

Stern, Isaac Apr 49 Feb 89

Stern, Leonard Mar 91

Stern, Martha Dodd see Dodd, Martha

Stern, Richard Jun 94

Stern, Robert A. M. Jun 2000

Sterne, Hedda Mar 57

Sterne, Maurice Apr 43 obit Oct 57

Stettinius, Edward R., Jr. Jul 40 obit Dec 49

Steuer, Max David obit Oct 40

Stevens, Edmund Jul 50 obit Jul 92

Stevens, George, Jr. Dec 65

Stevens, George Apr 52 obit May 75

Stevens, John Paul May 76

Stevens, Risë Nov 41

Stevens, Robert T. Jul 53 obit Mar 83

Stevens, Roger L. Dec 55 obit Apr 98

Stevenson, Adlai E., 3d Apr 74

Stevenson, Adlai E. Jan 49 Sep 61 obit Sep 65

Stevenson, Bryan Mar 96

Stevenson, E. Robert Jan 40

Stevenson, Elizabeth (WLB) Yrbk 56

Stevenson, George S. Dec 46

Stevenson, McLean Jun 80 obit Apr 96

Stevenson, William E. Nov 43 obit May 85

Stever, H. Guyford Jan 81

Stewart, Alice Jul 2000

Stewart, Anna Bird (WLB) Yrbk 48

Stewart, Donald Ogden Jul 41 obit Sep 80

Stewart, Ellen Jun 73

Stewart, George Craig, Bishop obit Jan 40

Stewart, George R. Jan 42 obit Nov 80

Stewart, Harris B., Jr. Mar 68

Stewart, James Apr 41 Dec 60 obit Sep 97

Stewart, Kenneth Dec 43

Stewart, Martha Aug 93

Stewart, Michael Sep 65 obit Jun 90

Stewart, Mrs. Gordon Neil see Johnson, Pamela Hansford

Stewart, Patrick Aug 94

Stewart, Potter Dec 59 obit Feb 86

Stewart, Rod Aug 79

Stewart, Thomas May 74

Stewart, William G. obit Sep 41

Stewart, William H. Apr 66

Stewart-Murray, John George, 8th Duke of Atholl see John George Stewart-Murray

Stickney, Dorothy Apr 42 [Lindsay, Howard; and Stickney, Dorothy] obit Aug 98

Stiebeling, Hazel K. Apr 50

Stieglitz, Alfred Jan 40 obit Sep 46

Stigler, George Joseph Jul 83 obit Feb 92

Stignani, Ebe Feb 49 obit Yrbk 91 (died Oct 74)

Stigwood, Robert Oct 79

Stikker, Dirk U. Feb 50 Feb 62

Stiles, Charles Wardell obit Mar 41

Still, Clyfford Sep 71 obit Aug 80

Still, William Grant Jan 41 obit Feb 79

Stiller, Ben Nov 99

Stillwell, Lewis Buckley obit Mar 41

Stilwell, Joseph W. May 42 obit Nov 46

Stilwell, Richard Feb 86

Stimson, Frederic Jesup obit Jan 44

Stimson, Henry L. Aug 40 obit Dec 50

Stimson, Julia Catherine Nov 40 obit Nov 48

Stine, Charles Milton Altland Jan 40 obit Sep 54

Stipe, Michael Apr 97

Stirnweiss, George Mar 46 obit Dec 58

Stock, Frederick obit Dec 42

Stockberger, W. W. Aug 41

Stockbridge, Frank Parker obit Jan 41

Stockhausen, Karlheinz Dec 71

Stockman, David Aug 81

Stockton, John Jun 95

Stockwell, Dean Feb 91

Stoddard, Alexandra Jun 96

Stoddard, Brandon Feb 89

Stoddard, Frederick Lincoln obit Mar 40

Stoddard, George D. Jul 46 obit Feb 82

Stoessel, Albert obit Jul 43

Stoessel, Mrs. Henry Kurt see Chastain, Madye Lee

Stoessel, Walter J., Jr. Jun 70 obit Feb 87

Stoica, Chivu Jan 59 obit Apr 75

Stokes, Anson Phelps, Jr. Jul 62 obit Jan 87

Stokes, Carl B. Apr 68 obit Jun 96

Stokes, Edward C. obit Dec 42

Stokes, I. N. Phelps obit Feb 45

Stokes, Richard R. Sep 51 obit Oct 57

Stokes, Thomas L. May 47 obit Sep 58

Stokowski, Leopold Feb 41 Jul 53 obit Nov 77

Stokowski, Olga Samaroff see Samaroff, Olga

Stolk, William C. Mar 53

Stoltenberg, Gerhard Sep 89

Stolz, Mary (WLB) Yrbk 53

Stolz, Robert Aug 43 obit Aug 75

Stone, Abraham Mar 52 obit Oct 59

Stone, Edward C. Feb 90

Stone, Edward D. Jun 58 obit Sep 78

Stone, Hannah obit Sep 41

Stone, Harlan Fiske Aug 41 obit Jun 46

Stone, I. F. Sep 72 obit Aug 89

Stone, Irving Dec 67 obit Oct 89

Stone, John Charles obit Jul 40

Stone, Matt May 98 [Parker, Trey; and Stone, Matt]

Stone, Oliver Jun 87

Stone, Robert Jan 87

Stone, Sharon Apr 96

Stone, W. Clement Feb 72

Stone, William S. Jun 60 obit Feb 69

Stonehaven, John Lawrence Baird, 1st Viscount see Baird, John Lawrence

Stookey, Charley Jan 40

Stoopnagle, Colonel Oct 47 obit Jul 50

Stoph, Willi Oct 60 obit Aug 99

Stoppard, Tom Jul 74

Storey, David Sep 73

Storey, Robert G. Nov 53

Storke, Thomas M. Dec 63

Storms, Harrison A., Jr. Jan 63 obit Sep 92

Storr, Anthony Jun 94

Storr, Vernon Faithfull, Rev. obit Yrbk 40

Stout, Rex Mar 46 obit Jan 76

Stout, Ruth A. Jan 59

Stout, Wesley Winans Jun 41 obit Jan 72

Stout, William Bushnell Mar 41 obit May 56

Stowe, Leland Jul 40 obit Mar 94

Stowell, Clarence Warner obit Jan 41

Strachan, Paul A. Jan 52

Strachey, John Jun 46 obit Sep 63

Straight, Michael Aug 44

Strait, George Feb 2000

Strakakis, Anastasia see Stratas, Teresa

Stranahan, Frank Sep 51

Strand, Paul Jul 65 obit May 76

Strang, Ruth Dec 60 obit Feb 71

Strasberg, Lee Oct 60 obit Apr 82

Strasberg, Susan May 58 obit Apr 99

Strasser, Otto Sep 40 obit Oct 74

Stratas, Teresa Jan 80

Stratemeyer, George E. Feb 51 obit Oct 69

Strathmore And Kinghorne, Claud George Bowes-Lyon, 14th Earl of see Bowes-Lyon, Claud George

Stratton, Dorothy C. Jun 43

Stratton, Julius A. May 63 obit Aug 94

Stratton, Samuel S. Jan 66 obit Jan 91

Stratton, William G. Apr 53

Straub, Peter Feb 89

Straus, Jack I. Mar 52 obit Nov 85

Straus, Michael W. Jun 52

Straus, Nathan May 44 obit Nov 61

Straus, Oskar Mar 44 obit Mar 54

Straus, Percy Selden obit May 44

Straus, Roger W., Jr. Aug 80

Straus, Roger W. Jul 52 obit Oct 57

Strauss, Anna Lord Nov 45 obit Apr 79

Strauss, Franz Josef Feb 57 Feb 87 obit Nov 88

Strauss, J. G. N. Jan 51

Strauss, Lewis L. Feb 47 obit Mar 74

Strauss, Richard Jul 44 obit Oct 49

Strauss, Robert S. Mar 74 Jul 92

Stravinsky, Igor May 40 Apr 53 obit May 71

Strawberry, Darryl Jun 84

Strawbridge, Anne West obit Nov 41

Streep, Meryl Aug 80 Mar 97

Street, James (WLB) Yrbk 46 obit Nov 54

Street, Jessie Sep 47

Street, Picabo Apr 98

Streeter, Ruth Cheney Jul 43 obit Jan 91

Strehler, Giorgio Mar 91 obit Mar 98

Streibert, Theodore C. Feb 55 obit Mar 87

Streicher, Julius obit Nov 46

Streisand, Barbra Jun 64

Streit, Clarence K. May 40 May 50 obit Sep 86

Streuli, Hans Apr 57

Stridsberg, Gustaf obit Dec 43

Strijdom, Johannes Gerhardus May 56 obit Nov 58

Strike, Clifford S. Nov 49

Stritch, Elaine Jun 88

Stritch, Samuel Apr 46 obit Sep 58

Stroessner, Alfredo Dec 58 Mar 81

Strömberg, Leonard, Rev. obit Sep 41

Strong, Anna Louise Mar 49 obit May 70

Strong, Lee A. obit Jul 41

Strong, Maurice F. Dec 73

Strong, William McCreery obit May 41

Strossen, Nadine Oct 97

Strouse, Norman H. May 60 obit Mar 93

Strout, Richard L. Apr 80 obit Oct 90

Struble, Arthur D. Nov 51 obit Jul 83

Strughold, Hubertus Jul 66

Struther, Jan Jan 41 obit Oct 53

Struthers, Sally Jan 74

Struve, Otto Oct 49 obit Jun 63

Stuart, Duane Reed obit Oct 41

Stuart, Gloria Apr 98

Stuart, J. Leighton Oct 46 obit Nov 62

Stuart, James Everett obit Feb 41

Stuart, Jesse Aug 40 obit Apr 84

Stuart, Kenneth Feb 44 obit Dec 45

Studebaker, John Ward May 42 obit Oct 89

Studebaker, Mabel Nov 48

Studer, Cheryl Apr 92

Stuhlinger, Ernst Nov 57

Stummvoll, Josef Jun 60

Stump, Felix B. Jan 53 obit Sep 72

Sturdee, V. A. H. Jul 42

Sture-Vasa, Mary Alsop see O'Hara, Mary

Sturges, Preston Apr 41 obit
Oct 59

Sturgis, Samuel D., Jr. Jan 56
obit Sep 64

Sturzo, Luigi Feb 46 obit Nov
59

Stutz, Geraldine May 83

Styne, Jule May 83 obit Nov
94

Styron, William Jul 68 Jun 86

Suárez González, Adolfo
May 77

Subah, Abdullah al-Salim al,
Sheikh see Abdullah, Al-
Salim Al Sabah, Sheikh of
Kuwait

Subandrio Mar 63

Suchocka, Hanna Jan 94

Sucksdorff, Arne Apr 56

Suenens, Léon Joseph, Cardinal May 65 obit Jul 96

Sues, Ralf May 44

Suesse, Dana May 40 obit Jan
88

Sueyro, Saba H. obit Sep 43

Suggs, Louise Jan 62

Sugiyama, Hajime obit Oct
45

Sugrue, Thomas Jun 48 obit
Feb 53

Suharto see Soeharto

Suhr, Otto Apr 55 obit Nov
57

Suhrawardy, H. S. Apr 57
obit Jan 64

Sui, Anna Jul 93

Suits, Chauncey Guy Feb 50
obit Oct 91

Sukarnoputri, Megawati Sep
97

Sukarno Sep 47 obit Sep 70

Sullavan, Margaret Jul 44
obit Feb 60

Sullivan, A. M. Dec 53 obit
Aug 80

Sullivan, Brian Dec 57

Sullivan, Ed Sep 52 obit Nov
74

Sullivan, Francis L. Jun 55
obit Jan 57

Sullivan, Gael May 47 obit
Jan 57

Sullivan, Harry Joseph see
Sullivan, Brian

Sullivan, Harry Stack Nov 42
obit Feb 49

Sullivan, Henry J. Jun 58

Sullivan, John L. Sep 48 obit
Oct 82

Sullivan, Leon H. Mar 69

Sullivan, Leonore Kretzer
Dec 54 obit Oct 88

Sullivan, Louis Wade Jul 89

Sullivan, Mrs. John B. see
Sullivan, Leonore Kretzer

Sullivan, Walter Sep 80 obit
Jun 96

Sullivan, William H. Aug 79

Sulloway, Frank J. Sep 97

Sultan, Daniel I. Jan 45 obit
Feb 47

Sultan of Brunei see Bolkiah,
Muda Hassanal

Sulzberger, Arthur Hays Mar
43 obit Feb 69

Sulzberger, Arthur O., Jr. Jan
97

Sulzberger, Arthur Ochs Nov
66

Sulzberger, C. L. May 44 obit
Nov 93

Sulzer, William obit Jan 42

Sumac, Yma Dec 55

Summer, Donna Jul 79

Summerfield, Arthur E. Sep
52 obit Jun 72

Summerskill, Edith Clara
Apr 43 Jul 63 obit Apr 80

Summerville, Slim obit Feb
46

Sumner, Cid Ricketts (WLB)
Yrbk 54

Sumner, James B. Jan 47 obit
Oct 55

Sumner, Jessie Jan 45 obit
Oct 94

Sumner, Mrs. G. Lynn see
Picken, Mary Brooks

Sun, Chingling see Sun Yat-
Sen

Sunay, Cevdet Mar 69 obit
Aug 82

Sunderland, Thomas E. Apr
62 obit May 91

Suner, Ramon Serrano see
Serrano Suner, Ramon

Sun Fo Oct 44 obit Dec 73

Sung Tzu-wen see Soong,
T.V.

Sun Myung Moon see Moon,
Sun Myung

Sununu, John H. May 89

Sun Yat-Sen Apr 44 obit Jul
81

Surles, Alexander D. Nov 45
obit Dec 47

Susann, Jacqueline May 72
obit Nov 74

Suslov, Mikhail A. Feb 57
obit Mar 82

Susskind, David May 60 obit
Apr 87

Sutherland, Donald Feb 81

Sutherland, George obit Sep
42

Sutherland, Graham Jan 55
obit Apr 80

Sutherland, Joan Dec 60

Sutton, George P. Jul 58

Sutton, Percy Mar 73

Suvero, Mark Di see Di
Suvero, Mark

Suydam, Edward Howard
obit Feb 41

Suyin, Han see Han Suyin

Suzman, Helen Nov 68

Suzman, Janet May 76

Suzuki, Chiyoko see Suzuki,
Pat

Suzuki, Daisetsu Teitaro Oct
58 obit Nov 66

Suzuki, David T. Jul 95

Suzuki, Kantaro, Baron Aug
45 obit May 48

Suzuki, Pat Jan 60

Suzuki, Umetaro obit Nov 43

Suzuki, Zenko Jan 81

Svanholm, Set Dec 56 obit
Dec 64

Sveda, Michael Dec 54 obit
Nov 99

Svinhufvud, Pehr Evind obit
Apr 44

Swados, Elizabeth Feb 79

Swaggart, Jimmy Oct 87

Swallow, Alan Feb 63 obit
Jan 67

Swank, Hilary Sep 2000

Swann, Donald Jan 70 obit
May 94

Swann, W. F. G. Feb 41 Dec
60 obit Mar 62

Swanson, Gloria Sep 50 obit
May 83

Swart, Charles R. Jun 60

Swarthout, Gladys Mar 44
obit Sep 69

Swartwout, Egerton obit Apr
43

Swayze, Patrick Mar 91

Swearingen, John E. Jan 79

Sweeney, James Johnson Mar
55 obit Jul 86

Sweeney, John J. Jun 96

Sweet, William Ellery obit Jul
42

Swenson, Alfred G. obit May 41

Swidler, Joseph C. Mar 64 obit Jul 97

Swift, Ernest John obit Dec 41

Swift, Gustavus F. obit Dec 43

Swift, Harold H. Feb 50 obit Sep 62

Swigert, Ernest G. Oct 57 obit Feb 87

Swing, Joseph M. Apr 59 obit Feb 85

Swing, Raymond Jan 40 obit Feb 69

Swings, Paul see Swings, Pol

Swings, Pol Dec 54

Swirbul, Leon A. Apr 53 obit Sep 60

Switzer, George obit Yrbk 40

Switzer, Mary E. Jan 62 obit Dec 71

Swoopes, Sheryl Jul 96

Swope, Gerard Sep 41 obit Feb 58

Swope, Herbert Bayard Nov 44 obit Sep 58

Syberberg, Hans Jürgen Apr 83

Sydney, Mrs. Basil see Keane, Doris

Sydow, Max Von Apr 67

Sykes, Charles H. obit Feb 43

Sykes, Eugene Octave obit Jul 45

Sykes, Richard Eddy, Rev. obit Nov 42

Syme, John P. Mar 57

Symes, James M. Dec 55 obit Sep 76

Symington, James W. Jun 68

Symington, Stuart Sep 45 Jul 56 obit Feb 89

Symons, Arthur obit Mar 45

Synge, Richard Lawrence Millington Nov 53

Syran, Arthur George Mar 50

Szasz, Thomas Stephen Jan 75

Szell, George Jun 45 obit Oct 70

Szent-Györgyi, Albert Jan 55 obit Jan 87

Szeryng, Henryk Jan 68 obit Apr 88

Szigeti, Joseph May 40 Mar 58 obit Apr 73

Szilard, Leo Jan 47 obit Jul 64

Szold, Henrietta Jan 40 obit Apr 45

Szyk, Arthur Nov 46 obit Oct 51

Tabb, Mary Decker see Decker, Mary

Taber, Gladys (WLB) Yrbk 52 obit May 80

Taber, John Feb 48 obit Jan 66

Taber, Louis J. Jun 42 obit Dec 60

Tabouis, Genevieve Jan 40

Tae Woo, Roh see Roh Tae Woo

Tafawa Balewa, Abubakar see Balewa, Abubakar Tafawa

Tafel, Richard L. Feb 2000

Taffin de Givenchy, Hubert see Givenchy, Hubert De

Taft, Charles P. Jul 45 obit Aug 83

Taft, Helen obit Jul 43

Taft, Horace D. obit Mar 43

Taft, Mrs. William Howard see Taft, Helen

Taft, Robert, Jr. Oct 67 obit Feb 94

Taft, Robert A. May 40 Apr 48 obit Oct 53

Tagliabue, Paul Oct 92

Tagliavini, Ferruccio Jun 47 obit Apr 95

Tagore, Rabindranath obit Oct 41

Tainter, Charles Sumner obit May 40

Takeshita, Noboru May 88 obit Nov 2000

Talal Jan 52 obit Sep 72

Talbert, Billy Mar 57 obit Jun 99

Talbert, William F. see Talbert, Billy

Talbot, A. N. obit May 42

Talbott, Harold E. Jul 53 obit May 57

Talbott, Philip M. Apr 58

Talbott, Strobe Jul 2000

Talese, Gay Jul 72

Tallamy, Bertram D. Mar 57 obit Nov 89

Tallant, Robert (WLB) Yrbk 53 obit Jun 57

Tallchief, Maria Nov 51

Talley, James obit Sep 41

Talley, Truman H. obit Mar 42

Talmadge, Eugene Sep 41 obit Feb 47

Talmadge, Herman E. Mar 47

Talvela, Martti Oct 83 obit Sep 89

Tamayo, Rufino Mar 53 obit Aug 91

Tambo, Oliver Apr 87 obit Jun 93

Tamm, Igor Dec 63 obit Jun 71

Tan, Amy Feb 92

Tanaka, Kakuei Dec 72 obit Feb 94

Tandy, Jessica Mar 56 Aug 84 obit Nov 94

Tange, Kenzo Sep 87

Tani, Masayuki May 56

Tannen, Deborah Jul 94

Tanner, Alain Jun 90

Tanner, Edward Everett, 3d May 59 obit Feb 77

Tanner, John Henry obit Mar 40

Tanner, Väinö Sep 60 obit May 66

Tao-ming, Wei see Wei Tao-Ming

Tàpies, Antoni Jul 66

Tarancón, Vicente Enrique see Enrique Tarancón, Vicente

Tarantino, Quentin Oct 95

Tarassoff, Lev see Troyat, Henri

Tarbell, Ida M. obit Feb 44

Tarchiani, Alberto Jan 50 obit Jan 65

Tardieu, Andre obit Oct 45

Tarkenton, Fran Sep 69

Tarkington, Booth obit Jun 46

Tarr, Curtis W. Sep 70

Tartikoff, Brandon Apr 87 obit Nov 97

Tassigny, Jean de Lattre de see Lattre De Tassigny, Jean

Tata, J. R. D. Dec 58 obit Jan 94

Tata, Jehangir Ratanji Dadbhoy see Tata, J. R. D.

Tate, Allen Nov 40 obit Apr 79

Tatekawa, Yoshitsugu obit Oct 45

Tati, Jacques Feb 61 obit Jan 83

Tatum, Edward L. Mar 59 obit Jan 76

Taubes, Frederic Mar 43

Taubman, A. Alfred Jan 93

Taubman, Howard Apr 59 obit Mar 96

Taufa'ahau Tupou IV Sep 68

Taussig, Frank William obit Yrbk 40

Taussig, Helen B. Sep 46 [Blalock, Alfred; and Taussig, Helen B.] Mar 66 obit Jul 86

Tavener, John Jun 99

Tavernier, Bertrand Jun 88

Tawes, J. Millard Oct 60 obit Aug 79

Tawresey, John Godwin obit Apr 43

Taylor, A. Hoyt Sep 45 obit Jan 62

Taylor, A. J. P. Nov 83 obit Nov 90

Taylor, Billy Oct 80

Taylor, Cecil Mar 86

Taylor, Charles A. obit May 42

Taylor, Charles Sep 92

Taylor, Deems Mar 40 obit Nov 66

Taylor, Edward T. obit Oct 41

Taylor, Elizabeth [actor] Jul 52 Oct 85

Taylor, Elizabeth [author] (WLB) Yrbk 48

Taylor, F. Chase see Stoopnagle, Colonel

Taylor, Francis Henry Jan-Feb 40 obit Feb 58

Taylor, George Braxton, Rev. obit Apr 42

Taylor, George W. May 42 obit Feb 73

Taylor, Glen H. Oct 47 obit Jul 84

Taylor, Harold Sep 46 obit Apr 93

Taylor, Henry O. obit Jun 41

Taylor, James Jun 72

Taylor, John W. Jan 54

Taylor, Laurette Jul 45 obit Jan 47

Taylor, Lawrence Jul 90

Taylor, M. Sayle obit Mar 42

Taylor, Maxwell D. Nov 46 Dec 61 obit Jun 87

Taylor, Mrs. John William Kendall see Taylor, Elizabeth

Taylor, Myron C. Feb 40 obit Jul 59

Taylor, Paul Jun 64

Taylor, Peter Apr 87 obit Jan 95

Taylor, Richard Jun 41 obit Jul 70

Taylor, Robert Lewis Dec 59 obit Jan 99

Taylor, Robert May 52 obit Jul 69

Taylor, Susan L. Feb 97

Taylor, Telford Dec 48 obit Aug 98

Taylor, Theodore B. Apr 76

Taymor, Julie Feb 98

Tchelitchew, Pavel Mar 43 obit Oct 57

Tcherkassky, Marianna Nov 85

Tchernichovsky, Saul obit Dec 43

Tead, Ordway May 42 obit Jan 74

Teagle, Walter C. Jun 42 obit Feb 62

Teague, Olin E. Mar 52 obit Apr 81

Teague, Walter Dorwin May 42 obit Jan 61

Teale, Edwin Way Dec 61 obit Jan 81

Tebaldi, Renata Apr 55

Tebbel, John (WLB) Yrbk 53

Tebbit, Norman Nov 87

Tedder, Arthur William Tedder, 1st Baron Jan 43 obit Oct 67

Teitgen, Pierre-Henri Jan 53

Teixeira-Gomes, Manuel obit Dec 41

Te Kanawa, Kiri Nov 78

Teleki, Paul, Count obit May 41

Telkes, Maria Nov 50 obit Oct 96

Teller, Edward Dec 54 Nov 83

Teller Jun 2000 [Penn and Teller]

Tello, Manuel Dec 59 obit Jan 72

Tempest, Marie obit Dec 42

Temple, Shirley see Black, Shirley Temple

Temple, William, Archbishop of Canterbury see Temple, William

Temple, William Apr 42 obit Dec 44

Templer, Gerald Jul 52 obit Jan 80

Templeton, Alec Mar 40 obit May 63

Templewood, Samuel John Gurney Hoare, 1st Viscount see Hoare, Samuel John Gurney

Tempski, Armine Von obit Jan 44

Tenby of Bulford, Gwilym Lloyd George, Viscount see Lloyd-George, Gwilym

Tener, John Kinley obit Jun 46

Tenet, George J. Aug 99

Teng Hsiao-ping see Deng Xiaoping

Teng Hsi-hsien see Deng Xiaoping

Teng Wen-pin see Deng Xiaoping

Tennant, William George Feb 45 obit Sep 63

Tennenbaum, Irving see Stone, Irving

Tennent, David Hilt obit Mar 41

Tennstedt, Klaus Sep 83 obit Mar 98

Tenzing Norkey Oct 54 [Hunt, John; Hillary, Edmund; and Tenzing Norkey] obit Jul 86

Ter-Arutunian, Rouben Jun 63 obit Jan 93

Terboven, Josef Nov 41 obit Jun 45

Teresa, Mother Sep 73 obit Nov 97

Tereshkova, Valentina Dec 63

Terhorst, Jerald F. Feb 75

Terhune, Albert Payson obit Apr 42

Terkel, Studs Nov 74

Ter Poorten, Hein Mar 42

Terra, Daniel J. Nov 87 obit Sep 96

Terra, Gabriel obit Nov 42

Terrell, Daniel V. Apr 54

Terrell, Mary Church Jun 42 obit Oct 54

Terrell, St. John Feb 66 obit Jan 99

Terry, C. V. see Slaughter, Frank G.

Terry, Luther L. Oct 61 obit May 85

Terry, Randall A. Jan 94

Terry-Thomas Mar 61 obit Mar 90

Thornburgh, Dick *see* Thornburgh, Richard L.

Thornburgh, Richard L. Oct 88

Thorndike, Edward L. Sep 41 obit Oct 49

Thorndike, Sybil Dec 53 obit Aug 76

Thorneycroft, Peter Dec 52 obit Aug 94

Thornhill, Arthur H. Apr 58 obit Mar 70

Thornton, Charles B. Feb 70 obit Jan 82

Thornton, Dan Feb 54

Thorp, Willard L. Jul 47 obit Jul 92

Thorpe, James Francis *see* Thorpe, Jim

Thorpe, Jeremy Oct 74

Thorpe, Jim Nov 50 obit May 53

Throckmorton, Cleon Sep 43 obit Dec 65

Thurber, James Mar 40 Oct 60 obit Jan 62

Thurman, Howard Jun 55 obit Jun 81

Thurman, Robert A. F. Sep 97

Thurman, Uma Aug 96

Thurmond, Strom Sep 48 Nov 92

Thurow, Lester C. Nov 90

Thurso, Archibald Henry Sinclair Macdonald, 1st Viscount *see* Sinclair, Archibald

Thye, Edward J. Oct 51 obit Nov 69

Thyssen, Fritz May 40 obit Mar 51

Thyssen-Bornemisza De Kaszon, Hans Heinrich Feb 89

Tiant, Luis Jun 77

Tibbett, Lawrence Feb 45 obit Oct 60

Tice, Merton B. Jun 55

Ticker, Reuben *see* Tucker, Richard

Tiegs, Cheryl Nov 82

Tien, Thomas May 46 obit Oct 67

T'ien Keng-hsin *see* Tien, Thomas

Tietjens, Eunice obit Nov 44

Tiger, Lionel Jan 81

Tijerina, Reies Lopez Jul 71

Tikhonov, Valentin *see* Payne, Robert

Tilberis, Elizabeth *see* Tilberis, Liz

Tilberis, Liz Nov 98 obit Jul 99

Tillich, Paul Mar 54 obit Dec 65

Tillinghast, Charles C. Feb 62 obit Oct 98

Tillstrom, Burr May 51 obit Feb 86

Tilson Thomas, Michael May 71 Jun 96

Tilzer, Harry Von *see* Von Tilzer, Harry

Timberlake, Charles B. obit Jul 41

Timberlake, Clare H. Jan 61

Timberlake, Justin *see* 'N Sync

Timerman, Jacobo Nov 81 obit Jan 2000

Timmerman, George Bell, Jr. Jan 57 obit Feb 95

Timoshenko, Semyon Aug 41 obit May 70

Tinbergen, Niko Nov 75 obit Feb 89

Tindemans, Leo Mar 78

Tinguely, Jean Jan 66 obit Oct 91

Tinker, Clarence L. Jun 42

Tinker, Grant A. Mar 82

Tinkham, George H. Apr 42 obit Oct 56

Tinney, Cal Feb 43

Tinney, Frank obit Jan 41

Tippett, Michael Sep 74 obit Mar 98

Tipton, Jennifer Jul 97

Tipton, Stuart G. Mar 67

Tisch, Laurence A. Feb 87

Tisdel, Alton P. obit Jul 45

Tiselius, Arne Apr 49 obit Dec 71

Tishler, Max Mar 52 obit May 89

Tiso, Joseph Mar 43 obit May 47

Tisserant, Eugene Apr 63 obit Apr 72

Titov, Gherman Dec 62

Titterton, Lewis H. Sep 43

Tittle, Y. A. Mar 64

Titulescu, Nicolas obit May 41

Tizard, Henry Jan 49 obit Dec 59

Tjarda *see* Starkenborgh Stachouwer, A. W. L., Tjarda Van

Tobe *see* Davis, Tobé Coller

Tobey, Charles W. Jun 41 Jul 51 obit Oct 53

Tobey, Mark Mar 57 obit Jun 76

Tobias, Channing H. Jul 45 obit Jan 62

Tobin, Daniel J. Nov 45 obit Jan 56

Tobin, Harold J. obit Aug 42

Tobin, James Oct 84

Tobin, Maurice J. Jun 46 obit Oct 53

Tobin, Richard L. Nov 44 obit Nov 95

Toch, Maximilian obit Jun 46

Todd, Alexander Mar 58 obit Mar 97

Todd, Lord *see* Todd, Alexander

Todd, Mike Dec 55 obit Jun 58

Todd, Richard [football player] May 82

Todd, Richard [actor] Dec 55

Todt, Fritz obit Apr 42

Toffler, Alvin Apr 75

Togliatti, Palmiro Nov 47 obit Oct 64

Tojo, Eiki *see* Tojo, Hideki

Tojo, Hideki Dec 41 obit Jan 49

Tokugawa, Iyesato, Prince obit Jul 40

Toland, Edmund M. obit Jul 42

Toland, Gregg Jul 41 obit Nov 48

Tolbert, William R., Jr. Mar 74 obit Jun 80

Tolbukhin, Fedor I. May 45 obit Dec 49

Toledano, Ralph De Dec 62

Toledano, Vicente Lombardo *see* Lombardo Toledano, Vicente

Tolischus, Otto David Jan 40 obit Apr 67

Tolkien, J. R. R. (WLB) Yrbk 57 Oct 67 obit Nov 73

Tollefson, Thor C. Feb 63

Tolstoi, Aleksei Nikolaevich, Count obit Apr 45

Tolstoy, Alexandra Apr 53 obit Nov 79

Tomás, Américo Deus Rod-
rigues Dec 58 obit Nov 87
Tomasi, Mari May 41
Tomasson, Helgi Apr 82
Tomba, Alberto May 93
Tomlin, Lily Sep 73
Tomorrow, Tom Apr 2000
Tompkins, Ewell *see* Ewell,
Tom
Tone, Franchot May 40 obit
Nov 68
Tong, Hollington K. Dec 56
obit Feb 71
Tooker, George Mar 58
Toon, Malcolm Jul 78
Tope, John Feb 50
Topping, Norman Feb 59 obit
Jan 98
Tormé, Mel Mar 83 obit Aug
99
Torn, Elmore, Jr. *see* Torn,
Rip
Torn, Rip Apr 77
Torp, Oscar Dec 52 obit Jul 58
Torre, Joe May 72 May 97
Torre, Victor Raul Haya de la
see Haya De La Torre, Víc-
tor Raúl
Torre-Bueno, Lillian de la *see*
De La Torre, Lillian
Torrence, Gwen Jul 96
Torres Bodet, Jamie *see*
Bodet, Jaime Torres
Torrey, E. Fuller Jul 98
Torrey, George Burroughs
obit Jun 42
Torrijos Herrera, Omar Jul 73
obit Sep 81
Tors, Ivan Feb 69 obit Aug 83
Torvalds, Linus Jul 99
Toscani, Oliviero Sep 97
Toscanini, Arturo Jun 42 May
54 obit Mar 57
Totenberg, Nina Mar 96
Totty, Charles H. Jan 40
Touré, Ahmed Sekou Jun 59
obit May 84
Tourel, Jennie Feb 47 obit Jan
74
Tournier, Michel Apr 90
Toussaint, Jeanne Feb 55
Tovey, Donald Francis obit
Sep 40
Tower, John G. Dec 62 obit
Jun 91
Towers, Graham F. Feb 52
Towers, J. H. Oct 41 obit Jun
55

Towle, Katherine A. Jan 49
obit May 86
Towne, Robert Jun 89
Townes, Charles H. Mar 63
Townsend, Edward Water-
man obit May 42
Townsend, Harry E. obit Oct
41
Townsend, Lynn A. Sep 66
obit Yrbk 2000
Townsend, Robert [execu-
tive] Nov 70 obit Mar 98
Townsend, Robert [actor]
May 94
Townsend, Willard S. Jan 48
Townshend, Pete Aug 83
Toy, Henry, Jr. May 52
Toynbee, Arnold Joseph Jul
47 obit Jan 76
Tozzi, Giorgio Oct 61
Trabert, Marion Anthony *see*
Trabert, Tony
Trabert, Tony Jul 54
Tracy, Spencer Apr 43 obit
Oct 67
Train, Arthur obit Feb 46
Train, Russell E. Oct 70
Trammell, Niles Sep 40 obit
May 73
Trampler, Walter Nov 71 obit
Jan 98
Traphagen, Ethel Dec 48 obit
Jun 63
Trapp, Maria Augusta May
68 obit Jun 87
Trask, James D. obit Jul 42
Traubel, Helen Jan 40 Feb 52
obit Oct 72
Trautman, George M. Oct 51
obit Sep 63
Travell, Janet G. Dec 61 obit
Oct 97
Travers, P. L. May 96 obit Jun
96
Travis, Randy Sep 89
Travolta, John Oct 78 May 96
Treanor, Tom obit Oct 44
Tree, Marietta Dec 61 obit Oct
91
Tree, Mrs. Ronald *see* Tree,
Marietta
Trefflich, Henry Jan 53 obit
Sep 78
Tregaskis, Richard Aug 43
obit Oct 73
Trenet, Charles Feb 89
Trenkler, Freddie Jun 71
Tresca, Carlo obit Mar 43
Trevino, Lee Nov 71

Trevor, William Sep 84
Trevor-Roper, H. R. Sep 83
Tribe, Laurence H. Jul 88
Trigère, Pauline Feb 60
Trigg, Ralph S. Nov 50
Trillin, Calvin Jun 90
Trilling, Diana May 79 obit
Jan 97
Trimble, David Jul 2000
Trimble, Vance H. Dec 60
Trinidad, Felix Feb 2000
Trintignant, Jean-Louis Jul 88
Trippe, Juan T. Aug 42 Feb 55
obit May 81
Troost, Laurens Jan 53
Trotsky, Leon obit Oct 40
Trotta, Margarethe Von Nov
88
Trotter, Frank Butler obit Apr
40
Trottier, Bryan Jun 85
Troubetzkoy, Amelie obit Jul
45
Trout, Robert Oct 65
Trowbridge, Alexander B.
Mar 68
Troyanos, Tatiana Aug 79
obit Oct 93
Troyat, Henri Mar 92
Trudeau, Arthur Gilbert Apr
58 obit Aug 91
Trudeau, Garry Aug 75
Trudeau, Pierre Elliott Nov
68
True, Rodney Howard obit
May 40
Trueba, Andrés Martínez *see*
Martínez Trueba, Andrés
Trueblood, D. Elton Jan 64
obit Mar 95
Truex, Ernest Jan 41 obit Sep
73
Truffaut, François Jan 69 obit
Jan 85
Truitt, Paul T. Sep 48
Trujillo Molina, Rafael
Leónidas Jul 41 obit Oct 61
Trulock, Mrs. Guy Percy Jan
57
Truman, Bess Feb 47 obit Jan
83
Truman, David B. Jan 72
Truman, Harry S. Jan 42 Apr
45 obit Feb 73
Truman, Margaret Jun 50 Jun
87
Truman, Mrs. Harry S. *see*
Truman, Bess

Trumbo, Dalton May 41 obit Oct 76

Trumka, Richard L. Apr 86

Trump, Donald J. Feb 84

Truscott, Lucian K. May 45 obit Nov 65

Trussell, C. P. Jul 49 obit Dec 68

Trussell, Ray E. Jan 71 obit Feb 2000

Trygger, Ernst obit Nov 43

Tryon, George Clement Tryon, 1st Baron obit Jan 41

Tryon, Thomas Jan 77 obit Nov 91

Tsai Yuan-pei see Cai Yuan-pei

Tsaldaris, Constantin Nov 46 obit Jan 71

Tsarapkin, Semyon K. Jun 60 obit Nov 84

Tschirky, Oscar Jan 47 obit Dec 50

Tshombe, Moise Dec 61 obit Sep 69

Tsiang, T. F. Jun 48 obit Dec 65

Tsongas, Paul E. Jul 81 obit Mar 97

Tsung-Hsi, Pai see Pai Tsung-Hsi

Tsung-Jen, Li see Li Tsung-Jen

Tubb, Ernest Oct 83 obit Oct 84

Tubman, William V. S. Jan 55 obit Sep 71

Tuchman, Barbara W. Dec 63 obit Mar 89

Tuck, William M. Dec 46 obit Aug 83

Tucker, B. Fain Dec 57

Tucker, Henry St. George Sep 43 obit Nov 59

Tucker, Richard Mar 56 obit Feb 75

Tucker, Sophie Apr 45 obit Mar 66

Tuckwell, Barry Jul 79

Tudjman, Franjo Sep 97 obit May 2000

Tudor, Antony Nov 45 obit Jun 87

Tufts, James Hayden obit Sep 42

Tugwell, Rexford G. Sep 41 Jan 63 obit Sep 79

Tully, Alice Jan 84 obit Feb 94

Tune, Tommy Jan 83

Tung, Hsien-kuang see Tong, Hollington K.

Tunnard, Christopher Jun 59 obit May 79

Tunney, Gene Sep 40 obit Jan 79

Tunney, John V. Jun 71

Tuomioja, Sakari Mar 54 obit Nov 64

Tupolev, Andrei N. Jan 57

Tupou IV, Taufa'ahau see Taufa'ahau Tupou IV

Turabi, Hassan al- Jan 99

Turbay Ayala, Julio César Jul 79

Turcotte, Ron Nov 74

Ture, Kwame see Carmichael, Stokely

Tureck, Rosalyn Sep 59

Turkle, Sherry Aug 97

Turnbull, Colin M. Sep 80 obit Sep 94

Turner, Ben obit Nov 42

Turner, Donald F. Jul 67 obit Sep 94

Turner, Ewald May 62

Turner, John Nov 84

Turner, Kathleen Jun 86

Turner, Lana Jun 43 obit Sep 95

Turner, Margaret Marian see McPartland, Marian

Turner, R. Kelly Apr 44 obit Apr 61

Turner, Robert Edward, 3d see Turner, Ted

Turner, Stansfield May 78

Turner, Ted May 79 Jun 98

Turner, Tina Nov 84

Turow, Scott Aug 91

Turpin, Ben obit Aug 40

Turpin, Randolph see Turpin, Randy

Turpin, Randy Sep 51 obit Jun 66

Turrell, James May 99

Turturro, John Oct 96

Tushingham, Rita Oct 65

Tuttle, Charles E. Jul 60 obit Aug 93

Tuttle, Emerson obit Apr 46

Tuttle, Merlin D. Jun 92

Tutu, Desmond Jan 85

Tvardovsky, Aleksandr May 71 obit Feb 72

Tweed, Harrison Jan 50 obit Jul 69

Tweed, Thomas Frederic obit Jan 40

Tweedie, Mrs. Alec obit May 40

Tweedsmuir, John Buchan, 1st Baron see Buchan, John

Twiggy Oct 68

Twining, Nathan F. Dec 53 obit May 82

Twombly, Cy Apr 88

Tworkov, Jack Mar 64 obit Oct 82

Tydings, Millard E. Jan 45 obit Apr 61

Tyler, Alice S. obit Jun 44

Tyler, Anne Jun 81

Tyler, Richard May 97

Tyler, Steven Aug 96

Tynan, Kenneth Dec 63 obit Sep 80

Tyner, McCoy Aug 97

Tyson, Cicely Aug 75

Tyson, Laura D'andrea Sep 96

Tyson, Mike Apr 88

Tyson, Neil de Grasse May 2000

Ubico, Jorge Jun 42 obit Jul 46

Uchida, Mitsuko Sep 91

Udall, Morris Apr 69 obit Mar 99

Udall, Stewart L. May 61

Ueberroth, Peter Apr 85

Ugarteche, Manuel Prado see Prado Ugarteche, Manuel

Uggams, Leslie Oct 67

Uhlmann, Richard F. Jan 49 obit Feb 90

Ulanova, Galina Apr 58 obit Jun 98

Ulbricht, Walter Jul 52 obit Oct 73

Ulio, James A. Sep 45

Ullman, Al Aug 75 obit Jan 87

Ullman, James Ramsey Oct 45 obit Sep 71

Ullman, Mrs. Egon V. see Kennelly, Ardyth

Ullman, Tracey Oct 88

Ullmann, Liv Dec 73

Ullstein, Hermann obit Jan 44

Ulman, Joseph N. obit May 43

Ulrich, Charles obit Aug 41

Ulyanov, Dmitri Ilyich obit Sep 43

Umberto II, King of Italy Oct 43 obit May 83

Unden, Bo Osten Feb 47 obit Apr 74

Underhill, Charles L. obit Mar 46

Underhill, Ruth M. Feb 54 obit Oct 84

Underwood, Bert E. obit Feb 44

Underwood, Cecil H. May 58

Undset, Sigrid Sep 40 obit Jul 49

Ungaro, Emanuel Jul 80

Unitas, John Feb 62

Unruh, Jesse M. Oct 69 obit Sep 87

Untermeyer, Louis Jan 67 obit Feb 78

Untermyer, Samuel Apr 40

Unwin, Stanley Mar 49 obit Dec 68

Updike, Daniel Berkeley obit Feb 42

Updike, John Feb 66 Oct 84

Upfield, Arthur W. (WLB) Yrbk 48 obit Apr 64

Upham, Francis Bourne, Rev. obit May 41

Upshaw, Dawn Feb 90

Upshur, William P. obit Sep 43

Urey, Harold C. Feb 41 Jul 60 obit Mar 81

Uris, Leon (WLB) Yrbk 59 Feb 79

Urquhart, Brian E. Jun 86

Urquhart, Robert E. Dec 44 obit Feb 89

Urrutia, Francisco Jun 58

Urrutia Lleo, Manuel May 59 obit Aug 81

Usery, W. J., Jr. Jun 76

Usher, Elizabeth R. May 67

Usman Ali, Nizam of Hyderabad Oct 48 obit Apr 67

Ustinov, Peter Dec 55

U Thant see Thant, U

Utley, Freda Dec 58 obit Mar 78

Utley, George B. obit Nov 46

Utrillo, Maurice Sep 53 obit Jan 56

Utterback, Hubert obit Jul 42

Vadim, Roger Jan 84 obit Aug 2000

Vagnozzi, Egidio Cardinal Mar 67 obit Feb 81

Vail, Robert W. G. Feb 45 obit Jul 66

Vaizey, John Jan 64

Vajpayee, Atal Behari Aug 2000

Valente, Benita Mar 88

Valenti, Jack Jan 68

Valentina Dec 46 obit Nov 89

Valentine, Alan Dec 50 obit Sep 80

Valentine, Lewis J. Jun 46 obit Feb 47

Valentine, Stephen see Allen, Steve

Valentino Nov 73

Valenzuela, Fernando Oct 82

Valera, Eamon de see De Valera, Eamon

Valery, Paul Ambrose obit Aug 45

Vallee, Rudy Jun 47 Apr 63 obit Aug 86

Valletta, Vittorio Jul 67 obit Jul 67

Valtin, Jan Apr 41 obit Jan 51

Van Acker, Achille see Acker, Achille Van

Van Allen, James A. Jan 59

Van Arsdale, Harry May 69 obit Apr 86

Vanbrugh, Violet obit Jan 43

Van Buren, Abigail May 60

Vance, Cyrus R. Dec 62 Nov 77

Vance, Harold S. May 49 obit Nov 59

Vance, John T. obit May 43

Vance, Marguerite (WLB) Yrbk 51 obit Jul 65

Vance, William Reynolds obit Yrbk 40

Van Damme, Jean-Claude Mar 99

Vandegrift, Alexander Archer Jan 43 obit Jun 73

Vandenberg, Arthur H. Nov 40 Jun 48 obit May 51

Vandenberg, Hoyt S. Mar 45 obit May 54

Van Den Haag, Ernest Oct 83

Vanderbilt, Amy Feb 54 obit Feb 75

Vanderbilt, Arthur T. Feb 47 obit Oct 57

Vanderbilt, Cornelius, III obit Apr 42

Vanderbilt, Gloria Jul 72

Vanderbilt, William K. obit Feb 44

Vandercook, John W. Apr 42 obit Feb 63

Van Devanter, Willis obit Mar 41

Vandiver, S. Ernest Jul 62

Vandivert, William Mar 63

Van Doren, Harold Livingston May 40 obit Apr 57

Van Doren, Irita Sep 41 obit Feb 67

Van Doren, Mark Jan 40 obit Feb 73

Vandross, Luther Sep 91

Van Druten, John Feb 44 obit Feb 58

Van Dusen, Henry P. Dec 50 obit Apr 75

Van Duyn, Mona Jan 98

Van Dyke, Dick Mar 63

Van Dyke, W. S., 2d obit Apr 43

Vane, John R. May 86

Vaness, Carol Sep 86

Van Fleet, James A. Apr 48 obit Nov 92

Van Hamel, Martine Sep 79

Van Heusen, Jimmy Jun 70 obit Apr 90

Van Heuven Goedhart, G. J. see Heuven Goedhart, G. J. Van

Van Horne, Harriet Dec 54 obit Mar 98

Van Houtte, Jean see Houtte, Jean Van

Vanier, George Philias Jan 60 obit May 67

Van Karnebeek, Herman Adriaan obit May 42

Van Kleffens, Eelco (Nicolaas) see Kleffens, Eelco Van

Van Konijnenburg, Willem Adriaan see Konijnenburg, Willem Adriaan Van

Van Loen, Alfred Feb 61

Van Loon, Hendrik Willem obit Apr 44

Van Mook, Hubertus J. Apr 42 obit Jul 65

Vann, Robert Lee obit Yrbk 40

Van Nuys, Frederick obit Mar 44

Vanocur, Sander Jan 63
Van Paassen, Pierre Oct 42 obit Mar 68
Van Peebles, Mario Nov 93
Van Pelt, John V. Dec 46 obit Sep 62
Van Royen, Jan Herman *see* Royen, Jan Herman Van
Van Sant, Gus Mar 92
Van Schmus, W. G. obit Mar 42
Vansittart, Robert Jul 41 obit Apr 57
Van Slyke, Donald D. Jan 43 obit Jul 71
Van Starkenborgh Stachouwer, Alidius Warmoldus Lambertus Tjarda *see* Starkenborgh Stachouwer, A. W. L., Tjarda Van
Van Volkenburg, J. L. Jan 55 obit Jul 63
Van Wagoner, Murray D. Nov 41 obit Aug 86
Van Waters, Miriam Mar 63 obit Apr 74
Van Zandt, James E. Nov 50 obit Mar 86
Van Zeeland, Paul *see* Zeeland, Paul Van
Varda, Agnès Jul 70
Vardaman, James K., Jr. Apr 51
Vargas, Getúlio Dornelles Aug 40 May 51 obit Oct 54
Vargas Llosa, Mario Feb 76
Varian, Dorothy Jan 43
Varmus, Harold E. Nov 96
Varnay, Astrid May 51
Varnedoe, Kirk Feb 91
Vasarely, Victor Feb 71 obit May 97
Vasilevsky, Alexander M. Oct 43 obit Mar 78
Vassallo, Ernesto obit Jan 40
Vatutin, Nikolai F. Feb 44
Vaughan, Guy W. Dec 48 obit Jan 67
Vaughan, Harry H. Mar 49 obit Jul 81
Vaughan, Sarah Nov 57 Apr 80 obit May 90
Vaughan Williams, Ralph Dec 53 obit Nov 58
Vaughn, Jack H. Apr 66
Vaughn, Robert Sep 67
Veeck, Bill Nov 48 obit Feb 86

Veeck, William Louis, Jr. *see* Veeck, Bill
Vega, Suzanne Aug 94
Veidt, Conrad obit May 43
Veil, Simone May 80
Veiller, Bayard obit Aug 43
Vejjabul, Pierra Mar 64
Veksler, Vladimir I. Jan 65 obit Nov 66
Velasco Alvarado, Juan Jun 70 obit Mar 78
Velasco Ibarra, José María Nov 52 obit May 79
Velázquez, Nydia M. Jul 99
Velde, Harold H. Mar 53 obit Jan 86
Velez, Lupe obit Feb 45
Velikovsky, Immanuel May 57 obit Jan 80
Vendler, Helen May 86
Venizelos, Sophocles Dec 50 obit Mar 64
Venter, J. Craig Feb 95
Ventris, Michael Jan 57
Ventura, Jesse May 99
Venturi, Ken Apr 66
Venturi, Robert Jul 75
Vera-Ellen Feb 59 obit Oct 81
Verdier, Jean, Cardinal obit May 40
Verdi-Fletcher, Mary Jan 97
Verdon, Gwen Oct 60
Verdy, Violette Dec 69 Oct 80
Vereen, Ben Apr 78
Verity, C. William, Jr. May 88
Vermeij, Geerat J. Jun 95
Vermilye, William Moorhead obit Oct 44
Vernon, Grenville obit Jan 42
Vernon, Lillian Mar 96
Veronese, Vittorino Jun 59
Verrett, Shirley Apr 67
Verrett-Carter, Shirley *see* Verrett, Shirley
Versace, Donatella Jun 98
Versace, Gianni Apr 93 obit Sep 97
Vertès, Marcel Apr 61 obit Jan 62
Verwoerd, H. F. Mar 59 obit Nov 66
Vezin, Charles obit May 42
Vian, Philip Aug 44 obit Sep 68
Vickers, Jon Mar 61
Vickery, H. L. Dec 43 obit May 46

Victor, Sally Apr 54 obit Jul 77
Victor Emmanuel III, King of Italy Jul 43 obit Jan 48
Vidal, Gore Feb 65 Jun 83
Videla, Gabriel González *see* Gonzalez Videla, Gabriel
Videla, Jorge Rafaél Apr 78
Vidor, King Feb 57 obit Jan 83
Vieira Da Silva, Maria Helena Dec 58 obit May 92
Vienot, Pierre obit Oct 44
Viereck, George Sylvester Nov 40 obit May 62
Viereck, Peter Apr 43
Vigneaud, Vincent du *see* Du Vigneaud, Vincent
Viguerie, Richard A. Jan 83
Vila, George R. Mar 63 obit Aug 87
Vilar, Jean Apr 62 obit Sep 71
Vilas, Guillermo Apr 78
Villain- Marais, Jean *see* Marais, Jean
Villa-Lobos, Heitor Apr 45 obit Jan 60
Villard, Oswald Garrison Aug 40 obit Nov 49
Villella, Edward Mar 65
Villemure, Gilles Apr 74
Villon, Jacques Jan 56 obit Jul 63
Vincent, Fay May 91
Vincent, Francis Thomas, Jr. *see* Vincent, Fay
Vincent, George Edgar obit Mar 41
Vincent, Leon H. obit Apr 41
Vine, Barbara *see* Rendell, Ruth
Vinson, Carl Apr 42 obit Jul 81
Vinson, Fred M. Aug 43 obit Nov 53
Vinton, Bobby Jul 77
Vinton, Stanley Robert, Jr. *see* Vinton, Bobby
Viola, Bill May 98
Vip *see* Partch, Virgil Franklin
Viscardi, Henry, Jr. Jan 54 Dec 66
Visconti, Luchino Jan 65 obit May 76
Vishinskii, Andrei May 44 obit Jan 55
Vishnevskaya, Galina Jul 66
Vishniac, Roman Feb 67 obit Mar 90

Visser 't Hooft, Willem Adolph May 49 obit Aug 85
Vogel, Hans Jochen Jan 84
Vogel, Herbert D. Dec 54
Vogel, Paula Jul 98
Vogelstein, Bert Jan 96
Vogt, William Mar 53 obit Sep 68
Voight, Jon Apr 74
Voigt, Deborah Jan 99
Voinovich, George V. May 97
Volcker, Paul A. Jul 73
Vollenweider, Andreas May 87
Volpe, John A. Feb 62 obit Jan 95
Volterra, Vito obit Yrbk 40
Von Arco, Georg Wilhelm Alexander Hans, Graf *see* Arco, Georg Wilhelm Alexander Hans Graf Von
Von Aroldingen, Karin *see* Aroldingen, Karin Von
Von Békésy, Georg *see* Békésy, Georg von
Von Bock, Fedor *see* Bock, Fedor Von
Von Brauchitsch, Heinrich Alfred Hermann Walther *see* Brauchitsch, Heinrich Alfred Hermann Walther Von
Von Braun, Wernher Jan 52 obit Aug 77
Von Brentano, Heinrich *see* Brentano, Heinrich Von
Von Däniken, Erich May 76
Von Dardel, Nils *see* Dardel, Nils Von
Von Einem, Gottfried *see* Einem, Gottfried Von
Von Frisch, Karl *see* Frisch, Karl Von
Von Fürstenberg, Diane Sep 76
Von Galen, Clemens August *see* Galen, Clemens August Von
Vo Nguyen Giap Feb 69
Von Hagen, Victor Wolfgang Mar 42
Von Hammerstein-Equord, Kurt *see* Hammerstein-Equord, Kurt Von
Von Hassel, Kai-Uwe *see* Hassel, Kai-Uwe Von
Von Hayek, Friederich A. *see* Hayek, Friedrich A. Von

Von Heidenstam, Karl Gustaf Verner *see* Heidenstam, Verner Von
Von Heidenstam, Rolf *see* Heidenstam, Rolf Von
Von Kallay, Nicolas *see* Kallay, Nicholas De
Von Karajan, Herbert *see* Karajan, Herbert von
Von Kármán, Theodore May 55 obit Jun 63
Von KleinSmid, Rufus B. *see* Kleinsmid, Rufus B. Von
Von Kleist, Paul Ludwig *see* Kleist, Paul Ludwig Von
Von Klenze, Camillo *see* Klenze, Camillo Von
Von Mannerheim, Carl Gustaf Emil, Baron *see* Carl Gustaf Emil
Von Manstein, Fritz Erich *see* Manstein, Fritz Erich Von
Vonnegut, Kurt Jul 70 Mar 91
Von Neumann, John Jul 55 obit Apr 57
Von Otter, Anne Sofie *see* Otter, Anne Sofie von
Von Paassen, Pierre *see* Van Paassen, Pierre
Von Papen, Franz *see* Papen, Franz Von
Von Parseval, August *see* Parseval, August Von
Von Reichenau, Walter *see* Reichenau, Walter Von
Von Ribbentrop, Joachim *see* Ribbentrop, Joachim Von
Von Rundstedt, Karl *see* Rundstedt, Karl Von
Von Sauer, Emil *see* Sauer, Emil Von
Von Seyss-Inquart, Artur *see* Seyss-Inquart, Artur Von
Von Stade, Frederica Aug 77
Von Stauss, Emil Georg *see* Stauss, Emil Georg Von
Von Sydow, Max *see* Sydow, Max Von
Von Szent-Györgyi, Albert *see* Szent-Györgyi, Albert
Von Tempski, Armine *see* Tempski, Armine Von
Von Thadden-Trieglaff, Reinold *see* Thadden-Trieglaff, Reinold Von
Von Tilzer, Harry obit Mar 46
Von Trapp, Maria Augusta *see* Trapp, Maria Augusta

Von Wagner-Jauregg, Julius *see* Wagner-Jauregg, Julius Von
Von Weingartner, Felix *see* Weingartner, Felix
Von Wicht, John Jan 63 obit Mar 70
Von Zell, Harry Jun 44 obit Jan 82
Von Zemlinsky, Alexander *see* Zemlinsky, Alexander von
Voorhees, Donald Feb 50 obit Apr 89
Voorhees, Tracy S. Feb 57 obit Nov 74
Voorhis, Jerry Aug 41 obit Nov 84
Voris, John Ralph Dec 48 obit Mar 68
Voronoff, Serge Jan 41 obit Oct 51
Voroshilov, Klementii Mar 41 obit Jan 70
Vorster, Balthazar J. Jun 67 obit Nov 83
Vorster, John *see* Vorster, Balthazar J.
Vorys, John M. Sep 50 obit Nov 68
Vosper, Robert Jul 65
Voulkos, Peter Nov 97
Voznesensky, Andrei Mar 67
Vranitzky, Franz Aug 89
Vrba, Elisabeth S. Jun 97
Vredenburgh, Dorothy M. Jul 48 [Vredenburgh, Mrs. Peter]
Vredenburgh, Mrs. Peter *see* Vredenburgh, Mrs. Dorothy M.
Vreeland, Diana Feb 78 obit Oct 89
Vukmanovic-Tempo, Svetozar Dec 58

Waart, Edo de *see* de Waart, Edo
Wachenheimer, Fred W. *see* Friendly, Fred W.
Wachner, Linda Nov 98
Wachuku, Jaja Apr 63
Waddington, C. H. Apr 62 obit Nov 75
Wade, Virginia May 76
Wadhams, Robert Pelton obit Feb 41

Wadiyar, Sri Krishnaraja, Bahadur Maharaja of Mysore obit Sep 40

Wadsworth, James J. Jun 56 obit May 84

Wadsworth, James W. Jul 43 obit Sep 52

Waesche, Russell R. Mar 45 obit Dec 46

Wagman, Frederick H. Jul 63

Wagner, Aubrey J. Jun 63

Wagner, J. Addington May 56

Wagner, Richard Apr 62

Wagner, Robert F., Jr. Feb 54 obit Apr 91

Wagner, Robert F. May 41 obit Jun 53

Wagner, Robert Jun 84

Wagner-Jauregg, Julius Von obit Nov 40

Wahlen, Friedrich T. Jun 61

Wainwright, Jonathan M. May 42 obit Nov 53

Waite, Alice Vinton obit May 43

Waite, Henry Matson obit Oct 44

Waite, Terry Sep 86

Waits, Tom Oct 97

Waitt, Alden H. Sep 47

Waitz, Grete Apr 81

Wajda, Andrzej Jul 82

Wakasugi, Kename obit Jan 44

Wakefield, Charles Cheers Wakefield, 1st Viscount obit Mar 41

Wakehurst, John De Vere Loder, 2d Baron see Loder, John de Vere

Wakeman, Frederic Sep 46

Wake-Walker, W. Frederick obit Oct 45

Waksman, Selman A. May 46 obit Oct 73

Walcott, Derek Apr 84

Walcott, Joe Jun 49 obit May 94

Wald, George May 68 obit Jun 97

Wald, Jerome Irving see Wald, Jerry

Wald, Jerry May 52 obit Sep 62

Wald, Lillian D. obit Oct 40

Wald, Patricia M. Jun 2000

Walden, Amelia Elizabeth (WLB) Yrbk 56

Walden, Percy Talbot obit May 43

Waldheim, Kurt May 72 Jan 87

Waldron, Hicks B. Mar 88

Wales, George Canning obit May 40

Walesa, Lech Apr 81 May 96

Walken, Christopher Oct 90

Walker, Alice Mar 84

Walker, Dan Aug 76

Walker, E. Ronald Dec 56

Walker, Eric A. Mar 59 obit Apr 95

Walker, Frank C. Oct 40 obit Nov 59

Walker, Herschel Mar 85

Walker, Jay Oct 2000

Walker, John May 57 obit Jan 96

Walker, Kara Mar 2000

Walker, Larry May 98

Walker, Margaret Nov 43 obit Jun 99

Walker, Mildred (WLB) Yrbk 47 obit Aug 98

Walker, Nancy Feb 65 obit May 92

Walker, Norma Ford Oct 57 obit Nov 68

Walker, Paul A. May 52 obit Jul 66

Walker, Ralph Dec 57 obit Mar 73

Walker, Stanley Nov 44 obit Jan 63

Walker, Stuart obit May 41

Walker, Walton H. Sep 50 obit Jan 51

Walker, Waurine Feb 55

Wall, Art, Jr. Dec 59

Wall, Evander Berry obit Jan 40

Wallace, Clayton M. Sep 48

Wallace, Dewitt Apr 44 [Wallace, Dewitt; and Wallace, Lila Acheson] May 56 obit May 81

Wallace, Euan obit Apr 41

Wallace, George C. Dec 63 obit Nov 98

Wallace, Henry A. Aug 40 Jan 47 obit Jan 66

Wallace, Irving Mar 79 obit Sep 90

Wallace, Lila Acheson May 56 [Wallace, Dewitt; and Wallace, Lila Acheson] obit Jul 84

Wallace, Lurleen B. Sep 67 obit Jul 68

Wallace, Mike Jul 57 Nov 77

Wallace, Myron Leon see Wallace, Mike

Wallace, Ruby Ann see Dee, Ruby

Wallace, Thomas W. obit Sep 43

Wallach, Eli May 59

Wallenstein, Alfred May 40 Apr 52 obit Mar 83

Waller, Fats Apr 42 obit Feb 44

Waller, Fred Feb 53 obit Jul 54

Waller, Robert James May 94

Waller, Thomas Wright see Waller, Fats

Wallerstein, Judith S. Nov 96

Wallgren, Mon C. Nov 48 obit Nov 61

Wallop, Douglass (WLB) Yrbk 56 obit Jun 85

Waln, Nora Jan-Feb 40 obit Nov 64

Walpole, Hugh obit Jul 41

Walsh, Bill Nov 89

Walsh, Chad Feb 62 obit Mar 91

Walsh, George Ethelbert obit Apr 41

Walsh, J. Raymond Nov 46

Walsh, James J. obit Apr 42

Walsh, Joseph obit Mar 46

Walsh, Lawrence E. Oct 91

Walsh, Mrs. Richard J. see Buck, Pearl

Walsh, William B. May 62 obit Mar 97

Walsh, William Henry obit May 41

Walsh, William Thomas Jul 41 obit Mar 49

Waltari, Mika Feb 50 obit Oct 79

Walter, Bruno Nov 42 obit Apr 62

Walter, Eugene obit Nov 41

Walter, Francis E. Jun 52 obit Jul 63

Walter, Wilmer obit Oct 41

Walters, Barbara Feb 71

Walters, Vernon A. Feb 88

Walton, Bill Mar 77

Walton, Ernest T. S. Mar 52 obit Sep 95

Walton, Sam Mar 92 obit Mar 92

Walton, William Mar 40 obit May 83

Walworth, Arthur Dec 59

Wambaugh, Eugene obit Sep 40

Wambaugh, Joseph Mar 80

Wambaugh, Sarah Apr 46 obit Jan 56

Wampler, Cloud Dec 52

Wan, Prince Jun 54

Wanamaker, Pearl A. Sep 46

Wang, An Jan 87 obit May 90

Wang, Ping-Nan Dec 58

Wang Chao-ming see Wang Ching-Wei

Wang Ching-Wei May 40 obit Jan 45

Wangchuk, Jigme Dorji, Druk Gyalpo of Bhutan Oct 56 obit Sep 72

Wanger, Walter Jun 47 obit Jan 69

Wang Shih-Chieh Sep 45 obit Jun 81

Wank, Roland Dec 43 obit Jul 70

Wapner, Joseph A. Sep 89

Warburg, James P. Apr 48 obit Jul 69

Warburton, Herbert B. Nov 51

Ward, Barbara Jan 50 Jan 77 obit Jul 81

Ward, Benjamin Aug 88

Ward, Christopher L. obit Apr 43

Ward, Donovan F. Mar 65

Ward, Douglas Turner Sep 76

Ward, Lem obit Jan 43

Ward, Maisie Jan 66 obit Mar 75

Ward, Mary Jane Jun 46

Ward, Paul L. Mar 62

Ward, Robert Jul 63

Ware, Wallace see Karp, David

Warhol, Andy Feb 68 Jul 86 obit Apr 87

Waring, Fred Sep 40 obit Sep 84

Waring, George J., Mgr. obit Apr 43

Waring, J. Waties Dec 48 obit Mar 68

Waring, Roane Dec 43 obit Dec 58

Warne, William E. Nov 52 obit May 96

Warnecke, John Carl Jul 68

Warner, Albert Jan 45 [Warner, Albert; Warner, Harry M; and Warner, Jack L.] obit Jan 68

Warner, Edward P. Oct 49 obit Sep 58

Warner, Harry M. Jan 45 [Warner, Albert; Warner, Harry M; and Warner, Jack L.] obit Oct 58

Warner, Jack L. Jan 45 [Warner, Albert; Warner, Harry M; and Warner, Jack L.] obit Nov 78

Warner, John Christian Oct 50 obit Jul 89

Warner, John W. Nov 76

Warner, Milo J. Nov 41

Warner, Ty Nov 98

Warner, W. Lloyd Dec 59 obit Jul 70

Warnke, Paul C. Aug 77

Warren, Althea Feb 42 obit Feb 60

Warren, Avra M. Feb 55 obit Mar 57

Warren, Diane Jun 2000

Warren, Earl Jan 44 Jan 54 obit Sep 74

Warren, Edgar L. Jul 47

Warren, Fletcher Jul 60 obit Mar 92

Warren, Fuller Dec 49

Warren, Harry Jun 43 obit Nov 81

Warren, Harry Marsh, Rev. obit Feb 41

Warren, Leonard Dec 53 obit Apr 60

Warren, Lindsay C. Nov 49

Warren, Robert Penn Jun 70 obit Nov 89

Warren, Shields Jun 50 obit Sep 80

Warren, Whitney obit Mar 43

Warren, William C. Jan 60 obit Yrbk 2000

Warwick, Dionne Feb 69

Wash, Carlyle H. obit Mar 43

Washburn, Bradford Jun 66

Washburn, Gordon Bailey Dec 55

Washington, Alonzo May 99

Washington, Denzel Jul 92

Washington, Harold Feb 84 obit Jan 88

Washington, Walter E. Jul 68

Wasilewska, Wanda Jul 44 obit Oct 64

Wason, Betty Aug 43

Wason, Edward H. obit Apr 41

Wason, Robert R. Jan 46 obit Sep 50

Wasserburg, Gerald J. Mar 86

Wasserman, Lew R. May 91

Wasserstein, Wendy Jul 89

Waste, William Harrison obit Jul 40

Waterlow, Sydney P. obit Jan 45

Waterman, Alan T. Jun 51 obit Feb 68

Waters, Ethel Apr 41 Mar 51 obit Oct 77

Waters, James R. obit Jan 46

Waters, John Jun 90

Waters, Maxine Nov 92

Waters, Muddy May 81 obit Jun 83

Waterston, Sam Sep 85

Watkins, Arthur V. Jul 50 obit Dec 73

Watkins, Gloria see Hooks, Bell

Watkins, James D. Mar 89

Watkins, Shirley (WLB) Yrbk 58

Watkinson, Harold Mar 60

Watrous, George Dutton obit Yrbk 40

Watrous, Harry Willson obit Jan 40

Watson, Arthur K. Sep 71 obit Oct 74

Watson, Burl S. Apr 57

Watson, Clarence Wayland obit Jul 40

Watson, Edwin M. obit Apr 45

Watson, Jack H., Jr. Nov 80

Watson, James D. Apr 63 Oct 90

Watson, John B. Oct 42 obit Dec 58

Watson, Lucile Dec 53 obit Sep 62

Watson, Mark S. Nov 46 obit Apr 66

Watson, Pearl Yvonne see Burke, Yvonne Brathwaite

Watson, Samuel Newell, Rev. obit May 42

Watson, Thomas J., Jr. Feb 56 obit Mar 94

Watson, Thomas J., Sr. Nov 40 Jul 50 obit Sep 56

Watson, Tom Jul 79

Watson-Watt, Robert Sep 45 obit Jan 74

Watt, Donald Jan 58

Watt, James G. Jan 82

Watt, Robert J. Mar 45 obit Sep 47

Wattenberg, Ben J. Jun 85

Wattleton, Faye Jan 90

Watts, Alan Mar 62 obit Jan 74

Watts, André May 68

Watts, Heather May 83

Watts, J. C. Jr. Mar 99

Watts, Julius Caesar *see* Watts, J. C. Jr.

Watts, Lyle F. Oct 46

Waugh, Auberon May 90

Waugh, Frederick Judd obit Oct 40

Waugh, Samuel C. Dec 55 obit Oct 70

Waugh, Sidney Jul 48 obit Sep 63

Wavell, Archibald, 1st Earl Mar 41 obit Jul 50

Waverley, John Anderson, 1st Viscount *see* Anderson, John

Waxman, Henry A. Jul 92

Wayans, Damon Nov 99

Wayans, Keenen Ivory Feb 95

Waymack, W. W. Mar 47 obit Jan 61

Wayne, David Jun 56 obit Apr 95

Wayne, John Feb 51 Jul 72 obit Aug 79

Weafer, Elizabeth Jan 58

Weafer, Mrs. Eugene C. *see* Weafer, Elizabeth

Weagant, Roy A. obit Oct 42

Weaver, Affie obit Jan 41

Weaver, Arthur J. obit Nov 45

Weaver, Dennis Nov 77

Weaver, Earl Feb 83

Weaver, Fritz Jan 66

Weaver, Robert Clifton Apr 61 obit Oct 97

Weaver, Sigourney Mar 89

Weaver, Sylvester L., Jr. Jan 55

Weaver, Walter Reed obit Dec 44

Weaver, Warren Apr 52 obit Feb 79

Webb, Aileen O. Dec 58 obit Oct 79

Webb, Beatrice obit Jun 43

Webb, Clifton Mar 43 obit Dec 66

Webb, Jack May 55 obit Mar 83

Webb, James E. Oct 46 May 62 obit May 92

Webb, James H., Jr. Aug 87

Webb, Loretta *see* Lynn, Loretta

Webb, Maurice May 50 obit Sep 56

Webb, Mrs. Vanderbilt *see* Webb, Aileen O.

Webb, Walter Loring obit Mar 41

Webb, Wellington E. Aug 99

Webb, William Flood Dec 48

Webber, Andrew Lloyd *see* Lloyd Webber, Andrew

Weber, Dick Jun 70

Weber, Joseph M. obit Jul 42

Weber, Louis Lawrence obit Mar 40

Weber, Max Jun 41 obit Dec 61

Webster, H. T. Mar 45 obit Nov 52

Webster, Margaret May 40 Sep 50 obit Jan 73

Webster, William H. Aug 78

Webster, William May 50 obit Jul 72

Wechsberg, Joseph Apr 55 obit Jun 83

Wecter, Dixon Nov 44 obit Sep 50

Wedel, Cynthia Clark Mar 70 obit Oct 86

Wedemeyer, Albert C. Jan 45 obit Feb 90

Wedgwood, C. V. Jan 57 obit May 97

Wedgwood, Josiah C. Apr 42 obit Sep 43

Wedgwood of Barlaston, Josiah Clement Wedgwood, 1st Baron *see* Wedgwood, Josiah C.

Weede, Robert Feb 57 obit Sep 72

Weeks, Edward Dec 47 obit May 89

Weeks, Sinclair Mar 53 obit Mar 72

Wegman, William May 92

Wegner, Nicholas H. Dec 49 obit May 76

Weicker, Lowell P., Jr. Jan 74 May 93

Weidenbaum, Murray L. Mar 82

Weider, Joe Jan 98

Weidlein, Edward R. Jul 48 obit Nov 83

Weidman, Charles Apr 42 [Humphrey, Doris; and Weidman, Charles] obit Sep 75

Weidman, Jerome Aug 42 obit Jan 99

Weigle, Luther Allan Mar 46 obit Oct 76

Wei Jingsheng Sep 97

Weil, Andrew Aug 96

Weil, Frank L. Feb 49 obit Jan 58

Weil, Lisl Jan 58

Weil, Richard, Jr. Jul 51 obit Jul 58

Weill, Kurt Dec 41 obit May 50

Weill, Sanford I. Jul 99

Wein, George Oct 85

Weinberg, Alvin M. Sep 66

Weinberg, Robert A. Jun 83

Weinberger, Caspar W. Jun 73

Weingartner, Felix obit Jun 42

Weinstein, Bob Mar 97 [Weinstein, Harvey; and Weinstein, Bob]

Weinstein, Harvey Mar 97 [Weinstein, Harvey; and Weinstein, Bob]

Weir, Ernest T. Jun 41 obit Oct 57

Weir, Peter Aug 84

Weis, Jessica McCullough Dec 59 [Weis, Jessica McCullough] obit Jun 63

Weis, Mrs. Charles W(illiam), Jr. *see* Weis, Jessica McCullough

Weisen, Jim *see* Palmer, Jim

Weisgal, Meyer W. Oct 72 obit Nov 77

Weiskopf, Tom Nov 73

Weiss, Paul A. Oct 70 obit Nov 89

Weiss, Paul May 69

Weiss, Peter Apr 68 obit Jul 82

Weiss, Soma obit Mar 42

Weiss, Ted Oct 85 obit Nov 92

Weisse, Faneuil Suydam obit Mar 40

Weissenberg, Alexis Jun 78

Weisskopf, Victor Frederick Nov 76

Wei Tao-Ming Dec 42

Weitz, John Sep 79

Weitzenkorn, Louis obit Mar 43

Weizman, Ezer Sep 79

Weizmann, Chaim Nov 42 Nov 48 obit Dec 52

Weizsäcker, Carl Friedrich Von Jan 85

Weizsäcker, Richard Von Mar 85

Welch, John F. Jan 88

Welch, Joseph N. Jun 54 obit Dec 60

Welch, Leo D. Dec 63 obit Jan 79

Welch, Raquel May 71

Welch, Robert Nov 76 obit Mar 85

Welch, William A. obit Jun 41

Weld, John May 40

Weld, Susan Ker see Weld, Tuesday

Weld, Tuesday Jul 74

Weld, William F. Feb 93

Weldon, Fay May 90

Welensky, Roland see Welensky, Roy

Welensky, Roy Jul 59 obit Feb 92

Welitsch, Ljuba May 49 obit Nov 96

Welk, Lawrence Feb 57 obit Jul 92

Welker, Herman Feb 55 obit Jan 58

Weller, Michael May 89

Weller, Thomas H. Jun 55 [Enders, John F.; Robbins, Frederick C.; and Weller, Thomas H.]

Welles, Orson May 41 Feb 65 obit Nov 85

Welles, Sumner Mar 40 obit Nov 61

Wellman, Frederick Creighton Feb 44

Wellman, Manly Wade (WLB) Yrbk 55

Wellman, Paul Iselin (WLB) Yrbk 49

Wellman, William A. Jun 50 obit Feb 76

Wells, Agnes Nov 49 obit Oct 59

Wells, Carolyn obit May 42

Wells, Gabriel obit Dec 46

Wells, H. G. obit Sep 46

Wells, H. Gideon obit Jun 43

Wells, Herman B Apr 66 obit Aug 2000

Wells, Julia Elizabeth see Andrews, Julie

Wells, Mary Jan 67

Wells, Peter Aug 42

Wellstone, Paul D. May 93

Welman, Joseph C. May 58

Welsh, Edward Christy Jan 67 obit Jun 90

Welsh, Herbert obit Sep 41

Welsh, Irvine Nov 97

Welsh, Matthew E. Jun 62 obit Aug 95

Welty, Eudora Jan 42 Oct 75

Wenckebach, Karel Friedrich obit Yrbk 40

Wenders, Wim Jul 84

Wendt, Gerald Louis Mar 40 obit Feb 74

Weng Wen-hao see Wong Wen-Hao

Wenner, Jann S. Jan 80

Wenner-Gren, Axel Oct 42 obit Jan 62

Wente, Carl F. Feb 54

Werblin, David A. Apr 79 obit Feb 92

Werblin, Sonny see Werblin, David A.

Werfel, Franz Yrbk 40 obit Sep 45

Werne, Isaac obit Mar 40

Werner, Max Dec 43 obit Feb 51

Werner, Oskar Jun 66 obit Jan 85

Werner, Theodor Dec 58

Werntz, Carl N. obit Dec 44

Werth, Alexander Apr 43 obit Apr 69

Wertham, Fredric Jul 49 obit Jan 82

Wertheimer, Linda Nov 95

Wertheimer, Max obit Dec 43

Wertmuller, Lina Sep 76

Wesker, Arnold Feb 62

Wesley, Charles Harris Mar 44 obit Oct 87

West, Annie Blythe obit May 41

West, Claudine obit May 43

West, Cornel Oct 93

West, Dorothy Feb 97 obit Feb 97

West, Jan DeGaetani see DeGaetani, Jan

West, Jessamyn Aug 77 obit Apr 84

West, Keith (WLB) Yrbk 47

West, Levon Feb 48 obit Jun 68

West, Mae Nov 67 obit Jan 81

West, Mary Jessamyn see West, Jessamyn

West, Morris L. Jan 66 obit Feb 2000

West, Nathanael obit Feb 41

West, Rebecca Jun 68 obit May 83

Westcott, John Howell obit Jul 42

Westheimer, Ruth Jan 87

Westin, Av Aug 75

Westley, Helen obit Feb 43

Westminster, Archbishop of see Hinsley, Arthur

Westmore, Perc Oct 45 obit Nov 70

Westmoreland, W. C. Jun 61

Weston, Brett Feb 82 obit Mar 93

Westwood, Vivienne Jul 97

Wetmore, Alexander Feb 48 obit Mar 79

Wetter, Ernst Feb 42

Wexler, Jacqueline Grennan Mar 70

Wexler, Nancy S. Aug 94

Wexner, Leslie Feb 94

Weyerhaeuser, Frederick E. obit Nov 45

Weyerhaeuser, George H. Jul 77

Weyerhaeuser, Rudolph M. obit Sep 46

Weygand, Maxime Jan-Jun 40 obit Mar 65

Weymouth, Frank E. obit Sep 41

Whalen, Grover A. Sep 44 obit Jun 62

Wharton, Clifton R., Jr. Feb 87

Wharton, Clifton R. Jul 58 obit Jun 90

Wheat, Alfred Adams obit Apr 43

Wheat, William Howard obit Apr 44

Wheaton, Anne Jan 58 obit May 77

Wheaton, Elizabeth Lee Jan 42

Wheeler, Burton K. Aug 40 obit Feb 75

Wheeler, Earle G. Nov 65 obit Feb 76

Wheeler, John Archibald Jan 70

Wheeler, Mortimer Mar 56 obit Sep 76

Wheeler, Mrs. Post see Rives, Hallie Erminie

Wheeler, Raymond A. Apr 57 obit Apr 74

Wheelock, Warren Mar 40 obit Oct 60

Wheelwright, Jere (WLB) Yrbk 52 obit Mar 61

Wheelwright, John B. obit Nov 40

Whelan, Wendy Oct 98

Wherry, Kenneth S. Apr 46 obit Jan 52

Whipple, Fred Lawrence May 52

Whipple, Maurine Mar 41

Whipple, Wayne obit Dec 42

Whitaker, Douglas Nov 51 obit Dec 73

Whitaker, Forest Feb 97

Whitcomb, Richard T. Dec 56

White, Alexander M. Jul 51 obit Jan 69

White, Betty Jun 87

White, Byron R. Dec 62

White, Charles M. Jun 50 obit Mar 77

White, E. B. Oct 60 obit Nov 85

White, Edmund Jan 91

White, Edward H., 2d Nov 65 obit Mar 67

White, Francis W. Jan 54 obit Jun 57

White, Frank [governor] obit May 40

White, Frank [broadcasting executive] Dec 50 obit Jan 80

White, Gilbert F. Mar 53

White, Harry D. Sep 44 obit Oct 48

White, Helen Constance Jul 45

White, Herbert S. May 68

White, Hugh L. Dec 55 obit Nov 65

White, I. D. Dec 58 obit Aug 90

White, Isaac Davis see White, I. D.

White, John F. Nov 67

White, John R. Jan 56

White, Josh Aug 44 obit Nov 69

White, Katharine Elkus Feb 65 obit Jun 85

White, Kevin H. Dec 74

White, Margaret Bourke see Bourke-White, Margaret

White, Mark Aug 86

White, Michael R. Mar 99

White, Nelia Gardner (WLB) Yrbk 50 obit Oct 57

White, Patrick Jun 74 obit Nov 90

White, Paul Dudley Dec 55 obit Dec 73

White, Paul W. Mar 40 obit Oct 55

White, Portia Mar 45

White, Reggie Nov 95

White, Robert E. May 84

White, Robert M., 2d Mar 60

White, Robert M. Mar 64

White, S. Harrison obit Feb 46

White, Stewart Edward obit Nov 46

White, Theodore H. Apr 55 Apr 76 obit Jul 86

White, Thomas D. Dec 57 obit Feb 66

White, Trumbull obit Feb 42

White, Vanna Jan 88

White, W. Wilson Jan 59 obit Jan 65

White, Wallace H., Jr. May 48 obit May 52

White, Walter Francis Apr 42 obit Jun 55

White, Wilbert Webster obit Oct 44

White, William Allen Nov 40 obit Apr 44

White, William Anthony Parker see Boucher, Anthony

White, William Jan 53 obit Jun 67

White, William Lindsay Jan 43 obit Oct 73

White, William S. Dec 55 obit Jun 94

Whitehead, Don Dec 53 obit Mar 81

Whitehead, Edward Jan 67 obit Jun 78

Whitehill, Walter Muir Jun 60 obit May 78

Whitehouse, Harold Beckwith obit Sep 43

Whitelaw, William Mar 75 obit Nov 99

Whiteman, Paul Aug 45 obit Feb 68

Whiteman, Wilberforce James obit Jan 40

Whitford, Harry Nichols obit Jul 41

Whitlam, Gough Jan 74

Whitman, Christine Todd Jun 95

Whitman, Marina Von Neumann Oct 73

Whitman, Meg Feb 2000

Whitman, Walter G. Feb 52 obit Jun 74

Whitmire, Kathryn Mar 88

Whitmore, James Sep 76

Whitney, A. F. Feb 46 obit Sep 49

Whitney, Courtney Jun 51 obit May 69

Whitney, Gertrude Jul 41 obit Yrbk 42

Whitney, John Hay Dec 45 obit Apr 82

Whitney, Phyllis A. (WLB) Yrbk 48

Whittaker, Charles Evans Dec 57 obit Jan 74

Whittemore, Arthur Jan 54 [Whittemore, Arthur; and Lowe, Jack] obit Feb 85

Whittemore and Lowe see Lowe, Jack; Whittemore, Arthur

Whittle, Christopher Feb 91

Whittle, Frank Jan 45 obit Oct 96

Whittlesey, Charles F. obit Feb 41

Whitton, Charlotte Apr 53 obit Mar 75

Whitton, Rex M. May 62

Whitty, May Dec 45 obit Jul 48

Whitworth, Kathy Apr 76

Whyte, William H. Jr. Jan 59 obit Mar 99

Wick, Charles Z. Mar 85

Wick, Frances G. obit Aug 41

Wickard, Claude Raymond Oct 40 obit Jun 67

Wickenden, Dan (WLB) Yrbk 51 obit Feb 90

Wickens, Aryness Joy Sep 62 obit Apr 91

Wicker, Ireene Apr 43 obit
Jan 88
Wicker, Tom Nov 73
Wickware, Francis Graham
obit Yrbk 40
Wideman, John Edgar Jan 91
Widmark, Richard Apr 63
Widnall, Sheila E. Oct 97
Wiedoeft, Rudy obit Mar 40
Wiener, Alexander S. May 47
obit Feb 77
Wiener, Norbert Mar 50 obit
May 64
Wiesel, Elie Nov 70 Feb 86
Wiesel, Eliezer *see* Wiesel,
Elie
Wiesenthal, Simon Jan 75
Wiesner, Jerome B. Dec 61
obit Jan 95
Wiest, Dianne Mar 97
Wigand, Jeffrey Apr 2000
Wiggam, Albert Edward Jul
42 obit Jun 57
Wiggen, Henry W. *see* Harris,
Mark
Wiggins, James Russell Nov
69
Wigglesworth, Richard B.
May 59 obit Dec 60
Wigman, Mary Jan 69 obit
Nov 73
Wigner, Eugene P. Apr 53 obit
Mar 95
Wigny, Pierre Dec 60
Wilbur, Bernice M. Sep 43
Wilbur, Dwight L. Jul 69 obit
May 97
Wilbur, Ray Lyman Nov 47
obit Sep 49
Wilbur, Richard Jan 66
Wilby, Francis B. Aug 45 obit
Jan 66
Wilcox, Clair Dec 48
Wilcox, Francis O. Apr 62
obit Apr 85
Wilcox, Herbert Nov 45 [Nea-
gle, Anna; and Wilcox,
Herbert] obit Jul 77
Wilcox, J. W., Jr. obit May 42
Wild, Earl Jul 88
Wilde, Frazar B. Apr 59 obit
Aug 85
Wilde, Louise K. Apr 54
Wilde, Patricia May 68
Wilder, Alec Jul 80 obit Feb
81
Wilder, Billy Feb 51 Oct 84
Wilder, Frances Farmer Jul
47

Wilder, Gene Apr 78
Wilder, L. Douglas Apr 90
Wilder, Laura Ingalls (WLB)
Yrbk 48 obit May 57
Wilder, Mrs. Almanzo J. *see*
Wilder, Laura Ingalls
Wilder, Thornton Aug 43
Nov 71 obit Feb 76
Wildmon, Donald Jan 92
Wile, Frederic William obit
Jun 41
Wile, Ira S. obit Nov 43
Wiles, Andrew J. Mar 96
Wiley, Alexander Apr 47 obit
Jan 68
Wiley, Richard E. Mar 77
Wiley, William Foust obit Oct
44
Wilgress, Dana Jan 54 obit
Oct 69
Wilgus, Sidney Dean obit
Mar 40
Wilhelm, Hoyt Jul 71
Wilhelmina, Juliana Louise
Emma Marie *see* Juliana,
Queen of The Netherlands
Wilhelmina, Queen of the
Netherlands *see* Wilhelm-
ina
Wilhelmina Jun 40 obit Jan
63
Wilkens, Lenny Jul 96
Wilkins, Dominique May 95
Wilkins, Hubert Jan 57 obit
Feb 59
Wilkins, J. Ernest Dec 54 obit
Mar 59
Wilkins, Maurice H. F. Jun 63
Wilkins, Robert W. Jul 58
Wilkins, Roger Aug 94
Wilkins, Roy Jun 50 Jan 64
obit Oct 81
Wilkins, T. Russell obit Feb
41
Wilkinson, Bud *see* Wilkin-
son, Charles
Wilkinson, Charles Apr 62
obit May 94
Wilkinson, Ellen Jul 41 obit
Mar 47
Will, George F. Sep 81
Willard, John obit Nov 42
Willes, Mark H. Mar 98
Willet, Anne Lee obit Mar 43
Willet, Henry Lee Mar 47
William II, Emperor *see*
Hohenzollern, Friedrich
Wilhelm Victor Albert

Williams, Alford Joseph Jr.
Oct 40
Williams, Andy Feb 60
Williams, Anthony A. Oct 99
Williams, Aubrey Willis May
40 obit Apr 65
Williams, Benjamin *see* Fair-
less, Benjamin F.
Williams, Betty Mar 79
Williams, Billy Dee Apr 84
Williams, Brian Jul 98
Williams, Camilla Jun 52
Williams, Clyde E. Jul 47
Williams, Dick Dec 73
Williams, Doug Feb 99
Williams, Edward Bennett
Jan 65 obit Sep 88
Williams, Edwin G. May 50
Williams, Emlyn Feb 41 Apr
52 obit Nov 87
Williams, Eric Feb 66 obit
May 81
Williams, Errick *see* Will-
iams, Ricky
Williams, Esther Feb 55
Williams, Francis, Baron *see*
Francis-Williams
Williams, G. Mennen Apr 49
Jun 63 obit Mar 88
Williams, Gluyas Jun 46 obit
Apr 82
Williams, Hank, Jr. Mar 98
Williams, Harrison A., Jr. Oct
60
Williams, Jay (WLB) Yrbk 55
obit Sep 78
Williams, Jody Mar 98
Williams, Joe Apr 85 obit Jun
99
Williams, John A. Oct 94
Williams, John Bell Mar 64
obit May 83
Williams, John D. obit May
41
Williams, John H. Jan 60 obit
May 66
Williams, John J. Jan 52 obit
Apr 88
Williams, John [guitarist] Jul
83
Williams, John [composer]
Oct 80
Williams, Joseph John,
Father obit Yrbk 40
Williams, Lucinda Mar 99
Williams, Mary Lou Nov 66
obit Jul 81
Williams, Myrna *see* Loy,
Myrna

Williams, Paul Jun 83
Williams, Paul R. Mar 41 obit Mar 80
Williams, Ralph E. obit Jul 40
Williams, Ralph Vaughan see Vaughan Williams, Ralph
Williams, Ricky Aug 99
Williams, Robert R. Sep 51 obit Dec 65
Williams, Robin Jun 79 Jan 97
Williams, Roger J. Jul 57 obit Apr 88
Williams, Shirley Oct 76
Williams, Ted Apr 47
Williams, Tennessee Jan 46 Apr 72 obit Apr 83
Williams, Theodore Samuel see Williams, Ted
Williams, Thomas Sutler obit May 40
Williams, Tom Apr 46 obit May 67
Williams, Vanessa May 84
Williams, W. Walter Nov 48
Williams, William Robert obit Jan 41
Williams, Wythe Oct 43 obit Sep 56
Williams of Barnburgh, Thomas Williams, Baron see Williams, Tom
Williamson, Kevin Apr 2000
Williamson, Marianne Feb 93
Williamson, Nicol Jan 70
Willingdon, Freeman Freeman-Thomas, 1st Marquess of obit Oct 41
Willis, Bruce Feb 87
Willis, Frances E. Jan 54
Willis, Kelly Oct 99
Willis, Paul S. Jan 51 obit Aug 87
Willison, George Findlay Jan 46
Williston, Samuel Dec 54 obit Apr 63
Willkie, Wendell L. Feb 40 obit Nov 44
Willoughby, Charles C. obit Jun 43
Wills, C. Harold obit Feb 41
Wills, Garry Jun 82
Wills, Maurice Morning see Wills, Maury
Wills, Maury Jun 66
Wills, Royal Barry Dec 54 obit Feb 62

Willson, Beckles obit Nov 42
Willson, Meredith Jun 58 obit Aug 84
Willstätter, Richard obit Sep 42
Wilmut, Ian Jun 97
Wilson, A. N. Aug 93
Wilson, Andrew Norman see Wilson, A. N.
Wilson, Angus Feb 59 obit Aug 91
Wilson, August Aug 87
Wilson, Carroll Louis May 47 obit Mar 83
Wilson, Cassandra Mar 98
Wilson, Charles E. [President of General Electric] Apr 43 Feb 51 obit Feb 72
Wilson, Charles E. [Secretary of Defense] Aug 41 Sep 50 obit Dec 61
Wilson, Colin Apr 63
Wilson, Donald R. Jan 52
Wilson, Donald V. Jan 54
Wilson, Don Aug 44 obit Yrbk 91 (died Apr 82)
Wilson, Dorothy Clarke (WLB) Yrbk 51
Wilson, Edmund Apr 45 Jan 64 obit Jul 72
Wilson, Edward Foss Mar 58 obit May 94
Wilson, Edward O. Oct 79
Wilson, Eugene E. Oct 45
Wilson, Flip Nov 69 obit Feb 99
Wilson, Frank J. Jun 46 obit Oct 70
Wilson, George Arthur obit Nov 41
Wilson, H. W. Dec 41 May 48 obit Apr 54
Wilson, Harold Feb 48 May 63 obit Jul 95
Wilson, Henry Maitland Wilson, 1st Baron Oct 43 obit Feb 65
Wilson, Hugh May 41 obit Feb 47
Wilson, I. W. Jul 52 obit Jan 78
Wilson, James Harold see Wilson, Harold
Wilson, John Burgess see Burgess, Anthony
Wilson, John Tuzo Apr 73 obit Aug 93
Wilson, Joseph C. Oct 66 obit Jan 72

Wilson, Kemmons Sep 73
Wilson, Kenneth Geddes Sep 83
Wilson, Lanford Mar 79
Wilson, Leroy A. Apr 48 obit Jul 51
Wilson, Logan Dec 56 obit Jan 91
Wilson, Louise Maxwell see Baker, Louise
Wilson, Malcolm May 74 obit Aug 2000
Wilson, Margaret Bush Oct 75
Wilson, Margaret Stevens obit May 43
Wilson, Michael H. Mar 90
Wilson, O. Meredith Jul 67 obit Feb 99
Wilson, O. W. Oct 66 obit Dec 72
Wilson, Pete Apr 91
Wilson, Peter Feb 68 obit Aug 84
Wilson, Robert Aug 79
Wilson, Robert R. Aug 89 obit May 2000
Wilson, Rufus H. Jun 55
Wilson, Sloan Sep 59
Wilson, Volney C. Jun 58
Wilson, William Julius Feb 96
Wilt, Fred Oct 52 obit Nov 94
Wiman, Dwight Deere Jun 49 obit Feb 51
Winant, John G. Feb 41 obit Dec 47
Winchell, Constance M. Jun 67 obit Sep 84
Winchell, Walter Jun 43 obit Apr 72
Winchester, Alice Feb 54
Windsor, Duke of see Windsor, Edward
Windsor, Edward Sep 44 [Windsor, Edward, Duke of; and Windsor, Wallis, Duchess of] obit Jul 72
Windsor, Wallis Warfield Sep 44 [Windsor, Edward, Duke of; and Windsor, Wallis, Duchess of] obit Jun 86
Windust, Bretaigne Mar 43 obit May 60
Winfield, Dave Jan 84
Winfrey, Oprah Mar 87
Wingate, Orde Charles obit May 44

Winger, Debra Jul 84

Winiarski, Bohdan Feb 62

Winkler, Henry Sep 76

Winpisinger, William W. Feb 80 obit Feb 98

Winpisinger, Wimp *see* Winpisinger, William W.

Winslow, Anne Goodwin (WLB) Yrbk 48

Winsor, Frederick obit Jan 41

Winsor, Kathleen Dec 46

Winster, Baron Feb 46

Winston, Harry Apr 65 obit Feb 79

Winter, Ella (WLB) Yrbk 46 obit Sep 80

Winter, Fritz Mar 58

Winter, George B. obit May 40

Winter, Paul Oct 87

Winters, Jonathan Mar 65

Winters, Shelley Apr 52

Winthrop, Beekman obit Yrbk 40

Wintour, Anna Jul 90

Wirth, Conrad L. Sep 52 obit Sep 93

Wirth, Timothy E. Mar 91

Wirtz, W. Willard Nov 46 Feb 63

Wise, James Decamp Apr 54 obit Apr 84

Wise, Robert Sep 89

Wise, Stephen S. Jul 41 obit May 49

Wiseman, Frederick Dec 74

Witherow, W. P. Apr 42 obit Mar 60

Witos, Wincenty obit Dec 45

Witt, James Lee Mar 2000

Witt, Katarina Jul 88

Witte, Edwin E. Jul 46 obit Sep 60

Witten, Edward Jun 97

Wodehouse, P. G. Nov 71 obit Apr 75

Wofford, Harris Apr 92

Wohl, Louis De *see* De Wohl, Louis

Woiwode, Larry Mar 89

Wojciechowska, Maia Sep 76

Wojtyla, Karol Jozef *see* John Paul II

Wolchok, Sam Oct 48 obit Mar 79

Wolcott, Jesse P. Dec 49 obit Apr 69

Wolf, Alfred, Rabbi Mar 58

Wolf, Naomi Nov 93

Wolfe, Deborah Partridge Dec 62

Wolfe, George C. Mar 94

Wolfe, Hugh C. Feb 50

Wolfe, Humbert obit Jan 40

Wolfe, Tom Jan 71

Wolfenden, John Oct 70 obit Mar 85

Wolfenden, Lord *see* Wolfenden, John

Wolfensohn, James D. May 2000

Wolfert, Ira Apr 43 obit Feb 98

Wolff, Geoffrey Jan 97

Wolff, Maritta M. Jul 41

Wolff, Mary Evaline *see* Madeleva, Sister Mary

Wolfit, Donald Mar 65 obit Apr 68

Woll, Matthew Jan 43 obit Sep 56

Wolman, Abel Feb 57 obit May 89

Wolman, Leo Sep 49 obit Dec 61

Wolper, David L. Oct 86

Woltman, Frederick Jul 47 obit Apr 70

Wonder, Stevie Mar 75

Wong Kar-Wai Apr 98

Wong Wen-Hao Nov 48

Woo, John Feb 99

Wood, Charles Erskine Scott obit Mar 44

Wood, Edward Frederick Lindley, 3d Viscount H *see* Halifax, Edward Frederick Lindley Wood, 1st Earl of

Wood, Grant Aug 40 obit Apr 42

Wood, Henry Joseph obit Oct 44

Wood, James Madison Feb 47 obit Dec 58

Wood, John Apr 83

Wood, John S. Jul 49 obit Nov 68

Wood, Kingsley Nov 40

Wood, Louise A. Jul 61 obit Jul 88

Wood, Natalie Apr 62 obit Jan 82

Wood, Peggy Jul 42 Dec 53 obit May 78

Wood, Philip obit Mar 40

Wood, Robert D. Dec 74 obit Jul 86

Wood, Robert E. May 41 obit Dec 69

Wood, Sam Nov 43 obit Nov 49

Woodard, Alfre Feb 95

Woodard, Stacy obit Mar 42

Woodbridge, Frederick James Eugene obit Jul 40

Woodbury, Charles Herbert obit Jan 40

Woodcock, Charles Edward obit Mar 40

Woodcock, George Feb 64 obit Jan 80

Woodcock, Leonard Nov 70

Wooden, John Jan 76

Woodham-Smith, Cecil Blanche Fitz gerald (WLB) Yrbk 55 obit Mar 77

Woodhouse, Barbara Feb 85 obit Aug 88

Woodhouse, Chase Going Mar 45 obit Apr 85

Woodley, Winifred *see* Hedden, Worth Tuttle

Woodlock, Thomas Francis obit Sep 45

Woodruff, Judy Sep 86

Woods, Bill M. May 66 obit Sep 74

Woods, Donald Feb 82

Woods, Eldrick *see* Woods, Tiger

Woods, George D. Jul 65 obit Oct 82

Woods, James Nov 89

Woods, Mark Mar 46

Woods, Tiger Nov 97

Woods, Tighe E. Oct 48 obit Sep 74

Woodsmall, Ruth F. Jul 49 obit Jul 63

Woodson, Carter G. Feb 44 obit Yrbk 84 (died Apr 50)

Woodsworth, J. S. obit May 42

Woodward, Arthur Smith obit Oct 44

Woodward, Bob Nov 76

Woodward, C. Vann May 86 obit Jun 2000

Woodward, Joanne Jun 58

Woodward, Patti *see* Darwell, Jane

Woodward, R. B. Feb 52 obit Sep 79

Woodward, Robert F. Dec 62

Woodward, Stanley Jun 51 obit Oct 92

Wooldridge, Dean E. Apr 58
[Ramo, Simon; and Wooldridge, Dean E.]

Woolf, Leonard Dec 65 obit
Oct 69

Woolf, Virginia obit May 41

Woollcott, Alexander Jun 41
obit Mar 43

Woollen, Evans, Jr. Dec 48
obit Apr 59

Woolley, Edgar Montillion
see Woolley, Monty

Woolley, Leonard Dec 54 obit
Apr 60

Woolley, Mary E. Mar 42 obit
Nov 47

Woolley, Monty Jul 40 obit
Jun 63

Woolton, Frederick James
Marquis, 1st Earl Oct 40
Oct 50 obit Feb 65

Woolwich, Bishop Suffragan
of see Robinson, John

Wootton, Barbara, Baroness
Wootton of Abinger Feb 64

Worcester, J. R. obit Jun 43

Worden, Edward Chauncey
obit Nov 40

Work, Hubert obit Feb 43

Work, Martin H. May 51

Wörner, Manfred Oct 88 obit
Oct 94

Worsham, Lew Jan 54 obit
Jan 91

Worsley, Frank Arthur obit
Mar 43

Worth, Irene May 68

Worthington, Leslie B. Oct 60
obit Oct 98

Wouk, Herman (WLB) Yrbk
52

Wozniak, Stephen Jul 97

Wray, John Griffith obit May
40

Wren, Percival C. obit Jan 42

Wright, Anna Rose (WLB)
Yrbk 52

Wright, Archibald Lee see
Moore, Archie

Wright, Benjamin F. Jul 55
obit Mar 77

Wright, Berlin H. obit Jan 41

Wright, Fielding L. Sep 48
obit Jul 56

Wright, Frank Lloyd Jan 41
Nov 52 obit Jun 59

Wright, Harold Bell obit Jul
44

Wright, Helen Mar 56 obit
Feb 98

Wright, Huntley obit Sep 41

Wright, Irving S. Oct 68 obit
Mar 98

Wright, James Claud, Jr. see
Wright, Jim

Wright, Jane C. May 68

Wright, Jerauld Feb 55 obit
Jul 95

Wright, Jim Apr 79

Wright, John J. Cardinal Feb
63 obit Oct 79

Wright, Louis B. Nov 50 obit
Jun 84

Wright, Loyd Jul 55 obit Jan
75

Wright, Martha Feb 55

Wright, Michael Jul 61

Wright, Mickey Jan 65

Wright, Mrs. Donald
McCloud see Meadowcroft, Enid

Wright, Orville Oct 46 obit
Mar 48

Wright, Peter Feb 88 obit Jul
95

Wright, Quincy Oct 43 obit
Dec 70

Wright, Richard Mar 40 obit
Jan 61

Wright, Robert Alderson Jul
45 obit Sep 64

Wright, Robert C. Jan 89

Wright, Russel Sep 40 Dec 50
obit Mar 77

Wright, Teresa May 43

Wright, Theodore P. Nov 45
obit Nov 70

Wrigley, Philip K. Apr 75 obit
Jun 77

Wrinch, Dorothy Jul 47

Wriston, Henry M. May 52
obit May 78

Wriston, Walter B. Nov 77

Wrong, Hume Oct 50 obit
Mar 54

Wu, Chien-Shiung Oct 59
obit Apr 97

Wu, Gordon Sep 96

Wu, Harry Feb 96

Wu, K. C. see Wu, Kuo-Cheng

Wu, Kuo-Cheng Feb 53 obit
Aug 84

Wu, Peter Hongda see Wu,
Harry

Wuorinen, Charles Apr 72

Wurf, Jerry Jun 79 obit Feb 82

Wurster, William Wilson Nov
46 obit Nov 73

Wu Yifang Aug 45 obit Jan 86

Wyatt, Jane May 57

Wyatt, John Whitlow Nov 41
obit Nov 99

Wyatt, Wilson W. Mar 46 obit
Aug 96

Wyeth, Andrew Apr 55 Nov
81

Wyeth, James Jan 77

Wyeth N. C. obit Nov 45

Wyler, William Jan 51 obit
Sep 81

Wylie, Max Jan-Feb 40 obit
Nov 75

Wyman, Jane Mar 49

Wyman, Thomas Jun 83

Wynder, Ernest L. Nov 74
obit Sep 99

Wynette, Tammy Jun 95 obit
Jun 98

Wynkoop, Asa obit Dec 42

Wynn, Ed Jan 45 obit Jul 66

Wynonna May 96

Wyszynski, Stefan Cardinal
Jan 58 obit Jul 81

Xenakis, Iannis Sep 94

Xiaoping, Deng see Deng
Xiaoping

Yadin, Yigael Feb 66 obit Aug
84

Yaffe, James (WLB) Yrbk 57

Yafi, Abdullah El- Jun 56

Yahya Khan, A. M. Jan 71
obit Oct 80

Yalow, Rosalyn S. Jul 78

Yamaguchi, Kristi Jun 92

Yamamoto, Isoroko Feb 42
obit Jul 43

Yamamoto, Yohji Nov 2000

Yamanaka, Lois-Ann Jun 99

Yamani, Sheik Ahmed Zaki
Sep 75

Yamasaki, Minoru Mar 62
obit Apr 86

Yamut, Nuri May 52

Yancey, Lewis Q. Alonzo obit
Jan 40

Yang, Chen Ning Nov 58

Yang, Jerry Oct 97 [Yang,
Jerry; and Filo, David]

Yang, You Chan Feb 53

Yankelovich, Daniel Mar 82

Yankovic, "Weird Al" Feb 99

Yankovic, Alfred *see* Yankovic, "Weird Al"

Yanks, Byron *see* Janis, Byron

Yaobang, Hu *see* Hu Yaobang

Yarborough, Cale Jan 87

Yarborough, Ralph W. Feb 60 obit Apr 96

Yard, Molly Nov 88

Yarmolinsky, Adam Mar 69 obit Jun 2000

Yaroslavsky, Emelyan obit Jan 44

Yarrow, William obit Jun 41

Yassin, Ahmed Jul 98

Yastrzemski, Carl May 68

Yates, Donald N. May 58

Yates, Elizabeth (WLB) Yrbk 48

Yates, Herbert Jul 49 obit Mar 66

Yates, Sidney R. Aug 93

Ybarra, Thomas Russell Jan 40

Ydígoras Fuentes, Miguel Nov 58

Yeager, Charles E. May 54

Yeager, Jeana May 87

Yeakley, Marjory Hall *see* Hall, Marjory

Yearwood, Trisha Jul 98

Yeats-Brown, Francis obit Feb 45

Yegorov, Boris Mar 68 obit Nov 94

Yeh, George K. C. Mar 53 obit Jan 82

Yeh Kung-chao *see* Yeh, George K. C.

Yellin, Samuel obit Nov 40

Yeltsin, Boris N. Jan 89

Yen, Y. C. James Jul 46 obit Mar 90

Yeoh, Michelle Jan 98

Yeoh Chu-Kheng *see* Yeoh, Michelle

Yepes, Narciso Oct 66 obit Jul 97

Yerby, Frank Sep 46 obit Mar 92

Yergan, Max Sep 48 obit Jun 75

Yergin, Daniel Nov 99

Yerushalmy, J. Mar 58

Yeutter, Clayton K. Jul 88

Yevtushenko, Yevgeny Feb 63 Mar 94

Yim, Louise Oct 47 obit Apr 77

Yimou, Zhang *see* Zhang Yimou

Ying-Chin, Ho *see* Ho Ying-Chin

Yingling, Ruth Knight *see* Knight, Ruth Adams

Yoakam, Dwight Nov 2000

Yoder, Albert Henry obit Nov 40

Yokich, Stephen P. Nov 98

Yon, Pietro A. obit Jan 44

Yonai, Mitsumasa Jan-Feb 40 obit Jun 48

York, Cyril Forster Garbett, Archbishop of *see* Garbett, Cyril Forster, Archbishop ofof York

York, Herbert F. Dec 58

York, Michael Apr 76

Yorke, Oswald obit Mar 43

Yorty, Sam Jan 67 obit Aug 98

Yoshida, Shigeru Sep 46 obit Jan 68

Yoshimura, Junzo May 56

Yost, Charles W. Mar 59 obit Jul 81

Yost, Fielding Harris obit Oct 46

Youlou, Fulbert Dec 62 obit Jun 72

Youmans, Vincent Apr 44 obit May 46

Young, Alan Jun 53

Young, Andrew Apr 77

Young, Art Feb 40 obit Feb 44

Young, Charles Jac obit Apr 40

Young, Coleman Sep 77 obit Feb 98

Young, Frank E. Oct 89

Young, Hugh obit Sep 45

Young, John A. Oct 86

Young, John W. Jun 65

Young, Joseph Louis Jul 60

Young, Karl obit Jan 44

Young, Loretta Mar 48 obit Nov 2000

Young, Marian Jun 52 obit Jan 74

Young, Milton R. Dec 54 obit Jul 83

Young, Nancy Wilson Ross *see* Ross, Nancy Wilson

Young, Neil Feb 80 Jan 98

Young, Owen D. Aug 45 obit Sep 62

Young, Philip Dec 51 obit Mar 87

Young, Robert *see* Payne, Robert Jul 50 obit Sep 98

Young, Robert R. Apr 47 obit Mar 58

Young, Rose obit Sep 41

Young, Sheila Jan 77

Young, Stanley (WLB) Yrbk 51 obit May 75

Young, Stephen M. Oct 59 obit Feb 85

Young, Steve Oct 93

Young, Whitney Moore Apr 65 obit Apr 71

Youngdahl, Luther W. Mar 48 obit Aug 78

Younger, Kenneth Sep 50

Youngerman, Jack Nov 86

Younghusband, Francis obit Sep 42

Youngman, Henny Oct 86 obit May 98

Yount, Robin Jun 93

Yourcenar, Marguerite Nov 82 obit Feb 88

Youskevitch, Igor Feb 56 obit Aug 94

Yu Hung-chin *see* Yui, O. K.

Yui, O. K. May 55 obit Sep 60

Yukawa, Hideki Jan 50 obit Nov 81

Yun-ho, Li *see* Jiang Qing

Yust, Walter Apr 43 obit Apr 60

Yu-tang, Lin *see* Lin, Yutang

Zabach, Florian Dec 55

Zabaleta, Nicanor Jun 71

Zablocki, Clement Jun 58 Jun 83 obit Jan 84

Zacharias, Ellis M. Mar 49 obit Oct 61

Zacharias, Jerrold Feb 64 obit Sep 86

Zadkine, Ossip Mar 57 obit Jan 68

Zaentz, Saul Mar 97

Zafrullah Khan, Choudri Mohammad Dec 47

Zaharias, Babe Didrikson Apr 47 obit Dec 56

Zaharias, Mildred Didrikson *see* Zaharias, Babe Didrikson

Zahedi, Fazlollah Feb 54 obit Nov 63

Zahir, Mohammed Shah *see* Mohammed Zahir Shah

Zail Singh *see* Singh, Giani Zail

Zajick, Dolora May 2000
Zaldivar, Fulgencio Batista y *see* Batista, Fulgencio
Zamora, Rubén Sep 91
Zander, Arnold S. Oct 47 obit Sep 75
Zandonai, Riccardo obit Aug 44
Zanft, Hattie Carnegie *see* Carnegie, Hattie
Zanuck, Darryl F. Aug 41 Mar 54 obit Feb 80
Zapf, Hermann Jan 65
Zápotock, Antonín Jun 53 obit Jan 58
Zappa, Frank Feb 90 obit Feb 94
Zarb, Frank G. Sep 75
Zaroubin, Georgi N. Apr 53 obit Jan 59
Zatopek, Emil Apr 53
Zeckendorf, William Mar 52 obit Nov 76
Zedillo Ponce De León, Ernesto Apr 96
Zeeland, Paul Van Mar 50
Zeeman, Pieter obit Dec 43
Zeffirelli, Franco Dec 64
Zeidler, Carl Frederick Jul 40 obit Feb 43
Zeineddine, Farid Feb 57
Zeisel, Hallie Burnett *see* Burnett, Hallie Southgate
Zellerbach, J. D. Dec 48 obit Nov 63
Zelomek, A. Wilbert Dec 56
Zemeckis, Robert Sep 97
Zemin, Jiang *see* Jiang Zemin
Zemlinsky, Alexander von obit May 42
Zenos, Andrew C. obit Mar 42
Zerbe, Karl Feb 59 obit Jan 73
Zernike, Frits Feb 55 obit Apr 66
Zevin, Ben David Sep 43 obit Feb 85

Zhabotinskii, Vladimir Evgenevich *see* Jabotinsky, Vladimir Evgenevich
Zhang Yimou Aug 92
Zhao Ziyang Jun 84
Zhirinovsky, Vladimir Nov 95
Zhivkov, Todor Jan 76 obit Oct 98
Zhou Enlai *see* Chou En-Lai
Zhukov, Georgi K. Feb 42 Apr 55 obit Sep 74
Zhukov, Georgy A. Oct 60
Zia Ul-Haq, Mohammad Jun 80 obit Sep 88
Ziegler, Karen Blanche *see* Black, Karen
Ziegler, Ronald L. Nov 71
Ziemer, Gregor Apr 42
Ziff, William B. Oct 46 obit Feb 54
Zilboorg, Gregory Sep 41 obit Nov 59
Zim, Herbert S. Sep 56 obit Feb 95
Zimbalist, Efrem, Jr. Feb 60
Zimbalist, Efrem Mar 49 obit Apr 85
Zimmer, Henry obit May 43
Zimmerman, Alfred F. M. obit Jul 40
Zimmerman, M. M. Jul 57
Zimmerman, Robert *see* Dylan, Bob
Zindel, Paul Jun 73
Zinn, Howard Aug 99
Zinn, Walter H. Dec 55 obit Aug 2000
Zinnemann, Fred Mar 53 obit Jun 97
Zinsser, Hans obit Oct 40
Zirato, Bruno Dec 59 obit Jan 73
Ziskin, Laura Oct 97
Ziyang, Zhao *see* Zhao Ziyang
Zog I Aug 44 obit Jun 61

Zoli, Adone Mar 58 obit Apr 60
Zolotow, Maurice May 57 obit May 91
Zook, George F. Feb 46 obit Oct 51
Zorach, William Feb 43 Feb 63 obit Jan 67
Zorbaugh, Geraldine B. Dec 56 obit Sep 96
Zorin, Valerian A. Mar 53 obit Mar 86
Zorina, Vera Jan 41
Zorlu, Fatin Rustu Dec 58 obit Nov 61
Zorn, John Aug 99
Zsigmond, Vilmos Oct 99
Zuazo, Hernán Siles *see* Siles Zuazo, Hernán
Zubiría, Alberto F. Dec 56
Zubrod, C. Gordon Jan 69 obit Jul 99
Zuckerman, Mortimer B. Jan 90
Zuckerman, Solly Jul 72 obit May 93
Zuckert, Eugene M. Apr 52 obit Yrbk 2000
Zukerman, Pinchas Nov 78
Zukor, Adolph Mar 50 obit Aug 76
Zulli, Floyd, Jr. Jan 58 obit Jan 81
Zuloaga, Ignacio obit Dec 45
Zumwalt, Bud *see* Zumwalt, Elmo R.
Zumwalt, Elmo R. Jun 71 obit Jun 2000
Zu Reventlow, Ernst, Graf *see* Reventlow, Ernst, Graf Zu
Zweig, Stefan obit Apr 42
Zwicky, Fritz Apr 53 obit Apr 74
Zwilich, Ellen Jan 86
Zworykin, Vladimir Kosma Dec 49 obit Sep 82
Zyuganov, Gennadi A. Oct 96